Pathways for Ecumenical and Interreligious Dialogue

Series Editor
Mark Chapman
Ripon College
University of Oxford
Oxford, UK

Building on the important work of the Ecclesiological Investigations International Research Network to promote ecumenical and inter-faith encounters and dialogue, the Pathways for Ecumenical and Interreligious Dialogue series publishes scholarship on such engagement in relation to the past, present, and future. It gathers together a richly diverse array of voices in monographs and edited collections that speak to the challenges, aspirations, and elements of ecumenical and interfaith conversation. Through its publications, the series allows for the exploration of new ways, means, and methods of advancing the wider ecumenical cause with renewed energy for the twenty-first century.

Cristina Lledo Gomez • Agnes M. Brazal
Ma. Marilou S. Ibita
Editors

500 Years of Christianity and the Global Filipino/a

Postcolonial Perspectives

palgrave
macmillan

Editors
Cristina Lledo Gomez
BBI-The Australian Institute of
Theological Education
Pennant Hills, NSW, Australia

Australian Centre for Christianity
and Culture
Barton, ACT, Australia

Ma. Marilou S. Ibita
Department of Theology and
Religious Education
De La Salle University
Manila, Philippines

Agnes M. Brazal
Department of Theology and
Religious Education
De La Salle University
Manila, Philippines

ISSN 2634-6591   ISSN 2634-6605 (electronic)
Pathways for Ecumenical and Interreligious Dialogue
ISBN 978-3-031-47499-6   ISBN 978-3-031-47500-9 (eBook)
https://doi.org/10.1007/978-3-031-47500-9

© The Editor(s) (if applicable) and The Author(s), under exclusive licence to Springer Nature Switzerland AG 2024
This work is subject to copyright. All rights are solely and exclusively licensed by the Publisher, whether the whole or part of the material is concerned, specifically the rights of translation, reprinting, reuse of illustrations, recitation, broadcasting, reproduction on microfilms or in any other physical way, and transmission or information storage and retrieval, electronic adaptation, computer software, or by similar or dissimilar methodology now known or hereafter developed.
The use of general descriptive names, registered names, trademarks, service marks, etc. in this publication does not imply, even in the absence of a specific statement, that such names are exempt from the relevant protective laws and regulations and therefore free for general use. The publisher, the authors, and the editors are safe to assume that the advice and information in this book are believed to be true and accurate at the date of publication. Neither the publisher nor the authors or the editors give a warranty, expressed or implied, with respect to the material contained herein or for any errors or omissions that may have been made. The publisher remains neutral with regard to jurisdictional claims in published maps and institutional affiliations.

This Palgrave Macmillan imprint is published by the registered company Springer Nature Switzerland AG.
The registered company address is: Gewerbestrasse 11, 6330 Cham, Switzerland

Paper in this product is recyclable.

Foreword

The volume you hold in your hands can be fruitfully read in three inter-connected ways: as a celebrative commemoration of the coming of Christianity to the Philippine Islands 500 years ago, as a postcolonial and feminist assessment of Philippine Christianity, and as a global, especially diasporic, contextualization of this Christianity.

It is customary to qualify the statement that Christianity forms but a tiny minority of the Asian population of 4.7 billion in 2023 with "except in the Philippines." According to the 2020 Census of Population and Housing issued by the Philippine Statistics Authority, of the 108,667,043 household population, nearly four-fifths, or 85,645,362 Filipinos, are Christians, of whom 78.8% reported Roman Catholicism as their religious affiliation. The Philippines is the fifth-largest Christian majority and the third-largest Catholic country in the world. These extraordinary numbers should be cause for national pride and commemorative celebrations. The Philippine Catholic Church can also point to its enormous impact on national politics, especially its contribution to national independence from Spanish colonial rule, the removal of Ferdinand Marcos from the presidency through the nonviolent People Power Revolution (the EDSA Revolution), the struggle for and with the poor, and the preservation of the environment. But the contributors to the volume are by no means blind to the failures of the Philippine Catholic Church, highlighting the *double vérité* and the shadows behind the light, such as cultural erasure behind evangelization, the rise of the *Iglesia Filipina Independiente* behind ecclesial unity, the lurking anti-Judaism behind the *Pasyon*, and the marginalization of Islam behind interreligious dialogue.

viii FOREWORD

The volume can also be read as an exemplification of a postcolonial, and within it, feminist approach to the half-a-millennium history of Philippine Christianity. Antonio Pigafetta's chronicles of the first Spanish Catholic missions to Cebu under the *Patronato Real* can and must be read against the grain, from the perspective of the Indigenous people, who were far more receptive to religious diversity than the colonists' exclusivist soteriology. The same thing must be said about the past evangelizing activities and ecclesiastical structures of the Filipino Catholic Church that were deeply tainted by colonialist policies and practices. Another anti-colonial practice that is suggested is "rebaptism" and "immersion" into a Christian spirituality rooted in the land and the traditions of the Indigenous ancestors. From a feminist approach, one essay seeks to free the devotion to Mary, a defining feature of the Philippine Catholic Church, from the anti-woman "political Marianism" rampant under the Marcos and Duterte regimes. Another essay examines *Pinay*'s (Filipina women) experience of colonial trauma and institutionalized and internalized sexism.

Finally, this volume can be read from the global perspective of the Philippine diaspora, albeit somewhat less developed than the two previous ones. The Philippine labor diaspora is one of the largest in the world, with around 10 million people, or 10% of the country's population, and more than 1 million leaving the country each year to work abroad. Migration poses huge problems of all kinds (but also economic benefits) to the country, to individual emigrants, to their families, and to the Philippine Catholic Church. The fact that the Philippine government bestows annually the *Bagong Bayani* (New Heroes) Awards on **the country's outstanding and exemplary Overseas Filipino Workers (OFWs)** is an indication of the huge financial contribution that Filipino migrants make to the national economy with their remittances (about US $33.5 billion in 2019). The two essays on diaspora and Babaylan Studies constitute initial gestures toward Filipino migration which deserves a more extended and sustained theology of migration in which the Christian God is seen as *Deus Migrator* accompanying all migrants in their quest for a better life.

A historical overview of a quincentennial of Christian presence, a postcolonial and feminist perspective, and a migration theology—these are the three ways this splendid collection of essays enriches our understanding of Philippine Christianity, and we are deeply grateful to the editors and contributors for their work.

The Ignacio Ellacuria Chair of Catholic Social Thought   Peter C. Phan
Department of Theology and Religious Studies
Georgetown University, Washington DC, USA

Acknowledgments

De La Salle University, Philippines
Libraries of the Katholieke Universiteit Leuven, Belgium
BBI-The Australian Institute of Theological Education
Libraries of Charles Sturt University, Australia
Berkeley Center for Religion, Peace & World Affairs, Georgetown University
International Grants, American Academy of Religion

Praise for *500 Years of Christianity and the Global Filipino/a*

"This groundbreaking volume interrogates the past, analyzes the present, and envisions decolonial Christianity for the Philippines. It discusses cultural hybridity, indigenous traditions, resistance movements, migration and diaspora, and environmental justice from postcolonial and feminist perspectives. It makes a critical contribution to the study of Asian and postcolonial Christianity."

—Kwok Pui-lan, *Dean's Professor of Systematic Theology, Candler School of Theology, Emory University, Author of "Postcolonialism, Feminism, and Religious Discourse"*

"In this illuminating volume, discover a celebrative commemoration of the arrival of Christianity in the Philippines. The different contributors offer a postcolonial and feminist critique, and a global perspective, especially within the Filipino diaspora. Uncover the extraordinary influence of the Philippine Catholic Church on national history, from independence struggles, survival under Martial Law to environmental preservation. However, this collection does not shy away from revealing the shadows behind the light, highlighting cultural erasure, the rise of alternative faiths, and interreligious challenges. This comprehensive exploration of Philippine Christianity offers a rich understanding of its complex history."

—Mary John Mananzan OSB, *Activist, Theologian, and Superior of the Missionary Benedictine Sisters in Manila, Author of "Shadows of Light: Philippine Church History Under Spain, A People's Perspective"*

"Owing to the COVID-19 pandemic, the Philippines failed to fully celebrate the significance and meaning of the 500th year anniversary of the arrival of Christianity to the islands in 2021. Fortunately, there are ongoing attempts to revisit and rethink our ancestors' encounters with the colonizers as well as to determine how we can pursue the tasks of decolonization and resistance. This book – a collection of 16 essays written from a Filipino-centric point of view while adopting postcolonial and feminist perspectives – provides the reader with a detailed assessment of what I have labelled as the chauvinist Christianity handed down to the present generations. Bravo to this book's writers and editors for this must-read book which will certainly hold a pride of place in *Filipiniana* collections."

—Karl Gaspar CSsR, *Anthropologist, Theologian, Artist, and Professor of Philippine Studies, Ateneo De Davao University, Author of "Handuman (Remembrance): Digging for the Indigenous Wellspring"*

"*500 Years of Christianity and the Global Filipino/a: Postcolonial Perspectives* challenges a great deal of what many of us have learned and taught in church history about Christianity in the Philippines. It also affirms a great deal of what we have learned and taught. The book does this by consistently engaging both colonizing and decolonizing historical experiences and forms of knowledge over the past five centuries in the Philippines, in all of their complexity. Along the way it provides us with access to multiple and competing colonial and indigenous narratives, experiences, epistemologies, and people. The compelling goal of the effort is decolonizing the Philippine nation and Filipino peoples globally, a moral imperative that guides the entire project. I consider it one of the most important books on Christianity in the Philippines to have been published in the last half-century."

—Dale T. Irvin *Professor of World Christianity, New School of Biblical Theology, Co-Editor, Journal of World Christianity*

CONTENTS

1 Philippine Christianity: 500 Years of Resistance and Accommodation   1
Agnes M. Brazal, Cristina Lledo Gomez, and Ma. Marilou S. Ibita

Part I Rethinking the Encounters   27

2 Indigenization as Appropriation (What Being Baptized Could Have Meant for the Natives of Cebu in 1521)   29
Pablo Virgilio S. David and Ma. Maricel S. Ibita

3 The Double Truth of (Colonial) Mission   47
Daniel Franklin E. Pilario

4 Rethinking Encounters and Re-imagining Muslim-Christian Relations in Post-colonial Philippines   65
Vivienne S. M. Angeles

5 The Glocal Filipin@s and the Pasyon Through the Lens of Ethnicity   83
Ma. Marilou S. Ibita

xiii

xiv CONTENTS

6 An Independent Catholic, Nationalist People's
Movement: The Iglesia Filipina Independiente (Philippine
Independent Church)   101
Eleuterio J. Revollido

7 Philippine, Independent and International: The
Relationship Between—*the Iglesia Filipina Independiente
and the Old Catholic Churches*   123
Peter-Ben Smit

Part II Reappropriation, Resistance & Decolonization 141

8 Indigenous Inculturation: A Hermeneutics of Serendipity 143
Antonio D. Sison CPPS

9 Decolonizing the Diaspora through the Center for
Babaylan Studies   161
Leny M. Strobel

10 Back from the Crocodile's Belly: Christian Formation
Meets Indigenous Resurrection Redux   179
S. Lily Mendoza

11 The Ygollotes' Pudong and the Insurrection of the Reeds
In the Post-Human Commune   199
Ferdinand Anno

12 Introducing Jeepney Hermeneutics: Reading the Bible as
Canaanites   209
Revelation Enriquez Velunta

13 Inang Diyos, Inang Bayan: The Virgin Mary and Filipino
Identity   227
Jamina Vesta M. Jugo

14	**Bangon Na, Pinays Rise Up: Reclaiming Pinay Power Dismantled by a Christian Colonial Past and Present** Cristina Lledo Gomez	249
15	**Re-Baptizing Spirit in Land and Ancestry: An Approach for Un-Doing Christian Colonialism** James W. Perkinson	271
16	**Toward Reclaiming the Wisdom of our Forebears: Nature and Environment from a Filipino Perspective** Ma. Florina Orillos-Juan	291

Index 311

Notes on Contributors

Vivienne S. M. Angeles recently retired from La Salle University in Philadelphia where she taught courses on Islam at the Department of Religion and Theology. She has published on the areas of Islam in the Philippines and Southeast Asia, Islam and gender, visual expressions of religion, and religion and migration. Angeles was a Fullbright scholar at the Center for Civilizational Dialogue at the University of Malaya and was president of the American Council for the Study of Islamic Societies. She was active at the American Academy of Religion where she served as co-chair of the Religion in Southeast Asia unit and was a member of the International Cooperation Committee. She was a Hamad Bin Khalifa Fellow for the Islamic Art symposium in Doha, Qatar, and was an affiliate of the Harvard Pluralism project. She received her PhD in Religion, major in Islamic Studies from Temple University.

Ferdinand Anno is an indigenous person belonging to the Bago-Kankanaey ethnolinguistic group. He taught Resistance Liturgics, Indigenous Peoples' Theologies, and practical theologies at Union Theological Seminary in the Philippines. He did his studies at the University of Leeds (PhD, 2006), the University of Edinburgh (MTh, 1998), Silliman University (MDiv, 1991), and Union Christian College (BA, 1987). Some of Anno's works on liturgy, resistance liturgics, and indigenous theologies have been published by Regnum, Wiley-Blackwell, ISPCK, Wipf, and Stock, among others. An ordained minister of the United Church of Christ in the Philippines, Anno is currently the chairperson of the UCCP Faith and Order Commission and president of Union

NOTES ON CONTRIBUTORS

Christian College. His other practical engagements include advocacies for the rights of indigenous peoples and ecological justice.

Agnes M. Brazal is a full professor and holder of the Br. Adelino Manuel FSC Professorial Chair for Religious Studies and Br. Flannan Paul FSC Professorial Chair for Rhetoric research fellow at the De la Salle University, Philippines. She is past president and founding member of the DaKaTeo (Catholic Theological Society of the Philippines) and past coordinator of the Ecclesia of Women in Asia (EWA). She is the author of *A Theology of Southeast Asia: Liberation-Postcolonial Ethics in the Philippines* (Orbis, 2019), co-author of *Intercultural Church: Bridge of Solidarity in the Migration Context* (Borderless Press, 2015), and co-editor of fourteen anthologies/journal special issues, on postcolonial, migration, feminist, and cyber ethics/theologies, which includes *Gender, Sexuality and Postcolonial Christianities in the Philippines* (*Intersections* 48, 2022) and *Toward a Bai Theology: Catholic Feminism in the Philippines* (Claretian, 2023). She obtained her MA/STL and PhD/SThD from the Katholieke Universiteit Leuven.

Pablo Virgilio S. David, Bishop of the Diocese of Kalookan in Metro Manila, hails from Guagua, Pampanga. He is a biblical scholar whose doctoral dissertation for the Katholieke Universiteit Leuven is on the Book of Daniel. As a storyteller, David's homilies are popular even on social media. He has published biblically rooted popular books like *Yeshua: Son of Man* and *The Gospel of Mercy According to Juan/a* and *The Gospel of Love According to Juan/a* written with N.L.B. Tomen. A mission-minded bishop, Kalookan's current **20** mission stations in cooperation with religious congregations embody the Church's reaching out to the poor. With *kenosis* as episcopal motto and Maximilian Kolbe and Oscar Romero as models, he courageously stands up for the victims of drug addiction and the drug war. As reelected president of the Catholic Bishops' Conference of the Philippines, David is also at the forefront of what the Church can do in the fight against climate change.

Cristina Lledo Gomez is a Filipina living on the lands of the Dharrug and Guringai peoples, also known as Hornsby, NSW, Australia. She is the Presentation Sisters Senior Lecturer in Theology at BBI-The Australian Institute of Theological Education and a Research Fellow for the Australian Centre for Christianity and Culture. Her role at BBI-TAITE is directed toward promoting women's spiritualities, feminist theologies, and ecotheologies. She is the author of *The Church as Woman and Mother* (2018) and a recipient of the Catherine Mowry Lacugna Award for her essay "Mother Language, Mother Church, Mother Earth" (2020) from the Catholic Theological Society of America. Her recent publications include "Narratives and Experiences of Racializing by Oceania Women" (2023), "Wives Submitting to Husbands: Domestic Violence, Women and the Christian Faith" (2022), and "Deleted and Reclaimed Borders: Embracing My Native Self" (2022). She is currently co-convener of the Women's Consultation for Constructive Theology at the Catholic Theological Society of America, Co-Chair of the Ecclesiological Investigations Network at the American Academy of Religion and board member for the College Theology Society.

Ma. Maricel S. Ibita, Associate Professor, Theology Department— Ateneo de Manila University (AdMU), researches on biblical narrative and poetry; feminist, liberation, social science, empire studies, trauma, and ecological-sustainability hermeneutics; and Jewish-Christian sources for biblical interpretation. She is currently the President of the Catholic Biblical Association of the Philippines. She co-chairs the research unit The Bible, Ecology, and Sustainability of the European Association of Biblical Studies. In 2018, 2019, and 2020–2022, she co-promoted Open Faculty Global Minds Project between AdMU, St. Vincent School of Theology-Adamson University, Department of Theology and Religious Education-De La Salle University and the KU Leuven in Belgium. She also co-promoted the multidisciplinary and multisectoral 2020–2022 Urban Poor Women and Children with Academics for Reaching and Delivering on UNSDGs in the Philippines—(UPWARD-UP) funded by VLIR-UOS, Belgium. She was awarded the 2022–2023 Rev. Joseph A. O'Hare SJ Endowed Professorial Chair in the Humanities, Ateneo de Manila University.

Ma. Marilou S. Ibita is an associate professor at the Department of Theology and Religious Education at the De la Salle University in Manila, Philippines. She is also Visiting Professor of Contextual Hermeneutical Approaches to the Bible at the Faculty of Theology and Religious Studies at Katholieke Universiteit Leuven (FTRS KU Leuven) in Belgium. Her primary research centers around biblical literature and Jewish-Christian dialogue. She is widely published, having contributed to edited books and journals, and has co-edited three books: *The Spirit, Hermeneutics and Dialogue* (Leuven: Peeters, 2019), *Theologizing in the Corinthian Conflict: Studies in the Exegesis and Theology of 2 Corinthians* (Leuven: Peeters,

xx NOTES ON CONTRIBUTORS

2013) and *Kindness, Courage, and Integrity in Biblical Texts and in the Politics of Biblical Interpretation* (Leuven: Peeters, 2023). Her recent publications include *The Johannine Peter's Trauma and Recovery: Characterization from the Lens of Trauma* (2021), *Contributing Voice: Women and Waiting at Table* (2021), *The Use of Luke 10:25-37 in Fratelli Tutti* (2021), and *Meals and Mission: A Contextual Reading of the Lukan Meal Scenes in the Filipin@ Context* (2021), *Dinner and Dissent in 1 Cor 11:17-24* (2023), and *Partaking of the Death-Proclaiming Meal for Life: Re-reading 1 Cor 11:17-34 from the Lens of Post-Traumatic Growth* (2024).

Jamina Vesta M. Jugo finished her doctorate in Political Science at the University of Goettingen. She is currently employed by the Catholic organization *Missio* in Aachen, Germany, and teaches classes in European Studies at the Ateneo de Manila University in the Philippines. She enjoys intersectional and interdisciplinary work and hopes to discover more ways to build bridges between Asia and Europe.

S. Lily Mendoza is a Kapampangan-born Filipina and currently resides in Waawiyatanong (aka Detroit), the traditional homeland of the Anishinaabe peoples, Wyandot Huron, Fox, Miami, and Sauk. She is Full Professor of Culture and Communication at Oakland University in Rochester, Michigan, and is known for her pathbreaking work on the politics of indigeneity particularly within the Philippine diasporic and homeland contexts. Currently, she serves as the executive director of the Center for Babaylan Studies (CfBS), a movement for decolonization and indigenization among diasporic Filipinos. Her most recent book publication is the co-edited volume, *Decolonizing Ecotheology: Indigenous and Subaltern Challenges* (Wipf & Stock, 2022).

Ma. Florina Orillos-Juan is an associate professor at the De la Salle University Department of History. Her research interests include environmental history of the Philippines, history of disasters, history of leprosy in the Philippines and Southeast Asia, the Spanish colonial period, culture during the Japanese Occupation, and general topics about history and geography. In 2012, she won the *Young Historian's Prize* of the National Commission for Culture and the Arts of the Philippines. Her book titled *Kasaysayan at Vulnerabilidad: Ang Lipunang Pilipino sa Harap ng Pananalanta ng Pesteng Balang, 1569-1949*, published by De La Salle University Publishing House won the 2019 Outstanding Book Award granted by the National Academy for Science and Technology (NAST) of the Philippines. She obtained her degrees in PhD History, MA History, and BA History from the University of the Philippines, Diliman.

James W. Perkinson has lived for 35 years as a white settler on Three Fires land in inner-city Detroit, currently teaching as Professor of Social Ethics at the Ecumenical Theological Seminary and lecturing in Intercultural Communication Studies at the University of Oakland (Michigan). He holds a PhD in theology from the University of Chicago, and is the author of *Political Spirituality for a Century of Water Wars: The Angel of the Jordan Meets the Trickster of Detroit; Political Spirituality in an Age of Eco-Apocalypse: Communication and Struggle Across Species, Cultures, and Religions; Messianism Against Christology: Resistance Movements, Folk Arts, and Empire; Shamanism, Racism, and Hip-Hop Culture: Essays on White Supremacy and Black Subversion;* and *White Theology: Outing Supremacy in Modernity* and two poetry books: *Dreaming Moorish;* and *A Secret Gift Outside the Door.* He is an artist on the spoken-word poetry scene and an activist in the struggle against water shutoffs.

Daniel Franklin E. Pilario is member of the Congregation of the Mission, professor of St. Vincent School of Theology in Quezon City, and the incoming president of Adamson University in Manila. His book, *Back to the Rough Grounds of Praxis,* earned the best research in humanities in Belgium in 2005. He contributed articles and edited or co-edited several anthologies—the most recent are *Philippine Local Churches after the Spanish Regime* (2015); *Faith in Action: Catholic Social Teaching on the Ground* (2015); *Second Plenary Council of the Philippines: Quo Vadis* (2015); *Theology and Peacebuilding* (2018); *Sexual Violence Against Women: Victim-Survivors and Faith-Based Approaches* (2023); *Fratelli Tutti: A Global Commentary* (2023). He belongs to the editorial board of philosophical and theological journals and is a former president and founding member of the Catholic Theological Society of the Philippines (DAKATEO). On weekends, he also serves as a minister of a garbage dump parish in Payatas, Quezon City.

Eleuterio J. Revollido (1960) studied theology and historical studies at St. Andrew's Theological Seminary, M.Div., Trinity University of Asia, AB Political Science (Quezon City, Philippines), South East Asia Graduate School of Theology, M.Th. (Philippines), and the Royal and Pontifical University of Santo Tomas, S.Th.D. (Manila, Philippines). Eleuterio published several articles in the publication series of the Old Catholic Seminary

xxii NOTES ON CONTRIBUTORS

Publication and the International Church Review of the Old Catholic Church; is recipient of the Archbishop Andreas Rinkel Prize from the Old Catholic Seminary, Utrecht, the Netherlands, 2019; a priest of the Iglesia Filipina Independiente and member of the Concordat Council in partnership with the Old Catholic Church of the Union of Utrecht and the Episcopal Church; elected treasurer of the Association for Theological Schools in South East Asia (ATESEA 2023–2026); and rector of Aglipay Central Theological Seminary (ACTS), Urdaneta City, Philippines.

Antonio D. Sison, CPPS, PhD, is the Vatican Council II Chair of Theology and Professor of Systematic Theology at Catholic Theological Union, Chicago. He is the author of the book *The Art of Indigenous Inculturation: Grace on the Edge of Genius* (Orbis Books, 2021) and editor-contributing author of the upcoming anthology *Deep Inculturation: Global Voices on Christian Faith and Indigenous Genius* (Orbis Books, Spring 2024). A Filipino-American scholar, Sison has spoken widely on the confluence of contextual-liberation theologies, postcolonial aesthetics, and inculturation. He was the featured speaker at the 2022 co-curation forum of Chicago's Field Museum (Anthropology department) and the Cathedral Filipino Network (CFN); the presentation theme was on "Ancestral Miracles: Catholic Faith, Indigenous Genius."

Peter-Ben Smit (Dr. theol. and Dr. theol. habil., Bern; ThD, General Theological Seminary, New York) is Professor by special appointment of Ancient Catholic Church Structures and the History and Doctrines of the Old Catholic Churches at Utrecht University, Professor of Contextual Biblical Interpretation at Vrije Universiteit Amsterdam, and a research associate at the University of Pretoria. He has published on the history of the Iglesia Filipina in particular, including the volumes *Old Catholic and Philippine Independent Ecclesiologies in History: the Catholic Church in Every Place* (Leiden: Brill, 2011), with W.H. de Boer, *"In necessariis unitas": Hintergründe zu den ökumenischen Beziehungen zwischen der "Iglesia Filipina Independiente", den Kirchen der Anglikanischen Gemeinschaft und den altkatholischen Kirchen der Utrechter Union* (Frankfurt: Lang, 2012) and with Ineke Smit, *The Iglesia Filipina Independiente: Being Church "Pro Deo Et Patria"* (Amersfoort: Pascal, 2022).

Leny M. Strobel is Professor Emerita in American Multicultural Studies at Sonoma State University in California. She is also a Founding Elder of the Center for Babaylan Studies. She is the author of *Coming Full Circle:*

The Process of Decolonization Among Post-1965 Filipino Americans, editor, *Babaylan: Filipinos and the Call of the Indigenous;* co-author with S. Lily Mendoza, *Back from the Crocodile's Belly: Philippine Babaylan Studies and the Struggle for Indigenous Memory.* Most of her publications, webinars, and podcasts are archived at her website https://www.lenystrobel.com/.

Revelation Enriquez Velunta is a professor of New Testament and Cultural Studies at Union Theological Seminary, Philippines. He also serves as director of UTS's Master of Theology Program. He has taught at the Pacific Theological College (Fiji), Lutheran Theological Seminary (Hong Kong), Yu-Shan Theological College and Seminary (Taiwan), Vanderbilt University (USA), Teologiska Hogskolan Stockholm (Sweden), Philippine Women's University, Philippine Christian University (Manila and Dasmarinas campuses), and Southern Christian College. Velunta studied at Union Theological Seminary, Princeton Theological Seminary, and Vanderbilt University. He is part of the International Scholars Program of the Society of Biblical Literature. Many of his works are available on Amazon and via his blog. Velunta is also a Certified Public Accountant.

LIST OF FIGURES

Fig. 8.1 Quiapo Black Nazarene, 2014. Photograph courtesy
of the author   146
Fig. 8.2 (*Santa Santita* © 2004 Unitel Pictures)   156

CHAPTER 1

Philippine Christianity: 500 Years of Resistance and Accommodation

Agnes M. Brazal, Cristina Lledo Gomez, and Ma. Marilou S. Ibita

In the Philippines, the "500th anniversary of the introduction of Christianity" is part of a bigger celebration called the 2021 Quincentennial Commemoration, organized by the Philippine government. This consists

---

A. M. Brazal
Department of Theology and Religious Education, De La Salle University, Manila, Philippines
e-mail: agnes.brazal@dlsu.edu.ph

C. Lledo Gomez (✉)
BBI-The Australian Institute of Theological Education, Pennant Hills, NSW, Australia

Australian Centre for Christianity and Culture, Barton, ACT, Australia
e-mail: cristina.lledogomez@bbi.catholic.edu.au

M. M. S. Ibita
Department of Theology and Religious Education, De La Salle University, Manila, Philippines
e-mail: ma.marilou.ibita@dlsu.edu.ph

© The Author(s), under exclusive license to Springer Nature Switzerland AG 2024
C. Lledo Gomez et al. (eds.), *500 Years of Christianity and the Global Filipino/a*, Pathways for Ecumenical and Interreligious Dialogue, https://doi.org/10.1007/978-3-031-47500-9_1

of three celebrations: (1) the role of the country in the Magellan-Elcano circumnavigation of the world; (2) the introduction of Christianity in the Philippines; (3) and the victory of Lapu-Lapu against the Spaniards in the Battle of Mactan. The Philippine national government aims to commemorate these encounters with the Spanish in 1521 from a Filipin@-centric point of view.

This Filipin@-centric point of view is in line with the postcolonial perspective that we adopt in this anthology. Postcolonial criticism recognizes and examines how colonial, neo-colonial, dominant interests have been ingrained in the reception of Christianity during and even after the period of colonization.

The tasks of postcolonial criticism include scrutinizing historical and biblical documents for their colonial entanglements, resurrecting or foregrounding suppressed voices such as that of dominated peasants and women, and interacting with and reflecting on hybridity, deterritorialization, and double or multiple identities resulting from these cultural encounters. The ultimate goal of postcolonial criticism is to decolonize knowledge and praxis of Christianity.

Our Filipin@-centrism from a postcolonial perspective does not mean romanticizing the "native" versus the Western. Rather, it highlights the liberating elements in the traditions that emerged from the colonized and/or marginalized groups, as well as, from the encounter between cultures. Lastly, the term postcolonial is not being used here in the temporal sense, as if colonialism has ended. Although many formerly colonized nations have attained formal independence, colonial/ neo-colonial or imperialist interests persist even after the period of colonization till today, both in the church and in the bigger society.

In this introductory chapter, we will focus on some highlights of Philippine Christianity as it developed in the colonial—333 years under the Spanish rule (1565–1898) and 48 years under the US-American regime (1898–1946)—as well as the post-colonial[1]context with particular focus on resistance and accommodation in the Philippines and the diaspora as this has been inspired by the Christian faith.

THE COLONIAL CONTEXT

The Initial Encounters

On behalf of the king of Spain, the Portuguese Ferdinand Magellan, initiated the first circumnavigation of the world from 1519 to 1522. Historian

Laurence Bergreen, author of *Over the Edge of the World: Magellan's Terrifying Circumnavigation of the Globe* referred to this as "the greatest sea voyage ever undertaken, and the most significant." [2] This is not an exaggeration as some of Magellan's contemporaries saw the voyage as suicidal and that sea monsters or killer fogs awaited them. Of the 243 men who started on the journey, only 35 men successfully made their way back to Spain. They perished not because of monsters or killer fogs but due to illness triggered by malnutrition while others were killed by the natives.[3]

As grade school students, we have been taught that it was Ferdinand Magellan who discovered the Philippines. The islands, however, have been known to Chinese[4] and Islamic traders even before the arrival of the Spanish colonialists. The Chinese have been trading in the Philippine islands centuries before the arrival of the Spaniards.

From the native perspective, it was actually our ancestors who discovered Magellan and his crew on March 18, 1521, in an island near Homonhon, Guiuan, Eastern Samar, extremely hungry, sick with scurvy, underfed, and dying.[5] Our ancestors fed and gave them food supplies to last till they reached Maluku which is now a part of Indonesia. Without their help, the Magellan-Elcano expedition would not have achieved its feat of circumnavigating the globe for the first time.

On April 14, 1521, the first baptism was held in Cebu, where the chieftain Rajah Humabon, and his wife, Hara Humamay, were baptized together with 800 others. The story was traditionally romanticized highlighting how the natives welcomed and accepted Christianity wholeheartedly. A more critical narrative reveals that Rajah Humabon agreed to be baptized to cement his alliance with Magellan against Lapu-Lapu, the ruler of Mactan, with whom he had some enmity. This mistake of Magellan who presumed that Humabon had sovereignty over a large territory would cost him his life.[6]

The Columban historian Martin Noone described the growing resentment against the Spaniards' demand for the people to convert, their intrusion into the people's lives, and even their treatment of women. This would explode in the battle of Mactan where Lapu-Lapu galvanized the help of other chieftains. Jesuit historian Jose Arcilla noted how Magellan grossly underestimated his enemies.[7] Magellan did not take the necessary precautions nor did he take time to get to know more about the terrain, nor allotted adequate firepower to support the battle. This led to the defeat of the Spaniards and Magellan's untimely demise.

The First Bishop and Synod

Forty-four years later in 1565 the Spanish conquistadores led by Miguel Lopez de Legaspi returned and established the first permanent settlement in Cebu. Domingo de Salazar, hailed as the Bartolome de las Casas of the Philippines, arrived 16 years later in 1581, to become the first bishop of Manila. Like his fellow Dominican Bartolome de las Casas, he championed the rights of the indigenous populations.

Informed by the natives themselves of the atrocities being committed, de Salazar described in his 1582 letter to the King of Spain the Spanish colonists' abuse of the indigenous population and the Chinese migrants in the islands.[8] While not contesting evangelization as justification for the conquest of the islands, he criticized the Spanish conquistadores who used the *encomienda* system solely to get rich quickly, by demanding gold tributes and by employing cruel and violent means of collecting tribute while failing in their duty to preach the gospel. In the *encomienda* system, the crown grants a conquistador, a soldier, an official or a number of natives, to exact tribute in gold, in kind, or in labor on the condition that they protect and evangelize the natives.[9] He pleaded for the reform of the *encomienda* system which had become a means for the cruel and violent collection of tributes, while failing to protect and evangelize the natives. The *encomienda* system which was envisioned to assist in the Christianization and Hispanization of the indigenous population was failing in its mission.

De Salazar also railed against the Spanish' unjust punishment of the Chinese merchants for small causes (e.g., going out at night to find provisions or because of their unclean belongings), as well as, forcing them to sell their goods to the authorities at a much-reduced price.[10]

De Salazar likewise complained that the rule against Spanish ownership of slaves was not being enforced, and thus the people resisted conversion and were more receptive to Islamic preachers from Mindanao and Borneo than the preachers of Christ: "This is different from our evangelizing, which comes accompanied by bad treatment and bad examples. [As a consequence] they say 'yes,' with words, but 'no' in their hearts, and if given a chance, they leave [the faith]."[11]

Within only a year of his arrival in the country, the Bishop convened the Synod of Manila that addressed the issue of forced labor, confiscation of land, as well as full restitution to the locals of whatever was taken from them.[12] The latter meant that if a Spanish conquistador stole property from a native, he had to pay back that farmer in full or return the confiscated land. The bishop then was responsible for the court prosecution of all offenses committed against the natives.[13]

The 1582 Synod of Manila laid a strong moral foundation for the new colony, at least in principle, holding the conquistadores accountable to help win the trust of the locals. It was also officially decided in the same synod to preach the gospel in the native languages.

The Clash with the Babaylans

The early history of evangelization in the islands is characterized by a clash on the one hand, between the indigenous religions led by *babaylan* or *catalonan* who are mostly older women with a few transgender females and, on the other hand, Christianity headed by an all-male priesthood.[14]

At the start of the seventeenth century, it is estimated that over half the population of the Philippines had heard the Gospel and one third had been baptized, but Christianity had not really taken deep roots. The people continued to go to the priestess for all their problems.[15]

The conversion of the babaylan was important to ensure the evangelization of the islands. The Spanish priests condemned them as priestesses of the devil. In accordance with the Instructions to Commissary of the Inquisition in the Philippines[16] young boys were removed from their families to live in a convent where they received catechism and baptism, and then employed to catechize the older generation, or if not, report their clandestine animist practices.[17]

The confessional box was especially useful for extracting information from the people, particularly the young boys, and in rooting out the babaylans and eradicating native religious beliefs. Through the labeling of native religious beliefs as *abusos* or *supersticiones* and using this as a guide for confession, the priests were able to locate the babaylans and their followers.[18] The babaylan tradition however was not completely eradicated. Indigenous religions and beliefs will merge with Christian beliefs to galvanize resistance against colonizers.

The Revolutionary Impact of Religious Ideas

While the national elites were influenced by liberal ideals from Europe, the masses drew their inspiration for the revolution in their hybrid religiosity. The postcolonial theorist Homi Bhabha developed the concept of hybridity in relation to the construction of culture and identity in the colonial context.[19] The colonial government hoped to reproduce in the colonized their culture but failed by producing instead a hybrid, an in-between. Hybridity in the postcolonial sense is not the same as acculturation and syncretism which may just be a benign combination. Hybridity is a product, in the context of unequal power relations, of both accommodation and resistance to colonial domination.

For example, Reynaldo Ileto, in his book *Pasyon and Revolution*, argued how the masses were inspired to resist colonial domination through the ritual singing of the *Pasyon*, in the latter period of Spanish colonization in the nineteenth century.[20] As powerful amulets are believed to emit light and make their possessors radiant, Christ himself has been described in the Pasyon as radiating with light. The peasants believed that only a person with a beautiful *loob* or inner self that attracts others could be a light to others. Aligned with this, the revolutionary nineteenth century Katipunan movement which fought against the Spanish colonizers has been imaged like Christ of the Pasyon, as radiating with light that leads to liberation.

Jesuit historian John Schumacher also highlighted as a major influence on the masses the Filipino clergy who were favorable to the Revolution. "Where the clergy gave their support and leadership, the masses remained faithful to the Revolution."[21]

In fact, the most crucial event that led to the Revolution against Spanish rule was the execution of three Filipino secular priests in 1872—Mariano Gomez, Jose Burgos, and Jacinto Zamora—allegedly for their involvement in a Cavite military mutiny.[22] They were leaders for the secularization, in effect the nationalization of Philippine parishes. It is believed that their being linked to the mutiny, instigated by Spanish friars, was a ploy to do away with the priests' demand for clerical equality.

The US-American Regime and the Establishment of the Iglesia Filipina Independiente

By 1898, the revolutionaries were winning the war against the Spaniards and had taken hold of most islands except Manila when as a result of the defeat of Spain in the Spanish-American War, Spain sold the Philippines to the USA for US$20 million. The USA justified its colonization of the islands as "benevolent assimilation" in order to civilize and Christianize the natives.[23] The Philippine-American War erupted in 1899 and lasted over three years till 1902, with a death rate of US-American soldiers comparable to that of the Vietnam War.

The radicalization of the nationalist movement among the clergy eventually took form in the establishment in 1902 of the *Iglesia Filipina Independiente* or the IFI. The IFI had as its dual aim the liberation "from the influence of foreign regular clergy" and the establishment of a church with a "Filipino face."[24] A number of Protestant missionaries who arrived with the US colonialists defended or, at the very least, spoke well of the IFI.

Within the Catholic Church, however, it was only in 1919 that the Church through Pope Benedict XV advocated for the thorough training of the native clergy as they could better understand their people and thus were able to more effectively introduce the faith to them. This training should be "excellent in all its phases" so they can take on the task of spiritual leadership.[25]

Even as the process of inculturation started from the beginnings of Christianity, it was only in the Second Vatican Council (1963–1965) that the Catholic Church officially acknowledged the need for the faith to be rooted in the wisdom of the people's culture, and once again allowed the use of the vernacular in liturgies.

On August 12, 2021, a Joint Statement from the *Iglesia Filipina Independiente* and the Roman Catholic Church was released noting that the "formation of the IFI was *not* against the Catholic Church, but rather against the continued domination of Spanish bishops and priests in the dioceses and parishes of the colony."[26]

The Post-colonial Context

The independence from the USA that the Philippines gained on July 4, 1946, did not mean the end of the colonial relations with its former colonizer. The Tydings-McDuffie law prescribed conditions that cemented the Philippines' neo-colonial relation with the USA. The first condition was the acceptance of the 1946 Philippine Trade Act that granted the following: (1) equal rights of US citizens to exploit the country's natural resources and to own public utilities and other types of businesses; (2) forbidding interference with foreign currency exchange with the peso pegged on the dollar; (3) removal of tariffs on imported US goods; and (4) "unlimited remittance of profits for U.S. corporations." [27] The Act passed Congress through the expulsion of left-leaning lawmakers. The second condition was the granting of supreme authority to the USA over its military bases through the approval of the 1947 US-Philippines Treaty of General Relations.

Martial Law, the Church, and the People Power Revolution

The declaration of Martial law by Ferdinand Marcos Sr. in 1972 was tacitly endorsed by the USA as he assured continued support for their economic interests in the country. Marcos Sr. used the threat of a communist take-over as justification for his declaration of Martial law, thus aligning with the USA in the Cold War geopolitics.

Between 1968 and 1972, a significant minority of Christian left emerged, influenced by the New Left, the Civil Rights movement in the USA, and the Latin American liberation theology.[28] The National Council of Churches in the Philippines (NCCP) which was formed in 1963 to give voice to progressive Protestant Filipinos was the "first religious body to officially condemn the Marcos regime in 1973."[29] The 20-year reign of Ferdinand Marcos Sr. as the country's President witnessed the gradual galvanization of forces within the different churches in the Philippines toward opposing the dictatorship.

On February 13, 1986, with the economy in shambles and with evidence of massive cheating in the snap elections called by Marcos Sr., the Catholic Bishops Conference of the Philippines issued a call to discern civil disobedience, that was read in all the Sunday masses. It stated:

> In our considered judgment, the polls were unparalleled in the fraudulence of their conduct....According to moral principles, a government that assumes or retains power through fraudulent means has no moral basis. If such a government does not of itself freely correct the evil it has inflicted on the people then it is our serious moral obligation as a people to make it do so....The way indicated to us now is the way of non-violent struggle for justice. [30]

This means active resistance to evil by peaceful means—in the manner of Christ. And its one end, for now, was that the will of the people be done through ways and means proper to the Gospel. Hildegard Myers-Goss[31] noted the significance of this event as this was the first occasion in modern times when a Catholic Bishops' Conference called the people to civil disobedience to overthrow an unjust system.

Sparked by a failed military coup against Marcos Sr., a three-day non-violent insurrection commenced on the evening of February 22 and ended on February 25, 1986. This People Power revolution can be seen as the culmination of years of conscientization, and various forms of resistance including massive trainings in active non-violence starting in 1984, side by side, with the growing Communist guerilla warfare. The US government, however, stood by Marcos Sr. until February 24, 1986, when US President Ronald Reagan endorsed the call of the public for Marcos Sr. to resign. Ronald Sider described the 1986 People Power revolution as "[t]he most stunning non-violent victory since Mahatma Gandhi and Martin Luther King"[32]

GLOBALIZATION AND THE CHRISTIAN DIASPORA

It was the thought of living under the oppressive martial law of Marcos Sr. and marching along with other Filipin@s on EDSA, in protest to this illegal government, which gave impetus for Cristina Lledo Gomez's parents to decide to migrate out of the Philippines. Their choices were Libya (Africa), Sydney (Australia), or somewhere in the USA. Her father visited Libya first and decided it was just as dangerous, if not more. Meanwhile, it seemed everyone was applying to move to the USA but US visa applications took longer to process than Australian visas. Her family entered Australia at the end of February 1986 (just days after the failed military coup against Marcos Sr.), via the 1986–1987 skilled migration program[33] pushed by the Australian government, in its attempts to increase its population; it seemed, at least, Australia needed engineers, and thus, gladly welcomed her father's experience and expertise in the area.

Like many migrants, her family experienced the troubles of starting with nothing but the few items they could bring. They had to acclimatize to the weather, the ways of the people, and even the language of the people given the differing accents between American English (which Filipin@s learned in school) and British-Australian English. It was the Catholic Church and a handful of Filipin@-Australian contacts who helped them to settle into a new land and its different ways of being. The Catholic community was a place of familiarity but also a place where one could find other Filipin@ migrants seeking to retain Philippine culture to pass on to future generations. After all, many if not most Filipin@s, whether in the Philippines or overseas, at the time were Catholic or from another Christian denomination. In terms of gifts to the Filipin@, as migrants, Christianity

10   A. M. BRAZAL ET AL.

has enabled Filipin@s all over the world to find a place of familiarity, of fellowship/community/ ready-made networks, of meaning and hope in the midst of the difficulties of being a migrant, and safety among one's own kind in places of unfamiliarity and even danger, especially as exploited overseas workers—as domestic workers, slave laborers in building and clothing industries, seafarers (notice how many cruise ship workers are Filipin@), and overworked nurses. Recognizing the troubles of migrating and the specific needs of different cultural groups, within the Philippine Catholic community at least, priest chaplains are assigned to various cultural groups, dedicated to helping them settle into their new lands and address ongoing issues particular to their cultural groups, or with the cultural sensitivity that only a person from that group could appropriately approach. With many international clergy in Western countries deriving from Asia and Africa, Filipin@s in Western countries almost always have had dedicated Filipino priest-chaplains attending to them.

According to the Philippine Commission on Filipinos Overseas (CFO) from 2010 to 2020, the top five countries for Philippine emigration were the USA, Canada, Japan, Australia, and Italy, with an overwhelming majority, that is, over 77% of Filipin@ emigrants who chose to move to the Americas/Trust Territories.[34] The CFO defines Philippine Emigrants as "those leaving the Philippines for family reunification, marriage migration, with an intention to stay for long term or permanently overseas. They are immigrants or permanent visa holders."[35] In total, 77.14% fell under the category of "Emigrants" while only 21.29% were considered "Spouses and other partners of Foreign Nationals," and 1.57%, "Immigrant Workers."[36]

The latest statistics on the number of Overseas Filipino workers (OFWs) estimate about 1.83 million between April and September 2021.[37] Overseas contract workers made up 96.4% (1.76 million) of the total OFWs and the majority (60.2% or 1.10 million) were women. Further, four in ten were employed for elementary occupations, that is, occupations that involved "...the performance of simple and routine tasks which may require the use of hand-held tools and considerable physical effort."[38] This includes "...cleaning, restocking supplies and performing basic maintenance in apartments, houses, kitchens, hotels, offices, and other buildings; washing of cars and windows; helping in kitchens and performing simple tasks in food preparations; delivering messages or goods; carrying luggages and handling baggage."[39] Of the 1.83 million OFWs, 41% "...sent remittance between 40 thousand pesos to less than 100 thousand pesos."[40] In total, between April and September 2021, the remittance sent to the Philippines by OFWs was 151.33 billion pesos.[41] This is 9.31% of Philippine GDP,[42] evidencing how much OFWs support the Philippine economy.

Whether viewed from the perspective of the top professions of the emigrant, or top occupations of immigrant workers, the professional nurse stands out as the largest labor export of the Philippines with 72% being female.[43] In addition, 91.05% of marriage migrants are female, and 97.45% of au pairs are also female, with over 50% being college graduates.[44] The top five occupations of emigrants prior to migration are students (26.91%); unemployed (22.59%); housewives (15.7%); professional, technical, and related workers (12.46%); and service workers (10.46%).[45]

Considering that Filipinas overseas are often stereotyped as being either nurses, mail-order brides (married to very elderly Westerners), or domestic workers, the statistics might explain why such stereotypes exist. Consider too, the number of Philippine migrants who are female and largely engaged in service industries, despite being college graduates. Slave labor, domestic violence, and trafficking are just some of the extra difficulties facing the Filipina migrant in addition to the usual difficulties of starting in a new land. This should be a cause for concern to Filipin@s all over the world. That is, the lot of the Filipina often found in service jobs, or other positions that make her vulnerable to abuse and exploitation.[46]

Regarding the dominant move of the Filipin@ toward the USA, California being their top destination, this might be explained by the pursuit of family reunification, but also, under the idea of colonial mentality (CM), where anything American is deemed superior, emigrating to the USA would be seen as achieving the ultimate success.[47] And yet once in America, the Filipin@ faces the realities of racism and exclusion. As Peter Jamero writes about his Filipino farm-labor camp experience from 1930 to 1944:

> It was as a "campo" boy [Filipino farm-labor camp] that I first learned of my ancestral roots and the adventuresome and sometimes torturous path that Filipinos took in sailing halfway around the world to the promise that was America...As a campo boy, I also began to see the two faces of America, a place where Filipinos were at once welcomed and excluded, were considered equal and were discriminated against.[48]

Interestingly, the experience of discrimination begins in the mother country, the Philippines, as psychology professors E.J.R. David and Kevin Nadal write in their 2005 article on the colonial context of Filipino American Immigrants' psychological experiences, observing that: "(a) Filipino American immigrants experienced ethnic and cultural denigration in the Philippines prior to their U.S. arrival, (b) ethnic and cultural denigration in the Philippines and in the United States [in turn] may lead to the development of colonial mentality (CM), and (c) that CM may have negative mental health consequences among Filipino American immigrants."[49] In Australia, mental health counselor, Candice Garcia, points to the reality of colonial mentality among Filipin@s, leading to "feelings of inadequacy that have been passed on to us from our ancestors."[50] These feelings of inadequacy have and can be measured through the Colonial Mentality Scale (CMs) and Colonial Mentality Implicit Association Test (CMIAT).[51]

Because of racism and discrimination, it is without surprise that first-generation migrants, whether as mothers and fathers, grandparents, or aunts and uncles might advise their children, grandchildren, and nieces and nephews to hide their Philippine ethnic identity, especially if only one of the parents is Filipin@ while the other is a Westerner (British, Scottish, a white-skinned American, a white-skinned Australian, or white-skinned European). For these elders, being Filipin@ is not only considered inferior to being Western but also as not safe—from racism, discrimination, and exclusion in Western countries. This has resulted in a number of second-, third-, and fourth-generation Filipin@ migrants seeking to recover and learn more about their Philippine roots through other means such as decolonizing groups with the Centre for Babaylan Studies, co-created by Leny Strobel and Lily Mendoza, who have contributed chapters to this anthology and speak in those chapters about the ways they have helped many Filipin@s in the diaspora, to decolonize and reindigenize. Young Filipin@s in the diaspora appear to seek their Philippine cultural roots in the same way an adopted child might seek their birth parents—until they reconcile with their heritage, ancestry, or cultural origins, they feel incomplete and unable to explain such things as their interest in the spirits or the Filipin@ transpersonal worldview, or are drawn toward natural healing such as their grandmother whom they might discover is the *arbularyo* (healer) of her village in the Philippines.

Amid the complex context of the migrant Filipin@, navigating two worlds, the carrying of internalized inferiority, and dealing with the difficulties of migration—where might the Christian church sit? As already indicated above, the Christian church appears as a place where the overseas Filipin@, whether as a temporary or permanent migrant, might find familiarity and even refuge from isolation and exclusion, as a new person, and even as a brown person in a society that once enforced an all-white citizenship through its laws, policies, and structures.[52] But the Christian church too must ask how it might participate in maintaining the hegemonies that oppress not just the migrant but other vulnerable persons in society. Such hegemonies include patriarchy, sexism, whiteness, racism, colonialism, religious intolerance, for example, as this anthology points out.

The 500th year anniversary of the entry of Christianity into the Philippines was the perfect time to reflect on the mixed heritage that Christianity brought to the Philippines and Filipin@s all over the world. On the one hand, it was because of Filipin@ bishops, priests, religious sisters and brothers, nuns, and committed lay people who believed in the dignity of the Filipin@ as God's creation, as God's *imago dei*, that they were encouraged to fight against the unjust Marcos regime, working with people in rural and urban settings, articulating the injustice involved in the voting of Marcos Sr. through the statement of the bishops, marching with them at EDSA, and even laying down their own bodies in front of military tanks—all eventuating into a People's Power Revolution/Movement that would model people's power movements around the world. It was and is because of Christianity that Filipin@s find hope amid hopelessness, living in endless cycles of poverty, corruption, and joblessness. It is through Christianity that Filipin@s find connection even when far away from their own families. On the other hand, as also pointed out in the first part of this introduction, it was because of Christian colonizers that the Filipin@ indigenous spirituality was demonized and its women spiritual healers and priestesses were demoted and denigrated. Such spirituality remained in the Filipin@ but was hidden as if it was a cause of shame or an indication of his/her inferiority to the Westerner who was not bidden to any spirits in the landscape—for they had Jesus (in addition to Western science, technology, and weapons). Belief in Jesus meant then that there was no need to believe in spirits as that belonged to primitive or unreasonable beliefs among 'undeveloped' societies. To this day, we continue to hear comments from Westerners (including male theology professors) about how ridiculous Filipin@s are because they talk to the spirits in the trees or to their loved ones as ancestor spirits, as if they were physically present. And yet, it is this same indigenous religious spirituality that is now being mined for its wisdom, in terms of saving our planet and creating better relationships between people and the land.[53]

(White European and White American) Christianity has much to answer for the way it has been utilized to denigrate Philippine indigenous religiosities and spiritualities, Philippine cultural values, and the overall Philippine self as the authors of this anthology discuss in this volume. The anthology hopefully provides impetus for reflection on how Christianity is a mixed gift to the Philippines. It also hopes to show that decolonizing does not mean returning to some pure state of existence before the colonizers arrived in the Philippines. All existences are mixed or maybe better imaged as matrices. Even the babaylans lived with syncretism, combining their own cultural beliefs and practices with other beliefs and practices of those they encountered. The Filipin@ in diaspora must grapple with the identity of being both Filipin@ and Australian/American/Canadian etc., of living in urban modern settings but having affinity with the land and the spirits, or inversely, living in rural settings but not untouched by modernity, and of Christian colonialism and yet aspects of Christianity as very much entangled with rich Philippine history and traditional cultural practices (e.g., the *Flores De Mayo*, a procession which is dedicated to the Virgin Mary, *Simbang Gabi*, the early morning nine-day mass attendance, before and in preparation for Christmas, *Sinakulo*, the theatrical performance of the life, cross, death and resurrection of Jesus, and the honouring of the Black Nazarene or *Poong Nazareno* through an annual mass and/or procession).

The Catholic Church has recently (March 2023) repudiated the Doctrine of Discovery, the US law used to this day to reject any indigenous claims to land. This law was based on fifteenth-century papal bulls that justified colonial takeover of "undiscovered lands" and dealing with natives in any manner that was deemed necessary for the building of God's kingdom. However, the implementation included treating them as slaves or converting them into Western ways. The papal bulls were later revoked in the late 1530s but its colonial mindset would remain in the consciousness of colonizers. Indigenous peoples all over the world called for an apology from the Church and after meeting with an indigenous delegate from Canada, the Pope did apologize for the harm caused to indigenous peoples by the doctrine (July 2022) but stopped short of formally rescinding the papal bulls that were the source of the doctrine.[54] The church itself exists as a paradox, on the one hand seeking to proclaim, protect, and fight for the dignity of the human person, the dignity of

God's creation, and the dignity of the indigenous person, even providing the vision and medium of grace to enable individuals and groups to fight for this dignity.[55] On the other hand, the church still has much work to do in terms of rooting out such things as internalized racism (through colonial mentality) and institutionalized oppression (the unsaid apology and rejection of the fifteenth-century papal bulls that justified a European race toward empire building and constiuted the bases for the Doctrine of Discovery). This volume hopes its readers will come to a better understanding of the post-colonial context of being Filipin@-Christian.

THE ESSAYS

Peter Phan who has graced this book with a foreword suggests it can be read in three ways—" as a celebrative commemoration of the coming of Christianity to the Philippine Islands 500 years ago, as postcolonial and feminist assessments of Philippine Christianity, and as a global, especially diasporic contextualization of this Christianity." It can also be read as articles addressing two main contexts, following the way in which the texts, as presentations, were divided in the webinar of the same name and which gave impetus for this book. The first part focuses on "Rethinking the Encounters" with seven contributions while the second part shifts the focus to "Reappropriation, Resistance & Decolonization" with eight more articles.

Part 1 begins with an exploration and rethinking of the encounters in various stages of the coming of the Catholic faith through the Spanish expedition led by Ferdinand Magellan to the different groups of locals that they encountered in the various islands. It is very apt to begin with "Indigenization as Appropriation: What Being Baptized Could Have Meant for the Natives of Cebu in 1521," the contribution of Bishop Pablo Virgilio S. David, who along with Ma. Maricel Ibita focused on the very beginning of the encounter between Magellan and his cohorts and the local communities in the islands where they landed. Given that the source of the accounts of the First Mass and the First Baptism on April 14, 1521, comes mainly from the Chronicles of Antonio Pigafetta, the authors suggest that the native ancestors were accommodating other faiths as long as they were given the space to decide on their own how to appropriate these foreign religions into their own religious worldview.

Daniel Franklin E. Pilario, a member of the Congregation of Mission (or Vincentians), brings up the issue of "The Double Truth of (Colonial) Mission." From a postcolonial lens, he scrutinizes the ambivalent and indeterminate directions of colonial missions employing the research of Filipino historians and following Pierre Bourdieu's notion of double verité (dual truths) argues that a pluralist view on mission is needed to uncover the monologic readings brought about by hegemonic colonial practice.

"Rethinking Encounters and Reimagining Muslim-Christian Relations in Post-colonial Philippines" is the contribution of Vivienne S. M. Angeles. She expands the horizon of the conversation on the fifth centennial of Christianity in her contribution by including the colonial and post-colonial government policies that affected Muslim-Christian relationships while highlighting the contemporary efforts by Muslims and Christians to promote interreligious understanding. This is an important read for the dominantly Christian Filipino/a nation and the need for greater understanding of its Muslim background and current relations.

Muslims were not the only ones affected by the Christianizing missions to the Philippines. Ma. Marilou Ibita focuses on how the Spanish colonial brand of Christianization also impacted the presentation of the Jewish people through the popular religious expression of the *pasyon*. In her piece, "The Glocal Filipin@s and the *Pasyon* Through the Lens of Ethnicity," Ibita holds that from a theological-pastoral perspective, the binary approach that pits the text of the *pasyon* against its chanting is unnecessary because they complement one another. Moreover, other pressing issues like the vilification of the Jews in the *pasyon* must be rejected by glocal (global and local) Filipin@s in the post-Holocaust and contemporary era where ethnic-based hatred continues such as the intensification of Jewish and Asian hate during the COVID-19 pandemic.

Aside from the interreligious challenges posed by the colonization and the Christianizing mission, it is also important to note the development of the Christian faith under the continued Spanish presence. Eleuterio J. Revollido's contribution presents a Filipin@ perspective on the ecclesial development among the locals in his chapter, "An Independent Catholic, Nationalist People's Movement—The *Iglesia Filipina Independiente* (Philippine Independent Church)," with emphasis on the meaning and understanding of "independent Catholicism" from a combination of political/social and ecclesial/theological angles.

Complementing Revollido's work is Peter Ben-Smit's "Old Catholic and Independent Catholic: Negotiation of Independent Catholic Identities: The Case of Old Catholic—*Iglesia Filipina Independiente* Contacts." The chapter draws on archival sources from the correspondence of church leaders including Gregorio Aglipay, Eduard Herzog,

Andreas Rinkel, and Michael Ramsey to focus on the variety of motifs showcasing the development of the relationship of the IFI with the (European) Old Catholic Churches since its proclamation in 1902.

The seventh contribution related to exploring and rethinking the encounters between Christianity and the peoples of the Philippine islands is by Antonio D. Sison, CPPS entitled "Indigenous Inculturation: A Hermeneutics of Serendipity." He proposes "serendipity"—a fortuitous "conspiracy of grace" between human and divine agency—as an interpretative lens to examining the devotion to the Quiapo Black Nazarene as an example of "Indigenous inculturation." For Sison, in a creative dialectic, the Filipin@ primal religion remains extant as a form of crypto-resistance that continues to find mutual assimilation with Christianity in folk Catholic piety.

In Part 2, the book's foci are on reappropriation, resistance, and decolonization. Leny M. Strobel's text, "Decolonizing the Diaspora Through the Center for Babaylan Studies," speaks of her journey as a Filipina-American migrant post-1965. This is shown in her struggles toward the founding of the Babaylan Studies Centre and her research and activism in the reclamation of the Philippine indigenous spirit as a diasporic, *kapampangan* woman in the Filipin@ American space. For the Filipin@s in diaspora, this chapter and the next, written by Strobel's sister, are rich source materials for the carving of Philippine diasporic decolonial discourses.

S. Lily Mendoza's contribution, "Back from the Crocodile's Belly: Christian Formation Meets Indigenous Resurrection Redux," continues the story of the struggle of the Filipin@ in diaspora. She asks: What happens when the "One True Story" encounters other faith stories? With insights from her co-edited book similarly titled, *Back from the Crocodile's Belly: Philippine Babaylan Studies and the Struggle for Indigenous Memory*, Mendoza narrates her personal journey and its intersection with the Philippine colonial history and its consequences for her and her people's struggle for wholeness and authenticity. These are accompanied by her reflections on the biblical story of Jonah (Jonah 1-11), with implications for sustainability and global co-existence issues.

The consideration of the development of rites as a response to Christianization is a vital aspect of reflecting on the fifth centenary of Christianity in the Philippines. Is there a connection between the planting of Magellan's cross and Philippine Christianity's silence about the destruction of our mountains and rainforests? Or have we reached the point

18 A. M. BRAZAL ET AL.

where we must uproot the cross and plant the *Pudo*ng of the Igorots instead? These are the questions that Ferdinand Anno's chapter, "The Ygollotes *Pudong* and the Leitourgia of the Post-human Commune" seeks to answer. He argues for the significance of the *Pudong* rite to the formation of an ecumenical/inter-faith spirituality of resistance vis-à-vis the continuing reality of development aggression in the Philippines, particularly the Gran Cordillera Central.

Continuing the theme of reappropriation, resistance, and decolonization, Revelation Velunta applies a specifically Filipin@ "reading in front of texts" in the pericopes of Matthew's Gospel, in "Introducing Jeepney Hermeneutics: Reading the Bible as Canaanites." This hermeneutical lens uses the metaphor of the transformation of the military jeep into a mass transportation in the Philippines as a form of resistance to imperialism and colonialism. This kind of reading aims to disrupt and challenge the hegemony of Western scholarship in biblical studies, especially in plural Asia. A special thanks goes to Marilou Ibita for her addition of extra resources relevant to this chapter in the footnotes.

The discussion of the 500 years of Christianity in the Philippines would be incomplete without a critical reflection on Mary. In Chap. 13, Jamina Vesta M. Jugo writes in "*Inang Diyos, Inang Bayan*: The Virgin Mary and Filipino Identity" about Marianism as a conduit for inculturated colonial religiosity, and, ultimately, for nation-building. She contends that Marianism laid the foundations for a sacrificial, ambiguously domestic notion of motherhood that Filipin@s, especially girls and women, must grapple with to this day not only in ecclesial but also the political aspect of lived religion. She suggests the exploration of a wider range of Marian narratives which can liberate rather than oppress the Philippines and its women.

Continuing the reflection of the experience of oppression of the Filipina, particularly as a Catholic migrant, Cristina Lledo Gomez expounds in "*Bangon Na*, Pinays Rise Up: Reclaiming Pinay Power Dismantled by a Christian Colonial Past" the effect of Christian colonization of the Philippines upon the *Pinay* (the Filipina). That is, the Pinay experience of intersectional oppression at the levels of the institutional, interpersonal, and internal. Lledo Gomez explores the use of Babaylans as a form of feminist *pinay* re-empowerment and model for decolonizing and suggests rather that for Filipina Christians, Jesus as "Christa" can be a possible alternate Christian feminist-*pinay* decolonizing model of liberation and empowerment.

The effect of the 500 years of Christianity to the Filipin@s is not limited to the human family alone but includes effects upon the wider creation. This helps us to remember the interconnection between people and the land, in indigenous spiritualities, thoughts, and practices. The final two contributions to this anthology serve fittingly in this resistance and decolonizing section, specifically against a Christianity that harms the planet (a colonizing empire-building approach), and rather toward a Christian faith that sees the dignity of all creation and promotes a sustainable future. James W. Perkinson's "Re-baptizing Spirit in Land and Ancestry: An Approach for Un-doing Christian Colonialism" recounts the lessons learned and questions raised by his exposure to development interests in Luzon to face Filipin@ "Doctrine of Discovery" decimation of the indigenous Ayta homeland. Perkinson turns to a re-reading of the biblical tradition to center both the wild and living human and non-human biblical characters. He argues that the first task of Christian vocation is to *be* baptized—into both land wisdom and indigenous practice of such—for the sake of an anti-colonial vision of a future that is actually viable and worthy of the planet.

Finally, Ma Florina Orillos-Juan's contribution, "Towards Reclaiming the Wisdom of our Forebears: Nature and Environment from a Filipino Perspective," argues that the early Filipin@s were able to evolve into a complex civilization and culture, rooted in their relationship with nature and the environment, albeit neglected because of favoring the more rational and scientific European and Western epistemologies. She foregrounds the Filipin@ indigenous system of knowledge concerning nature, the environment, and disasters to highlight the early Filipinos who developed a profound ecological wisdom and environmental stewardship.

We hope that the collection in this book that remembers and analyzes critically the pre-colonial, colonial, and postcolonial developments of Christianity in the Philippines and the diaspora, with all the intertwining movements of resistance and accommodation, will inspire continuous conversation and engagement among Filipin@s and other conversation partners for a more meaningful, more liberating, more life-giving and sustaining Christian faith in the Philippines and beyond in the coming years.

Notes

1. Post-colonial with a "hyphen" is being used here in the temporal sense, that is, after the period of colonization or from the time of independence and beyond.
2. Laurence Bergreen, *Over the Edge of the World: Magellan's Terrifying Circumnavigation of the Globe*, reprint ed. (Perennial: HarperCollins, 2004).
3. Fundacion Elkano, "Death and Disease on the First Circumnavigation of the World," https://artsandculture.google.com/story/death-and-disease-on-the-first-circumnavigation-of-the-world/vQWxOWN1pDjbJA.
4. Edgar Wickberg, *Early Chinese Economic Influence in the Philippines, 1850-1898*, East Asian Series, Reprint no. 3 (Lawrence, Kansas: Center for East Asian Studies, The University of Kansas, https://kuscholarworks.ku.edu/bitstream/handle/1808/1072/CEAS.1962.n3.pdf;jsessionid=E0F5968E473B21489B54A1C9BADB5D30?sequence=1.
5. Xiao Chua, "When our Ancestors Discovered Magellan," March 18, 2020, https://nqc.gov.ph/en/resources/when-our-ancestors-discovered-magellan/.
6. Luis H. Francia. The Contagion of History," https://usa.inquirer.net/source/inquirer-net-u-s-bureau.
7. Quoted in Karl M. Gaspar, *Handumanan/Remembrance: Digging for Indigenous Wellspring* (Quezon City: Claretian Publications, 2021).
8. Christina H. Lee, "Domingo de Salazar's Letter to the King of Spain in Defense of the Indians and the Chinese of the Philippine Islands (1582)," in *The Spanish Pacific, 1521-1852: A Reader of Primary Sources*, ed. Christina H. Lee and Ricardo Padron (Amsterdam: Amsterdam University Press, 2020), 37–52.
9. Cf. Eric A. Anderson, "The encomienda in early Philippine colonial history," *Asian Studies* 14, no.2 (1976): 25–36.
10. Lee, "Domingo de Salazar's Letter," 46.
11. Lee, "Domingo de Salazar's Letter," 44.
12. See Nathalie Cobo, "Creating Authority and Promoting Normative Behaviour: Confession, Restitution, and Moral Theology in the Synod of Manila (1582–1586)," in *The School of Salamanca: A Case of Global Knowledge Production,* ed. Thomas Duve, Jose Luis Egio, and Christianne Birr (Leiden: Nijhof/Brill, 2021), 210–244.
13. Charles H. Cunningham, The Ecclesiastical Influence in the Philippines (1565-1850), *American Journal of Theology* 22, no. 2 (April 1918): 161–186, 168.
14. For a critique of this view, see Sarah Ngu, "Gender-Fluidity and Shamanism in Spanish Philippines," *Intersections,: Gender, Sexuality, and Postcolonial Christianities*, ed. Agnes M. Brazal, Michael Sepidoza Campos, and Marilou Ibita, 48 (November 2022).

15. For instance, the 1633 letter of the Jesuit priest Fr. Juan de Bueras describes how lowland Catholic communities in Mindoro have returned to their pre-Christian beliefs and practices. John Blanco, "Idolatry and Apostasy in the 1633 Jesuit Annual Letter," in *The Spanish Pacific*, 115–130.

16. Pedro de los Rios, et al. "Instructions to commissary of the Inquisition [in the Philippines," Mexico: 1 March 1585, cited in Medina (fn 5, p. 300 Brewer)]. The Bolinao [Zambales] manuscript (1679–1685) is a documentation of the interrogation of the Filipin@ babaylans and their sexual practices. See Carolyn Brewer, *Holy Confrontation: Religion, Gender and Sexuality in the Philippines, 1521-1685* (Manila: Institute of Women's Studies, St. Scholastica's College, 2001), 309–350.

17. Brewer, *Holy Confrontation*, 292.

18. Vicente L. Rafael, *Contracting Colonialism: Translation and Christian Conversion in Tagalog Society under Early Spanish Rule* (Durham, NC: Duke University Press, 1988), 108.

19. Homi Bhabha, *The Location of Culture* (New York: Routledge, 2004; 1st ed. 1994), 159, 162–163.

20. Reynaldo Clemeña Ileto, *Pasyon and Revolution: Popular Movements in the Philippines, 1840-1910* (Quezon City: Ateneo de Manila University Press, 1979).

21. John Schumacher, *Revolutionary Clergy: The Filipino Clergy and the Nationalist Movement, 1850-1903* (Quezon City: Ateneo de Manila University Press, 1981).

22. Chris Antonette Piedad-Pugay, "The Two Faces of the 1872 Cavite Mutiny," September 5, 2012, https://nhcp.gov.ph/the-two-faces-of-the-1872-cavite-mutiny/.

23. Stuart Creighton Miller, *"Benevolent Assimilation:" The American Conquest of the Philippines, 1899-1903* (New Haven: Yale University Press, 1982).

24. Paul Rodell, "The founding of the Iglesia Filipiniana Independiente (The Aglipayan Church): An Histographical Review," *Philippine Quarterly of Culture and Society* 16, nos. 3 & 4 (1988): 213.

25. Benedict XV, *Maximimum illud* in *Acta apostolicae sedis* 11 (Città del Vaticano: Typis Polyglottis Vaticanis, 1919), 14.

26. "Celebrating the Gift of Faith: Learning from the Past and Journeying Together" https://cbcpnews.net/cbcpnews/celebrating-the-gift-of-faith-learning-from-the-past-and-journeying-together/.

27. E. San Juan Jr., "Tracking the Spoors of Imperialism and Neocolonialism in the Philippines: Sketch of a Synoptic Reconnaissance," February 2, 2015, https://portside.org/2015-02-02/tracking-spoors-imperialism-neocolonialism-philippines-sketch-synoptic-reconnaissance.

28. Dennis Shoesmith, "Church and Martial Law in the Philippines: The Continuing Debate," *Southeast Asian Affairs* (1979): 246–257, 246.
29. *Protestant Christianity in the Philippines,* Harvard Divinity School, Religion and Public Life, https://rpl.hds.harvard.edu/faq/protestant-christianity-philippines.
30. Catholic Bishops Conference of the Philippines (CBCP), *Post-Election Statement* (Manila, 13 Feb 1986), https://cbcponline.net/post-election-statement/.
31. Hildegard Myer and Jean Goss are a French couple and leaders of the International Fellowship of Reconciliation, who in 1984, helped crystalized interests in the non-violent option with the initial visit and seminars they conducted. Ronald J. Sider, *Non-violent Action: What Christian Ethics Demands but Most Christians Have Never Really Tried* (Grand Rapids, MI: Brazos, 2015). They shared the philosophy of "active nonviolence" (ANV) with members of the clergy that include Jaime Cardinal Sin, Bishop Francisco Claver, SJ, and Jose Blanco, SJ, as well as prominent lay leaders in politics. This led to the conduct of trainings in ANV both in Catholic and Protestant circles.
32. Ronald J. Sider, *Non-violence: the Invincible Weapon* (Nashville: Tennessee: Word Publishing, 1989), 55.
33. Mr. Hurford (Minister for Immigration and Ethnic Affairs), *Ministerial Statement, Migration Program 1986-87 Parliament of Australia* (10 April 1986), https://parlinfo.aph.gov.au/parlInfo/search/display/display.w3p;db=CHAMBER;id=chamber%2Fhansardr%2F1986-04-10%2F0001;query=Id%3A%22chamber%2Fhansardr%2F1986-04-10%2F0021%22.
34. "Filipino Emigrants per Continent (2010-2020)" in Office of the President of the Philippines Commission on Filipinos Overseas (CFO), *CFO Statistics on Philippine International Migration (Permanent residents, marriage migrants, US J-1 visa holders and other CFO programs for the period 2010–2020),* https://cfo.gov.ph/wp-content/uploads/2023/03/compendium-2020_Feb-14-2023_smaller.pdf. See also Office of the President of the Philippines Commission on Filipinos Overseas, *Number of Registered Filipino Emigrants by Major Country of Destination: 1981-2020,* https://cfo.gov.ph/statistics-2/.
35. "Emigrants" in CFO, *CFO Statistics on Philippine International Migration.*
36. "Percentage per Category of Registered Filipino Emigrants (2010-2020)" in CFO, *CFO Statistics on Philippine International Migration.*
37. Philippine Statistics Authority (PSA), *2021 Overseas Filipino Workers (OFWs) (Final Results)* (2 Dec 2022), https://psa.gov.ph/content/2021-overseas-filipino-workers-final-results.
38. PSA, *2021 OFWs.*
39. PSA, *2021 OFWs.*

40. PSA, *2021 OFWs.*
41. PSA, *2021 OFWs.*
42. The Global Economy: Business and economic data for 200 countries, *Philippines: Remittances as percent of GDP* (2021), https://www.theglobaleconomy.com/Philippines/remittances_percent_GDP/.
43. "Top 5 Professions of Registered Emigrants prior to Migration (2010-2020)" and "Top 5 Occupation of Immigrant Workers (2010-2020)," CFO, *CFO Statistics on Philippine International Migration.*
44. "Sex Percentage of Filipino Marriage Migrants (2010-2020)," "Sex Percentage of Au Pairs (2012-2020)," "Number of Registered Au Pair Participants by Educational Attainment: 2012-2020)" in CFO, *CFO Statistics on Philippine International Migration.*
45. "Number of Filipino Spouses and other Partners of Foreign nationals by Occupation: 2010-2020," CFO, *CFO Statistics on Philippine International Migration.*
46. See chapter in this anthology, Cristina Lledo Gomez, "*Bangon Na,* Pinays Rise Up," and Cristina Lledo Gomez, "Wives submitting to husbands: Domestic violence, Women, and the Christian faith," in *Theology Without Borders: Essays in Honor of Peter C. Phan,* ed. Leo Lefebure (Washington DC: Georgetown University Press, 2022), 83-106.
47. See the explanation on the Filipin@ colonial mentality in this anthology in Cristina Lledo Gomez, "*Bangon Na:* Pinays Rise Up"
48. Peter M. Jamero, *Growing Up Brown: Memoirs of a Filipino American* (Washington DC: University of Washington Press, 2006), pp. 1–2. The 1920s and 1930s saw Filipin@s moving to the Americas to attend to its vast agricultural fields and they would be known to help build the farm workers movement in the USA. See Dennis Arguelles, "Remembering the Manongs and Story of the Filipino Farm Worker Movement," *National Parks Conservation Association* (25 May 2017), https://www.npca.org/articles/1555-remembering-the-manongs-and-story-of-the-filipino-farm-worker-movement and H. Brett Melendy, "Filipinos in the United States," *Pacific Historical Review* vol.43, no.4 (1974): 520–547.
49. E.J.R David and Kevin L. Nadal, "The colonial context of Filipino American Immigrants' psychological experiences," *Cultural Diversity and Ethnic Minority Psychology* 19 (2013): 298.
50. Nikki Alfonso-Gregorio, "Decolonising the mind: Why colonial mentality is a difficult attitude to abandon," *SBS Filipino* (17 January 2022), https://www.sbs.com.au/language/filipino/en/article/decolonising-the-mind-why-colonial-mentality-is-a-difficult-attitude-to-abandon/nhjtcjj1m.
51. For a colonial mentality scale fitted to the Filipino@, see E. J. R. David & S. Okazaki, "The Colonial Mentality Scale (CMS) for Filipino Americans:

Scale construction and psychological implications," *Journal of Counseling Psychology,* 53(2) (2006): 241–252.

52. For example, Australia and Canada have had their own "whites-only" policies in which non-white persons could not migrate into the countries and even forced out of the countries if they were already there. Those laws were only abolished much less than a century ago, around the 1960s. Meanwhile, in America a long history of racial segregation beginning with the slavery of non-white persons, the Jim Crow era, and the "separate but equal" doctrine applied to non-whites meant that the otherness and inferiority of the non-white person is something the country has been grappling with for centuries. See Ellen Jane Kennedy, *No Asians Allowed: The "White Australia" and "White Canada" Immigration Policies* (PhD Thesis, University of Minnesota, 2001), https://www.proquest.com/openview/b472d042388c52bb3bce7fe3972f6d66/1?pq-origsite=gscholar&cbl=18750&diss=y; Terrance Macmullan, "The American Redoubt and the Coyolxauqui Imperative: Dismembering America through Whiteness, Remembering America with Gloria Anzaldúa," *Cross Currents* vol71. No.2 (2021): 175–195. For how multiracial identities are disrupting and maintaining whiteness in the Americas, see Lauren Davenport, *Politics beyond black and white: biracial identity and attitudes in America* (Cambridge: Cambridge University Press, 2018).

53. See, for example, the way the United Nations has taken up the Pacific Islander indigenous approach of *Talanoa* as its framework to tackle the problem of climate change in United Nations Climate Change, *2018 Talanoa Dialogue Platform,* https://unfccc.int/process-and-meetings/the-paris-agreement/the-paris-agreement/2018-talanoa-dialogue-platform. See also the adoption of indigenous fire burning practices to manage bushfires in Australia in Royal Commission into National Natural Disaster Arrangements, *Background Paper: Cultural burning practices in Australia* (20 Feb 2020), https://naturaldisaster.royalcommission.gov.au/system/files/2020-06/Cultural%20burning%20practices%20in%20Australia%20-%20Background%20Paper.pdf.

Pope Francis himself has acknowledged that the Catholic Church could learn a lot from indigenous peoples in how to integrally develop our fractured society and save our earth, in Pope Francis, *Final Document: The Amazon: New Paths for the Church and for an Integral Ecology* (Oct 2019), http://secretariat.synod.va/content/sinodoamazonico/en/documents/final-document-of-the-amazon-synod.html and Pope Francis, *Querida Amazonia* Post-Synodal Exhortation (2 Feb 2020), http://secretariat.synod.va/content/sinodoamazonico/en/documents/post-synodal-apostolic-exhortation%2D%2Dquerida-amazonia-.html.

54. Bill Chappell, "The Vatican repudiates 'Doctrine of Discovery' which was used to justify colonialism," *NPR* (30 Mar 2023), https://www.npr.org/2023/03/30/1167056438/vatican-doctrine-of-discovery-colonialism-indigenous. For the story on the youth delegate who called on the pope to apologize to Canadian indigenous, see Rob Gillies and Nicole Winfield, "'Rescind the Doctrine' protest greets pope in Canada," *The Associated Press* (29 July 2022), https://apnews.com/article/pope-francis-latin-america-canada-world-news-religion-9e266815081da9f7b38710b6b6e4dec6.

55. See, for example, Pope John Paul II's speech to the Australian indigenous in which he says:

> You are part of Australia and Australia is part of you. And the Church herself in Australia will not be fully the Church that Jesus wants her to be until you have made your contribution to her life and until that contribution has been joyfully received by others. (n.13)

In John Paul II, *Address of John Paul II to the Aborigines and Torres Strait Islanders in Blatherskite Park* (29 Nov 1986), https://www.vatican.va/content/john-paul-ii/en/speeches/1986/november/documents/hf_jp-ii_spe_19861129_aborigeni-alice-springs-australia.html#:~:text=Dear%20Aboriginal%20people%3A%20the%20hour,and%20those%20of%20your%20fellowman.

PART I

Rethinking the Encounters

CHAPTER 2

Indigenization as Appropriation (What Being Baptized Could Have Meant for the Natives of Cebu in 1521)

Pablo Virgilio S. David and Ma. Maricel S. Ibita

Sometime before Mount Pinatubo erupted in 1991,[1] in one of the settlements of the indigenous Aetas of Porac, Pampanga on a hill along the Zambales mountain range,[2] a group of Korean Evangelical Christians did their evangelizing mission with one tribal community called *Sapang Uwak*. The Koreans were very impressed about the way they were accommodated by the Aetas, and how easy it was for them to invite the community to their Evangelical Christian Worship Service. They found the natives so endearing. They not only gave them Bibles, taught them praise music, gifted them regularly with Korean groceries, they even built for them a little chapel. After several weeks of preaching the Gospel to them with the help of an Aeta interpreter who knew a smattering of English, the Koreans

---

P. V. S. David
Roman Catholic Diocese of Kalookan, Caloocan City, Philippines

M. M. S. Ibita (✉)
Department of Theology, Ateneo de Manila University, Quezon City, Philippines
e-mail: mibita@ateneo.edu

© The Author(s), under exclusive license to Springer Nature Switzerland AG 2024
C. Lledo Gomez et al. (eds.), *500 Years of Christianity and the Global Filipino/a*, Pathways for Ecumenical and Interreligious Dialogue, https://doi.org/10.1007/978-3-031-47500-9_2

29

thought the community was ready to be fully converted to their evangelical religion, meaning, to be "born again." They told them during the preparation for their "Baptism in the Spirit" that, if they had already accepted Jesus as their personal Lord and Savior, they should renounce their "tribal superstitions" and "destroy their idols."

The natives fell silent when they realized what they were being asked to do. Their village chieftain asked that they be given some time to discuss about it among themselves. The discussion did not even take much time. When the chieftain came back, accompanied by the tribal elders, they politely returned to the Korean missionaries all the gifts that they had received and explained that they were doing so because they could not do what they were being asked to do. The idols that they were being asked to destroy were actually representations of their ancestors that stood side-by-side with images of the Santo Niño, Our Lady of Fatima, and St. Martin de Porres who had earlier been introduced to them by an old Roman Catholic priest who used to visit them.

The village chieftain told the Korean missionaries that they had also been visited by people of other faiths from the lowland, that every one of them was welcome, as long as they did not require them to repudiate their God whom they called *Apu Namallari* and their ancestors and saints, as well as the nature spirits for whom they offered animal sacrifices every now and then. The Koreans were surprised about this change of demeanor and left the village puzzled. They realized that the indigenous Aetas whom they thought to be ready for conversion to their "born again" religion were willing to accommodate their faith but *in their own terms.* They had misunderstood their hosts' friendly and welcoming disposition.[3]

THE EVENTS THAT LED TO THE FIRST MASS AND FIRST BAPTISM IN 1521

The natives whom Magellan and his men encountered in the Visayan islands were friendly and hospitable, according to the chronicler, Antonio Pigafetta.[4] There was no comparing them with other indigenous peoples they had earlier met along the coasts of Africa, South America, and Guam, who mostly tended to be hostile to strangers like them.[5]

Pigafetta recalls how impressed the captain general was about the way they had been treated by a group of fishermen from Suluan in Samar. He was particularly fascinated by the innate religiosity of the two chieftains,

2 INDIGENIZATION AS APPROPRIATION (WHAT BEING BAPTIZED COULD... 31

the brothers, Rajah Kolambu and Rajah Siani, and the way they and their families had conducted themselves when they celebrated Mass on Easter Sunday, March 31, 1521, on the island Pigafetta identified as Massaua.[6] Pigafetta describes Kolambu and Siani's indigenous religious gestures:

> When I had landed, the king *raised his hands to the sky*, and turned to us two, and we did the same as he did ... Their fashion of drinking is in this wise, they first *raise their hands to heaven*, then take the drinking vessel in their right hand, and extend the left hand closed towards the people. ... The king, before we went away, was very gay, and *kissed our hands, and we kissed his*.[7]

Not only did the natives help in constructing a bamboo platform on which they could hold the Eucharist; they also joined the celebration and reverently followed all the religious gestures that their foreign guests were making, including kneeling at the consecration, folding their hands in prayer, bowing their heads, kissing the cross, etc. At Massaua, Pigafetta records:

> ...when the offertory of the mass came, the two kings went to kiss the cross like us,... Then he [Magellan] had a cross brought, with the nails and crown, *to which the kings made reverence*... Besides this, the captain told them that it was necessary that this cross should be placed on the summit of the highest mountain in their country, so that seeing it every day they might adore it, and that if they did thus, neither thunder, lightning, nor the tempest could do them hurt. *The kings thanked the captain, and said they would do it willingly.* Then he asked whether they were Moors or Gentiles, and in what they believed. They answered that *they did not perform any other adoration, but only joined their hands, looking up to heaven, and that they called their God, Aba.* Hearing this, the captain was very joyful, on seeing that, *the first king raised his hands to the sky and said that he wished it were possible for him to be able to show the affection which he felt towards him*.[8]

When the captain spoke about wanting to plant a cross on their island, the chieftains also volunteered to assist them. They likewise assisted Magellan in burying some members of his crew who had died:

> Wednesday morning, because the night before one of our men had died, the interpreter and I, by order of the captain, went to ask the king for a place where we might bury the deceased. We found the king accompanied by a good many people, and, after paying him due honour, we told him of the death of our man, and that *the captain prayed him that he might be put into the ground. He replied that if he and his people were ready to obey our master,*

32   P. V. S. DAVID AND M. M. S. IBITA

> *still more reason was there for his land and country being subject to him. After that we said we wished to consecrate the grave in our fashion and place a cross on it. The sovereign said that he was content, and that he would worship that cross as we did.* The deceased was buried in the middle of the open space of the town, as decently as possible, and performing the above-mentioned ceremonies to set them a good example, and in the evening we buried another.[9]

At some point, Pigafetta narrates how the captain general began to speak to them about the Christian faith and his desire to get his native hosts to know his faith better.

> The captain spoke at length on the subject of peace, and prayed God to confirm it in heaven. These people replied that they had never heard such words as these which the captain had spoken to them, and *they took great pleasure in hearing them. The captain, seeing then that those people listened willingly to what was said to them, and that they gave good answers, began to say a great many more good things to induce them to become Christians.*[10]

Like Magellan, Pigafetta expressed surprise that the natives seemed genuinely interested and even suggested that the captain general might want to leave behind two of his men to remain for a while and explain their faith to them more extensively.

> The people heard these things *willingly, and besought the captain to leave them two men to teach and show them the Christian faith, and they would entertain them well with great honour.* To this the captain answered that for the moment he could not leave them any of his people, but that *if they wished to be Christians that his priest would baptise them, and that another time he would bring priests and preachers to teach them the faith.* They then answered that they wished first to speak to their king, and then would become Christians. Each of us wept for the joy which we felt at the goodwill of these people, and the captain told them not to become Christians from fear of us, or to please us, but *that if they wished to become Christian they must do it willingly, and for the love of God, for even though they should not become Christian, no displeasure would be done them,* but those who became Christian would be more loved and better treated than the others. Then *they all cried out with one voice, that they did not wish to become Christians from fear, nor from complaisance, but of their free will.* The captain then said that if they became Christians he would leave them the arms which the Christians use, and that his king had commanded him so to do. At last they said they did not know what more to answer to so many good and beautiful words which

2 INDIGENIZATION AS APPROPRIATION (WHAT BEING BAPTIZED COULD... 33

he spoke to them, but that they placed themselves in his hands, and that he should do with them as with his own servants. Then the captain, with tears in his eyes, embraced them.[11]

From here on, Pigafetta would note how Magellan would shift from being a mercenary to practically behaving like a missionary. He describes how elated the captain general was about the apparent "interest" of the native chieftains Kolambu and Siani, and later also of Humabon of Cebu, in the Christian religion.

Humabon hosted the Baptism in Cebu on the second Sunday of Easter, April 14, 1521. But it is important to note that before they submitted themselves to baptism, Pigafetta narrates that Rajah Humabon first invited the captain general to a native ritual we now refer to as a "blood compact," followed by an exchange of gifts.

> Then the king said that he was content, and as a greater sign of affection *he sent him a little of his blood from his right arm, and wished he should do the like.* Our people answered that he would do it. Besides that, he said that all the captains who came to his country had been accustomed to make a present to him, and he to them, and therefore *they should ask their captain if he would observe the custom.* Our people answered that he would; but as the king wished to keep up the custom, let him begin and make a present, and then the captain would do his duty.[12]

It is important to note that all of this is being narrated from the point of view of Pigafetta and his captain general whom he is deliberately portraying as a hero. Like Magellan, Pigafetta interpreted the hospitality and the friendly gestures of their native hosts to be an expression of their desire to "convert to the Christian religion" and turn their backs on their own faith.

> Then the captain began to speak to the king through the interpreter to incite him to the faith of Jesus Christ, and told him *that if he wished to be a good Christian, as he had said the day before, that he must burn all the idols of his country, and, instead of them, place a cross, and that everyone should worship it every day on their knees, and their hands joined to heaven: and he showed him how he ought every day to make the sign of the cross.* To that the king and all his people answered that they would obey the commands of the captain and do all that he told them.[13]

Pigafetta also narrates how Magellan had affirmed the gift of the Santo Niño which Pigafetta had given the wife of Humabon on behalf of the captain general, and how the captain had advised her to "put it in place of her idols." He wrote, "The captain on that occasion approved of the gift which I had made to the queen of the image of the Infant Jesus and recommended her *to put it in the place of her idols, because it was a remembrancer of the Son of God. She promised to do all this, and to keep it with much care.*"[14] However, Pigafetta himself would later explain that they found out later that the natives had not exactly done what the captain general had instructed them to do if they were to embrace the Christian faith—namely, "destroy their idols." Pigafetta recounts,

> The captain-general, who had informed the king and all those who had been baptised of the obligation they were *under of burning their idols, which they had promised to do, seeing that they retained them and made them offerings of meat, reproved them severely for it.* They thought to excuse themselves sufficiently by saying that *they did not do that now on their own account, but for a sick person, for the idols to restore him his health.* ... Having heard this, the captain, seized with zeal for religion, said that *if they had a true faith in Jesus Christ, they should burn all the idols,* and the sick man should be baptised, and he would be immediately cured, of which he was so certain that he consented to lose his head if the miracle did not take place. *The king promised that all this should be done, because he truly believed in Jesus Christ.* Then we arranged, with all the pomp that was possible, a procession from the place to the house of the sick man. We went there, and indeed found him unable to speak or to move. "We baptised him, with two of his wives and ten girls. The captain then asked him how he felt, and he at once spoke, and said that by the grace of Our Lord he was well enough. This great miracle was done under our eyes. The captain, on hearing him speak, gave great thanks to God. He gave him a refreshing drink to take, and afterwards sent to his house a mattress, the sheets, a covering of yellow wool, and a cushion, and he continued to send him, until he was quite well, refreshing drinks of almonds, rosewater, rosoglio, and some sweet preserves.[15]

Was there some miscommunication? Is it possible that they had not really understood each other? Or could the Malay slave Enrique have failed in his task of interpreting for Magellan and his companions?[16]

We will attempt in this brief chapter to deconstruct the narrative of Pigafetta and try to reinterpret the supposed "conversion," not from the viewpoint of Magellan or his chronicler, but from the natives' viewpoint, using as a parallel the story of the encounter of the Indigenous Aeta Community of Sapang Uwak with the group of Korean evangelical lay missionaries. Admittedly, the gap of five centuries can immediately cast doubt on the relevance of the parallelism. Nevertheless, knowing how the Aetas have continued to maintain the same precolonial communal life that was lived by our native ancestors five centuries ago, and the fact that their guests were also foreigners who at some point became too eager to "convert" the natives into their own religion, we dare insist that the parallelism is very relevant.

Anyone who reads Pigafetta critically should begin by asking who his intended reader/s was/were and what he intended to achieve through his narrative. It does not take much exegesis to be able to sift the facts from the embellishments. One can easily read between the lines and sense that some of the embellishments could not have actually happened. The following narration, for example, bears the obvious objective of portraying Magellan as a champion of the Christians. Pigafetta recounts how Magellan had the sick person baptized and healed, and how he was able to prove his point that his God was more powerful than those of the natives, and that these "false gods" therefore had to be destroyed:

> On the fifth day the convalescent rose from his bed, and as soon as he could walk, *he had burned, in the presence of the king and of all the people, an idol which some old women had concealed in his house. He also caused to be destroyed several temples constructed on the sea shore, in which people were accustomed to eat the meat offered to the idols. The inhabitants applauded this, and, shouting "Castile, Castile," helped to throw them down, and declared that if God gave them life they would burn all the idols they could find, even if they were in the king's own house.*[17]

This narration, for example, bears the obvious objective of portraying Magellan as a champion of the Christians. Pigafetta recounts how Magellan had the sick person baptized and healed, and how he was able to prove his point that his God was more powerful than those of the natives, and that these "false gods" therefore had to be destroyed. This same person would later be seen, according to Pigafetta, leading away the very priest who had baptized him earlier, in order to be included among the whole group that was to be massacred by Humabon, whom Magellan gave the baptismal name "Carlos." Here's how he would reminisce the tragic events that happened before he hurriedly left on May 1, 1521:

36 P. V. S. DAVID AND M. M. S. IBITA

Juan Carvalho, with the chief of police, who also were invited [i.e., to Humabon's treacherous dinner], *turned back, and said that they had suspected some bad business, because they had seen the man who had recovered from illness by a miracle, leading away the priest to his own house.*[18]

Fr. Pedro de Valderrama became one of the victims of the gruesome massacre.

INDIGENIZATION AS APPROPRIATION

How are we to interpret the religious accommodation that the native chieftains, Kolambu, Siani, and Humabon, had apparently extended toward Magellan and his men? Are we to presuppose as Pigafetta obviously does, that within a matter of a few days from the moment they started to open their doors to their alien guests, the natives were able to decide to abandon their indigenous faith in favor of a foreign faith called Christianity? For the sake of brevity, we will limit our observations of the parallelism between the native chieftains and their communities and Magellan and the Spaniards with the experience of the indigenous community of Aetas and the Korean evangelical missionaries.

First Observation: The foreigners were treated as guests in the indigenous community.

The foreigners came as human beings; they were welcomed as human beings. Hospitality to strangers is something Filipinos value in our native culture. There is actually something universal about it. This value is encountered both in the Semitic and in the Greek cultures present in the Judaeo-Christian tradition.[19] One hears, for instance about Abraham and Sarah welcoming three guests who are ultimately revealed as divine messengers, later rewarding the couple of a son for their hospitality (Gen 18). One also encounters in the Greek tragedies' accounts of Greek gods and goddesses visiting their favored humans incognito.[20] Thus, Barnabas and Paul were mistaken for Zeus and Hermes, respectively, when they visited Lystra and healed a crippled man (Acts 14:8–14). This value became more pronounced in early Christianity, on account of Mt 25:40 which says that what we do for the least, we do for Christ. There eventually emerged a tradition of hospitality to strangers, especially the poor, as hospitality to Christ himself (*Hospes venit; Christus venit*).

No doubt, as in any other culture, there is the natural fear of strangers, too, such as toward those who might be like wolves in sheep's clothing. In the native Filipino culture, the unwritten rule for hospitality is clear in the stranger's plea (*Tao po!* Literally, "A human being here!") and the host's response (*Tuloy po!,* "Come in!").[21] This means that the stranger is welcome if he comes as a human person, not a treacherous predator. He or she is expected to knock and identify him/herself and the purpose first—that he/she comes as a *tao* with an authentic human being's purpose. Then he/she leaves the prospective host free to discern his/her motives and make a judgment, either to open the door or to beg the visitor to leave. Even begging one to leave has to be done in a humane way. The homeowner says, *"Patatawarin po,"* seeking forgiveness from the guest that, within the given circumstances, the house owner cannot open the door.

Even more unique than the other ethnic cultures within the Philippines, like those of the Cebuanos, Samarenos, and Tagalogs, is the Kapampangan culture. In Pampanga, there is an alternative plea, aside from *"Tao po!"* for strangers who knock at the door; they say *"Dispu!,"* which is a contraction of *"Diyos po!"* (It is God!) K. Montalvo explains, *"Tao po"* is just saying there is someone at your gate or door. But *"Dispu"* is asking permission or blessing in reference to God to enter one's house, or to proceed with whatever transaction you may have with that person. Asking for one's blessing is considered very vital in Kapampángan and biblical culture.[22] It could be surmised that this expression could already be a product of later evangelization—the idea that the stranger who knocks at the door might be God in disguise.

An Aeta chieftain once said, "A stranger from the lowlands who comes to our place has to make a huge effort to climb mountains, cross rivers, and pass through jungles. If they made such a sacrifice to visit us, they must mean well." Apparently, the visitors arrived drenched in sweat, their feet full of blisters, and their clothes soiled with dust. It did not take much for the Indigenous peoples to discern whether or not these strangers might harm them. They came as human beings; they were welcomed as human beings. They served them spring water and freshly boiled sweet potatoes.

Magellan and his men could not have struck the natives as harmful strangers. The natives were accustomed to having Arab and Chinese traders who sailed in bigger boats called junks. L. Bergreen describes Pigafetta's narration of the encounter as a break from the travails of the expedition.[23] The traumatic events of dealing with rebellions, the dangers of the sea, and the resistance or aggression by some natives in the areas they traveled to were met by a reasonable openness by the Indigenous peoples of the island which Magellan called Lazarus as their fleet landed there on the Fifth Sunday of Lent, dedicated to the story of Lazarus (John 12). In a roundabout way, they managed to communicate that they were just passing through, that they needed to buy food and drink and other provisions in order to get to the Moluccas islands, and that they had sick and dead crew members to attend to.

Second Observation: Both native hosts and foreign guests spontaneously expressed their own culture and religious worldview.

Since they came as human beings, they comported themselves as human beings. This means that they had to show basic respect for each other's culture and religion. Pigafetta tells his readers that when Rajah Humabon escorted his foreign guests to his island, the first thing that he did upon arrival was to lift up his arms to heaven in thanksgiving for arriving safely. He looked at his guests and the guests, realizing that this was an important gesture for their host, imitated him. The effort obviously warmed the heart of Kolambu. A whole series of other events would introduce the foreign guests to the religious worldview of their hosts, such as the kissing of hands of the elders and authorities, the *tagay* when they drank palm wine,[24] the blood compact,[25] and the exchange of gifts. With a little help from a Malay interpreter who was coming from a not-so-different kind of culture and religious worldview, the foreign guests had passed the indigenous community's tests of how to be a human being, *pagpapakatao*.[26]

Pigafetta gives us enough details to suggest that part of the religious-cultural worldview of the natives were such values as reverence for the dead, respect for parents and elderly people, offering of sacrifices for the healing of the sick, elaborate rituals for the slaughtering of animals, recognition of the dignity even of children (Santo Niño), reverence for sacred symbols with hierophanic value, such as the cross, religious images, rituals of friendship and covenanting, expressions of worship, and others.

It is not incomprehensible to assume that because Magellan and his companions had respected the religious expressions of their native hosts, this was reciprocated by them with the same respect when requesting assistance in order to build a bamboo platform on which to offer their Easter Sunday Mass, and plant a cross in one of the hills. It is also not incomprehensible to assume that Humabon's willingness to submit himself and his family to baptism was an effort on his part to reciprocate Magellan's willingness to join him in his own religious ritual of a blood compact. According to Pigafetta, it was followed by an exchange of gifts, which, as far as the natives were concerned were probably done as part of their own religious rituals of covenanting.[27]

Third Observation: A friendly accommodation is the beginning of religious appropriation.

Inevitably, much of the "others'" religious expressions remained strange, both from the perspective of the native hosts and from the perspective of the foreign guests. The Aetas accommodated the Korean evangelical missionaries in the same way they had earlier accommodated a Roman Catholic priest, some Buddhists from the Tzu Chi Foundation, and the Iglesia ni Cristo church members. They were even willing to worship with them and accommodate their own religious symbols. Nevertheless, the indigenous community continued to worship their heavenly God called *Apo Namallari* in addition to venerating their ancestors and the nature spirits around them. They had no problem accepting Bibles from the Protestants, singing religious hymns of the Iglesia Ni Cristo and Evangelicals, or even worshiping and dancing the charismatic way. They accepted the religious worldview of their guests but appropriated them *in their own terms.*

The wife of Humabon, when offered religious symbols as gifts, chose the Santo Niño rather than the complete Madonna and Child image.[28] She may have found the Madonna too big for her own altar, and the Santo Niño just the right size in comparison to her other *anitos.* When Magellan instructed her to put the image of the Infant Jesus "in place of her anitos," most likely she understood it as "in *the* place of her anitos." That is, not as a replacement but alongside her anitos. Thus, she acceded to the instruction without difficulty.

It is unlikely that the natives took their submission to Baptism to mean a repudiation of their own indigenous faith in favor of this foreign religion. In all likelihood, as we have already pointed out earlier, they perceived the baptismal ritual to be the equivalent for their foreign guests of their own blood compact. There is a strong possibility that Magellan was aware that they understood it this way. He remained consistent with his effort to reciprocate the hospitality of his hosts.

40   P. V. S. DAVID AND M. M. S. IBITA

But one also has to be mindful of the fact that Pigafetta was narrating all of these stories for a specific audience, for people who were not there with them.[29] He did not want to give the impression that his captain general had merely used the expressions of the Roman Catholic Christian faith as gestures for mutual accommodation. Common sense dictates that Magellan could not have simply thrown his weight around, telling the natives to burn their "idols" and their religious shrine and to repudiate their own native faith. As we have earlier pointed out, one must be able to read between the lines written by Pigafetta in order to sift the grain from the chaff. Pigafetta is deliberately portraying his captain general as a hero,[30] not only for the king of Spain but also for the Roman Pontiff whose support for future expeditions he considered most essential.

Fourth Observation: The distinction being made by Pigafetta between Moors and Gentiles is a projection of their own background of Spanish trauma with the Arab Moors.

In the Middle Ages, the Arab Moors had occupied huge parts of the Iberian peninsula and had taken over their Churches and turned them into mosques.[31] They were familiar with the intolerance of the Moors toward Christians and Jews and tended to treat them with the same tendencies toward intolerance. As far as they were concerned, the other religions which they simply classed together as "Gentiles" tended to be more tolerant and accommodating than either the Jews or the Muslims, as long as they treated them with the same amount of tolerance and respect.

This instance can be labeled as the more humane approach to evangelization, the willingness to make space for mutual accommodation and for intercultural dialogue. The basic exchange of goodwill becomes the fertile ground for evangelization, the recognition that, at the very base, the strangers can be our friends, too. That they are as capable as we are of love, care, and compassion. That before one presumptuously "brings God" to them, one must have the humility to "find God" already present among them. Mutual accommodation gives the other the space to interpret the faith of the other, whether rightfully or wrongfully, in their own terms. After all, the other has no other way of interpreting the worldview that the guests bring with them than in their own indigenous worldview and culture, and vice versa.

Accommodation makes way for indigenization, and hopefully for appropriation. It is a process that is, of course, fraught with tensions because one or the other may react vehemently to the manner of appropriation as wrong, disrespectful, blasphemous, syncretistic, or perhaps even outright heretical. Is not this the case with Filipino Catholic popular religious practices?[32]

CONCLUSION

What are the *karakols* (among the Tagalogs),[33] or the *curaldals* (in Pampanga),[34] but sincere efforts on the part of the natives to accommodate the faith of their foreign guests by weaving them into their indigenous fertility dances and collective rituals of exorcism? What are the musical *Pasyons* and the drama of *Sinakulos* if not the efforts of the natives to appropriate the faith of the foreign guests in their own terms by allowing them to take the place of the epic chants, laments, and dirges of their own *babaylanes* while also later on serving as resistance literature against oppression brought by colonization and globalization?[35] Even in Mexico, the Lady of Guadalupe and her shrine became a convenient indigenous appropriation of Christian symbols into their worship of *Pachamama*.[36]

The Christian faith never exists in a vacuum. Even the Christianity brought by the Spaniards to the indigenous peoples of the Philippines came in a cultural vessel that was European. The Western colonizers inculturated Christianity was likewise primarily an appropriation of a faith that evolved from a Semitic Asian faith into a Greco-Roman faith through a long process of intercultural dialogues that paved the way for new forms of accommodation and appropriation. It is the task now of contemporary believers to appropriate, inculturate, and recontextualize the faith received to the planetary, global, national, communal, and individual levels as we face the challenges of these critical times.[37]

NOTES

1. Jean-Christophe Gaillard, "Was It a Cultural Disaster? Aeta Resilience Following the 1991 Mt Pinatubo Eruption," *Philippine Quarterly of Culture and Society* 34, no. 4 (2006): 376–399.
2. For a contemporary overview of how Aetas live, see Mhirone Jemel V. Dizon et al., "Analysis on Household Income to the Indigenous Aetas of Pampanga Philippines," *Journal of Economics, Finance and Accounting Studies* 3, no. 2 (2021): 202–219, https://doi.org/10.32996/jefas.2021.3.2.20.

3. For an observer's view on the dynamics between contemporary foreign missionaries and lowland Filipino Christians, see Kenneth D. Mulzac, "Cultural and Religious Dynamics of the Church in the Philippines," *Andrews University Seminary Studies* 46, no. 1 (2008): 109–119.
4. Antonio Pigafetta, *The First Voyage Around the World by Magellan: Translated from the Accounts of Pigafetta and Other Contemporary Writers*, trans. Lord Stanley of Alderley (London: Hakluyt Society, 1874), http://ia600501.us.archive.org/9/items/firstvoyageround00piga/firstvoyageround00piga.pdf; See also Antonio Pigafetta, *The First Voyage Round the World by Magellan: Translated from the Accounts of Pigafetta and Other Contemporary Writers*, ed. Henry Edward John Stanley, Cambridge Library Collection (London: Cambridge University Press, 2010), http://ia600501.us.archive.org/9/items/firstvoyageround00piga/firstvoyageround00piga.pdf. In this contribution, the 2010 edition will be used and emphases will be indicated by italicized phrases or sentences.
5. For more information on Christianity and colonization in these places, see John Lynch, *New Worlds: A Religious History of Latin America* (Yale University Press, 2012); Richard Elphick and Rodney Davenport, eds., *Christianity in South Africa: A Political, Social, and Cultural History* (Berkeley and Los Angeles, CA: University of California Press, 1997); Francis X. Hezel, *From Conquest to Colonization: Spain in the Mariana Islands, 1690 to 1740*, Occasional Historical Papers Series 2 (Saipan: Division of Historic Preservation, 2000).
6. On the debate on whether the first mass in 1521 was conducted in Limasawa or in Butuan, see Peter Schreurs, *The Location of Pigafetta's Mazaua, Butuan, and Calagan, 1521-1571: A Bibliographic and Cartographic Evidence* (Manila: National Commission for Culture and the Arts, National Historical Institute, 2000); Rene R. Escalante, "NHCP's Latest Ruling on the 1521 Easter Sunday Mass Controversy" (National Historical Commission of the Philippines, August 18, 2020), https://drive.google.com/file/u/1/d/1mExTClwb_z7AMjS3Hvpds75W-LoKLNnYh/view?usp=sharing&usp=embed_facebook. The NHCP's latest ruling favors the Limasawa theory since it has more solid supporting evidences.
7. Pigafetta, *First Voyage*, 2010, 78.
8. Pigafetta, 80. 81.
9. Pigafetta, 90.
10. Pigafetta, 88.
11. Pigafetta, 88–89.
12. Pigafetta, 86.
13. Pigafetta, 92.
14. Pigafetta, 94.

15. Pigafetta, 95–96.
16. For a brief overview on Enrique, the faithful slave of Magellan, see Danilo Madrid Gerona, "Enrique de Malacca: Pagsasalin Sa Imperyalismong Español," *Katipunan: Journal Ng Mga Pag-aaral Sa Wika, Panitikan, Sining at Kulturang Filipino* 0, no. 7 (2021): 143–162, https://doi.org/10.13185/KA2021.00709.
17. Pigafetta, *First Voyage*, 2010, 96.
18. Pigafetta, 104.
19. Jakub Walczak, "The Conditions of Christian Hospitality," *The Way* 60, no. 3 (2021): 85–97.
20. See, for example John Taylor, *Classics and the Bible: Hospitality and Recognition*, Classical Literature and Society (Bloomsbury Publishing, 2011); Joshua W. Jipp, *Divine Visitations and Hospitality to Strangers in Luke-Acts: An Interpretation of the Malta Episode in Acts 28:1-10* (Leiden: Brill, 2013); M.J.O. Verheij, "Hospitality & Homicide.: Violation of Xenia in Euripides' Electra," *Mnemosyne: A Journal of Classical Studies*, 2015, 1–25, https://doi.org/10.1163/1568525X-12341582.
21. For a brief background on this Filipino concept, see *Tao Po! Tuloy! Halina Sa Loob Ng Tao*, Magisterial Lectures - Arete (Ateneo de Manila University, Quezon City: Arete, 2020), https://www.youtube.com/watch?v=VEvVVJe-dgc.
22. Kevin Montalbo, "Basic Kapampángan Greetings - How to Greet in Kapampángan," Sínupan Singsing: Center for Kapampángan Cultural Heritage, January 12, 2019, https://sinupan.org/greetings.
23. See Laurence Bergreen, *Magellan: Over the Edge of the World* (New York: Roaring Brook Press, 2017), 100–101.
24. For Gideon Lasco, "Tagay: Why There's No Tagalog Word for 'Cheers' and Other Notes on Filipino Drinking Culture," January 6, 2015, https://www.gideonlasco.com/2015/01/tagay-why-theres-no-tagalog-word-for.html: "it seems that *tagay* [sharing of the glass for drinking alcoholic beverage to enact social relationship] has always been part of Filipino drinking culture, as it appears in the earliest Spanish-Tagalog dictionaries. In the Miguel Ruiz *vocabolario* of 1630, an entry for tagay is as follows: *La racion de vino ya echada en la escudilla que se da y deputa para uno....*"
25. Pigafetta, *First Voyage*, 2010, 86.
26. For a deeper exploration of this concept of being human, see Florentino H. Hornedo, *Pagpapakatao and Other Essays in Contemporary Philosophy and Literature of Ideas* (Manila: UST Publishing House, 2002); Fleurdeliz R. Altez-Albela, "Phenomenologizing Filipino Organic Thought: Florentino H. Hornedo's Philosophical Anthropology," *KRITIKE: An Online Journal of Philosophy* 10, no. 2 (December 2016): 61–67. For linguistic analyses of pagpapakatao in connection with social relations, see

Roberto E. Javier, Jr.., "Madaling Maging Tao, Mahirap Magpakatao! Paninindigan, Pagpapakatao at Pakikipagkapwatao," *Malay* 22, no. 2 (2010): 45–56; Roberto E. Javier Jr., "Ang Tao Sa Ka-Taw-an at Sa Ka-Tau-Han: Pag-Uugnay Sa Pagpapakatao, Pakikipagkapuwa-Tao, at Pagkatao: The Person in the Human Body: Being Human, Becoming a Human Person, Sharing the Self with 'Other' Selves.," *Malay* 30, no. 1 (2017): 70–85.

27. Pigafetta, *First Voyage*, 2010, 86.
28. For the varying documentations of this story and a postcolonial critical reading, see Christina H. Lee, "Santo Niño in Recoding the History of the Spanish Conquest," in *Saints of Resistance: Devotions in the Philippines Under Early Spanish Rule* (New York, NY: Oxford University Press, 2021), 15–38.
29. See, for example, Matteo Salonia, "Asian Ceremonies and Christian Chivalry in Pigafetta's 'The First Voyage Around the World,'" in *Travel Writings on Asia: Curiosity, Identities, and Knowledge Across the East, c. 1200 to the Present*, ed. Christian Mueller and Matteo Salonia, Palgrave Series in Asia and Pacific Studies (Singapore: Springer Nature, 2022), 83–110, https://doi.org/10.1007/978-981-19-0124-9_4.
30. Salonia, 86, 97.
31. For more information on the socio-cultural, religious, and political inter-relations of sixteenth-century Spain, see Mark D. Meyerson and Edward D. English, eds., *Christians, Muslims, and Jews in Medieval and Early Modern Spain: Interaction and Cultural Change*, Notre Dame Conferences in Medieval Studies 8 (Notre Dame, IN: University of Notre Dame Press, 2000).
32. Jayeel S. Cornelio, "Popular Religion and the Turn to Everyday Authenticity: Reflections on the Contemporary Study of Philippine Catholicism," *Philippine Studies: Historical and Ethnographic Viewpoints* 62, no. 3–4 (2014): 471–500.
33. In their study, Lorenzo Alvin T. Capio and Susana R. Reyes, "A Phenomenological Inquiry on the Devotees of the Miraculous Image of San Agustin De Tanza, Philippines," *Journal of Advanced Research in Social Sciences and Humanities* 4, no. 1 (2019): 9–16 noted that this prayerful dance depicting devotion to the miraculous image of San Agustin de Tanza allows the devotees to manifest their own experience of God's revelation, an expression of cosmic religiosity.
34. Sir Anril Pineda Tiatco, "Imag(in)ing Saint Lucy: The Narrative and Performative Construction of the Kuraldal in Sasmuan, Philippines," *Philippine Humanities Review*, January 6, 2022, 124–150 explains that participants in this religious street dancing are usually childless couples whose participation is an act of panata (religious pledge and sacrifice) to

Apung Lucia (Saint Lucy), the patroness of the town who is believed to be an effective intercessor for conception and child-bearing.

35. See Jim Perkinson and S. Lily L. Mendoza, "Indigenous Filipino 'Pasyon' Defying Colonial Euro-Reason," *Journal of Third World Studies* 21, no. 1 (2004): 117–137, https://doi.org/10.2307/45198365.

36. See Sabine Dedenbach-Salazar Sáenz, "Deities and Spirits in Andean Belief: Towards a Systematisation," *Anthropos* 112, no. 2 (2017): 443–453; Lynette Yetter, "Virgin Mary/Pachamama Syncretism: The Divine Feminine in Early-Colonial Copacabana," *Western Tributaries* 4 (2017): 1–14.

37. Didier Pollefeyt and Jan Bouwens, "Framing the Identity of Catholic Schools: Empirical Methodology for Quantitative Research on the Catholic Identity of an Education Institute," *International Studies in Catholic Education* 2, no. 2 (2010): 193–211, https://doi.org/10.1080/1942253 9.2010.504034; Catholic Bishops' Conference of the Philippines, "*Salubong*: The Philippine Catholic Church Synodal Report" (Catholic Bishops' Conference of the Philippines, August 15, 2022), https://synod-philippines.com/wp-content/uploads/2022/08/Philippines_National-Synodal-Report.pdf.

CHAPTER 3

The Double Truth of (Colonial) Mission

Daniel Franklin E. Pilario

We know that the past is not past. Its ghosts continue to haunt us. The debate is not only about "what the past was" but also "if the past is really past." Edward Said writes:

> Appeals to the past are among the commonest strategies in interpretations of the present. What animates such appeals is not only disagreement about what happened in the past and what the past was, but uncertainty about whether the past really is past, over and concluded, or whether it continues, albeit in different forms, perhaps.[1]

This struggle for the politics of the meaning of the past becomes apparent in postcolonial discourse.

Mishra's and Hodge's distinction between the hyphenated and unhyphenated version of post(-)colonialism can help us in this regard.[2] On the one hand, the "post-colonial" hyphenated version is prevalent in post-independent colonies within recent post-revolutionary situations. Mostly located in Third World contexts, its main concern is both temporal and

---

D. F. E. Pilario (✉)
Adamson University, Manila, Philippines

© The Author(s), under exclusive license to Springer Nature
Switzerland AG 2024
C. Lledo Gomez et al. (eds.), *500 Years of Christianity and the
Global Filipino/a*, Pathways for Ecumenical and Interreligious
Dialogue, https://doi.org/10.1007/978-3-031-47500-9_3

47

48   D. F. E. PILARIO

ideological; its struggle is located in the racial, linguistic, and political fields after the colonial period as it deals with the ravages and consequences of colonial rule. The North American white settler colonies do not anymore exhibit these issues as compared to Latin American, African, and Asian post-colonies. In these colonies of the Third World, the temporal "post" lingers even for centuries. On the other hand, the "postcolonial" unhyphenated version does not refer mainly to the temporal "post" since the discursive struggle can be located within the colonial itself. It is the "always present underside" of colonization parallel to the rebellion of a child against the father or the "ghost that stalks the parents' literary history,"[3] thus, can be traced back to the initial colonial encounters. The unhyphenated version traces subversion, fracture, interlanguage, hybridity, and polyglossia within colonial practices. In other words, while the hyphenated version (post-colonialism) focuses its analysis on the aftermath of colonial domination, the unhyphenated form (postcolonialism) centers on the discursive practices of domination both during the colonial period and its complex history.

It might be useful to use these two senses in our reading of the discourses and practices of Christian colonial evangelization in the Philippines. On the one hand, since we are clearly located in the temporal "post," it is thus helpful to do a post-colonial (hyphenated) assessment of the vestiges of colonial discourse and practices after 500 years. On the other hand, we can also read it back postcolonially (unhyphenated), thus, locating both its hegemonic cooptation and creative resistance from within the colonial discourse itself.

This article[4] examines the ambivalent and indeterminate directions of the colonial mission. Using the research of Filipino historians and following Pierre Bourdieu's notion of *double verité*, I argue that colonial missionary enterprises contain dual truths. I will do this in three parts. First, I will examine many divergent readings of colonial evangelization and expose their problematic and/or productive consequences. Second, I will expose the socio-political context of *Patronato Real* and its ambivalent consequences upon the missionary—being both the defender of the King and the rights of the "natives." Third, I will look into specific missionary approaches, e.g., colonial territorial management, catechetical instruction, sacramental practices, and investigate their double truths and ambivalences. Such a plural view is necessary so as to unmask the monologic readings brought about by hegemonic colonial practice.

DOUBLE TRUTH: READING HISPANIC COLONIAL EVANGELIZATION

There are two general directions on how to read Spanish colonial mission. On the one hand, we have the Hispanophiles—mainly Catholic writers—who argue that the Spanish missionaries and their evangelical methods brought "civilized ways, salvation, and unity to the island."[5] To use the words of Pablo Fernandez, a famous Dominican historian, the missionaries "were able, at [the] cost of so much sacrifice, to keep them for Christ and for Spain."[6] His book, *Church History in the Philippines* (1979), has become a classic church history book taught in the many seminaries in the Philippines. On the other hand, we have the so-called nationalists. An example is Renato Constantino's classic work, *Philippines: A Past Revisited* (1977),[7] which certainly is a reference book to many history students and was hailed as the "new interpretation of Philippine History."[8] Constantino argues that the Church's role was transformed from a mere colonial accessory to a principal apparatus of colonial exploitation. This view which started from the revolutionary era against Spain is not without basis. However, it also possesses the tendency to "demonize" the systems and actors—missionaries included—of the Spanish regime.

Beyond these two divergent readings, I argue that all practices—colonial practice included—possess a "double truth." In the words of the French sociologist, Pierre Bourdieu, practices are both "structured structures" and "structuring structures."[9] Just as these practices are consequences of their socio-political contexts (structured), they can also be creative and innovative within the bounds of their own historical limits (structuring). On the one hand, cultural practice is a product of social structures of which it is a part—including its abuses and asymmetries. On the other hand, it also generates ingenious revolutionary elements, being a part of creative human practice. These opposites must be held in tension in order to account for the real "logic of practice." If we consider the Christian faith as "gift" to the Philippines in the last 500 years—thus, having been gifted, we also need to give as the celebration's motto suggests[10]—it is necessary that we consider the "double truth" of such a gift-exchange. Bourdieu writes:

> On the one hand, it is experienced (or intended) as a refusal of self-interest and egoistic calculation, and an exaltation of gratuitous, unrequited generosity. On the other hand, it never entirely excludes awareness of the logic of

exchange or even confession of the repressed impulses and, intermittently, the denunciation of another, denied, truth of generous exchange—its constraining and costly character.[11]

Thus, to understand these historical events and colonial missionary experiences, there is a need to be open to their ambivalence, imprecision, and indeterminacy, that is, their double truth, as these same practices also contain unintended "surplus of meaning" beyond the conscious intentions of their historical agents.

PATRONATO REAL AND THE HUMAN RIGHTS OF THE "NATIVES"

The work of evangelization in the Philippines during the Spanish regime can be understood within the framework of Church-State relations called the *Patronato Real de las Indias*—"a series of agreements entered into by the Holy See and the Spanish monarchy... [later] developed by Spanish jurists and theologians into a body of law and of standard practices and procedures which remained in force until the dissolution of the Spanish empire in the late XVIII and XIX centuries."[12] In brief, Spain shall promote, maintain, and defend the Catholic religion in all its colonies (i.e., to support the whole work of evangelization) in exchange for being recognized by the Holy See as the "patron" of the Church of the Indies (i.e., to possess a legitimate "title to the colonies it had conquered"). This entitles the monarchy to certain rights in ecclesiastical administration, e.g., (1) the right to assign religious congregations the territories for them to evangelize; (2) the privilege to approve missionaries to be sent or be retained in the colonies; (3) the right to nominate bishops with the understanding that these nominations were *pro forma* which the Holy See should automatically accept; (4) the right to approve the parish priests appointed to parishes by their local bishops; (5) the right to censor communication between the Holy See and the Church in the Indies; communications shall be coursed through the King's Council to the Indies which has the power "to allow or not to allow such communications to be forwarded to those to whom they were addressed"; (6) the right to assign civil functions to parish priests, that is, compiling a tribute list, supervising elections or public works and others.[13]

"*El servicio de ambas Majestades*" (the service of both Majesties)—a phrase present in many official documents—explains the relationship

3 THE DOUBLE TRUTH OF (COLONIAL) MISSION   51

between Church and politics during the Spanish colonial regime in the Philippines. The Filipino Jesuit historian, Horacio de la Costa, writes:

> This is what claimed the entire allegiance of Spanish subjects everywhere, from the highest to the lowest, from Manila to Madrid: in the temporal order, the majesty of the King, and in the spiritual order, the majesty of God. The Church was primarily concerned, of course, with the service of God, the State with the service of the King; but it would be a great mistake to imagine this meant a division of labor or of powers. In the constitution of Spain and the Spanish empire each served both Majesties, God and King, Church and State might be distinct, but they were not divided. They were integral parts of one massive structure, which might be viewed either as a civilizing Church or a missionary State.[14]

The evangelization project made possible by the *Patronato Real* was both missionary and civilizing. The friar's task was both evangelical and political. At once, he was the empire's civil servant and God's missionary. In the midst of this tension-filled arrangement, the Church continued in its mission of preaching the Gospel. By placing itself "at the service of both Majesties"—of God and of the king—the colonial Church already locates itself at the crossroads of potential tension between two contending powers. On the one hand, this location also automatically makes the Church complicit with imperial power. The rights granted to the monarchy over the church affairs by the *Patronato Real* announced not only future conflicts but also real collusion with colonial intentions. The last right, for instance, "the privilege of assigning civil functions to church personnel, especially parish priests, such as that of drawing the tribute lists, supervising municipal elections, and directing public works,"[15] makes the priest a direct vassal of the Crown, thus, making his missionary work, no matter how well-intentioned, an ambivalent accessory to the colonial project. On the other hand, this dual loyalty gives the Church the possibility of defending the conquered peoples from the unconscionable subjugation by the *conquistadores*. Since it has access to institutions of power, it can shape the priorities of the system toward the defense of the natives.

The exaction of tribute, forced labor, military service, and *bandala* (annual quotas to sell products to the government at lower prices) were direct instruments of exploitation and pacification. While it is true that the friars were not directly in charge of their implementation, they were closely connected with the system as they were increasingly entrusted with civil duties—inspector of schools and taxation, of health units and public works, certifier of *cedulas*, auditing and partitioning of lands, among others.[16] Despite being monks who could not own properties, the pope exempted them from this monastic rule so that they can administer the parishes in the absence of the secular clergy. Canonical collation—the act of bestowing ecclesiastical posts with a fixed amount of property or income—proved to be one source of corruption among the friars. This arrangement transformed the friar-missionaries into landowners gradually amassing large tracts themselves—some through the confiscation of mortgaged lands, others through outright land-grabbing. These properties came to be called in Philippine history as "friar lands" which, together with other friar abuses, fueled the Filipino revolution against Spain.

Pierre Bourdieu can easily agree with Renato Constantino's assessment that colonial mission has its political and economic intentions and consequences. Constantino's main argument is precisely that: "conquest is business."[17] Evangelization was a mere "religious garb" to mask Spain's economic interests. If there were infighting between the friars and *encomenderos*, it was equivalent to what Bourdieu calls the "palace wars"—the battle regarding who gets the greater spoils of the conquest. In Bourdieu's frame, this is precisely what symbolic violence means—economic interests masquerading as generous giftedness of faith and civilization.

But if Constantino's Marxist-structuralist reading is the only interpretation, it cannot account for other real experiences that also form part of colonial history on the ground. For example, it cannot account for the role of the Dominican, Domingo de Salazar (1512–1594), the first bishop of Manila and his lifetime fight for the human rights of the colonized natives.[18] De Salazar came from the famous school of Salamanca whose renowned theologians, Francisco de Vitoria (c. 1480–1546) and Francisco Suárez (1548–1617), advocated for the natural rights of indigenous peoples long before the modern discussion on the international human rights put into question the right of monarchs to colonize peoples even for missionary purposes. The Dominicans Antonio de Montesinos (c. 1475–1545) and Bartolome de las Casas (1484–1566), missionaries of the Americas, also came from the Salamanca school and were at the forefront of defending the rights of the Indians in the Americas.

From the years De Salazar first stepped on the Philippines until the time of his death, the bishop defended the rights of the Filipinos against Spanish sovereignty, particularly against the abuses of the *encomenderos* (Spanish rulers) in their desire to enrich themselves quickly through the violent extortion of tribute, the ownership of slaves by the colonial masters against the anti-slavery legislation in Spain, and the harsh maltreatment of the *Sangleys* (Chinese). The first Synod of Manila (1582–1586), which he himself presided upon his arrival, tackled the thorny issue of the right of the Spanish Crown on a conquered people. [19] His presence on the ground made his reports to the King of Spain concrete, convincing, and credible. In one of those extant letters, he wrote:

> Because all the *encomenderos* bring their stocks when they go to collect [their tributes], and there they whip and torment them until they are given everything they demand. The wife or daughter of the chief is taken if he does not appear. Many chiefs have died due to torture for the causes that have been mentioned. When I was at the port of Ibalon, some chiefs came to see me and the first thing they said was that a man who collected tributes in that settlement had killed a chief, and the same Indians demonstrated the way in which he was killed, which was crucified, with his arms hung.[20]

After a long fight with colonial rulers in the Philippines, he went back to Spain in 1591 to put his lifetime advocacy in front of the King: "It is clear then that the dominion over those Islands could not have come to belong to the King our lord either by title of election or of just war."[21] However, he died before the issue was resolved. And the same cause was taken on by another Dominican, Miguel de Benavides, his successor, who was with him on the trip. But earlier than Salazar or Benavides, the first Augustinian friars who came with Legaspi in 1565 were already opposed to the conquest of the Philippines in the name of the Spanish monarchs. Foremost among them was Fray Andrés de Urdaneta who did not want Legaspi's expedition to continue. When he and his companions arrived on the islands—they were only told of their final destination while sailing on the high seas—they were constantly updating the King on the abuses of the colonists. The envoy sent to represent them to the King, Fray Martin de Rada, categorically stated: "I have taken all the opinions of all the Fathers who were to be found here. They unanimously affirm that none among all these islands have come into the power of the Spaniards with just title."[22]

These narratives on Salazar, Benavides, and other missionaries who fought for the human rights of the "natives" hardly feature in the Marxist-structuralist radar of Renato Constantino, just as he dismisses the propaganda movement (of Diego Silang, Jose Rizal, Marcelo del Pilar, and others) as "reformist" and "elitist," or revolution of the masses inspired by the *Pasyon* as merely "magical."[23] While the *Hispanophiles* viewed colonial evangelization as liberation of the Filipino from the "power of the devil"—which is a ridiculous narrative—the nationalist versions of the same events also reject other legitimate revolutionary voices that do not fit this structuralist straightjacket.

REDUCCIÓN AND TRADUCCIÓN

Located in scattered spaces within the more than 7000 islands, the native population has been described by the Spanish chroniclers as living "without polity" (*sin policia*).[24] For the Spaniards, civilization is connected with the city—a concept that harks back to the existence of the Greek *polis*. To be without polity is to be barbaric. Thus, to spread civilization and to facilitate "spiritual conquest," the dispersed population needed to be congregated, "reduced" into compact villages, to live "*bajo de la campana*," that is, within hearing of the church bell. *Reducción* was the term used to describe the same project in colonial Mexico and Peru. This administrative reconfiguration of space was also implemented in the Philippines from the 1580s to the 1590s. There were many factors that led to the *reducción* project being vehemently resisted by the Filipinos. The first was economic: since Filipinos were subsistence farmers, there was no reason for them to leave their small farms and transfer to compact villages. Secondly, new congregated villages became easy targets of Moro raids, especially in the Visayas area. Though military coercion was sometimes employed to force people to relocate, the colorful ritual celebrations of the Church on Holy Week, Christmas, or patronal feasts were mainly used to attract them to come to the *cabecera* (town center). With it, there developed the elaborately vibrant popular Catholicism and religiosity that characterizes Philippine Christianity until today. But since these celebrations were only occasional, people still went back to their farms and only returned for the next liturgical season—making the Philippine version of the *reducción* project quite unique with the existence of the *cabecera-visita* complex. The *cabecera* was most often in the lowlands where the parish priest resided; the *visitas* were small chapels at the outskirts or mountain areas which the priest would visit occasionally most often during their annual patronal feasts. This basic ecclesiastical structure is still recognizable in our times. How successful was this project? Phelan comments: "The results certainly were not as sweeping as the missionaries wanted, but preconquest decentralization was sufficiently reduced so that Filipinos were brought into some social contact with Hispanic culture"[25] and the Christian faith.

Another creative colonial missionary instrument is the *Doctrina Christiana* (1593) written by Fray Juan de Plasencia and was the first book printed in the Philippines.[26] It is a catechetical book which contains the basic prayers (the Our Father, Hail Mary, Creed, and Salve Regina); the articles of faith, seven sacraments, seven capital sins, Ten Commandments, five commandments of the Church, and the acts of general confession. The pamphlet was not meant for general distribution due to the high cost of printing but mainly served as a catechetical guide for parish priests. Chronicles narrate how, after the Sunday masses, the children were made to recite the contents of the *Doctrina* in the church. Creative adaptations followed. The Jesuits, for instance, translated it into Bisayan verses adapted to the local traditional chants for planting and rowing.[27] But since Filipinos learned the doctrines in a recitative parrot-like manner, many missionaries also doubted the depth of the believers' comprehension of the tenets of the faith.

It is in this context that the schools became necessary. Schumacher writes: "The missionaries realized the difficulties of securing great depth in understanding among the older people and often had to content themselves with merely a basic knowledge of Christian teachings and the memorization of fundamental prayers. But the younger generation could not only be thoroughly grounded in the faith from their childhood, but the work of the schools with them also served to attract and teach their elders. Though the schools seem to have been an ordinary adjunct of the parishes, in the large towns the so-called *seminario de Indios,* or boarding schools, were set up for the boys from neighboring districts, where they lived together and received a thorough foundation in Christian life and doctrine,"[28] reading, writing, music, and other arts.

Both the colonial reconfiguration of space (*reducción*) and the reconfiguration of language (*doctrina*) involve the act of "translation." Instead of teaching natives the Spanish language, the first missionaries who were few in number decided to use the native languages in order to preach the Christian faith. Translation was the first act. The Spanish-based *Doctrina Christiana* was translated into Tagalog in its Romanized and *baybayin* scripts. Local terms had to be found to express theological categories. Creative adaptations of the tenets of faith, for instance, through songs and chants, made the learning and appreciation of doctrines easier and more

56   D. F. E. PILARIO

effective. Through these, one can appreciate the zeal and creativity of the first missionaries who became the first authorities of diverse local languages with their dictionaries and grammar books. Long before the term "cultural adaptation" or "inculturation" found itself into our sociological and theological vocabularies, the friars were already effectively practicing it in the field.

However, Vicente Rafael also alerts us to the semantic relationship between *traducción* (translation), *conversión* (conversion), and *conquista* (conquest). "To translate" is synonymous with "to convert." Conquest means both an aggressive entry into another's territory and winning over the other's confidence and affection. "Conversion [also] literally means the act of changing a thing into something else; in its more common usage, it denotes the act of bringing someone over to religion or practice. Conversion, like conquest, can thus be a process of crossing over into the domain—territorial, emotional, religious or cultural—of someone else and claiming it as one's own."[29]

Translation and conversion thus are ambivalent realities. On the one hand, they make the foreign Christian faith accessible to ordinary Filipinos and the local culture accessible to foreign missionaries. It is through these acts that we receive the faith. On the other hand, as we were converted, we were also "conquered," as it were. Spain has converted our identities to serve its colonial interests. "For a conqueror consolidates his position over the people he has conquered to the degree that he persuades them to defer to his interests – converts them to the view that they serve their own interests when they serve someone else's."[30]

What occurs at the semantic level becomes clearly visible in the socio-political sphere. Just as the Tagalog language needed to be translated and converted through the Castilian grammatical rules, the dispersed population and native bodies also needed to be "reduced" into the imperial grid so that it would be easier for the ruling body to subjugate. On the one hand, the time-tested missionary strategy of the *reducción* adopted from the experience of the New World proved helpful for easier transmission of the Christian message. The few available missionaries necessitated such a pastoral strategy. Moreover, to live away from the town—recounted one Spanish friar—generates "much spiritual and temporal damage" because, in those dispersed places, natives often live with "too much liberty of conscience."[31] On the other hand, Rafael argues that this reconfiguration of space also made it easier for colonizers to convert them "into arbitrary elements that could be made to fit into divinely sanctioned order characterized by the hierarchization of all signs and things in the world." Indigenous family names were also changed into Spanish-sounding ones for easier recall and profiling. The missionaries thus arrogated unto themselves the privilege to regulate "the placement, location, and movement of the converted populace with reference to the larger concerns of evangelization and colonial administration."[32] In other words, just as translation converts and adjusts the local language into a foreign configuration of grammar, tenses, and declensions, making it ready for colonial consumption, so does the reduction of the population into town centers (*cabeceras*) prepares them for easier management and supervision by the ambassadors of God and the King.

CONVERSION AND RESISTANCE

Conversion to the new faith was not a spontaneous response to the foreign missionaries' incursion into the indigenous religion. Distrust, violent resistance, and indifference characterized these initial encounters. Missionaries often discovered their huts burned, their belongings stolen, or the source of their drinking water poisoned. Thus, they resorted to more creative strategies other than coercion and violence in order to attract people to the faith. For instance, baptism was projected not only as purging the soul of its sin but also as healing the body of its ailments.[33] Chronicles in fact narrated miraculous healings brought about by the baptismal waters. Since healing is always a fundamental need, people started to request for baptism. The school became a central tool for catechetical classes. Once the children were indoctrinated, the chieftains and elders also became curious and were persuaded. "With the conversion of the leaders of the community, the baptism of their followers came as a matter of course."[34] Though there were instances when baptism was hastily celebrated with little preparation, most missionaries were careful in administering the sacrament and, in some cases, even postponed them. This makes post-baptismal catechesis and ongoing education in the faith very important.

There were many cultural obstacles to receiving the sacraments—polygamy, divorce, usury, slavery, sexual practices, drunkenness, etc.—customs traditionally practiced by pre-conquest Filipinos. Missionaries were careful not to admit to baptism those who have not fully imbibed the tenets of Christian faith and morals. If these obstacles were present for baptism, it was also true for the sacraments of marriage. Since polygamy and divorce were rampant, matrimony would only be celebrated if the couples deny these practices and uphold the Christian ideal. Phelan thinks that the acceptance of matrimonial demands "represents one of the most enduring achievements of the Spanish religious." With the work of the missionaries, "a new standard of premarital and marital morality was set up. Like all such norms, this one was not always observed, but it was a standard destined to exercise continuing influence through the coming centuries."[35] It was already difficult to convince the population to give in to the demands of the new Catholic morality, let alone live by them. In general, some parts of the population were converted; the majority remained in their traditional ways. On the one hand, these demands of the new religion were a colonial imposition. On the other hand, the "natives" had a way of resisting colonial rules and negotiating with hegemonic powers for reasons of cultural and, most often, physical survival. John Leddy Phelan has this quite somber and nuanced conclusion:

> As the 17th century wore on, the inadequacies of the missionary effort became increasingly apparent. Three sacraments – confirmation, extreme unction and holy orders – were of slight importance in the spiritual life of the Filipinos. In the case of penance and the Eucharist only the minimum requirements established by the Church were met... Yet the Filipinos were Christianized in the face of severe handicaps of a shortage of priests and a dispersed population speaking a bewildering variety of languages.[36]

Another occasion for indoctrination toward the new Christian morality was the sacrament of penance. Converts were enjoined to confess once a year. *Confessionarios*—detailed guides to the examination of conscience—were given to priests as they tried their best to elicit the "truth" from the penitent through some sort of question-and-answer interrogation process. Once accustomed to the practice, Filipinos needed no prompting as they literally flocked to the confessionals with eagerness and enthusiasm sometimes to the point of begging the priest on their knees—as many missionaries attested.

However, there is more to this eagerness and enthusiasm than what appears on the surface. While some missionaries were happy about this "rush to the confessional," others were more skeptical. Murillo Velarde complained about the Filipino's tendency toward "quibbling and contradictions [that] created labyrinths which confused even the most experienced confessors."[37] Instead of strictly following the *confessionarios,* the penitents turned this event into something else as they confessed not their own sins but the sins of their husbands or wives, their mothers-in-law, or those whom they considered enemies. Does this mean that the natives did not have the capacity to understand the theological intentions of this sacrament? Or was it a different game altogether?

Vicente Rafael's reflection might give us a hint as to what was really happening.[38] The Tagalog word for asking for forgiveness in confession is *tawad* which also means "to bargain, to haggle, and to use evasions (in Castillian *regatear*)." In other words, the practice of confession which was used by colonial authorities to control minds and bodies was also effectively employed by the natives to bargain with totalizing hegemonic power—the most accessible representative of whom is the parish priest. Beyond the colonial intention of reducing bodies into imperial designs through confession, the natives "responded by performing token payments designed to appease the figure of authority and deflect the force of hierarchy… What emerged was a confession without 'sin', conversion in a state of distraction."[39] In this reading, the truth of the practice contains a "surplus" that goes beyond the original intentions of its social agents— that is, the confessor and the penitent, the colonizer and the colonized— and overflows toward its unintended social consequences within the highly hegemonic colonial contexts.

As with confessions, so it was with other sacraments and religious practices in times of colonial domination. Another example is the recitation of the *Pasyon* (from the Passion of Jesus Christ)—a Tagalog extended verse form of salvation history from Genesis to Revelation chanted by people in their homes during the Holy Week. On the one hand, this activity can be viewed as an attempt by the colonizers to form the colonized minds into submission in the emulation of Jesus' resignation to suffering and death. On the other hand, Reynaldo Ileto—another Filipino historian—thinks that the peoples' chanting of the *Pasyon* had provided a narrative that served as a rallying symbol for their hopes and aspirations of liberation. Beyond the obvious intentions of the colonizers, the *Pasyon* contains a double truth which, to their surprise, was ingeniously and dexterously utilized by popular leaders to foster solidarity among the oppressed. As these unlettered masses dutifully chanted the narrative of the suffering of Jesus during Holy Week to the pleasure of the missionaries, these popular revolutionaries were also given the language and vision to articulate their longings for an alternative world far from what the colonizers had ever imagined.[40]

CONCLUSION

As a conclusion to his celebrated book, the Jesuit historian, Miguel Bernad, writes:

> [T]he achievement of Spain and of the missionaries was a substantial one. First of all, they made of these islands one nation, fusing the various regions and the innumerable barangays into one people sharing a common national identity and a common faith. Secondly, despite all the obstacles, natural and man-made, they succeeded in creating a Christian nation that eventually overthrew Spanish rule without rejecting the Christian faith. In the theological view of history, that is an achievement that could not have been accomplished without the abundant help of divine grace.[41]

However, Renato Constantino argues differently. He writes:

> [T]he attitude of the natives to the Church in the course of its economic and political ascendancy changed from initial obedience due to awe and fear; to loyalty and subservience arising from acceptance of the Catholic religion and experience with the power of priests within the colonial hierarchy, but accompanied by personal resentments; to generalized and group hostility because of the common experience of economic exploitation by the friars; and finally, to the violently anti-friar sentiments of the masses during the Revolution... It is very clear that this transition in the realm of consciousness was a response to a material stimulus — that transformation of the Church from a colonial accessory to the principal apparatus of colonial appropriation and exploitation.[42]

I have shown that these two conclusions are not without basis. But taken in isolation, each assertion sound like a swift generalization that neglects other socio-historical details which do not fit one's ideological straightjacket, thus, also overlooking the *doublé-verite* of practice. Bourdieu's theory of "double truth" also leads us to history's "surplus of meaning"—to borrow the phrase of Gadamer and Ricoeur or—if you wish to use Christian language—the presence of grace despite human sinfulness. It might be more helpful to heed a warning from another great historian, Horacio de la Costa: "It serves no useful purpose to conceal the fact that the record of the Church in the Philippines is a spotted one. It accomplished great things; it was also subject from time to time to great abuses."[43]

NOTES

1. Edward Said, *Culture and Imperialism* (London: Vintage, 1994), 1.
2. Vijay Mishra and Bob Hodge, "What is Post(-)colonialism," *Colonial Discourse and Post-colonial Theory: A Reader*, ed. Patrick Williams and Laura Chrisman (New York: Columbia University Press, 1994), 276–290.
3. Mishra and Hodge, "What is Post(-)colonialism," 288.
4. This is a revised version of my earlier article entitled "Das Evangelisierungs werk auf den Philippinen während der Kolonialzeit. Die missionarischen Methoden und ihre Ambivalenz," in *Evangelisierung: Die Freude des Evangeliums mitein anderteilen*, ed. Klaus Krämer and Klaus Vellguth (Freiburg, Basel, Wien: Herder, 2015), 40–65. This article was later translated as "Revisiting Evangelization Work in Colonial Philippines: The Ambivalence of Missionary Methods," in *Evangelization: Sharing the Joy of the Gospel*, ed. Klaus Krämer and Klaus Vellguth (Quezon City: Claretian Publications, 2016), 19–38.
5. Reynaldo Ileto, "Rizal and the Underside of Philippine Revolution," in idem, *Filipinos and their Revolution: Event, Discourse and Historiography* (Quezon City: Ateneo de Manila University Press, 1998), 32.
6. Pablo Fernandez, *History of the Church in the Philippines, 1521–1898* (Manila: National Book Store, 1979), 26.
7. Renato Constantino, *The Philippines: The Past Revisited*, vol. 1 (Quezon City: Tala Publications, 1975).
8. Jonathan Fast, "A New Interpretation of Philippine History," *Journal of Contemporary Asia* 7. No. 4 (1977): 535.
9. Pierre Bourdieu, *Pascalian Meditations* (London: Polity, 2000), 188–205; idem, *Outline of a Theory of Practice* (Cambridge: Polity Press, 1977); idem, *The Logic of Practice*, trans. R. Nice (Stanford, CA: Stanford University Press, 1990); idem, *Practical Reason: On the Theory of Action* (Stanford, CA: Stanford University Press, 1998), 92–123. For its application in theology, see D. F. Pilario, *Back to the Rough Grounds of Praxis: Exploring Theological Method with Pierre Bourdieu* (Leuven: Peeters, 2005).
10. Catholic Bishops' Conference of the Philippines (CBCP), "Pastoral Letter Celebrating the 500th Year of Christianity in the Philippines," in https://500yoc.com/wp-content/uploads/2021/03/500-YOC-CBCP-Pastoral-Statement-Final.pdf.
11. Pierre Bourdieu, *Pascalian Meditations*, 191.
12. Cf. Horacio de la Costa, "Church and State under the *Patronato Real*," *Horacio de la Costa, S.J.: Selected Studies in Philippine Colonial History*, comp. and ed. Roberto Paterno (Quezon City: Ateneo de Manila University Press), 50–65.
13. De la Costa, "Church and State under the *Patronato Real*," 51–52.

62 D. F. E. PILARIO

14. Horacio de la Costa, *Readings in Philippine History* (Makati: Bookmark, 1992 [1965]), 58.
15. De la Costa, "Church and State under *Patronato Real*," 52.
16. Renato Constantino, *The Philippines: A Past Revisited – Pre-Spanish to 1941*, Vol. 1 (Manila: n.p. 1975), 39–48, 58–71.
17. Constantino, *The Philippines: A Past Revisited*, 21.
18. Cf. John Schumacher, "Bishop Domingo de Salazar and the Manila Synod of 1582," in idem, *Growth and Decline: Essays in Philippine Church History* (Quezon City: Ateneo de Manila University Press, 2009), 1–21; Horacio de la Costa, "Bishop Salazar and the Colonial Episcopate," *Horacio de la Costa, S.J.: Selected Studies in Philippine Colonial History*, comp and ed. Roberto Paterno (Quezon City: Ateneo de Manila University Press), 66–92.
19. Cf. For an account of the first Synod of Manila, see John Schumacher, *Readings in Philippine Church History* 2nd ed. (Quezon City: Loyola School of Theology, Ateneo de Manila University, 1987), 28–35.
20. "Memorial of the Things Happening in These Philippine Islands of the West and of their Condition, and of What Must be Remedied, Written by Friar Domingo de Salazar, Bishop of the Said Islands; to be Read by Your Majesty and the Lords of the Royal Council of the Indies (1582)," Cf. Christina Lee, "Domingo de Salazar's Letter to the King of Spain in Defense of the Indians and the Chinese of the Philippine Islands (1582)," in *The Spanish Pacific, 1521–1815: A Reader of Primary Sources*, ed. C. H. Lee and R. Padrón (Amsterdam: Amsterdam University Press, 2020), 37–52.
21. Schumacher, *Readings in Philippine Church History*, 36.
22. J. Gayo Aragón, "The Controversy over Justification of Spanish Rule in the Philippines," in *Studies in Philippine Church History*, ed. Gerald Anderson (Ithaca and London: Cornell University Press, 1969), 7.
23. John Schumacher, "Re-reading Philippine History: Constantino's A Past Revisited," *Philippine Studies* 23, no. 4 (1975) 465–481.
24. Cf. John Leddy Phelan, *The Hispanization of the Philippines: Spanish Aims and Filipino Responses* (Madison: University of Wisconsin Press, 1959), 44–49.
25. Phelan, *The Hispanization of the Philippines*, 49.
26. The cover page reads: *Doctrina Christiana en Lengua Espanola Y Tagala corregida Reglos por Los Religiosos de las Ordenes Impressa con Licencia en (San) Gabriel de las Orden de (Santo) Domingo. En Manila, 1593* (Christian Doctrine in Spanish and Tagalog Language), with correct rules for the Religious Order. Printed with License in Saint Gabriel of the Holy Dominican Order. In Manila, 1593.
27. Phelan, *The Hispanization of the Philippines*, 58.
28. Schumacher, *Readings in Philippine Church History*, 48.

29. Vicente Rafael, *Contracting Colonialism: Translation and Christian Conversion in Tagalog Society under Early Spanish Rule* (Quezon City: Ateneo de Manila University Press, 1988), ix.
30. Rafael, *Contracting Colonialism*, ix.
31. Rafael, *Contracting Colonialism*, 89.
32. Rafael, *Contracting Colonialism*, 90.
33. John Leddy Phelan, "Prebaptismal Instruction and the Administration of Baptism in the Philippines during the Sixteenth Century," in *Studies in Philippine Church History*, ed. Gerald Anderson (Ithaca and London: Cornell University Press, 1969), 22–43.
34. Phelan, *The Hispanization of the Philippines*, 55.
35. Phelan, *The Hispanization of the Philippines*, 65.
36. Phelan, *The Hispanization of the Philippines*, 71.
37. Pedro Murillo Velarde, *Historia de la provincia de Philippinas de la compaña de Jesus* (Manila, 1749), 5 cited in Phelan, *The Hispanization of the Philippines*, 66.
38. Rafael, *Contracting Colonialism*, 132.
39. Rafael, *Contracting Colonialism*, 135.
40. Cf. Reynaldo Ileto, *Pasyon and Revolution: Popular Movements in the Philippines, 1840-1910* (Quezon City: Ateneo de Manila University Press, 1979).
41. Miguel Bernad, *The Christianization of the Philippines: Problems and Perspectives* (Manila: Filipiniana Book Guild, 1972), 348.
42. Constantino, *The Philippines*, 81–82.
43. de la Costa, *Readings in Philippine History*, 56.

CHAPTER 4

Rethinking Encounters and Re-imagining Muslim-Christian Relations in Post-colonial Philippines

Vivienne S. M. Angeles

As a child growing up in an overwhelmingly Catholic town, our views of Muslims were defined and colored by the stories we read and heard about people who, as my grade schoolteacher in the parochial school told us, were "bad because they did not convert to Christianity." The only Muslim I had seen up to that time was an itinerant vendor selling pearls who came to my hometown. My neighbor told us later that we could never be sure if the pearls were real because Muslims could not be trusted. The next Muslim I met was a former student (the only Muslim in school so far at the time) who returned to visit his teachers when I was a senior in high school. The librarian introduced him to us, emphasizing that he was "a Moro, but a good Moro." In other words, an exception. These personal narratives happened decades ago, but are, in a way, among the many

---

V. S. M. Angeles (✉)
Department of Religion and Theology, La Salle University,
Philadelphia, PA, USA

© The Author(s), under exclusive license to Springer Nature
Switzerland AG 2024
C. Lledo Gomez et al. (eds.), *500 Years of Christianity and the Global Filipino/a*, Pathways for Ecumenical and Interreligious Dialogue, https://doi.org/10.1007/978-3-031-47500-9_4

65

66   V. S. M. ANGELES

indicators of how Muslims were viewed in a country that prides itself as one of two dominantly Catholic countries in Asia.

This chapter explores the colonial and post-colonial policies and practices that affected Muslim-Christian relations in the Philippines. In the 500 years since the Spanish arrived in the Philippines in 1521, the colonists, political authorities, and religious leaders, through their policies and practices, functioned as the arbiters of Muslim-Christian relations. The policies were numerous, but I will mention selected instances and colonial practices that helped shape and influence Muslim-Christian relations in the colonial and post-colonial periods. To understand this relationship, this chapter will touch on the following themes: first, Islam in the pre-colonial Philippines; second, Christianity as a colonial export and a tool of the colonists' "civilizing" mission; third, post-colonial policies affecting Muslim-Christian relations; and fourth, contemporary efforts of Christians and Muslims on promoting inter-religious understanding.

Critical to understanding Muslim-Christian relations is the Spanish use of the term "Moro" for Philippine Muslims and its corresponding connotations that survived from colonial times to the present. The word is from "Moors" which they used for Muslims who ruled southern Spain from 711 to 1492. Burkhardt notes that the Moors or Mauritanians are simply inhabitants of the Maghreb that extends from Spain to Tunisia.[1] In the Philippine setting, however, the Spanish use of the term had pejorative connotations, as indicated in colonial writings, which will be discussed below.

ISLAM IN PRE-COLONIAL PHILIPPINES

Scholars note that there were already Muslim settlements in Sulu in the last quarter of the thirteenth century.[2] In the succeeding years, Arab and other Asian traders continued to arrive, eventually intermarrying with the locals, and settling in Sulu. Among the Arab and Gujarati traders were Sufis,[3] who also functioned as missionaries. They brought Islam to Malaysia and Indonesia, and from there, to Sulu and other parts of the Philippines.[4] Information on the arrival of Islam to Sulu from traditions and *tarsilas*[5] (genealogies) which, while lacking specific dates, indicate the succession of sultans and their lineage which in turn legitimized their position as head of the political structure. *Tarsilas* also include information on the arrival of important personages in the history of Islam in the Philippines like Tuan Masha'ika and Karim ul Makhdum who settled in Sulu, with the latter credited as having built the first mosque in the Philippines. Traditions, particularly the one narrated by Haji Butu Abdul Baki, note the coming of Abu Bakr who overcame the people's initial rejection of his teachings about God and the Qur'an, but succeeded in converting people to Islam.[6] Other traders/missionaries followed Abu Bakr to the rest of Mindanao, thus paving the way for Islam to eventually become the dominant religion in Sulu and other areas in Mindanao.

By the time the Spanish came to the Philippines in 1521, there were already functioning sultanates in Sulu and Maguindanao with sultans exercising both political and religious leadership and participating actively in commercial activities in the Malay world. As head of the political structure and religious leader, the sultan also symbolized the community of the faithful on earth and their membership and participation in the *Dar al Islam* (world of Islam).[7] With the title *Zil Allah fil 'ard* (the Shadow of God on Earth),[8] the sultan was considered the defender of the faith and protector of the *Shari'ah* (Islamic law). He appointed the *qadi* (judge) who was usually a foreign Muslim from neighboring countries or from the Middle East and India and learned in Shafi'i law.[9] The other appointees of the sultan were the mosque officials: the *imam* (prayer leader), *bilal* (caller to prayer), and the *khatib* (recorder). In the sultanate where political and religious functions merged, the sultan invoked the teachings of the Qur'an and assumed the responsibility of keeping his subjects knowledgeable in Islam. The Sultan attended the *Jumaat* (Friday prayers) and had the right to have his name mentioned in the *khutbah* (sermon).[10] Islam in this situation functioned like a state religion, embedded within the socio-political structure of the state, providing a sense of identity to the people.

Islam, however, was not confined to Sulu and Mindanao in pre-colonial Philippines. Testimonies of friar missionaries around 1580[11] mention that when the Spanish arrived in Manila in the sixteenth century, they found chiefs, like Rajah Soliman who were Muslims. These chiefs were related to the ruling families of Borneo and Brunei—suggesting the existence of political, economic, and religious linkages between the Manila and Malaysian Muslim royalties.[12] Magad-China, a resident of Balayan, on the island of Luzon, testified to the Spanish Governor, Francisco Sande, that the people of Balayan, Manila, Mindoro, and Bonbon became Muslims through the efforts of Bornean preachers sent by the King of Borneo. He also reported that he had seen the "Alcoran" (Qur'an) and that preachers said that they are "enemies of Christians" although they intended to convert Christians to Islam.[13] In both the Christian and Muslim sides then,

68   V. S. M. ANGELES

the other was viewed negatively but seen as prospective converts. Considering the presence of Muslims in Manila, Bataan, and surrounding areas, Antonio de Morga noted that if the Spanish had delayed their arrival, Islam would have spread further in the Philippines, and it would have been more difficult to convert the people to Christianity.[14] Islam, at the time of Spanish contact, had already taken the form of an indigenous religion.

CHRISTIANITY: A COLONIAL EXPORT AND A TOOL OF THE COLONISTS' "CIVILIZING" MISSION

Spanish colonial ambitions can be summarized in three Cs: Conquest, Commerce, and Christianization. Conquest of lands for the Spanish crown, participation in the lucrative commercial activities, and Christianization of whatever peoples they encountered. For the Spanish colonizers, Christianity was the only legitimate religion, and it was necessary to convert the conquered peoples to Christianity as a way of saving their souls and civilizing them. Religious affiliation became an identity marker and a criterion for one's place in the social structure, with the Spanish occupying the top strata, Filipino Christians at the bottom, and the Muslims and other unconverted indigenous peoples outside of it.

Members of the religious orders and secular colonial officials promoted Christianity as part of their colonial undertaking. Considering the insular nature of the country where missionaries were usually the ones willing to venture to remote regions, the dual duties of converting people and administering the pueblo then fell into the hands of members of various religious orders like the Dominicans, Augustinians, Jesuits, and Franciscans. The accounts of missionaries acknowledged that the people they encountered were Muslims but considering their own religious orientation and colonial goals, there was an immediate bias against Islam and Muslims, with Francisco Combes, a Jesuit missionary, noting that the people of Mindanao are "treacherous and of little faith, as they are now swayed by the impious worship of Mahomet [sic]." Combes was critical of the level of religiosity of Muslims, claiming that they were "barbarous atheists."[15] Other Spanish missionaries and chroniclers shared this evaluation and described Philippine Muslims only in terms of their dietary habits and marriage practices.[16] Since Muslims practiced slavery and polygamy, the Spanish saw these practices as further justifying their view of Islam as a false religion and intensifying the need to convert Muslims to Christianity and deliver them from what they considered uncivilized practices. Combes, however, took exception to the Maguindanao sultan, Qudarat, and other leading datus (chief or petty ruler), who, he conceded, followed the teachings of Islam, and required the people to attend the mosque.[17] Combes had expected the religious experiences of people to be on the same level and did not allow for varieties of religious experiences even within the same religion. Other missionaries wrote to their superiors in Spain, describing Philippine Muslims as "cunning, hypocrites, traitors, swindlers, suspicious, accommodating and persistent…They are headstrong in their beliefs, and it is practically impossible to convert them to Christianity."[18]

Specific Spanish colonial government policies toward the Muslims are embodied in several instructions of the King and Spanish officials. In 1569, King Philip II directed the colonists to "reduce the Indians and convert them willingly to our Catholic faith and the Christian religion by means of religious and other good men."[19] By 1577, Christianization of the indigenous peoples in Luzon and Visayas had progressed so that, King Philip II decided that the evangelization of the country was "sufficiently advanced" to merit the establishment of an Episcopal See in Manila. However, the situation in the southern Philippines was different. After attacking Brunei in 1579, Governor Francisco Sande instructed Esteban Rodriguez de Figueroa to proceed from Borneo to Jolo and Mindanao and to pursue several objectives which included converting the natives to Christianity.[20] Sande also explicitly instructed Figueroa to order the natives to refrain from admitting more Muslim preachers, since "the teachings of Muhammad are evil and false and that alone of the Christian is good."[21] Muslim preachers were to be seized, and the mosques burned and destroyed. Although Figueroa met very limited success, Sande's instructions guided the Spanish in their relationship with Muslims in the succeeding centuries. In the later expeditions sent by Governor Hurtado de Corcuera to Mindanao and Sulu, Spanish soldiers destroyed copies of Islamic manuscripts and tombs of earlier sultans.[22]

Spanish attempts at conquering and converting the Muslims in Mindanao and Sulu were complicated by what Muslims saw as intrusions into their commercial activities. The Sultan of Sulu was a major participant in the global trade which catered to the demands of China and Europe for maritime products. The need for workers for the expanded maritime activities resulted in increased slave raiding activities, especially by the Iranun and Balangini Samals[23] who traded the slaves needed for maritime

70   V. S. M. ANGELES

industries. Although slave raiding was considered a legitimate profession in the Iranun's cultural-historical perspective,[24] it had devastating effects, particularly on the coastline communities, thus generating strong military reactions from the Spanish authorities. At the same time, it also led people affected by the raids to cooperate with the Spanish military to protect themselves and their properties.[25] The Iranuns and Balangingi Samals were the ones mainly involved in raiding and piratical activities but since the Spaniards lumped all the Muslims despite their tribal differences, under the umbrella term of "Moros," piracy and slave raiding became associated with all Muslims, no matter the tribe and their means of livelihood.

The Muslim-Spanish tension was a complicated one reflecting religious, political, and economic issues throughout Spanish rule in the Philippines. Both sides envisioned converting the other, they launched military attacks against each other, and both enslaved captive soldiers and civilians.[26] When organized armed resistance by Muslims against Spain failed, the responsibility then fell into individuals who took it upon themselves to protest colonial policies by engaging in *parang sabil*—a form of ritual suicide, sacralized by actions that involved praying with the *imam*, reading passages from the Qur'an, being primed for the attack which included the use of white clothing, and then early the next day, striking in public spaces, killing random people that may include soldiers, non-Muslims or even Muslims while being aware that they themselves would be killed by the soldiers. Although the Qur'an prohibits suicide,[27] several *parang sabil* happened during the Spanish and American colonization as a form of individual resistance against colonial practices. Also referred to as *juramentado, parang sabil*[28] strengthened the colonial views of Muslims as prone to "violent action"—and images of Muslims running with a bladed weapon were ingrained in Filipino minds as children who had never even met Muslims.

An event, however, that raised hopes of converting Muslims to Christianity, was the supposed "conversion" of Sultan Azim ud Din. The sultan acceded to the request of the Spanish King Philip V that Christian missionaries be allowed to preach in Jolo, but his subjects opposed the idea. This contributed to the tensions within the sultanate leading to the deterioration of the political situation in Sulu and prompted Sultan Azim ud Din to sail to Manila and seek the help of the Spanish authorities. While in Manila, he asked to be baptized a Christian and after due deliberation from Spanish officials and members of the religious hierarchy, he was baptized and given the name Don Fernando Azim ud Din, Catholic Sultan of Jolo. Spain was interested in having a Christian Sultan in the hope of facilitating the conquest of the area but that was not to be. There was strong mutual distrust and suspicions between the Spanish and the Sultan's followers leading the Spanish authorities to realize that Sultan Azim ud Din never really abandoned Islam.[29] While en route to Sulu, he was returned to Manila, as a prisoner.

The missionary zeal of the Spanish made them seek another peace treaty with Sultan Jamalul Kiram of Sulu which, among other things, gave the status of the sultanate as a protectorate where customs, laws, and the religion of the people were to be left alone. The treaty also gave Spain the right to send missionaries provided they informed the sultan of their presence. To Spain, it was necessary to Christianize the Muslims so that they would be loyal to the crown—a position enthusiastically supported by the religious orders but in the end, although Spain was able to establish some alliances with some sultans, they had to content themselves with leaving the Muslims to their faith.

The complex interplay of religion, commerce, and politics that involved military encounters made for the lack of missionary success in Mindanao and Sulu despite heavy Jesuit missionary presence in the area. Since there were Christianized Filipinos who were part of the Spanish forces, Muslims came to envision them as tools of Spanish colonial ambitions. Negative descriptions of Muslims in colonial literature (which became the basis of early Philippine history books), the piracy and slave trading, and resistance to what Christianized Filipinos have come to believe as the true religion, together with representations of Muslims in a theater form called *Komedya* or *Moro-Moro*[30] reinforced the negative image of Muslims and left a legacy of mutual suspicion between Muslims and Christians that continued even during post-independence times. Religion also became a salient feature of identity in the Philippines and Muslims became the "other" in Philippine society.

Although the Spanish officials and missionaries were not able to Christianize Mindanao and Sulu, they were very successful in Luzon and Visayas, so that by the time the United States took over the Philippines under the terms of the Treaty of Paris in 1898, Christianity, the Catholic version, had become the majority religion in the country. Cognizant of Spain's experience in the country, the Americans were more intent on their pacification campaign and tried not to touch on Islam for fear of violent opposition. Actions and policies of American administrators, however, reflected an understanding of Islam and Muslims through the lenses of the Spanish colonists and missionaries.

Shortly after the Philippines became a US colony, President William McKinley announced in a meeting with Protestant clergymen at the White House, that it was the obligation of the United States to "educate the Filipinos, and uplift and civilize and Christianize them, and by God's grace do the very best we could by them, as our fellow-men for whom Christ also died."[31] Despite the religious tone in McKinley's statement, the doctrine of separation of church and state in the US Constitution precluded it from officially supporting a religion and engaging in conversion activities. However, there were indications of American preference for Christianity in various colonial policies.

In 1916, the American colonial government created the Bureau of Non-Christian Tribes. Dean C. Worcester, secretary of the Interior from 1901 to 1913, acknowledged the awkward use of the term non-Christian but noted that the one characteristic that the numerous tribes had in common was "their refusal to accept the Christian faith, and their adherence to their ancient religious beliefs, or their lack of such beliefs as the case may be."[32] The major task of the bureau was to integrate non-Christian and Christian populations of the whole country and one of the ways the government implemented this program was through the establishment of agricultural colonies in Mindanao. Instead of promoting integration, however, the program generated confrontations between Muslims and Christians because Muslims claimed that they had ancestral rights to the land allocated by the colonial government to the settlers. The Christians, on the other hand, maintained that they had legal rights by virtue of legal titles to the lands granted to them by the government.[33] The independent government also launched a variation of the land allocation program, and it had the same effects on the relationship between the Muslims and the Christian settlers.

Muslims benefitted from American rule notably in the areas of health and education but there continued to be tensions in Muslim-American relations. The sultan was reduced to a religious head, but the laws which Muslims believed were based on the Qur'an as administered by the sultan were substituted by what they saw as secular laws. In principle, the Americans superimposed a judicial system that varied from their understanding of *adat* (custom) laws and the *Shari'ah*.

The American colonial government established public schools in Muslim areas, but the initial reaction of Muslims was suspicion, thinking that the schools might convert the students to Christianity. They opened up a girls' school and while it was not mentioned at the time, Governor John Pershing's Christian bias was manifested in his report in 1913 where he said that they were making an effort to bring the Muslim girls under the "elevating moral influence" of the American Christian women teachers, otherwise, they could only become wives or concubines of the *datus*.[34] Since Christian Filipino teachers were reluctant to accept assignments in Muslim areas, Pershing believed that supervision of education in Muslim areas should be in the hands of Americans. The government encouraged the children of sultans and *datus* to attend the school as they believed that since these girls were from royal families, others would follow their lead in being educated. Governor Pershing opposed a suggestion that Islam be taught in the schools, saying that the presence of Arabian and "Muhammedan" [sic] teachers was detrimental to good government.[35] He talked about the social evolution of the Muslims and reasoned that having Christian teachers would help facilitate this evolution. Governor Frank Carpenter, who succeeded Governor Pershing, noted that the government would not promote a religious objective but felt that it would be politically and economically expedient that all peoples of the Philippines share the same beliefs, standards, and ideals.[36] At the time, majority of the Filipinos were already Catholic.

Christian missionaries of different denominations came to Mindanao during the American period and while some had experienced initial resistance from the local people, others achieved some measure of success in dealing with Muslims, establishing Christian churches and schools in Mindanao and Sulu. Frank Laubach of the American Board of Commissioners for Foreign Missions established a school and created a literacy program involving the use of Latin script for the Maranao language. He invited *hajjis*[37] to teach him about Islam in what may have been among the early efforts at inter-religious dialogue in Mindanao. In his preaching, he appropriated teachings of the Qur'an that are compatible with Christian values and way of life.[38] The work of Laubach inspired the establishment of Dansalan College,[39] the majority of whose students are Muslims.

The tensions between the local populations in Mindanao and the Americans were at times high, resulting in armed confrontations due to several colonial policies and actions that Muslims viewed as disadvantageous to them. Because of the religious identity of the persons involved, the conflicts tended to be viewed as basically a Muslim-Christian religious conflict even if they involved more complicated factors rather than simple religious differences, like protests regarding the head tax, the road tax, and the agricultural colonization program, among others.

Post-colonial Government Policies and Muslim-Christian Relations

By the time the independent Philippine government was established in 1946, the negative views of Islam and Muslims as defined by the colonial governments had already become entrenched in the consciousness of both Philippine Christians and Muslims. The government implemented a version of the agricultural colonization programs in Mindanao, but this time, land was allotted to former members of the Huk movement, a communist group involved in uprisings against the government in the early 1950s.[40] The same issue of Muslim ancestral lands was involved, thus reviving the earlier conflicts between Muslims and Christian settlers. Christian Filipinos continued to govern Muslim areas, and Christian missionaries continued with their activities in Mindanao and Sulu, while these Muslim areas continued to lag in terms of economic indices—poverty, lower literacy rates, and underdevelopment.

Citing government neglect and discrimination against Muslims as well as an incident famously called the Jabidah massacre where Muslim military trainees were killed,[41] Muslim leaders and other non-Muslim sympathizers launched the Moro National Liberation Front (MNLF) in 1969 and called for the creation of an Islamic state.[42] President Ferdinand Marcos cited this rebellion as one of the reasons he declared martial law in 1972. The early 1970s witnessed death, destruction, and displacement of people as the Philippine military and the MNLF engaged in armed conflicts in various parts of Mindanao and Sulu. The Philippine government had to address both the situation of the Muslims and the demands of the liberation front to stop the devastation caused by the war. The martial law government implemented not only social and economic programs but also policies that were conducive to the practice of Islam, like the declaration in 1973 that Islam is part of Filipino heritage. The government claimed that its policy on Mindanao is guided by the preservation and advancement of Islamic culture and traditions as well as the promotion of the well-being of Muslim communities, including the rights to their ancestral lands.[43]

Over and against the Spanish heritage of religious intolerance, the Philippine government now sought to give Islam a rightful place in a predominantly Catholic country with presidential decrees recognizing Muslim holidays as Philippine holidays, regulation of working hours during the Muslim fasting month of Ramadan, the creation of the Amanah Bank based on the Islamic principle of prohibiting interest, the sponsorship of Qur'an recitation contests, the sponsorship of the pilgrimage to Mecca, and the codification of Muslim Personal Laws, among others. In addition, the government not only paid for the reconstruction of mosques destroyed during the war but also built a mosque in the heart of Manila and the Maharlika Village. The government referred to these as cultural centers, claiming that Muslims are cultural minorities who happened to be Muslims and therefore deserved government support. The government also established the Institute of Islamic Studies at the University of the Philippines—the first public university program that focused on the study of a religion and a religious minority in the Philippines. The Department of Public Information also produced reading materials and videos on Islam and Muslims.

It was also in the 1970s when the government, in response to employment problems in the country, launched an overseas workers program that exported Filipino labor to various parts of the world. The Middle East was a choice destination for Filipino workers because the wage was higher than in other countries. A majority of the overseas workers were Christians, and this employment program exposed them to a religion and culture that was unfamiliar to many of them. In places like Saudi Arabia where the public practice of a religion other than Islam is not allowed, conversions were not unusual and upon the return of the worker to the Philippines, many of them continued not only to practice their new religion but converted members of their family as well. In my interviews with some of them, they spoke about how their preconceived ideas about Islam and Muslims were changed by their experiences in the Middle East and their understanding of Islam.[44]

The government programs and policies, while intended to rectify previous anti-Muslim bias from colonial to post-colonial times, also provided an environment conducive to Islamic resurgence in the country. There were questions raised about martial law government policies for Muslims and the doctrine of separation of church and state enshrined in the Philippine Constitution[45] but there was no vigorous and organized action against government programs and policies favoring Muslims. With the policies promulgated and institutions created, the government had become an interpreter of Islam in the Philippines.

Although the policies implemented during martial law created a better opportunity for expressing the religious experiences of Muslims and for inter-religious understanding between Muslims and Christians, the sporadic clashes between the military and various groups claiming to represent Muslim interests continue. Some of these groups, like the Abu Sayyaf, have been influenced by the outside fundamentalist groups like Al Qaeda, and ISIS (Islamic State of Iraq and Syria), so their activities in the southern Philippines re-ignite colonial negative perceptions of Muslims.

CONTEMPORARY EFFORTS AT INTER-RELIGIOUS UNDERSTANDING

Five hundred years after Spain brought Christianity to the Philippines, many changes have occurred in the country's religious landscape. Roman Catholicism continues to be the dominant religion in the Philippines, but there are now many variations of Christianity, some of them the result of American colonialism and others the outcome of local interpretations of Christian teachings. Islam has become a plural religion too, with the presence in the Philippines of Sunnis, Shi'a, Jami'at Tabligh, and the more recent Balik-Islam,[46] among others. Muslims, who were concentrated in the southern part of the country, now live all over the Philippines and there are now mosques in practically every province. Where people in the Luzon islands hardly saw Muslims in the 1970s, now they could be neighbors, classmates, or co-workers, or they could encounter Muslims as overseas workers in the Middle East. This proximity between Muslims and Christians allows for more interaction and opportunities for inter-religious understanding which their respective global religious leaderships have already initiated.

The Catholic church, which was intolerant of other religions in the 1500s, promulgated *Nostra Aetate* (Declaration on the Relation of the Church to non-Christian Religions), in 1965, at the Second Vatican Council. The document calls for dialogue and respect toward the major non-Christian religions of the world: Judaism, Islam, Hinduism, and Buddhism. In dealing specifically with Islam, the document says that the "Church regards Muslims with esteem" and although Muslims do not believe Jesus is God, there are other teachings that the two religions share.

Cognizant of the tensions between Christians and Muslims in the past, the document calls for working toward mutual understanding and the promotion of social justice, moral welfare, peace, and freedom.[47] Islam does not have a monolithic structure that issues pronouncements for all Muslims, but individual Muslim leaders have also made efforts toward promoting inter-religious understanding. Many Muslim leaders have signed the Common Word document, an interfaith initiative for Muslims and Christians, and participated in various programs promoting relationships between the two religions.

Christians and Muslims in the Philippines have followed through the initiatives of their global leaders. Various groups like the Bishop-Ulama Conference, the Silsilah Dialogue Movement, and the Philippine Council for Islam and Democracy as well as other NGOs have organized seminars and dialogues on topics like learning about Islam and Christianity, the conflict situation in the Philippine south and working on strategies for understanding each other's religion and promoting a culture of peace in Mindanao. Universities like Notre Dame of Cotabato and Ateneo de Zamboanga have offered courses on Islam and Christianity as well as seminars and discussions on inter-religious understanding.

Despite the leadership of various Christians and Muslims in promoting inter-religious understanding that could help foster better relations, my random interviews of ordinary Catholics through the years have informed me that although *Nostra Aetate* was promulgated almost 60 years ago, many Catholics in the Philippines are not aware of this document and much less of its provisions. If the Church is to live up to the message of *Nostra Aetate*, then it must be creative in sharing the message at the grassroots level, using modern technology and through activities that allow members to engage, not just tolerate other religious groups. *Nostra Aetate* calls for forgetting the past quarrels and hostilities between Christians and Muslims[48] so there is a need to break away from negative colonial perceptions of Muslims and Christians toward each other and dialogue with openness and freedom. My random interviews of Philippine Muslims on relations with other religions generated varied responses—from emphasizing the truth of Islam over other religions to citing Qur'an 5:47[49] as an injunction to engage in inter-religious dialogue. Hopefully, the inter-religious initiatives will provide more positive interactions between Muslims and Christians in an atmosphere of religious pluralism which calls for engagement while respecting each other's differences.

Conclusion

In the last five hundred years, the policies and actions of the colonial and post-colonial governments affected the relationship between Muslims and Christians. Although Moro wars have often been seen as what defines Muslim-Christian relations in the Philippines, Crailsheim reminds us that the initial contact between the two peoples was peaceful, until the Spanish settled in Manila and the missionary activities intensified.[50] Spanish colonization was a complex situation where their aims of conversion, commerce, conquest, and their view of Muslims as the enemy who was expelled after the fall of Granada in 1492 in Spain converged. On the side of Muslims, there was also the merging of various factors such as religion, intrusion into their commercial activities, resources, and protection of their way of life that determined their responses to Spanish colonial ambitions. They conducted missionary activities themselves, in pursuit of their belief in the truth only of their religion. However, the raids, which were either part of the trading activities, attacks, or retaliations against Spanish forces, caused devastation not only to Spanish commercial interests but also to the lives of the indigenous population, thus explaining one of the reasons why there were locals who fought with the Spanish against the Muslims.

The American government and the Philippine post-colonial government did not enforce a religion, but they viewed the Muslims through the lenses of Spanish colonial literature and demonstrated biases toward Christianity in their policies and actions toward the Muslims. It had to take a Muslim rebellion and a demand for an Islamic state in the late 1960s for the Philippine government to adopt policies favorable to Muslims and conducive to Islamic resurgence in the country. Such policies treaded on the issue of separation of church and state although they did not generate an organized protest from the citizens during the time of martial law. Through the many decrees enforced during that time, the government became the interpreter of Islam for all Filipinos. While there have been significant changes through the years that brought about greater participation of Muslims in the socio-political and economic life of the community, and there has been a growing recognition of religious pluralism, there are still lingering issues of discrimination and prejudice against Muslims due to the rise of Islamic fundamentalism and the military conflicts that continue to happen sporadically in southern Philippines. Such incidents trigger old perceptions of Muslims from Spanish colonial periods. Part of the inter-religious discourse should also recognize the fact that Islam is not a monolithic religion, there are varied interpretations of the texts by different Muslims, and even among Muslims themselves, the question of which is the authentic Islam is also an ongoing exploration.

NOTES

1. Titus Burkhardt, *Moorish Culture in Spain* (Louisville: Fons Vitae, 1999), 7.
2. Cesar A. Majul, *Muslims in the Philippines* (Quezon City: University of the Philippines Press for the Asian Center, 1973), 63.
3. Muslim mystics.
4. See Bernard M. Vlekke, *Nusantara: A History of Indonesia* (New York and Bandung: Van Hoeve, Ltd.1960), 83; B. Schrieke, *Indonesian Sociological Studies* (The Hague: Van Hoeve, 1955), Pt II, 283–4; Cesar A. Majul, *Muslims in the Philippines*, 49.
5. Genealogical accounts; from the Arabic *silsilah.*
6. Haji Butu Abdul Baki, "Traditions, Customs and Commerce of the Sulu Moros," *The Mindanao Herald* (February 3, 1909): 21.
7. James Warren, *The Sulu Zone 1768-1898: The Dynamics of External Trade, Slavery and Ethnicity in the Transformation of a Southeast Asian Maritime State* (Quezon City: New Day Publishers, 1999), xxvii.
8. Majul, *Muslims in the Philippines*, 320.
9. Of the four major schools of law (Maliki, Hanbali, Hanafi, and Shafi'i), Shafi'I is the dominant school in Southeast Asia.
10. Sermon or oration delivered during the *Jumaat* (Friday) congregational prayers.
11. Marcelo de Ribadeneria, *Historia delas Islas del archipelago Filipinas y reinos dela gran China Tartaria Cochin China, Malacca, Siam, Cambodge y Japon*, ed. Juan R. de Legisma (Madrid:1947), 91, cited in Majul, *Muslims in the Philippines,76.*
12. Majul, *Muslims in the Philippines*, 73.
13. Francisco Sande, "An Account of the Expedition to Borneo, Jolo and Mindanao, January 15, 1579," in *The Philippine Islands* IV, ed. Emma Blair and James A. Robinson (Ohio: Arthur Clarke and Co., 1903), 150–151,　　　　https://www.fulltextarchive.com/book/ The-Philippine-Islands-1493-1898-Vol-4-of/#content.
14. Antonio de Morga, *The Philippine Islands, Moluccas, Siam, Cambodia, Japan and China at the close of the Sixteenth Century*, trans. Henry Stanley (London:1868), 307–388, cited in Majul, *Muslims in the Philippines,76–77.*

80   V. S. M. ANGELES

15. Francisco Combés, S.J., "The Natives of the Southern Islands" [From his *Historia de Mindanao y Ioló* (Madrid: Retana Edition, 1887)], 104, https://www.gutenberg.org/files/30253/30253-h/30253-h. htm#app2.
16. See Sande, "An Account of the Expedition to Borneo, Jolo and Mindanao," 148–150; Antonio Pigafetta, "First Voyage Around the world," in *The Philippine Islands*, XXXIII, ed. Emma Blair and James A. Robertson (Ohio: Arthur Clarke and Co., 1903), 148–150; J. S. Arcilla, ed., *Jesuit Missionary Letters from Mindanao: The Zamboanga-Basilan-Jolo Mission* (Quezon City: University of the Philippines, 2000).
17. Combes, "The Natives of the Southern Islands," 134.
18. J. Montero y Vidal, *El Archipelago Filipinas y las islas Marianas, Carolinas y Palao* (Madrid: Manuel Tello, 1886), 383–384.
19. Phillip II, "Reply to Legazpi," in *The Philippines*, XXXIV, ed. Emma Blair and James A. Robertson (Ohio: Arthur Clarke, 1906), 235–238.
20. The other objectives were to make the inhabitants recognize Spanish sovereignty, command the people to settle down, be peaceful agriculturists, develop the pearl industry, and cease to be pirates.
21. Sande, "Account of the expedition to Borneo, Jolo and Mindanao," 141.
22. Majul, *Muslims in the Philippines*, 84.
23. Iranuns and Samals are 2 of the 13 Muslim tribes in the Philippines.
24. James F. Warren, *Iranun and Balangingi: Globalization, Maritime Trading and the Birth of Ethnicity* (Quezon City: New Day Publishers, 2002), 43.
25. See Eberhard Crailsheim, "Fortalecer la Cohesion Interna? El "Peligro Moro" En Las Filipinas Coloniales en la Segundamitad det Siglo XVIII," in *Filipinas, siglo XIX: Coexistencia y interaccion entre comunidades en el imperio Español*, ed. Maria Dolores Elizalde y Xavier Huetz de Lemps (Madrid, 2017), 421. https://www.academia.edu/35260825/_ Fortalecer_la_cohesi%C3%B3n_interna_El_peligro_moro_en_las_ Filipinas_coloniales_en_la_segunda_mitad_del_siglo_XVIII.
26. Eberhard Crailsheim, "Missionaries and Commanders: the Jesuits in Mindanao, 1718-68," *Journal of Jesuit Studies*, 9 (2022): 209.
27. Qur'an, 4:29: "O believers! Do not devour one another's wealth illegally, but rather trade by mutual consent and do not kill 'each other or' yourselves. Surely Allah is ever Merciful to you."
28. See Majul, *Muslims in the Philippines*, Appendix B, 353–360.
29. Horacio dela Cuesta, *Jesuits in the Philippines, 1581-1768* (Cambridge: Harvard University Press, 1967), 543–549; Majul, *Muslims in the Philippines*, 219–222.
30. There are many versions of *Moro-Moro* but the theme is always the same: conflict between Muslims and Christians and the eventual defeat of the Muslims and eventual conversion to Christianity. The Jesuits staged the

first *Moro-Moro* in 1637, re-enacting the victory of Governor General Corcuera over Sultan Qudarat in Maguindanao. See Nicanor Tiongson, *Komedya* (Quezon City: University of the Philippines Press, 1999).

31. General James Rusling, "Interview with President William McKinley," *The Christian Advocate* 22 January 1903, 17, reprinted in *The Philippines Reader,* ed. Daniel Schirmer and Stephen Rosskamm Shalom (Boston: South End Press, 1987), 22–23.

32. Dean C. Worcester, *The Philippines: Past and Present* (New York: MacMillan, 1914), 533, https://www.gutenberg.org/files/41918/41918-h/41918-h.htm#ch24.

33. Klaus Hausherr, "Agricultural Colonization in the Kapatagan, Lanao del Norte, Mindanao, Philippines," *Yearbook of the Southeast Asia Institute, Heidelberg University 1968-1969* (Wiesbaden: Otto Harrassowitz, 1969), 111.

34. *Reports of the Governor of Moro Province* (1913), 32, cited by Peter Gowing, *Mandate in Moroland* (Quezon City: University of the Philippines Press, 1977), 216.

35. Gowing, *Mandate in Moroland,* 216–217.

36. Vivienne SM. Angeles, "Philippine Muslim Women: Tradition and Change" in *Islam, Gender and Social Change,* ed. Yvonne Y. Haddad and John Esposito (New York: Oxford University Press, 1998), 212–213.

37. Muslims who have made the pilgrimage to Mecca.

38. Midori Kawashima, "Islamic Reformism and an American Protestant Missionary: Contest over the Publication of Qur'an verses in Mindanao under US Colonial Rule," *Sophia Journal of Asian, African and Middle East Studies* (December, 2016): 192–199.

39. Dansalan College's Marawi campus was attacked by dissidents in 2017. Operations of the college have been moved to its campus in Iligan.

40. Benedict Kirkvliet, *The Huk Rebellion: A Study of Peasant Revolt in the Philippines* (Berkeley: University of California Press, 1977).

41. "Camp Massacre Bared," *The Manila Times,* 21, March 1968, 1.

42. Moro National Liberation Front, *Rise and Fall of Moro Statehood,* n.p., n.d.

43. Republic of the Philippines, Department of Public Information, "Seeking Solutions to the South" (January, 1956), 3.

44. Vivienne SM. Angeles, "From Catholic to Muslim: Changing Perceptions of Gender Roles in a Balik-Islam Movement in the Philippines," in *Gender and Islam in Southeast Asia: Women's Rights Movements, Religious Resurgence and Local Traditions,* ed. Susanne Schroeter (Leiden: Brill, 2013), 192.

45. Article IX Section 8 of the 1973 Philippine Constitution and Article III, Sec. 5 of the 1987 Constitution provides: "No law shall be made regarding the establishment of a religion or the free exercise thereof...".

82   V. S. M. ANGELES

46. Balik-Islam means "return to Islam." This refers to converts to Islam. This notion of return stems from the belief that Islam, which means submission, is the first religion of man and because Islam was already the dominant religion in the Philippines before the Spaniards introduced Christianity.
47. Declaration on the Relation of the Church to non-Christian Religions, *Nostra Aetate*, proclaimed by his Holiness Pope Paul VI on October 28, 1965, 3, https://www.vatican.va/archive/hist_councils/ii_vatican_council/documents/vat-ii_decl_19651028_nostra-aetate_en.html.
48. Nostra Aetate, 3.
49. "...And had God willed, he would have made you one community, but He willed otherwise, that he might try you in that which he has given you. So, vie with one another in good deeds. God shall be your return all together...."
50. Eberhard Crailsheim, "Fortalecer la Cohesion Interna? El "Peligro Moro" En Las Filipinas Coloniales en la Segundamitad det Siglo XVIII," in *Filipinas, siglo XIX: Coexistencia y interaccion entre comunidades en el imperio Español,* ed. Maria Dolores Elizalde y Xavier Huetz de Lemps (Madrid, 2017), 395. https://www.academia.edu/35260825/_Fortalecer_la_cohesi%C3%B3n_interna_El_peligro_moro_en_las_Filipinas_coloniales_en_la_segunda_mitad_del_siglo_XVIII.

CHAPTER 5

The Glocal Filipin@s and the Pasyon Through the Lens of Ethnicity

Ma. Marilou S. Ibita

Is the chanting of Christ's passion, the *pasyon*,[1] still relevant for the glocal (global and local) Filipin@s of the twenty-first century? Pastorally, while there seems to be a waning tradition on the localized *pasyon* chanting during Holy Week in the Philippines, the expansion of the practice has reached the digital space to accommodate the needs of Filipino workers abroad who do not have access to Roman Catholic churches inland and those in seafaring jobs.[2]

Academically, a debate between the textual or performance focus on the *pasyon* is ongoing. This is exemplified in a recent publication by Julius Bautista in his book entitled *The Way of the Cross*.[3] It is based on his ethnographical study from Pampanga on the Filipin@s' sense of suffering selfhood and analyzes self-inflicted pain commemorating Christ's suffering and death in what he calls the Filipino passion rituals by focusing on three examples, namely:

Ma. M. S. Ibita
Department of Theology and Religious Education, De La Salle University, Manila, Philippines
e-mail: ma.marilou.ibita@dlsu.edu.ph

© The Author(s), under exclusive license to Springer Nature Switzerland AG 2024
C. Lledo Gomez et al. (eds.), *500 Years of Christianity and the Global Filipino/a*, Pathways for Ecumenical and Interreligious Dialogue, https://doi.org/10.1007/978-3-031-47500-9_5

the *pabasa* (a "reading"), in which groups of people endure long hours of continuously chanting Christ's Passion story; the *pagdarame* ("to empathize"), in which hundreds of people self-flagellate onto open wounds on their backs as they go on a walking journey around the province; and the *pamamaku king krus* ("nailing on the cross"), in which steel nails are driven through the palms and feet of ritual practitioners.[4]

This chapter will tackle only the public reading of the *pasyon* (Christ's passion story) or the *pabasa* and the issue of primacy between the text and its performance in the recent debate. From a theological-pastoral perspective, I will argue that instead of a binary approach and given the growing presence and participation of the Filipin@s in the glocal community, where ethnic hate abounds, there is a need to recognize and challenge the textual and performance issues related to the topic of ethnicity found in the theological-pastoral language of the *pasyon* toward a more ethnicity-inclusive theological-pastoral approach that shows solidarity with the marginalized, poor, and outcasts rather than the ongoing denigration of the collective character of the Jews in this material. The chapter has three parts: (1) the diverging views on the text and the performance of the *pasyon*; (2) problematizing the theological-pastoral language of the *pasyon* through the lens of ethnicity; and (3) recontextualizing the *pasyon* for an ethnicity-inclusive theological-pastoral solidarity with the glocal Filipin@s.

PASYON: TEXT OR PERFORMANCE?

Rene Javellana describes the "*Pasyon*" as "the generic term for a type of religious verse that narrates the life of Jesus Christ the Savior."[5] The earliest version is in Tagalog, the *Mahal na Pasion ni Jesuchristong Panginoon Natin na Tola*, written by Gaspar Aquino de Belen in 1703 and its fifth edition in 1760 is the oldest extant copy.[6] Javellana's genealogical study shows that the Tagalog was directly translated into Filipino languages like Pangasinan (1855), Bicol (1867), Pampangan (1876), Iloko (1889), Hiligaynon (1892), Samareño (1929), and Ibanag (1948).[7] A broken line links the Cebuano to the Tagalog from 1929. My study uses a Tagalog version, a reprint 212 pages long, by Luna and Sons, generally accessible to contemporary readers as *Awit at Salaysay ng Pasiong Mahal ni Hesukristong Panginoon Natin Sukat Ipag-alab ng Puso ng Sinumang Babasa (Pasiong Henesis)* or the so-called *Pasyon Pilapil*.[8] This retelling of the salvation story begins with Genesis 1-4 (Adam and Eve, Cain and

Abel) and covers Jesus' life from conception based on the gospel stories to his Last Judgment taken from the perspective of John's Apocalypse, and continues until the story of Empress Helen's discovery of Jesus' cross and the crucifixion nails. This most popular version, and at times the only known version in rural areas,[9] is similarly the basis of the *Sinakulo*, the theatrical presentation of Christ's passion.[10]

Despite being the most popular version, historian Reynaldo Ileto recognizes that the *Pasyon Pilapil* is "a highly imperfect composition, one that probably does not deserve much attention from a literary or theological standpoint" but it was "for all purposes, the social epic of the nineteenth-century Tagalogs and probably other lowland groups as well."[11] Ileto contends that the *pasyon* text has a vital role in forming the poor and uneducated segment of the Filipin@s to revolt against Spain:

> Through the text and associated ritual, people were made aware of a pattern of universal history. They also became aware of the ideal forms of behavior and social relationships of crisis- economic, political, real or imagines -- there was available asset of ideas and images with which even the rural masses could make sense out of their condition. Popular movement and revolts were far from being blind reactions to oppression. They became popular precisely because leaders were able to tap existing notions of change; the pasyon was freed from its officially sanctioned moorings in Holy Week and allowed to give form and meaning to the people's struggle for liberation.[12]

As Bautista noted, Ileto's text-focused approach in analyzing the *pasyon* and its impact on the subaltern highlight how "Catholicism was subject to processes of local resistance and reinterpretation."[13] In contrast, Joseph Scalice critiques what he considers as Ileto's flawed, mainly elitist textual focus and argues for the primacy of the performance since the *pasyon* as *awit* was "not the reading material" of the nineteenth-century Filipino peasantry but that their access was through the performance of the *pasyon*, and yet experienced differently by the masses and the elite.[14] "Performers sung the *pasyon* in *punto*, a pattern of chanting that varied with the characters whose lines were being sung. Christ was sung in a slow and meek manner, and Mary in *tagulaylay*, a mournful singsong chant residual from the performance of pre-Hispanic epics."[15]

Other scholars consider Ileto's work as needing ethnographic analysis to provide more depth, a gap which Bautista attempts to fill with his insights from contemporary *pasyon* chanters and hearers.[16] Bautista starts his in-depth discussion of the Filipino passion rituals with a chapter on "The Ensounded Body: The Aural Environment of Passion Chanting."[17] He describes how the Pampanga *pabasa* happens: from the organization by the host family who vowed to have a *pabasa*, the venue, the set-up to amplify the sound of the *pasyon* chanting using a microphone, and the bodily processes and discomfort experienced by the performers/chanters of the *pasyon* who take turns in the uninterrupted lamentation-like singing-reading all day and all night.[18] Bautista considers the *pasyon* as an "aural representation of culture," analyzing it from the intersection of "sounded anthropology" and "sociology of emotions."[19]

Bautista offers two important observations in the chanting of the *pasyon*. First, "pious agency does *not exclusively (or even primarily) result from acts of biblical exegesis* but is, like Makeniman suggested, responsive to sonically projected deployments of emotions" (italics added).[20] Bautista notes the importance of the text and the process of reading it in the section of "*Pasyon* and the Cultivation of Passion" where he discusses the granting of indulgence by the archbishop of Manila to those who *read and chanted it* and the attractiveness to both men and women of the public reading of the *pasyon*.[21] Bautista cites Ileto's argument that it is in the reading and chanting of the *pasyon* that the Filipinos could connect the "meanings of Christ's suffering with their own status as oppressed colonial subjects, orienting themselves toward a new kind of collective soteriology premised on the deferred rewards of martyric suffering."[22] Bautista's interview with flagellants reveal the motivational centrality of the text of the *Pasiung Henesis* or *Pasiung Pilapil* "when passages from these versions are sung or chanted with expressions of grief, tearful weeping, and sometimes wailing," which help them to identify with Christ's suffering and self-sacrifice.[23]

Second, Bautista observes that the chanters' *lub* (pious inner state) is communicated through their singing and provides an "emotional contagion" to those within the hearing range of the *pabasa*, resulting in enhanced group solidarity and togetherness including the self-flagellants.[24] At first, he reiterates the prioritization of the performance over the text, saying, "More than just words read out loud, I would argue that the pabasa is *primarily a visceral form* of devoutness, one that commemorates Christ's martyric episode through the body's projection of and saturation in an aural sensorium" (italics added).[25] However, later in his discussion, he opposes the text and the chanting when he changes his position from the earlier "*not exclusively (or even primarily)*" linked to the text into the claim that "the ritual efficacy of the *pabasa* is predicated *not on a person's ability to reflect upon or even decipher the text of the pasyon* but on something more embodied, emotional, visceral" (italics added).[26] He reaffirms this division in the section on the Passion Chanter's Ensounded Body: "The efficacy of the pabasa, however, is not contingent upon a general cognition of the precise details of the pasyon text. Indeed, its visceral impact is independent of the referential function of language to express sentiments of grief and mourning."[27]

I appreciate Bautista's anthropological and sociological viewpoint on the *pasyon*. However, from theological-pastoral perspectives, Bautista's clear separation and opposition of the text from the embodied and emotional chanting seems unnecessary. I posit that the *pasyon* text does not need to be subjugated to and contrasted with the performance of the *pasyon*. It is in and through the chanting of the discernible *pasyon* text, no matter how incomplete the chanters' understanding of it is, which make those who participate synchronously onsite and even far away local hearers or digital participants remember the passion, death, and resurrection of Christ. The effect of the chanting of this passion text is enhanced by the temporal setting of the Holy Week, the most intense time to remember the paschal mystery. Some obscure Tagalog and Latin words might render the *pasyon* not fully intelligible today.[28] However, it is through the chanting of the *pasyon* text *per se* and not just a random text, that the inculturated lamentation for and solidarity with the suffering Christ vis-à-vis the chanters and hearers' own suffering and need for salvation in their lifetime that make the *pasyon* ritual a form of prayer. If an unconnected text to Christ's passion is chanted using the melody of the *pasyon*, will there be the same effect on the emotional and ensounded body? I argue that without the text of the *pasyon,* there will be no performance and bodily ensounding by the chanters and hearers. Other tunes of chanting the pasyon are experimented upon by the young people, albeit with some resistance from the older generation.[29] Yet, the text and the chanting must be done together not only for the ritual effectiveness but similarly for growing in what Bautista calls "emotional and sentimental investments" toward a reciprocal relationship with God for a favorable response to their needs in their lifetime.[30] These concerns are not only anthropological and sociological but also theological-pastoral.

The chanter's difficulty in vocalizing for a long time coupled with bodily strain becomes part of the embodiment of Christ's sacrifice because

88 MA. M. S. IBITA

what they are chanting is the *pasyon* text.[31] Bautista notes that those who hear the *pasyon* acoustic become fellow mourners in sound since the "meaningfulness of the pabasa is directly related to pakikiramay as a specific kind of intersubjectivity and fellow-beingness."[32] It is amplified with emotional contagion that happens involuntarily and promotes social solidarity.[33] These observations make sense because the chanter and the hearers of the chant, even from far away, despite the indecipherable words of the *pasyon* that they are hearing, cannot but recall the passion of Christ rather than any other event. They associate the tune to Christ's passion story and are helped by the temporal impact of the Holy Week as a commemoration of Jesus' suffering and death. Thus, the text and the chant cannot be set apart. One of Bautista's interviewees articulates the meaning of her chanting of the *pasyon* as "an arena for the cultivation of mournful emotions that uses the text of the pasyon as a template for communal, intersubjective bereavement and group solidarity."[34] Another explains that the *pasyon* becomes the right "soundtrack" for those who made a vow to self-flagellate, those who carry the cross, and others with self-inflicted pain in what Bautista calls an "interactive ritual chain."[35] The importance of the text *per se* is highlighted by the official book title of the *Pasyon Pilapil, Awit at Salaysay ng Pasiong Mahal ni Hesukristong Panginoon Natin Sukat Ipag-alab ng Puso ng Sinumang Babasa (Pasiong Henesis)*, which may be translated generally as "Song and Story of the Precious Passion of our Lord Jesus Christ that will Enflame a Reader's Heart." Thus, theologically and pastorally speaking, the efficacy of the *pasyon* as a ritual form of chanted prayer is contingent and in synergy with the details and understood meaning of the *pasyon* text, no matter how inadequate the chanters' and the hearers' understanding of some of the archaic words of the *pasyon*.

PASYON AND ETHNICITY

The previous section argues for a bridge between the historical-textual focus (Ileto) and the historical-ethnographical concentration on performance (Scalice, Bautista). Ileto's work was past-oriented and geographically local in its focus by highlighting how, as mentioned earlier, the "*pasyon* was freed from its officially sanctioned moorings in Holy Week and allowed to give form and meaning to the people's struggle for liberation."[36] Bautista's ethnographic work among the chanters in Pampanga is present-oriented and returns the *pasyon* to the Holy Week context. My research scrutinizes the *pasyon* text used in the *pabasa* during Holy Week and the engagement of glocal Filipin@s with present and future implications.

From a theological-pastoral view, keeping the *pasyon* text and the performance of the *pabasa together* helps in understanding some of the manifold roles the *pasyon* plays to promote liberation and solidarity for generations of chanters and hearers on the glocal stage. This section will continue tracing these themes with the combined emphasis on text and chanting but with the added lens of ethnicity. It is in and through remembering the suffering Christ and character identification with him as they chant the *pasyon* that the Filipino glocal chanters and hearers promote liberation and solidarity in the ensounded and embodied decisions and actions that they make which impact their lives and those they care about, in the present and their desired future life. As Bautista gathered from his interviewees, the *pabasa* of the *pasyon* along with other passion rituals are like "investments" aimed toward the hope that God would respond reciprocally and favorably with benefits that they and their loved ones can enjoy in their lifetimes.[37] This is seen among those who are in the Philippines and the Overseas Filipino Workers (OFWs). It is in consideration of these glocal Filipino contexts that onsite and online *pabasa* are found in the country and abroad. As noted earlier, since 2011 the Catholic Bishops' Conference of the Philippines offers an online *pasyon* recording especially for OFWs in places where there are no churches like the Middle East and those at sea.[38]

Following the same line of synergy between text and chanting performance, the problem of the ethnic depiction of the *Hudyo,* the Jews, as the ethnic representation of all the antagonists of Jesus in the *pasyon* needs to be recognized, challenged, and corrected given the glocal presence of the Filipin@s and the danger of their perpetuation of this ethnically denigrating reading of the *pasyon* in the lands of their migration. Scalice pointed out that the *pabasa* is the origin of the dramatic performance of the *pasyon*-based *Sinakulo* where the character of the *Hudyo* is depicted as one who

> pranced about the stage, gloating, boasting, and were the entertainment of the performance. Innovation in performance was strongly discouraged, and the holier the character represented, the stricter was the adherence to text and tradition. Only the *hudyo,* for whom variation in acting and changes in dialogue were not looked upon as blasphemous, engaged in comic behaviour and innovation.[39]

90   MA. M. S. IBITA

While these actions of the *Hudyo* character were not considered blasphemous, play the comic role, and show innovation in the *Sinakulo*, this combined characterization led to the caricature of the *Hudyo*. One of the effects of this caricature is seen in the admonition to a lowland Filipino Catholic who engages in many activities and/or seems playful, noisy, and/ or rowdy in the enactment of the *pasyon during the Holy Week*. The admonition can come in the form of a negative and accusatory ethnic-based question: "Ano ka, *Hudyo*?" (What are you, a Jew?) This negative caricature of the Jews among Filipino Catholics, shaped by the *pabasa* of the *pasyon* and the *Sinakulo*, needs to be critically assessed by scrutinizing the popularly used *pasyon* text in contemporary *pabasa* toward a more active form of constructing glocal Filipin@ Christian identity and strengthening one's commitment to solidarity with the marginalized and liberation for them in a plural, post-Holocaust, post-pandemic world.

Let me elaborate on the problem with this ethnic-based characterization of the *Hudyo* in the *pasyon*. In the *Pasyon Pilapil's* currently available version, the word *Hudyo* is mentioned 77 times including 11 in the section titles. Compound words include *sangkahudyohan* (2x) or *kahudyuhan* (1x) to refer to all Jews. The first *Hudyo* reference, found in the section of Jesus' conception, affirms and acknowledges the Jews as those who recognize the Creator God (15:10).[40] This positive *Hudyo* characterization presents them as a monotheist group constantly tested in the Old Testament. Next, the *Hudyo* appears in the words of the magi who came to worship the king of the *Hudyo* (24:13, based on Mt 2:2). The collective *Hudyo* celebrates the Passover and recalls their liberation from Egypt (81:11).[41] This reference serves as a backdrop for Jesus' entry to Jerusalem. These are the only instances where the *Hudyo* is positively presented. They are recollections of biblical stories without necessarily claiming literary dependence.

The ethnicity-based problem worsens from the fourth mention of "*Hudyo*" in the *pasyon* text under study, presenting them thereon negatively. The predominantly damaging Jewish portrayal in the *pasyon* happens in three ways. First, the *pasyon* subsumes all the antagonists into the character of the *Hudyo* regardless of ethnicity and religion even if the biblical accounts differentiate the Jewish actors (Pharisees, scribes, priests, crowd). The Roman soldiers are also mistakenly considered as *Hudyo*.[42]

Consequently, the second way the *Hudyo* is wrongly portrayed is in being assigned the primary role of torturing and killing Jesus. The non-Jewish Roman soldiers are identified as *Hudyo*. They strip Jesus' clothes, crown him with thorns, strike him, and taunt him as the king of the Jews such as in 130:7 and 131:5-6. There is a conflation of the passion stories from the various gospels since they have no access to it (Mk 15:16-20// Mt 27:27-31) as seen in the titles of the passion sections and the details in the stanzas about Jesus' torture. The section on his crucifixion and death is described as carried out by the "Hebrews" and the Pharisees (154: 1,6) and not by the Roman soldiers (contrast with Mk 16:1-25 and parallels). The Pharisees, cited 58 times, actively persecute Jesus along with the scribes who are mentioned 25 times. In contrast with the biblical stories, the priests' (*saserdote*) role in Jesus' passion and death is only mentioned twice, downplaying greatly their participation in it by only noting their anger over Jesus' teaching in the temple (69:14) and as he was carrying the cross (139:7). The collective *Hudyo* conspires to have Jesus' tomb guarded lest his disciples take his body away. Cleofas, one of the disciples walking back to Emmaus with the unrecognized risen Jesus, speaks the most dangerous attribution to the *Hudyo* as the killers of the Son of God (185:11).[43] It is a detail not found in any biblical account, not even in Lk 24:19-20, but with a very profound impact on the vilification of the Jews in medieval times and even to this day in different media of communication with horrendous, fatal consequences for the non-biblical, living Jews especially during the Holocaust.[44]

Third, employing negative adjectives intensifies the damaging portrayal of the Jews in the *pasyon* text. Examples include *hunghang* (foolish, silly, ignorant, stupid, 85:1; 201: 4,6; 202: 8), *ganid* (cruel, hard-hearted, severe, 125:15), and *malupit* (cruel; 125:15). The *pasyon* also uses *taksil* (traitor) to describe Judas (111:1) and the collective Jews repeatedly such as in the scenes with Pilate (example, 114:3; 133:3). It employs *buhong* (haughty, rude, shameless, impudent; example, 131:5) and *sukaban* (treacherous, faithless, infidel, false, inconstant, traitorous, perfidious[45]) as an alternative description instead of naming the Jews (example, 141:3). The most numerous is the adjective *lilo* (unfaithful, treacherous, disloyal, perfidious or infidel), used 56 times for the Jews, either as an adjective with the noun or as synonymous with the Jews to underscore how Jesus is betrayed by them (example: 95:4; 96:3, 7,16). The *pasyon's* traitor theme is intensified with the link between *lilo* and the devil to demonize the Jews (109:12; 111:14; 117:16).

These three ways denigrated the *Hudyo* in the *pasyon*. But what is the basis of the *pasyon* for this kind of characterization of the *Hudyo*? We cannot forget that the time of the Spanish colonization of the islands under

King Philip II's name coincided with the anti-Jewish campaign during and after the reconquest of Spain.[46] Javellana's study shows that the earliest version of the *pasyon* written by Aquino de Belen reflects his struggle to articulate "a topic not endemic to his native culture but one learned from the foreign missionaries."[47] Javellana suggests that Aquino de Belen's sources did not consist of first-hand knowledge of the biblical text in Latin but instead consist of literature that included devotional practices like the *Siete Palabras* (Seven Last words of Jesus) and books with paraphrases and conflation of the Gospels that incorporate citations from the Vulgate such as the 1585 *Retablo de la Vida de Cristo hecho en verso,* a work of the Carthusian monk Juan de Padilla.[48] However, Javellana notes that while they have a similar outline, they differ in some topics. The *Mahal na Pasion* includes incidents not found in the *Retablo* like the Last Supper and foot washing, the Jews mocking Jesus, Mary encountering and speaking with Jesus on the road to Calvary, and the story of Longinus.[49] Conversely, absent from the *Pasyon* are the *Retablo's* story about the Jerusalem women's encounter with Jesus, John's invitation to Mary to go to Calvary, the long dialogue between Jesus and Mary at Calvary, and the Jews' mockery of Mary. It is notable that in both materials the Jewish mocking of Jesus and Mary are present and paint the Jews negatively in their own ways. The *Retablo* and the *Pasyon* reflect the anti-Jewish bias in Castillan literature on Jesus' passion amidst the popularity of passion spirituality in the late fifteenth and sixteenth centuries after the 1492 expulsion of the Jews from Spain.[50] As a descendant of the *Mahal na Pasyon* and its sources, the *pasyon* edition used here similarly reflects traces of the same anti-Jewish bias as shown above. This *pasyon text* does not use the word *Hudyo* for Jesus, his mother, and his disciples.

Recontextualizing the *Pasyon* for Glocal Filipin@s

But why should glocal Filipin@s care about this *Hudyo* problem: the traces of anti-Jewish themes in the *pasyon* text and as chanted in the *pabasa*? Why does the *pasyon* need to be recontextualized? Let me provide two important reasons.

First, the chanted text of the *pasyon* has a theological-pastoral didactic function. It is underlined by the storytelling from Genesis to Jesus' eschatological judgment and the "*Aral*" (Teaching) that comes strategically after the select group of sections of the *pasyon*. Javellana notes that the verse narratives of the *pasyon* include "short sermonettes of a doctrinal or moral nature which seek to explain or apply a particular episode or saying of Jesus' life to the life of the reader. Thus, it can be said that the *pasyon* has not only narrative but also didactic verses."[51] Pilapil's *Pahiwatig* (Notice) in the printed book shows conviction back then that it was thoroughly correct but likewise says, "*Kung may pagkakamali naman makatuwiran lamang na ito'y ipawalang halaga at ihagis sa apoy*" (If there is a mistake, it is right to consider this book worthless and throw it into the fire). After more than a century of use, much has changed in the reality of Catholics in the world. Corrections have to be made since chanters and hearers now have access to the biblical text which is the fundamental source of the stories about Jesus' passion. Moreover, with the new theological-pastoral perspectives ushered in by Vatican II and the consequent academic advances which reveal this ethnically denigrating reading and its larger context, it is no longer acceptable to disregard Jesus' ethnicity as a Jew himself and to allow character conflation that misleads contemporary Catholics in understanding the ethnicities of biblical characters like the Romans identified as *Hudyo*.[52] Unfounded claims against the Jews like the use of negative adjectives for them, particularly the accusation that they are "Christ-killers" must be rectified. As *Nostra Aetate* 4 teaches:

> True, the Jewish authorities and those who followed their lead pressed for the death of Christ; still, what happened in His passion cannot be charged against all the Jews, without distinction, then alive, nor against the Jews of today. Although the Church is the new people of God, the Jews should not be presented as rejected or accursed by God, as if this followed from the Holy Scriptures. All should see to it, then, that in catechetical work or in the preaching of the word of God they do not teach anything that does not conform to the truth of the Gospel and the spirit of Christ.[53]

Thus, it is very crucial to take up the challenge to revise the *Pasyon Pilapil*. As Bishop Pablo David, current president of the Catholic Bishops Conference of the Philippines said even in 2017, it is not only time to check the *pasyon* for its anti-Semitic (or more appropriately, anti-Jewish) content, "It's about time we correct them."[54]

Second, the *pasyon's* didactic function is toward moral living and demands solidarity, especially with the suffering Christ and contemporary sufferers, Jews and others included. Ileto said:

94   MA. M. S. IBITA

One characteristic of such Tagalog sources as narrative poems and songs is their apparent disregard for accurate description of past events. (…) when errors proliferate in a patterned manner, when rumors spread 'like wildfire,' when sources are biased in a consistent way, we are in fact offered the opportunity to study the workings of the popular mind.[55]

Peterson also notes that the *Hudyo* is an "abstract category" that is most likely related to the very minimal presence of the Jews in the Philippines and influenced by the Spanish empire's treatment of the Jews during the Inquisition.[56] The "popular mind's" idea negatively drawn by the *pasyon's* chanted text must be replaced with biblically corrected non-anti-Jewish text that will be better ensounded and embodied because the Filipin@s are now also exposed to real, living Jews, not only those known through the *pasyon* and the recollected biblical stories. A corrected version of the *pasyon* text would serve as a very good basis for engendering embodied solidarity with the poor from the perspective of ethnicity around the world. In a post-Holocaust setting, Filipin@s cannot forget the welcome it extended to the Jews persecuted for being Jews by the Nazis.[57] However, it is important to note that it was not totally unopposed.

> President Quezon faced the formidable task of winning over the anti-Semitic members of his own cabinet as well as those in the political opposition led by Gen. Emilio Aguinaldo who viewed Jews as "Communists and schemers" bent on "controlling the world". In a letter written in August of 1939, Alex Frieder wrote of Mr. Quezon's response: "He assured us that big or little, he raised hell with every one of those persons. He made them ashamed of themselves for being a victim of propaganda intended to further victimize an already persecuted people." To the members of his own Catholic Church who were prejudiced against Jews, Quezon asked: "How can we turn our backs on the race that produced Jesus Christ?"[58]

With the Holocaust over, is the *pasyon's Hudyo* problem still a concern for glocal Filipi@s? If the Philippines is the sole Asian country to vote for the creation of the State of Israel and the Anti-Defamation League currently notes that the Philippines is the second country with the lowest antisemitism Index Score (3%), do glocal Filipin@s still need to advocate against anti-Jewish issues? Definitely. During the COVID-19 pandemic, there was an observable increase in real-life and virtual anti-Semitism due to conspiracy theories and misinformation multiplying on the Internet and social media, widely consumed by so many unwitting people isolated by the pandemic.[59] Here, the warning for what happens to the "virtual Jew" should be heeded. The "virtual Jew" was vilified in medieval literature that influenced passion literature like the *pasyon* resulting in concrete, life-threatening consequences for the actual Jews.[60] Today ethnic hatred in the digital space spills over to real life. The Filipin@s are among the many overseas workers caring for Jews, especially in Israel. Anything that impacts the Jews will likewise affect the Filipin@s caring for them considering personal safety and economic security, and, by extension and impact, their families in the Philippines, too. Moreover, the ethnicity-based animosity is not limited to the Jews. The pandemic similarly showed a widespread sharp increase of Asian hate through social media but with real-life consequences to Asians including Filipin@s.[61]

CONCLUSION

In this chapter I showed the continuing importance of chanting the *pasyon* text among glocal Filipin@s. The academic debate on whether to prioritize the text or the performance through chanting apart from the text has to be overcome. The *pasyon* text and its chanted performance are both needed for the theological-pastoral goals of the *pabasa* ritual as an important prayer of solidarity for the suffering Christ and other sufferers during Holy Week. Given the synergy and significance of the *pasyon* text and its chanting, I problematize instead the negative depiction and caricature of the *Hudyo* in the chanted *pasyon* from the perspective of ethnicity by subsuming all of Jesus' antagonists into the collective *Hudyo*, by charging them primarily with the violence and killing of Christ, and by the repeated negative adjectives connected with them. I demonstrated that these negative descriptions of the *Hudyo* are due to the influence of the medieval European portrayal of the Jews particularly in Spain which was brought to the Filipino Christians through the Iberian colonial and evangelization project. Noting the changed context of a post-Holocaust, post-Vatican II, and post-COVID-19 reality in which the glocal Filipin@s find themselves, it is high time to recognize, challenge, and correct the anti-Jewish theme in the *pasyon* to make it a more effective, ensounded, and incarnated ritual prayer of solidarity in a plural world. Since ethnic-based hatred remains a constant threat, "[I]t is too simplistic to consider the Jew in the Christian imagination without attention to living Jews at the same time."[62]

NOTES

1. *Pasyon* or *pasion* are written interchangeably in the literature. I will use *pasyon* in this work and employ *pasion* when used in citations.
2. See Agence France-Presse, "'Pasyon' Now Online," ABS-CBN News, April 18, 2011, https://news.abs-cbn.com/lifestyle/04/18/11/pasyon-now-online; Catholic Bishops Conference of the Philippines, "Pasyon," *Visita Iglesia* (blog), March 10, 2017, https://cbcpnews.net/visitaiglesia/pasyon/.
3. Julius Bautista, *The Way of the Cross: Suffering Selfhoods in the Roman Catholic Philippines* (Honolulu, HI: University of Hawaii Press, 2019), 28, https://doi.org/10.1515/9780824881047.
4. Bautista, 1.
5. Rene B. Javellana, "Pasyon Genealogy and Annotated Bibliography," *Philippine Studies* 31, no. 4 (1983): 451.
6. Javellana, 453–459.
7. Javellana, 451, 458–459.
8. Mariano Pilapil, *Awit at Salaysay Ng Pasiong Mahal Ni Hesukristong Panginoon Natin Sukat Ipag-Alab Ng Puso Ng Sinumang Babasa (Pasiong Henesis)* (Manila: Ignacio Luna and Sons, 1949). The authorial attribution to Pilapil is found on the "Pahiwatig" (p. 2) with a claim that the text is found to have no error in faith. However, see Javellana, "Pasyon," 462 which notes that the authorial link to Fr. Mariano Pilapil is an erroneous presupposition.
9. Vitaliano R. Gorospe, "Sources of Filipino Moral Consciousness," *Philippine Studies* 25, no. 3 (1977): 278–301, 291.
10. Javellana, "Pasyon," 462; Doreen Fernandez, "Philippine Theater and the Medieval World: Notes for Further Research," *Philippine Studies* 44, no. 4 (1996): 533.
11. Reynaldo Clemena Ileto, *Pasyon and Revolution: Popular Movements in the Philippines 1840-1910* (Manila: Ateneo de Manila Press, 1979), 13–14.
12. Ileto, 254.
13. Bautista, *Way of the Cross*, 10; Bautista was referring to these works: Ileto, *Pasyon*; John D. Blanco, *Frontier Constitutions: Christianity and Colonial Empire in the Nineteenth-Century Philippines* (Berkeley, CA: University of California Press, 2009); Filomeno Aguilar, *Clash of the Spirits: The History of Power and Sugar Planter Hegemony on a Visayan Island* (Honolulu, HI: University of Hawaii Press, 1998); Vicente Rafael, *Contracting Colonialism: Translation and Christian Conversion in Tagalog Society Under Early Spanish Rule* (Ithaca, NY: Cornell University Press, 1988).

14. Joseph Scalice, "Reynaldo Ileto's Pasyon and Revolution Revisited, a Critique," *Sojourn: Journal of Social Issues in Southeast Asia* 33, no. 1 (2018): 49–50.
15. Scalice, 43.
16. Bautista, *Way of the Cross*, 10.
17. Bautista, 31–45.
18. Bautista, 31–32.
19. Bautista, 32.
20. Bautista, 33.
21. Bautista, 35.
22. Bautista, 35.
23. Bautista, 35–36.
24. Bautista, 39–42.
25. Bautista, 33.
26. Bautista, 34.
27. Bautista, 37.
28. See, for instance, Rene B. Javellana, "Gaspar Aquino de Belen's Poetic Universe: A Key to His Metaphorical Theology," *Philippine Studies* 38, no. 1 (1990): 28–44.
29. See Zaphyr Iral, Ronald Mendoza, and Alvin Perez, "Will the Pasyon Survive?," Philstar.com, accessed May 27, 2023, https://www.philstar.com/news-commentary/2014/04/15/1312955/will-pasyon-survive. They report that apart from the five traditional *pasyon* tunes, the organizers and youth participants also introduced other tunes based on "Sta. Clarang Pinung-Pino," "De Colores," "My heart will go on," Voltes V theme song, and even a rap version at various times with mixed reviews.
30. See Bautista, *Way of the Cross*, 7.
31. Bautista, 38–39.
32. Bautista, 40–41.
33. Bautista, 40.
34. Bautista, 41–42.
35. Bautista, 43.
36. Ileto, *Pasyon*, 254.
37. Bautista, *Way of the Cross*, 9.
38. See Agence France-Presse, "Pasyon"; Catholic Bishops Conference of the Philippines, "Pasyon". For the discussion of OFW and passion rituals yet without mentioning the *pasyon*, see Bautista, *Way of the Cross*, 96–105.
39. Scalice, "Reynaldo Ileto's Pasyon," 43.
40. See Pilapil, *Awit*. To facilitate the reference and analysis, the first number refers to the page and the second to the stanza number on that page, separated by a column. Manual counting in the pdf version was used for the statistics mentioned here.

41. Pilapil, 81.
42. See Scalice, "Reynaldo Ileto's Pasyon," 54, n. 13; William Peterson, "Three Tagalog Sinakulos: The Repertoire and the Scenario," in *Places for Happiness: Community, Self, and Performance in the Philippines*, ed. William Peterson (Hawaii: University of Hawai'i Press, 2016), 29–30, https://doi.org/10.21313/hawaii/9780824851637.003.0002.
43. Pilapil, *Awit*, 185.
44. See Jeremy Cohen, *Christ Killers: The Jews and the Passion from the Bible to the Big Screen* (Oxford University Press, 2007).
45. For the issue of the use of the adjective "perfidious" for the Jews found in the Roman Catholic Good Friday liturgy and its removal in as well as the complication brought about by the renewed Good Friday prayer for the Jews by Pope Benedict XVI in 2008, see Marianne Moyaert and Didier Pollefeyt, "Israel and the Church: Fulfillment Beyond Supersessionism," in *Never Revoked: Nostra Aetate As Ongoing Challenge for Jewish-Christian Dialogue*, ed. Marianne Moyaert and Didier Pollefeyt (Leuven/ Walpole, MA; Grand Rapids, MI: Peeters/Eerdmans, 2010), 159–183.
46. Jessica A. Boon, "Violence and the 'Virtual Jew' in Castilian Passion Narratives, 1490s–1510s," *Journal of Medieval Iberian Studies* 8, no. 1 (January 2, 2016): See, https://doi.org/10.1080/17546559.201 5.1077987; for the role of mendicant orders during this time, see Jeremy Cohen, *The Friars and the Jews: The Evolution of Medieval Anti-Judaism* (Ithaca, NY): Cornell University Press, 1982).
47. Rene B. Javellana, "The Sources of Gaspar Aquino de Belen's Pasyon," *Philippine Studies* 32, no. 3 (1984): 305.
48. Javellana, 310.
49. See Javellana, 311.
50. See Boon, "Violence." On the history of Christians calling the Jews 'perfidious' in the Good Friday prayers, see footnote 45.
51. Rene B. Javellana, "Pasyon Genealogy and Annotated Bibliography," *Philippine Studies* 31, no. 4 (1983): 451–467, 451.
52. See, for instance, Rex Fortes, "'The Judeans' for Οἱ Ἰουδαῖοι? Contested Ethnicity in the Fourth Gospel," 2022; Wally V. Cirafesi, "John within Judaism: Religion, Ethnicity, and the Shaping of Jesus-Oriented Jewishness in the Fourth Gospel," in *John within Judaism* (Brill, 2021), https://brill.com/display/title/60162.
53. See Second Vatican Council, "Nostra Aetate," accessed June 13, 2023, https://www.vatican.va/archive/hist_councils/ii_vatican_council/documents/vat-ii_decl_19651028_nostra-aetate_en.html.
54. See Minerva Generalao, "Time to Check Pabasa for Anti-Semitic Content, Says Caloocan Bishop," INQUIRER.net, April 13, 2017,

https://newsinfo.inquirer.net/888866/time-to-check-pabasa-for-anti-semitic-content-says-caloocan-bishop.

55. Ileto, *Pasyon*, 11.

56. See Anna Foa, "Limpieza versus Mission: Church, Religious Orders, and Conversion in the Sixteenth Century," in *Friars and Jews in the Middle Ages and Renaissance*, ed. Steven McMichael and Susan Myers, vol. 2, The Medieval Franciscan (The Netherlands: Brill, 2004), 299–311, https://doi.org/10.1163/9789047400219_019; Maria Pilar Lorenzo, "Jewish Migration in the Philippines," in *Radical Definitions: State - Society - Religion*, ed. Xaver Hergenröther, Oana Ursulesku, and Dana Bădulescu, vol. 3, Seggau School of Thought (Graz: Grazer Universitätsverlag, 2018), 29–36.

57. For the difficulty in settling the Jewish refugees in Mindanao, see Frank Ephraim, "The Mindanao Plan: Political Obstacles to Jewish Refugee Settlement," *Holocaust and Genocide Studies* 20, no. 3 (2006): 410–436, https://doi.org/10.1093/hgs/dcl020.

58. Rodel Rodis, "Philippines: A Jewish Refuge from the Holocaust," INQUIRER.Net, April 13, 2013, https://globalnation.inquirer.net/72279/philippines-a-jewish-refuge-from-the-holocaust.

59. For example, see Kelly W. Sundberg, Lauren M. Mitchell, and Dan Levinson, "Health, Religiosity and Hatred: A Study of the Impacts of COVID-19 on World Jewry," *Journal of Religion and Health* 62, no. 1 (February 1, 2023): 428–443, https://doi.org/10.1007/s10943-022-01692-5.

60. See Boon, "Violence"; Sylvia Tomasch, "Postcolonial Chaucer and the Virtual Jew," in *The Postcolonial Middle Ages*, ed. Jeffrey Jerome Cohen, The New Middle Ages (New York: Palgrave Macmillan US, 2000), 243–260, https://doi.org/10.1057/9780230107342_14.

61. See Joshua Uyheng and Kathleen M. Carley, "Bots and Online Hate During the Covid-19 Pandemic: Case Studies in the United States and the Philippines," *Journal of Computational Social Science* 3, no. 2 (November 1, 2020): 445–468, https://doi.org/10.1007/s42001-020-00087-4.

62. Boon, "Violence," 117. For further discussion on responding to the challenge of Anti-Semitism, see Mary Doak, *A Prophetic, Public Church: Witness to Hope Amid the Global Crises of the Twenty-First Century* (Collegeville, MN: Liturgical Press, 2020), 39–74.

CHAPTER 6

An Independent Catholic, Nationalist People's Movement: The Iglesia Filipina Independiente (Philippine Independent Church)

Eleuterio J. Revollido

This chapter will first outline pertinent aspects of the proclamation of the *Iglesia Filipina Independiente* (Philippine Independent Church; abbrev.: IFI) as an independent church in 1902, then analyze its understanding of independence in its foundational documents, survey its concept of nationalism inherent to its understanding of independence, and finally outline its understanding of catholicity. In doing so, a contribution will be made to the study of the "only church of catholic liberation that was formed out of a people's yearning for dignity, freedom and recognition,"[1] and to research on the IFI as part of the religious history of the Philippines. Given the representative nature of the documents and the need to limit the scope of this contribution, the historical focus will remain on the proclamation in

---

E. J. Revollido (✉)
Iglesia Filipina Independiente/Rector, Aglipay Central Theological Seminary, Urdaneta City, Philippines

© The Author(s), under exclusive license to Springer Nature Switzerland AG 2024
C. Lledo Gomez et al. (eds.), *500 Years of Christianity and the Global Filipino/a*, Pathways for Ecumenical and Interreligious Dialogue, https://doi.org/10.1007/978-3-031-47500-9_6

101

102   E. J. REVOLLIDO

1902 and its immediate aftermath, with incidental use of illustrative materials from a later date. The broader religious studies framework, as outlined in the introduction to this edited volume is presupposed and not repeated on these pages.

THE PROCLAMATION OF THE *IGLESIA FILIPINA INDEPENDIENTE* IN HISTORICAL PERSPECTIVE

In order to understand what "independence" means for the IFI, first a survey of its historical origins is needed. These origins are very particular in nature, when it is considered that the meeting at which it was founded was that of the labor union *Unión Obrera Democrática* (UOD),[2] by the prominent politician and activist Isabelo de los Reyes, Sr. (1864–1938),[3] and that its first leading bishop ("Obispo maximo") was a former guerilla general and (excommunicated) Catholic priest, Gregorio Aglipay y Labayan (1860–1940).[4] Unique as this may be as a historical event, it is also expressive of the intertwining of religious and socio-political factors in the emergence of the IFI, a social force (labor union) that saw it fit to proclaim a church and to appoint a (retired) priest-guerillero as its head. In this context, it is also of interest that this event was appealing to many: soon after its proclamation it comprised of a membership of approximately 10% of the population at its peak.[5] Two historians of the IFI, Pedro de Achutegui and Miguel Bernad, opined that the establishment of this church "was numerically large enough to constitute a major change in the religious picture… (it) was in fact a major revolution, with important political and economic repercussions."[6]

However unusual the combination of agents may be in the proclamation of the IFI, the broader historical context makes them perspicuous. For this, attention needs to be given to some particularities of Spanish colonial rule over the Philippines, as it ended with the Spanish-Philippine war of 1896–1898, and of the subsequent American-Philippine War of 1899–1902.

Concerning the Spanish colonial rule and religious matters, it is necessary to emphasize the intertwined nature of Spanish political rule and the operation of the Roman Catholic Church in the Philippines. Three examples may suffice. First, on the basis of the royal right of patronage,[7] bishops in the Philippines were factual appointments by the Spanish crown and stood in the service of colonial rule. Second, the Roman Catholic

6 AN INDEPENDENT CATHOLIC, NATIONALIST PEOPLE'S MOVEMENT... 103

church in the Philippines, in particular the main religious orders operating in the colony (Franciscans, Dominicans, Augustinians and Augustinian Recollects, Jesuits), operated as major landowners and, therefore, as political forces were to be reckoned with. Third, discrimination on the basis of ethnicity was a characteristic of the Spanish colonial system as a whole and, consequently, also of colonial church life; indigenous priests could not rise in the ecclesial hierarchy. All of this leads to a situation in which the political and the religious are inextricably intertwined. As soon as the Philippine revolution started in earnest, the revolutionaries were, therefore, keen to organize the religious life of the liberated Philippines on the basis of this newly found freedom; religious independence was expressive of national independence—clergy like Aglipay also were keen to play a role in the revolution, both as a priest and as a soldier.[8]

When the results of the successful Philippine revolution were made undone in the Philippine-American war, the interrelationship between political and religious freedom remained for many, if not all Filipinos. This sentiment was difficult to grasp for the new colonial rulers of the Philippines, who ruled the country on the basis of a separation of church and state. Yet, the following political contextualization of the proclamation of the IFI by Ranche speaks to this point:

> The end of the Filipino-American war as officially proclaimed by then US President Theodore Roosevelt on July 4, 1902 did not mean the end of Filipino resistance or in a more positive manner, the Filipino desire for liberty. The laws passed by the Philippine Commission could be seen as evidence of continuing Filipino aspiration for liberty. Three of these would be the Sedition Law (1901) which forbade advocacy even by peaceful means; the Brigandage Act (1902) which classified all armed resistance as pure banditry; and the Reconcentration Act (1903) which gave legal justification for hamletting to deny the guerilla's support from the populace. A later one would be the Flag Law (1907) which prohibited the display of the Flag and the playing of the Philippine National Anthem. The Filipinos' expressions of their desire for liberty were varied and these laws could be seen as a response to these speculations/expressions... In this period of continuing resistance when the (institutional and missionary) churches were cooperating (explicitly or otherwise) with the established colonial government, the *Iglesia Filipina Independiente* was founded.[9]

This background makes apparent a church that emphasized independence and it must have appeared as suspect in the eyes of the American rulers of

104   E. J. REVOLLIDO

the Philippines.[10] In line with this, critics of the newly proclaimed church suggested that the "Aglipayan Church was nothing but a facade for a movement to oust the American sovereignty in the Philippines under the cloak of religion."[11] Both of these in fact proved to be true: the IFI was advocating Philippine independence, and misunderstood the role of religion in Philippine society completely, evaluating it from the perspective of a society with a separation between church and state as a constitutional principle. An example of this would be a comment in *The Manila American* of August 17, 1902, on the occasion of the arrest of De los Reyes, Sr., because of the unrest caused by the proclamation of the IFI: "Oh, my! Oh, my! Oh, my! Here is the head of the new Iglesia Filipina, the national church of the Filipinos, in a cell of a police station, charged with a criminal offense against the peace and dignity of the state!"[12] With this background, another apparent anomaly from the early history of the IFI can serve to illustrate the kind of context in and the concerns out of which it was founded. The anomaly, widely commented upon in the (pro-American) press of the time,[13] was that Aglipay hesitated considerably to accept the leadership of the IFI to which he had been nominated. He didn't want to cause a schism and intended to exhaust all means to negotiate with Rome for a church under indigenous (and elected) leadership in the Philippines.[14] Aglipay only accepted the leadership of the IFI when it became clear that both the desired political reforms (e.g., redistribution of land owned by religious orders)[15] and ecclesial changes would not be forthcoming.[16] This incident illustrates one issue very clearly: the context in which the IFI was proclaimed was one dominated by resistance against oppression by the colonial powers of first Spain and subsequently the USA and a church (hierarchy) that worked hand-in-glove with these colonial powers (under American rule, Spanish bishops were simply replaced with American ones). Given this historical background, it is now possible to outline the IFI's understanding of "independence."

UNDERSTANDING "INDEPENDENCE" IN THE EARLY DOCUMENTS, GOVERNANCE, AND WORSHIP OF THE IFI

The IFI issued a number of documents in its earliest days, notably the six *Epistolas Fundamentales* ("Fundamental Epistles"), written between the period of 1902–1903 and the *Doctrinas y Reglas Constitutionales* (Doctrine and Constitutional Rules) of 1903 primarily authored by Isabelo de los

Reyes, Sr.[17] In these documents, a characteristic understanding of independence can be found. In the next paragraphs, this will be outlined, with a focus on what the IFI wanted to be independent from (and what it did not), what this particular emphasis on independence meant for its self-organization, and finally for its worship.

First, the IFI's understanding of independence is expressed well in one of the earliest statements of the IFI's position issuing from the new church. It can be found in a confession of faith by the first IFI bishop, Pedro Brillantes, the so-called Bacarra Formula of October 1, 1902, that declares, "Peter in mind and heart, not however in the diplomatic Peter" [*"Fides in Petrum in mente et corde, non diplomaticum"*].[18] In this confession of the faith, bishop Brillantes also expresses his intentional position "to guard inviolate the Catholic Faith, Scripture, Tradition, the Sacraments, the veneration of the saints and in particular of the Blessed Virgin Mary."[19] By stating its faith in consonance with that of Peter (i.e., the See of Rome, the Catholic Church) but not its politics means the IFI's continued acceptance of the Catholic faith on the one hand, and its declaration of independence by rejecting "Peter's," that is, the pope's, administrative claims vis-à-vis the Philippine Church and its people. That this succinct statement of the IFI's position resonated well with statements by more representative bodies of the church is apparent from the first Fundamental Epistle (September 22, 1902), which advised the elected bishops of the IFI to have strong convictions, being a new Filipino church, reminding them that they were masters of their own destiny, in which the old condition of bondage had changed into a new life in freedom. In this context, the epistle also took the following position:

> In the new Filipino Church, then, everything should be new except what is Divine, and if we are now to seek Greek, Russian, Anglican or Protestant bishops to consecrate ours, as many may propose, this would show that we do not really mean to emerge from our slavery, that having shaken off the crushing yoke, we are already looking for new masters who, no doubt, will be no better than the first. In so doing, we will be proving that we are not equal to the circumstances, nor fit to be the champion of a far-reaching religious revolution. Like the apostles, progressives always advance and never retreat.[20]

This quotation makes clear again how intertwined ecclesial and national independence are. The IFI does not wish to seek consecration of its

106   E. J. REVOLLIDO

bishops from non-Filipino bishops, given that this might mean submission to foreign powers again. Independence is an administrative issue, therefore, not a doctrinal one. The IFI would pay a high price for this policy: until 1947, when its bishops received reordination through the Episcopal Church, its bishops would remain outside of a recognized form of apostolic succession.[21] A very similar sentiment can be found in the second "Fundamental Epistle," of October 2, 1902, as in it the IFI positions itself vis-à-vis the claim that it would be in schism with Rome:

> In good faith, we believe that there is no real schism, because our painful separation is based on sound reason and above all on the natural need to protect our rights and our national dignity.[22]

The logic is expressive of the IFI's position, even if it would have failed to convince others. There is an organizational matter at stake and the way the IFI has arranged things is reasonable and expressive of the Filipino people's national dignity. Therefore, there is real schism (and, as is implied—no doctrinal disagreement). Religious and national identity again appear to be fused here, as are matters of religiosity and national dignity. These examples sufficiently demonstrate the initial position of the IFI in these matters. Even if later substantial doctrinal disagreements would arise, these are in many ways secondary to the original inspiration guiding the proclamation of the IFI in 1902—even if they are also an example of the exercise of religious freedom.[23] The coat of arms and heraldic motto of the IFI, as it was adopted in these years, is expressive of this attitude. The coat of arms features the national flag of the Philippines, a map of the country, episcopal insignia, and the phrase "*Pro Deo et patria*" as well as the four words "*libertas*," "*scientia*," "*caritas*," and "*scripturae*."

Second, the IFI's emphasis on independence and freedom also gave rise to a different approach to church government. In fact, it was emphasized from the very start that the IFI, as a church proclaimed by the people (as represented by the Unión Obrera Democrática), ought to be governed by the people as well.[24] Also in the communication around the election of the first bishop of the IFI, Pedro Brillantes (taking possession of his diocese on October 1, 1902), it was emphasized that he "was chosen and elected by the Clergy, the people and the faithful belonging to different political parties in Manila, who represented the masses of the Filipino nation."[25] Being a church of a free nation implied also that this free nation and its inhabitants had a role to play in the governance of the church. This was

6 AN INDEPENDENT CATHOLIC, NATIONALIST PEOPLE'S MOVEMENT...

institutionalized in the 1903 *Doctrine and Constitutional Rules* of the IFI, as it made the following provision: "men's committee and the ladies commission of the Philippine Independent Church (and) shall be consulted in all that pertains to the people and their customs, their assistance and the conduct of parishes and other subjects of lay character."[26] The members of these commissions were entrusted with considerable responsibility as well. The same constitution of the IFI also stated they:

> [S]hall promote everything conducive to the moral and material well-being of those he represents [that is, on the commission]. He shall see that they observe Christian conduct and customs, keep them from gambling, and prevent drunkenness, licentiousness, and other vices or ugly customs. He shall take interest in the education of the children and the youths... he shall be in charge of both receiving and expressing the desires of those he represents.[27]

Third, how the IFI understood its independence can also be traced in the liturgical renewal that it embarked upon soon after its proclamation. In its 1903 Doctrine and Constitutional Rules, the church is very outspoken about this aim:

> The object of the founding of the Philippine Independent Church is principally to respond to the imperative need to restore the worship of the one true God in all its splendor and the purity of his most holy Word which under the reign of obscurantism had been diluted and distorted in a most disheartening manner for any Christian of even moderate education.[28]

This urgent need was connected in the same document to the necessity of being able to pray in the vernacular:

> It is impossible to pray with devotion if we address ourselves to God in a language we do not understand. God always wants us to speak of a Religion in a language which we understand; thus it was that he sent the Holy Spirit to the Apostles that they might make themselves understood in local languages. We must therefore pray and preach in the language of the people whom we are addressing.[29]

National independence and being a national independent church therefore translates itself into "liturgical nationalism" as well, in the sense of moving toward an independent and national liturgy. Here, as virtually always in the early history of the IFI, national and religious identities appear in a very intertwined manner. The question of liturgical language, as framed by the IFI (see the quotations above) is one indication of this. Another indication is that the IFI formally canonized Filipino saints, in particular, four revolutionary heroes. On November 2, 1902, just a few days after Bishop Aglipay performed his first public religious service, he announced to "set aside this date for a special commemorative service for the heroes of the Philippine Revolution."[30] The following year on September 24, 1903, the "Act of Canonization of the Great Martyrs of our country Dr. Jose Rizal, the priests Frs. Jose Burgos, Mariano Gomez and Jacinto Zamora" were approved in the plenary meeting of the bishops' conference of the IFI. The criterion for their canonization was based on the nationalistic spirit, saying that:

> In their private and public life, they stood guard and uphold exemplary the Christian conduct and by their sole love of country, for justice, for progress and for humanity, they died martyrs... by offering to the people a Christian and envious death.[31]

Such an act of canonization and the liturgical commemoration connected well with Philippine catholic spirituality, which revolved—and continues to revolve—much around the saints and their veneration. The interrelationship between national and religious independence, the former in terms of patriotism, is articulated well by Foronda in his study of the canonization of Rizal, when commenting on the (ecclesial) canonization of the three priests and Rizal:

> Patriotism therefore, appears to have been the main consideration for the canonization of Rizal and the three priests...patriotism is sacred and holy within the realm of the Independent Church; in itself it is a religious act.[32]

The same tendency that is apparent here also continued in later years, when the IFI produced and encouraged the use of liturgical calendars that include the commemoration of events pertaining to the heroes of Philippine history and to the history of the revolution in particular.[33] Foronda encapsulates the gist of these calendars as follows:

> These calendars contain the catalogue of saints and the feast days as observed in the Catholic Church with additions of important events of Philippine

6 AN INDEPENDENT CATHOLIC, NATIONALIST PEOPLE'S MOVEMENT... 109

History like the founding of the Katipunan, the birth and death anniversaries of Philippine heroes. Also included are the equivalents in the vernacular of the accepted names in Spanish like *Pag-asa* for Esperanza.[34]

The purpose of these calendars went beyond a historical interest as such: by affirming key events pertaining and personalities that played a key role in the Philippine struggle for independence, the IFI positioned itself as the advocate of this independence. In the context of the American attempts to gain fuller control over the Philippines, such publication bordered on the rebellious. This also applied to the subsequent decoration of churches with images of these heroes or significant figures for the IFI, rather than of the traditional saints. Yet, also traditional saints received a reinterpretation. A key example is the attempts of Aglipay to introduce and promote the cult of the so-called *Birhen sa Balintawak*, the Virgin of Balintawak. In 1925, Aglipay published the *Novenario de la Patria*, using a highly popular genre of religious text, used frequently in Philippine Catholicism,[35] in which he provides the liturgical materials for a novena in honor of this particular representation of Mary. The "Virgin of Balintawak" commemorates Mary as she appeared in a dream of the Katipunero leader Andrés Bonifacio in Balintawak in 1896, prior to starting their revolution against Spain there. The point of the veneration is expressed well in the following quotation from the 27th reading for this Novena, written by Aglipay:

> The Virgin is the Mother of Balintawak who would symbolize our country and the Divine Infant as the child member of the Katipunan who would represent the Filipino people, the rising generation who long for their independence, and both figures shall remind you constantly of the immense sacrifices of the redeemers of our country and inescapable obligation of imitating them; also doing on our part all the possible sacrifices in order to obtain our independence.[36]

An appertaining image, the original of which is kept in the church dedicated to Maria Clara in Sta. Cruz, Manila,[37] shows this Mary as a recognizably Filipina woman, attired in traditional dress, accompanied by her son, who is dressed as a Katipunero fighter. This image and the *Novenario* that promotes its veneration is, therefore, dedicated to an indigenous Mary, depicted as the mother of a nation fighting for its independence.

110　E. J. REVOLLIDO

Also the new liturgical materials published by the IFI, notably in the 1906 service book *Oficio Divino*, provided ample opportunity for further interrelating political and religious independence.[38] For instance, newspapers reported in 1911 on a Mass in honor of the heroes of the revolution (*Misang Parangal Para sa mga Bayani ng Himagsikan*) presided over by Aglipay, during which people were moved to tears when Aglipay chanted the following lines in the Eucharistic prayer: "Therefore, Our Father, we the Filipino priests humbly beseech you and pray you to allow the rising of the joyful day of our freedom, independence and prosperity."[39]

Also hymnological materials were developed, revolving around the Filipino people's struggle for independence (*pagsasarili*), freedom (*kalayaan*), and prosperity (*kaginhawahan*). Such hymns came into existence through the Philippines, with some of them still in use today. [40]

Beyond such liturgical texts, which could be read as transgressions of the 1901 "Sedition law," another liturgical innovation in the early years of the IFI can easily be understood as a subversion of the "Flag law" (1907), forbidding the use of the national flag. In response to this law, IFI clergy began to use liturgical vestments, especially chasubles, in the color and design of this very flag. Aglipay personally used such vestments and his chasuble in this style has been preserved.[41] In doing so, the IFI made use of the newly introduced separation between church and state under American colonial rule to precisely act subversively vis-à-vis that rule.[42] In a very similar manner, another liturgical custom was developed: the singing of the (forbidden) national anthem of the Philippines at one of the most central moments of the Mass: the elevation of the consecrated host.[43]

Thus, the IFI's intention "to respond to the imperative need to restore the worship of the one true God in all its splendor and the purity of his most holy Word which under the reign of obscurantism" took on a very particular shape, which was religious and political at the same time, or, probably more accurately put: made visible the political aspect of religion as it is always there, even when religious groups took a supposedly non-political stance, thereby factually supporting whoever was in charge. By doing the reverse, the IFI makes visible the political nature of the religious, in terms of its understanding of independence, of its internal organization, and of its liturgical life. From this background, we can now explore further the way in which nationalism and religious identity was interrelated in the IFI in its foundational phase.

A National and Nationalist Catholic Church

One of the more intriguing aspects of the history of the IFI is its positioning as both a national and *nationalist* church. Whereas most national churches, certainly as they arose in alliances with nation states in the context of the nineteenth century, did have a nationalist tendency, few are so outspoken about it as the IFI and even fewer combine it with such direct political involvement as this church. Many Philippine church historians also viewed that the forces at work that gained the momentum toward the advance of the IFI "was the intense wave of nationalism that swept the country at the time of the Revolution against Spain and war of resistance against America."[44] This opinion was supported by one of the first Western historians of the IFI, William Henry Scott when he wrote that: "Nationalism was the vitality that held the Philippine Independent Church through its many trials and setbacks."[45] Probing the question of what "nationalism" means for the IFI at its inception is therefore a promising way to further research this church's identity. In doing so, it can be shown that the IFI's nationalism is characterized by a conviction to be (a) a church of and for the people and (b) on that basis an emphatically politically oriented church. This contribution agrees thus with Smit, when he wrote that "the IFI in its proclamation subscribed to an ecclesiology of the national church in which it is hard to distinguish neatly between issues pertaining to the rights of the Philippine church and the Philippine people, a state of affairs that may be illustrated by the first part of the IFI's heraldic motto "*Pro Deo et Patria*.""[46] Exploring this question will also shed further the IFI's particular understanding of "catholicity," given that this is an identity marker that this church continues to stress, even after its involuntary separation from Rome.

First, from its inception, its establishment being proclaimed at a meeting of a union, the IFI considers the people the basis of the church. "The people" is a concept in which the people *qua* people of the Philippines and the people *qua* people of God merge. This is apparent from the following formulation from the 1903 *Doctrine and Constitutional Rules*:

> Our Church is Catholic, or Universal, because it considers *all men without distinction children of God*, and it bears the designation "Philippine Independent" to *identify this association of free men* who, within the said universality, *admit servility to no one*.[47]

112 E. J. REVOLLIDO

This definition illumines the IFI concept of a church as the "people of God" and at the same time describes its nationalist identity. The IFI considers itself as "children of God," not a hierarchy, identified with free people and in constant opposition to any kind of slavery. This "bottom up" understanding of the church found, as already outlined above, expression in the election of bishops by the people, rather than by their appointment, for instance by the pope. Election by the people was, therefore more than just an assertion of independence (as discussed above), but also an indication of the IFI's intention to be a church of the people, in which the people fully participate and act on behalf of the entire community. This latter assertion leads to the second aspect of the IFI's nationalism: its emphasis on political agency.

The self-understanding of the IFI as a national church is one that has an activist character. Given that much of its "DNA" stems from a politician, journalist, and labor organizer such as Isabelo de los Reyes, Sr., the first *Obispo Maximo*, Gregorio Aglipay, with his background as a "guerilla padre," and the politicians and thinkers behind them (notably Apolinario Mabini), this may not come as a surprise, yet it is worth exploring as it is so characteristic for the IFI. A retrospective remark of Aglipay from 1933, which at the same time points forward to his participation in the presidential elections of the Philippine Commonwealth in 1935, sums up the IFI's attitude, as it was also embodied by Aglipay, succinctly in an interview for the *Herald Week Magazine*:

> I believe that the Church should take part in politics, for it is part of our national life and any political changes that take place here are not unlikely to affect the affairs of the Church. Moreover, the Aglipayan Church, since its inception, has always been identified with the libertarian movement, and since its genesis is the revolt against foreign despotism. It would be recreant to the memory of Burgos, Zamora, del Pilar, Andres Bonifacio, and other immortals, should it not now take part actively in the fight for independence...Beneath their religious robes, the priests of the Philippine Independent Church are Filipinos. That ever present fact should not be discounted. Like the rest of the Filipinos, they cannot remain indifferent to the independence movement.[48]

The fact that the IFI is a church consisting of Filipinos, served by Filipino clergy, therefore leads to solidarity with the Philippines and a commitment to shaping Philippine society, including politically and not simply spiritually in an apolitical sense (which to the IFI would be an unconvincing understanding of what spirituality amounts to). Such political involvement, based as it was on being part of the same people and agitating against colonial rule with its discriminatory and unjust distribution of resources, often took a left-leaning shape—in contrast to other, right-leaning kinds of nationalism. For instance, in the 1903 constitution of the IFI, communal ownership of property was advocated, opposing the (American colonial) emphasis on private property and capitalism.[49] Quite in line with this initial commitment and suggesting that such a line of thought had remained characteristic for the IFI, or at least for its leadership, for a longer period of time, Aglipay made the redistribution of land and the nationalization of Philippine industry part of his 1935 campaign for the presidency of the Philippine Commonwealth.[50]

This understanding of ecclesial nationalism and political involvement in the life of the nation also sheds light on IFI's notion of "catholicity." The quotation from the 1903 constitution of the IFI, namely, sets out to explain why the IFI is "catholic or universal" (see above). Catholicity is subsequently understood in terms of universality, in terms of an identity of all as "children of God" and in terms of being free, or, in any case, of not existing in servility. The first aspect of catholicity as it is understood in this early constitution of the IFI is closely connected to its understanding as a national church: it is a church for everyone, the entire nation—consequently, the IFI also acts on behalf of this nation. The heraldic motto of the IFI, as it was introduced in this foundational period, *Pro Deo et Patria* is expressive of this understanding of catholicity. The second part of the 1903 blueprint of catholicity under consideration here, the reference to everyone one being a child of God, may strike one first as a religious cliché. Yet, with the background of colonial rule in the Philippines and the discrimination inherent to it, it is a strikingly emancipatory statement. As the entire 1903 constitutes and breathes an atmosphere of confidence in the abilities of the Filipino people, an apologetic tone is not altogether absent: although the IFI may consider all people, including Filipinos, children of God, they still need to live up to their dignity and implied abilities, as the constitution puts in it its section 2.X:

> We recommend much altruism and saintliness of behavior to our brothers, especially during these times of trial through which we are passing and it is essential that foreigners be unable to say that we separated from Rome sim-

114   E. J. REVOLLIDO

ply to hide or continue our debilities; let us demonstrate the benefits of having broken our secular chains, and may God be with us all.[51]

In a similar and connected manner, the question of freedom, or "servility to no one" is elaborated in this constitution. In a somewhat dramatic section, the following is said about it, connecting freedom with the ability to live up to the high standards that the constitution sets, and connecting servitude with debilitation and the inability to live up to one's dignity and talents:

> Ah Liberty! It's worth is understood only when it is lost; it can only be loved in the "saddest darkness of prison cells". A free man is a *complete man,* dignified, honorable, of lofty sentiments, attended by all his rights and by his unavoidable duties as well; but a man of his own free will becomes a slave in a man with a vile heart, a deceitful, abject sycophant - a person, in short deserving of pity.[52]

Catholicity is, therefore, understood in a sense that sustains community of all with all, in particular that of the national church, which consists of the people of a nation and acts on its behalf, that has the dignity of all as its point of departure and, in order to allow this dignity to come to full fruition, underlines freedom and rejects servitude. Thus, when the IFI was proclaimed in 1902 and gave itself a constitution in 1903, it understood itself to perform not an act of separation but a declaration of liberation from bondage and a noble deed of claiming the freedom that was forcibly denied from them. They gathered together as educated, organized, and ethical people for the love of God and country and it was action worthy of being called "catholic." As they gather together for a common journey of struggle they want to show to the world their difference in saying,

> In good faith, we believe that there is no real schism, because our painful separation is based on sound reason and above all on the natural need to protect our rights and our national dignity.[53]

This assertion failed to convince many, but, for the purpose of this contribution it is of significance. Also, it is again apparent how the political and the religious are fully merged here, albeit with a rather different, emancipatory, and liberative accentuation than it was the case under Spanish colonial rule. In an intriguing way, precisely the intertwining of state or politics and religion that was so oppressive during Spanish colonial rule becomes in this reinterpretation a tool for the struggle for independence under American colonial rule with its emphasis on a separation between church and state. The nationalism propagated by the IFI consists of an aspiration and a struggle motivated by love of country toward the attainment of one nation that is truly sovereign and independent from foreign domination. This nationalism is not an aggressive nationalism that seeks to conquer others but one that seeks for independence of a country and a church from foreign rule, in order to allow the people of the appertaining nation to thrive at their fullest potentiality.

CONCLUSION

In sum, the "independence" of the IFI is of a very particular kind. In it, catholicity is a concept that is understood as referring to a community of all acting on behalf of all, in particular of a people, in this case the people of the Philippines. In order to do this, these people and the church need to be free. This freedom is understood in an emancipatory sense, not in an aggressive way vis-à-vis against foreign players. Both the nation and the church need to be of the free, independent people. In order to achieve this, political and religious freedom must be advocated and campaigned, both by religious and political institutions, even via military aims. The IFI is therefore both a church that understands its catholicity as both requiring freedom and as an incentive to struggle for freedom for the people out of which it considers itself to have been born. The heritage of the Spanish colonial rule, with its intertwining of religion and colonial rule, receives a new interpretation through leaders such as De los Reyes, Sr., and Aglipay: the close relationship between the two is maintained, also when the new American colonial rulers introduced a separation between church and state. But it is now used on behalf and for the benefit of the Filipino people, furthering their independence, rather than as a means for exercising colonial power over these people. Independent Catholicism is in the case of the IFI closely connected to be a national church and the independence involved is both political and religious, with its aim the creation of a truly "catholic" community, in which all are given their full dignity and can live in freedom. Among the various independent catholic communities, the IFI is probably the only one that not only has such a forceful, left-leaning nationalistic interpretation of Catholicism, but also has sought to put this into practice.

NOTES

1. Franz Segbers and Peter-Ben Smit, *Catholicity in Times of Globalization: Remembering Alberto Ramento, Martyred Bishop of Workers and Peasants,* (Lucerne: Edition Exodus, 2011), 22.

2. The Unión Obrera Democrática was the first federation of labor unions in the Philippines founded on February 2, 1902, under the leadership of Don Isabelo de los Reyes, Sr. See: William Henry Scott, *The Unión Obrera Democrática: First Filipino Labor Union* (Quezon City: New Day, 1992). See for a report of the proclamation: *La Iglesia Filipina Independiente Revista Catolica* 1, 2 (18 October 1903), 6–7. See also: Pedro de Achutegui and Miguel Bernad, *Religious Revolution in the Philippines* 1–4 (Manila: Ateneo de Manila, 1960–1972), vol. 1, 183 (paraphrase).

3. On him, see: José de los Reyes y Sevilla, *Biography of Senator Isabelo de los Reyes, Father of Philippine Labor, Proclaimer of the Philippine Independent Church* (Manila: Nueva Era, 1947). The inscription accompanying the portrait of him in the main building of the University of Santo Tomas (Manila) is indicative of his manifold activities, celebrating him as follows: "Isabelo de los Reyes, Sr., Vigan, I.S., July 7, 1864 – October 10, 1938, graduated law at UST, journalist, scholar-author, publisher, labor leader, nationalist and politico-social leader, author of books on history, folklore, politics and social problems. Despite imprisonment for involvement in the Philippine Revolution, he was later appointed to responsible positions in the Spanish government. Founder, labor movement and co-founder, Philippine Independent Church, served as senator of the Philippines." A full biography of this key figure from Philippine history is still lacking.

4. That the establishment of this church was not an initiative by Aglipay himself is also documented by his recollection of the events: he was absent from the meeting, even asleep somewhere else in Manila. As he writes in a letter to the apostolic delegate Guglielmo Piani, dated February 17, 1932, published in *El Pueblo* of February 24, 1932, and the *Herald Week Magazine* of September 27, 1933, quoted in William Henry Scott, *Aglipay Before Aglipayanism* (Quezon City: National Priest Organization, 1987), 40–41: "The Filipino people is my witness that I am not the author of the Filipino Independent Church, neither did I intervene in its preparation. I was sleeping in Ezpeleta Street when I was awakened and told that in a meeting at the Centro de Bellas Artes in Manila, August 3, 1902, the Filipino people proclaimed the new church ... The Philippine Independent Church was founded by the people of our country. It was a product of their initiative, a product of their desire for liberty, religiously, politically and socially. I was only one of the instruments of its expression." For further reading on Aglipay as revolutionary, see Scott, *Aglipay Before Aglipayanism.*

6 AN INDEPENDENT CATHOLIC, NATIONALIST PEOPLE'S MOVEMENT... 117

5. See: Samuel H. Moffett, *A History of Christianity in Asia. Volume II 1500–1900* (Maryknoll: Orbis, 2005), 565–566.
6. Achutegui and Bernad, *Religious Revolution in the Philippines*, 234.
7. On which, see the brief overview of this in the context of the renewal of Catholicism around the Council of Trent by Robert Bireley, *The Refashioning of Catholicism 1450–1700* (Washington, D.C.: Catholic University of America, 1999), p. 78. The bull *Inter Caetera Divinae*, issued by Pope Alexander VI (May 3, 1493) regulated the right of patronage in the colonies of Portugal and Spain, see for example, Friedrich Huber, *Das Christentum in Ost-, Sud- und Sudostasien sowie Australien* (Leipzig: Evangelische Verlagsanstalt, 2005), 38–39.
8. See Scott, *Aglipay Before Aglipayanism.*
9. Apolonio Ranche (ed.), *Our Heritage our Response* 1 (Manila: IFI, 1993), 2.
10. On the character of this rule, see for instance: Daniel B. Schirmer and Stephen Rosskamm Shalom (ed.), *The Philippine Reader: A History of Colonialism, Neo-Colonialism, Dictatorship and Resistance,* (Quezon City: Ken Incorporated, 1987), 15–19. The human cost of the war from 1900 to 1901 was "over 600,000 in Luzon alone had been killed or had died of disease...," according to Patricio N. Abinales and Donna J. Amoroso, *State and Society in the Philippines* (Pasig City: Anvil, 2005), 117. They believe that "The Philippine-American War has been described as the United States' first Vietnam war because of its brutality and severity. Historians have cited conflicting figures, but according to the Philippine-American War Centennial Initiative (PAWCI), an organization dedicated to compiling information on the conflict, roughly twenty-two thousand Philippine soldiers and half a million civilians were killed between 1899 and 1902 in Luzon and Visayan Islands, while one hundred thousand Muslims were killed in Mindanao." See also William Henry Scott, *Cracks in the Parchment Curtain* (Quezon City: New Day Publisher, 1982), 285–299, for an outline of the anti-colonial stance of the first leaders of the IFI.
11. Scott, *The Union Obrera Democratica*, 62.
12. The pro-colonial newspaper, *The Manila American*, made the following sarcastic comments: "Oh, my! Oh, my! Oh, my! Here is the head of the new Iglesia Filipina, the national church of the Filipinos, in a cell of a police station, charged with a criminal offense against the peace and dignity of the state!" *The Manila Times,* June 8, 1902; quoted in Scott, *The Union Obrera Democratica*, 46.
13. On August 17, 1902, the *Manila American* announced that the *Iglesia Filipina Independiente* seemed to have died before it was born. See: Mary Dorita Clifford, "Iglesia Filipina Independiente: The Revolutionary

Church," in: Gerald Anderson (ed.), *Studies in Philippine Church History*, (Itchaca/London: Cornell University, 1969), 223–255, 239.

14. See the reporting in: *Libertas*, August 11, 1902; *La Democracia*, March 20, 1904, quoted in Clifford, "Iglesia Filipina Independiente," 238.

15. See for documentation of the political negotiations concerning this matter: Clifford, "Iglesia Filipina Independiente," 240.

16. On (disappointing) discussions about ecclesial reforms, see, e.g.: Teodoro Agoncillo, *History of the Filipino People*, Quezon City: R.P. Garcia Publishing Co., 1977, 238–239. See also De Achutegui and Bernad, *Religious Revolution in the Philippines* 1, 190–192.

17. The *Six Fundamental Epistles* written between the period of 1902–1903 contained the doctrinal tenets and the organizational aspects of the new Church. These Epistles guided the IFI in her first year of existence, together with a temporary constitution of October 1, 1902, until a more comprehensive constitution was adopted called *Doctrinas y Reglas Constitutionales* (DRC) on October 23, 1903. This was the doctrine and constitution of the IFI until it was superseded by the 1947 Constitution that was highly influenced by the Protestant Episcopal Church in the USA, and consequently the IFI's return to the historic Trinitarian Christianity. See for an overview of these developments: Peter-Ben Smit, *Old Catholic and Philippine Independent Ecclesiologies in History: The Catholic Church in Every Place*, (Leiden: Brill, 2011).

18. Published in: De Achútegui and Bernad, *Religious Revolution in the Philippines* 4, 137. It was in Bacarra, Ilocos Norte where Father Pedro Brillantes took possession of his Bishopric of Saint James the Greater. See Ambrosio Manaligod, *The Ecclesiality of the Philippine Independent Church* (National Priest Organization: Quezon City, 1988), 87–88. See also: Smit, *Old Catholic and Philippine Independent Ecclesiologies in History*, 149. – The position of Brillantes was shared more widely, see, e.g., the "Ultimatum of seventeen Ilocano Priests to the Apostolic Delegate appointing Aglipay as their Leader" stating that: "We the undersigned priests will fight for the exclusive right of the Filipino clergy to occupy the position of archbishops and bishops in the Philippines. If this right is violated by the Apostolic Delegate, we will secede from the Roman Church and form an independent Filipino Church, teaching the same dogmas as the Roman." See: De Achútegui and Bernad, *Religious Revolution in the Philippines*, 121.

19. De Achútegui and Bernad, *Religious Revolution in the Philippines* 4, 137.

20. See for this translation: Apolonio M. Ranche (ed.), *Doctrine and Constitutional Rules Important Documents, Various Articles and Chronology of the Iglesia Filipina Independiente* (Manuscript, 1996; photocopy – Special Collections, Aglipay Central Theological Seminary Library, Urdaneta City), 33.

6 AN INDEPENDENT CATHOLIC, NATIONALIST PEOPLE'S MOVEMENT... 119

21. See on this, e.g., Peter-Ben Smit, "The Road Towards Full Communion Between the Philippine Independent Church and The Episcopal Church," *Anglican & Episcopal History* 84:2 (2015), 1–45.
22. Translation in: Ranche (ed.), *Doctrine and Constitutional Rules*, 35.
23. See for an overview: Smit, *Old Catholic and Philippine Independent Ecclesiologies in History*, 233–278. Aglipay embarked on rather radical doctrinal and liturgical revisions in the four decades that he would serve the IFI as "Obispo Maximo." As interesting as these revisions are, the speed with which the IFI reverted to its first liturgical books and subsequently adopted other, notably Episcopalian, liturgical materials and doctrinal standards following Aglipay's death in 1940 gives rise to the impression that Aglipay's innovations were his, but not the church's.
24. As such, the IFI can be numbered among a larger group of popular religious movements in the Philippines, cf. Reynaldo Ileto, *Pasyon and Revolution. Popular Movements in the Philippines*, 1840–1910 (Quezon City: Ateneo de Manila University, 1979).
25. De Achútegui and Bernad, *Religious Revolution in the Philippines* 4, 137–138. See also: Manaligod, *The Ecclesiality of the Philippine Independent Church*, 87–88.
26. Translation in: Ranche (ed.), *Doctrine and Constitutional Rules*, 16.
27. Translation in: Ranche (ed.), *Doctrine and Constitutional Rules*, 17.
28. Translation in: Ranche (ed.), *Doctrine and Constitutional Rules*, 1.
29. Translation in: Ranche (ed.), *Doctrine and Constitutional Rules*, 6.
30. Clifford, "Iglesia Filipina Independiente," 243–244.
31. *La Iglesia Filipina Independiente. Revista Catolica* 1 (October 11, 1903), 2.
32. Marcelo A. Foronda, "The Canonization of Rizal," *The Journal of History* 8 (1960), 1–48, 19.
33. See for instance the following publication: *Calendario de la Iglesia Filipina Independiente para del Ano 1916* (Manila: Imp. Y Lit. de Juan Fajardo, 1915). The broader collection of such liturgical calendars kept at the IFI Archives at St. Andrew's Seminary shows that the publication was not done on a yearly basis, but nonetheless consistently over a number of years.
34. Foronda, "The Canonization of Rizal," 34.
35. See: *Novenario de la Patria (La patria se simboliza en la soñada madre de Balintawak) escrito por el Emmo. Sr. Gregorio Aglipay y Labayan, aprobado por el Consejo Supremo de Obispos. Editor: Monseñor Isabelo de los Reyes y López, Obispo rector de la parroquia de María Clara, en San Lázaro, Manila* (Manila, 1926). In general, see: Francis A. Gealogo, "Time, Identity and Nation in the Aglipayan Novenario ng Balintawak and Calendariong Maanghang," *Journal of Philippine Studies* 58 (2010), 147–168.
36. Translation by the author.

120   E. J. REVOLLIDO

37. Maria Clara is a fictional character out of Philippine national hero José Rizal's iconic novel *Noli me tangere* (1887), and an idealized representation of the Filipina *per se* (a notion that has not been without its critics, given Maria Clara's stereotypical "feminine" portrayal).
38. *Oficio Divino de la Iglesia Filipina Independiente* (Barcelona, 1906).
39. *El Ideal,* March 12, 1911, 4. Translation by the author.
40. The most popular songs that were composed in different regions, like the *Filipinas, Nadayag a Filipinas* in Ilocos, *Dayawon* of Iloilo, *Senor Sto. Nino* of Cebu and *Bathalang Maykapal* in the Tagalog areas, were examples of how the said nationalist themes were being propagated and used in the common worship of the people. These songs are known in the different regions where they belong and still popular in many other IFI parishes. They are being sung during special occasions like the annual proclamation anniversary of the IFI.
41. It is currently preserved in the IFI Archives at Aglipay Central Theological Seminary (ACTS) in Urdaneta City, Pangasinan.
42. Alfredo N. Salanga, "Aglipayan Aggiornamento," *Panorama* (April 29, 1984), 39.
43. Salanga, "Aglipayan Aggiornamento," 39.
44. De Achútegui and Bernad, *Religious Revolution in the Philippines* 1, 234–235.
45. William Henry Scott, "Philippine Independent Church in History," *Silliman Journal* 10 (1963), 298–310, 300.
46. Smit, *Old Catholic and Philippine Independent Ecclesiologies in history,* 149.
47. Translation in Ranche (ed.), *Doctrine and Constitutional Rules.* Emphasis mine.
48. "Interview with Bishop Gregorio Aglipay," *Herald Week Magazine,* September 23, 1933, 2.
49. Chapter 2 of the 1903 Constitution expressed the IFI's ethical position in relation to ownership of property saying: "Our promise will not be in vain to implement on our part and insofar as it is practicable nowadays, the communal ownership of property which Jesus preached and the apostles practiced (Acts 4:32,34–35), especially since it is the faithful compliance with this Christian doctrine which is the whole secret of the formidable power of the religious orders all over the world...We will begin by pooling the ecclesiastical wealth of all our bishops, parish priests, and other clergy, and in time even their private wealth by requiring those who enter the ministry of the Church to contribute all their property to the sacred treasury of the Church, in the manner of the religious orders...The universalization of property is not a mere utopian dream, first, because if it were, Jesus Christ would not have wished to introduce it; and second, because it will be no more than a collective society, though universal, and the capital

6 AN INDEPENDENT CATHOLIC, NATIONALIST PEOPLE'S MOVEMENT... 121

contributed will be unequal." Translation in: Ranche (ed.), *Doctrine and Constitutional Rules*, 22.

50. Partido Komunista ng Pilipinas, *Communism in the Philippines: The PKP* (Manila: Historical Commission, Partido Komunista ng Pilipinas, 1996), 231–232. Aglipay's election program contained the following items: (1) An independence that will bring happiness. (2) Uplifting the condition of the working classes and farmers by providing decent wages for them, securing for them and their children useful education; giving generous help to the unemployed, the sick, the aged, and the invalid; and calling upon those by the labors and farmers associations to take part in the direction of a democratic and liberal government. (3) To provide lands, means, and all possible facilities to all who may have need of the national patrimony. (4) To promote new industries and to Filipinize them, granting sufficient credit and subsidies, at low rate of interest to deserving merchants and industrialists who may need them. (5) Absolute economy in the government; all unnecessary expenditures to be eliminated; high salaries to be reduced, but merit will be done justice; and the Civil Service to be extended so that judicial positions will be filled through competitive examination. (6) Full investigation of all the sources of national wealth and the exploitation of the same, but care will be taken to avoid oppressing taxpayers; land tax will be reduced; and recreation centers will be made to pay just license fees. (7) To make the Tagalog language one of the official languages.

51. Translation in: Ranche (ed.), *Doctrine and Constitutional Rules*, 41.

52. Translation in: Ranche (ed.), *Doctrine and Constitutional Rules*, 53. Emphasis mine.

53. Translation in: Ranche (ed.), *Doctrine and Constitutional Rules*, 35.

CHAPTER 7

Philippine, Independent and International: The Relationship Between—*the Iglesia Filipina Independiente and the Old Catholic Churches*

Peter-Ben Smit

Christianity in the Philippines is, in many ways, an heir of the Spanish and (to a lesser extent) US-American colonial periods. Vis-à-vis the colonial overlords of the archipelago, churches positioned themselves rather differently. A particularly striking example of a church that positioned itself in the political landscape of the colonial Philippines is the *Iglesia Filipina Independiente*. As its history is discussed elsewhere in this volume, in Revollido's contribution, here the focus will be on one particular aspect of the negotiation of its identity: the establishment of relationships with churches from the global north. As it will become clear in what follows, both "purely" theological motifs and more (church) political concerns

---

P.-B. Smit (✉)
Vrije Universiteit Amsterdam, Amsterdam, Netherlands

Faculty of Theology, University of Pretoria, Hatfield, South Africa
e-mail: p.b.a.smit@uu.nl

© The Author(s), under exclusive license to Springer Nature Switzerland AG 2024
C. Lledo Gomez et al. (eds.), *500 Years of Christianity and the Global Filipino/a*, Pathways for Ecumenical and Interreligious Dialogue, https://doi.org/10.1007/978-3-031-47500-9_7

123

about intellectual and institutional autonomy, characteristic of a church that wishes to be fully Filipino as well as fully catholic, played a role in the development of these relationships. Eventually, this led to the international ecumenical recognition of the *Iglesia Filipina Independiente* on own its terms (and not on those of its partners), thereby showcasing how autonomy and indigenousness can be paired with a global ecumenical and catholic outlook. The relationship that will be studied here is that with the Old Catholic Churches of the Union of Utrecht, as it lends itself particularly well to demonstrating the dynamics just described. As this is a relatively small and little-known international communion of churches, it will be introduced first, before proceeding with the discussion of the relationship between the *Iglesia Filipina Independiente* and the Old Catholic Churches.

THE OLD CATHOLIC CHURCHES OF THE UNION OF UTRECHT: HISTORY AND BACKGROUND

Established in 1889 and with a membership that has seen slight variation in the course of time, the Union of Utrecht of Old Catholic Church (a name that postdates its actual founding) is the key and ecumenically recognized worldwide communion of Old Catholic Churches, its members having been co-founders of the World Council of Churches in 1948.[1] The current membership consists of the Old Catholic Churches of the Netherlands, Switzerland, Germany, Austria, the Czech Republic, and the Polish Catholic Church in Poland, all as autocephalous (autonomous) churches, and the Old Catholic Church of Croatia and the Mission Vieille Catholique Francophone as bodies without full autonomy (due to size and degree of organizational stability). By and large, these churches can be grouped into three groups as far as their origins are concerned, albeit these groups are very dissimilar in size. To begin with, the Old Catholic Church of the Netherlands, considering itself the historical continuation of the church that was founded in the Netherlands by Willibrord in the late seventh century, has its origins in the ("Jansenist") schism of Utrecht of 1723/1724, at which point Dutch Catholics elected a new Archbishop of Utrecht, the pope having failed to appoint one.[2] A second contingent of churches includes those churches that emerged in the wake of the First Vatican Council (1869–1870/1960), consisting of those Catholics who were unable to accept the doctrinal definitions concerning papal infallibility (*"ex sese, non autem ex consensu Ecclesiae"*) and universal papal jurisdiction contained in the dogmatic constitution *Pastor Aeternus* of this council (1870). These Catholics, under the leadership of theologians and scholars such as Ignaz von Döllinger and canonists like Johann Friedrich von Schulte, were forced to organize themselves in churches of their own, the successors of which include the contemporary Old Catholic Churches. A final group of churches originates in the Polish migration to the United States in the nineteenth century. These immigrants established their own autonomous catholic church (not under the jurisdiction of non-Polish bishops and with much authority for the [lay] people that had built up the church) under the leadership of, amongst others, Franciszek (Francis) Hodur (1866–1953). The resulting Polish National Catholic Church in turn established a mission in Poland, which, following the Second World War, became autonomous as the Polish Catholic Church. The latter church is still a member of the Union of Utrecht of Old Catholic Churches, its mother church ceased to be a member in 2006, over a dispute concerning the ordination of women to the apostolic ministry. The Dutch and post-Vatican I churches established the aforementioned international communion in 1889, and the other (Polish) churches joined at a later stage (1907 and 1951). The foundational document of this communion of churches is the so-called Declaration of Utrecht, while the relationships between the churches are regulated by means of a statute, which regulates the communion's central organ: the International Bishops' Conference, an episcopal synod by means of which the churches, represented by their bishops, express their communion and engage in common discernment.[3]

Old Catholic Interaction with the *Iglesia Filipina Independiente*

Throughout the history of the Union of Utrecht, its member churches and bishops have developed a strong ecumenical commitment, in particular with churches that are, as they are, both autonomous and catholic. This also provided the impetus for seeking to develop a relationship with the nascent *Iglesia Filipina Independiente* after its proclamation in 1902. Formal communion between the churches was established in 1965. This took place after an interaction that lasted nearly six decades and which resulted in a lively exchange of persons and ditto cooperation toward the end of the millennium.[4] Prior to the establishment of communion, the

126 P.-B. SMIT

relationship went through two phases, the first of which ended with the winding down of communications, and the second led to the formal establishment of communion.

Recapitulating some of what Revollido discusses, the Philippine Independent Church, or, *Iglesia Filipina Independiente*, came into existence in the context of the (eventually lost) struggle for Philippine independence in the late nineteenth and early twentieth centuries. Following the conclusion of the Philippine-American war, Filipinos, led by the politician and journalist Isabelo de los Reyes, Sr., proclaimed the *Iglesia Filipina Independiente* as a church that was to be free of the Roman Catholic (colonial) hierarchy and as an instrument for the struggle for the political independence of the Philippines. They invited a person who embodied both of these aspects to lead the new church as its leading bishop, or *Obispo Maximo*: Gregorio Aglipay (1860–1940), a Filipino priest who had previously fought as a *guerillero*. Under his leadership, the *Iglesia Filipina Independiente* organized itself, while he himself became a person of national significance and of some international renown, especially in circles of political and religious liberalism.[5] This development was, in many ways, programmatic, as can be deduced from the name that he used for his particular worldview: "religious Philippinism."[6] In this notion, Philippine nationalism and Philippine history and religious tradition, and a modern, philosophical, and "scientific" approach, were meant to go together and lead to the development of a religion that is both modern and authentically Filipino; such an outlook is also reflected in the coat of arms of the *Iglesia Filipina Independiente*, in which the heraldic motto consists both of "*pro deo et patria*" and of the striking keywords "*scientia*" and "*libertas*" in addition to the more traditional "*scripturae*" and "*caritas*." The embrace of all of this also amounts to the embrace of an emphatically postcolonial identity, in the sense of wishing to move beyond a situation of direct or indirect colonial rule. How this played out in the relationship with the Old Catholics can be studied now, based on documentary sources.

Geographical and Theological Antipodes: A First Phase of Old Catholic–Philippine Independent Contacts

The round of contacts between the Old Catholic Churches of the Union of Utrecht, represented by the secretary of its International Bishops' Conference, the (first) bishop of the Old Catholic Church of Switzerland, Eduard Herzog (1841–1924),[7] and the *Iglesia Filipina Independiente*,

7 PHILIPPINE, INDEPENDENT AND INTERNATIONAL: THE RELATIONSHIP...   127

represented by its first *Obispo Maximo*, started in 1903, when the former wrote the following to the latter on 1 December:

> Pax tecum!
> Dear Lord and Brother,
> I have read with very much satisfaction your article in *The Independent* of 29 October 1903.
> May God be with your Lordship and your Church!
> You don't know perhaps that there are in Switzerland, Germany, Holland, Austria similar catholic national Churches as you have organized so happily in your Islands. We hold the catholic faith, the catholic sacraments, the catholic liturgy, the catholic constitution of the church, but we are independent from the Pope and especially we deny the Vatican Decrees.
> It seems to me, that those national Churches should be in brotherly union to show the world that it is possible to be catholic everywhere without being submitted to Rome. As a sign of my brotherly feelings I send you the list of my clergy.
> I would accept your communications always with gratitude.
> Wishing you every grace of God our Father, I am with much respect your Brother in Christ O[ur] L[ord].
> + Edward Herzog, Bishop. (Herzog 1903a)

This is a promising beginning, of connection, indeed, with a clear intention of forging an international witness to a catholicity that is authentic and full but does not incorporate submission to the See of Rome. Herzog soon followed up this first letter with a second one on 12 December 1903, not yet having received a response from Manila, but apparently having studied *The Independent* in somewhat more detail:

> Right Reverend and Dear Sir,
> I see in 'The Independent' that you have your own official paper '*La Verdad*'. Would you have the kindness to send me the paper regularly. I will send you our weekly gazette '*Der Katholik*'. Perhaps you know German or you will find a man who understands it.
> The next summer we shall have here at Berne an international Congress to which all independent catholic Churches are invited. I shall send you an invitation as soon as the time of the gathering is fixed. It would be very important if you and some other bishops could come.
> In the '*Katholik*' of this day I have spoken of your work. To our readers it would be most interesting to know by whom and where you have received your Episcopal consecration.

128   P.-B. SMIT

> We are very anxious to show to the world that our independence from Rome does not hinder us to be good Catholics.
> Believe me, Right Reverend and dear Brother in O[ur] L[ord] J[esus] C[hrist],
> Yours very sincerely
> + E. Herzog, Bishop (Herzog 1903b)

Here, Herzog pursues a slightly different approach, even if his program, as indicated in the sentence "We are very anxious ... good Catholics" remains the same, as he not only invites Aglipay to a regular exchange of information and persons, but also asks a rather vital question: the provenance of Aglipay's episcopal consecration. Aglipay responds to Herzog on 26 February 1904. In his letter,[8] Aglipay mentions a number of things, and in particular, inquires as to the foundations of the faith of the Old Catholics and suggests that attendance of the upcoming International Old Catholics Congress might be an option. Herzog responds[9] requesting a copy of the foundational documents of the *Iglesia Filipina Independiente* in return. While letters continue to go back and forth, Herzog writes a particularly interesting letter on 4 June 1904, in which he indicates his joy about the possibilities for communion between the churches, assuring Aglipay that this would not diminish the autonomy of his church, but did inquire what the provenance of his episcopal consecration was, given that Roman Catholic newspapers indicated that it might not be within the apostolic succession and it would be a shame if Aglipay had given up that mark of catholicity.[10] Most of these topics also appear in a letter from the entire International Bishops' Conference of the Union of Utrecht of Old Catholic Churches to Aglipay, sent in 1904.[11] In the letter, the adherence of the Old Catholic bishops to the faith and order of the early church (excluding the 1870 doctrinal definition of the ministry of the pope, as well as their respect for the autonomy of the national churches) is stressed,[12] which, without a doubt, is meant to have a positive effect on Aglipay. Yet, also, one question is reiterated:

> Without wishing to derogate from the independence of your church or to forestall your own judgement as to that which benefits your church, we beg to call your attention above all to our adhering to the apostolic succession, that a church can only be considered a Catholic church, if its bishops have been consecrated by other Catholic bishops. If the bishops of your church should hitherto not have received the Catholic consecration, we would address to you the urgent entreaty, to be mindful of supplying this want.[13]

7 PHILIPPINE, INDEPENDENT AND INTERNATIONAL: THE RELATIONSHIP... 129

Such a consecration has two aspects, to be sure. One is to make the orders of a church valid from a catholic perspective, the other is just as important: it is an expression of communion (and therefore recognition as a catholic church) with other churches in the catholic tradition. In response to this communication, a number of representatives of Aglipay and of the Old Catholics in Bern meet, resulting in the following letter:

> Right Reverend and Dear Sir
> I have received with high satisfaction the visite [sic] of Mr. Emil Barrel, your delegate in the question of your consecration. In the conference of the 24th February we regulated the conditions under which the old catholic Bishops of Europe can give, as I believe, the catholic consecration to your episcopate.
> With this letter I have the pleasure to send you
> 1. the protocol of our conference.
> 2. the declaration of faith which we have.
> 3. the convention by which the intercourse between the old catholic bishops is regulated.
> 4. some Notes to explain the declaration of faith.
> If your Lordship can accept the conditions indicated in these documents, I shall be very happy to propose to my brother Bishops your consecration and to cooperate at this most important and holy occasion.
> Expecting your kind answer I am with brotherly feelings truly yours in J[esus] Ch[rist].
> Edward Herzog. Bishop.[14]

What the correspondence did *not* state, was what must have been discussed at the meeting: the kind of episcopal consecration Aglipay already possessed, one performed by a bishop who had been consecrated by seven priests. Instead, the focus was on (a) an agreement in the faith; and (b) a proper course of action with regard to the preparations for Aglipay's consecration. The latter was outlined in the minutes of the meeting, at which five conditions were stipulated:[15] (a) a complete curriculum vitae of the candidate; (b) notarized proof of his election; (c) a description of the current state of affairs concerning the church (statistics, etc.); (d) acceptance of the "Declaration of Utrecht"; (e) acceptance of the rules and regulations governing the International Bishops' Conference's life. The "Declaration of Utrecht" is the foundational doctrinal declaration of the Union of Utrecht of Old Catholic Churches.[16] With that, the aim then seems to have not been just to provide Aglipay with a valid consecration,

130 P.-B. SMIT

but also to include him and his church into the Union of Utrecht by incorporating him into the International Bishops' Conference.

Following this letter, the correspondence became somewhat confusing to Herzog, it seems, as Aglipay did not address his questions, even appearing to be unaware of the negotiations that took place in Switzerland. The letter also did not come with the various documents requested by Herzog. This led Herzog to make further inquiries in the Philippines, especially concerning Aglipay's reputation and that of his church.[17] To Herzog's warning to Aglipay that he needed to address the various points raised by him first, before he, as he announced somewhat surprisingly in September 1905, traveled to Switzerland for his consecration in the summer of 1906.[18] Following this last exchange of letters, the correspondence dwindled, even if Herzog remained an ardent observer of developments in the *Iglesia Filipina Independiente*, notably when it concerned matters of doctrine, reporting on this to his synod, for instance in 1910, when he commented on the ongoing influence of Isabelo de los Reyes, Sr., on the church, especially in theological matters. He was not in favor of this influence and hoped that De los Reyes would not speak on behalf of the church formally.[19] About two years later, in 1912, there was a final exchange of letters between the two bishops that deserves attention here. In that year, Aglipay sent Herzog, in a letter dated 2 August of that year, marking the ten-year anniversary of the proclamation of the *Iglesia Filipina Independiente*, a copy of the new catechism of his church (Aglipay 1911). This document recorded the speedy theological development that *Iglesia Filipina Independiente* had gone through in its first decennium. Herzog consequently responded with a letter that left nothing to be desired as far as clarity concerning his view of Aglipay's theological position was concerned:

My Lord

I have received the book 'Catequesis' which you have so kindly sent me. If I am not mistaken, this book is now the Confession of Faith of your Church. You know, that, in [the] geographical sense, we are antipodes. With deepest sorrow I must say [to] you that we are antipodes also in the religious and ecclesiastical sense. You are so far from us that even a discussion between us is impossible.

Will you allow me only some remarks:

7 PHILIPPINE, INDEPENDENT AND INTERNATIONAL: THE RELATIONSHIP... 131

1. The author of 'Catequesis' seems to believe that in the Old Testament we have to darn [?] natural science and history. That is not the case [that] should distinguish between the and the eternal religious and moral truth. The doctrine of evolution is not in opposition to the divine revelation of religion. Darwin was a churchman; Häckel is not even an authority to the naturalists.

2. I am astonished that the author of 'Catequesis' does so little [to] understand the language of the New Testament and especially of the Holy Gospels. It is not allowed to take parables in an eternal sense.

3. Strauss and Renan are forgotten. If the author of [the] 'Catequesis' had the intention to found his faith not on J[esus] Chr[ist], but on some instructed man of our time, he had to name Harnack and others.

4. I see on page 40 the words *'También han enviado sus plácemes los arzobispos independientes de Paris, de Antioquia, de Suiza'* [Ebenfalls haben geschickt ihre Zustimmung die unabhängigen Erzbischöfe von Paris, Antiochia, der Schweiz], I don't know the names of those arzobispos, but I think the author of 'Catequesis' has in view Vilatte, Houssay, the so called Donkin, 'Bishop of Holy Cross in Antiochia and Vicaire Apostolique of Southern Switzerland', Miraglia. These men have no Church; Donkin was not even priest, but he has deceived during many years Romans and Anglicans; he was often in prison as a swindler; he is now dead. The Old Catholics have no connection with these people.

   I regret very much that you are responsible for the 'Catequesis'. I am now 44 years Professor of Exegesis, but I have kept the faith and hope to do so until my end.

   Yours in X.

   Ed. Herzog, Bishop.

Aglipay responded to Herzog in kind,[20] fully confirming Herzog's view of things regarding his church and arguing that his church, free as it was, had the liberty to explore and take into account the latest and most modern insights—Herzog shouldn't think that such insights were unavailable to Filipinos![21] In other words, Aglipay confirmed Herzog's view that his church was deviating from the catholic tradition as Herzog understood it and that he had every right, even as a Filipino, to do so. Thus, there was a clear anti-colonial sentiment to Aglipay's interpretation of his own theological development: freedom and independence, as modern values, implied the reception of all modern insights available and the revision of one's creed in a fitting manner. With this last letter of Aglipay, the exchange between the two bishops came to an end and it is possible to draw some conclusions as to the way in which the Old Catholics negotiated their

132   P.-B. SMIT

identity vis-à-vis another, major, independent catholic church. The following criteria seemed to be at play: (a) ecclesial substance and reputation; (b) adherence to the faith and order of the early church in a recognizable manner to Herzog (and his fellow bishops), including matters of doctrine and church order (notably the manner of the election of a bishop). What did not seem to be a major obstacle to Herzog's desire to dialogue with Aglipay is the way in which Aglipay had been consecrated bishop earlier on. As soon as one of the two sets of criteria above, the second one to be sure, was no longer fulfilled, due to Aglipay's embrace of the latest insights in religious studies and their incorporation into his religious worldview in an anti-colonial mode, the conversations ceased.

What can be observed throughout this correspondence is the negotiation of a catholic and independent identity on the part of the *Iglesia Filipina Independiente* in a postcolonial context, in the course of which it valued international ecumenical contacts, but was not inclined whatsoever to allow others to determine how it ought to be a catholic church, let alone to be incorporated into another communion of churches. The result of this is a breakdown of a promising ecclesial relationship. Yet, this would not be the end of this story.

OLD CATHOLICS AND THE *IGLESIA FILIPINA INDEPENDIENTE*: PART II

Following 1912, the year in which the last contact between Herzog and Aglipay took place as discussed above, the history of the *Iglesia Filipina Independiente* was fairly turbulent. When summarizing it, it can be said that Aglipay, often in collaboration with Isabelo de los Reyes, Sr., further pursued the path toward "religious Philippinism" (as it was described above). However, upon his death in 1940, it turned out that his path was in reality not one pursued by the *Iglesia Filipina Independiente* as a whole; both out of the church's own volition and under the increasingly strong influence of the Episcopal Church and its jurisdiction in the Philippines, Aglipay's "religious Philippinism" was discarded and replaced by a statement of faith that very closely resembled that of the Episcopal Church in 1947. Meanwhile, in 1948, Episcopal bishops undertook the (subconditional) consecration of a number of bishops of the *Iglesia Filipina Independiente* in order to have them pass on these orders to the entire clergy of the church.[22] The church then made a successful attempt to establish communion with the Episcopal Church, the Churches of the Anglican Communion, and the churches in communion with these, including the Old Catholics (cf. Smit 2015 for an outline). This project was "spindoctored" and largely executed through the agency of the executive officer of the Anglican Communion, the American bishop, Stephen F. Bayne, who provided the various churches involved with the new doctrinal and liturgical books of the *Iglesia Filipina Independiente* and an accompanying request to establish communion with this church.[23] In this context, the Church of England consulted with the Old Catholic Churches of the Union of Utrecht, in particular with one of their leading theologians, archbishop Andreas Rinkel of Utrecht (1889–1979; archbishop: 1937–1970).[24] On the request of archbishop Michael Ramsey, the Church of England also forwarded the various documents of the *Iglesia Filipina Independiente* to Rinkel, requesting him to verify their doctrinal soundness. In his response, which was subsequently published as a formal statement of the Old Catholic Churches on the matter, Rinkel fully confirmed the catholicity of the *Iglesia Filipina Independiente*.[25] In 1964, this letter was published in the key Old Catholic academic journal, the *Internationale Kirchliche Zeitschrift*. Its relevant sections read as follows (in translation):

2. the statement of faith [of the IFI, pbs] is healthily catholic. We note that the "Tradition" is not sufficiently mentioned and that too little emphasis has been given to the fact that the Ph.I.C.C. [sc. Philippine Independent Catholic Church, pbs] strives to go back to the Church of the first millennium and the great Ecumenical Councils and that it wants to be the direct and legitimate continuation of the early Church. We have the impression that this omission is based on a scientific ignorance, because otherwise all the elements of faith of the undivided Church are mentioned (…).

It would have been better if the "filioque" clause (…) had been omitted and the confession itself had been identified with the words of the original Creed.

4. calling the sacrament of repentance a "confession of sins" is not exactly a correct interpretation of the sacrament of "metanoia" or "reconciliatio", since the confession of sins is only a part of the action.

…

6. from historical accounts we get the impression that the Ph.I.C.C. is still quite "Roman" in its liturgical practice and discipline, while at the same time it is theoretically, according to its confession and ideal, well Catholic.

We believe that there is nothing serious to prevent the Church of England from declaring the Ph.I.C.C. to be a true Catholic Church, a sincere witness

134 P.-B. SMIT

to the Gospel of the Lord and to the Church of the Apostles and of the first ten centuries, and from entering into a concordat of "full ecclesiastical communion" with that Church.

We would like to advise the Church of England as well as the Episcopal Church of the USA to intensify in some way the relations with the Ph.I.C.C., so that the Catholic line in the sense of the Old Ecumenical Church will be preserved and strengthened!

We are convinced that the Ph.I.C.C., which once strayed from its Catholic origin to the wrong path of liberalism and unitarianism—although not in its ordinary faithful—has found its way back to true Catholicism.[26]

A very similar letter, addressed by Rinkel to the *Obispo Maximo* of the *Iglesia Filipina Independiente* in that period, Isabelo de los Reyes, Jr., one of the many children of Isabelo de los Reyes, Sr., was published in the Philippines in the summer of 1964, stating:

Some days ago I received your valuable set of books, Missal, Ritual and Prayer Book, where for I bring you great thanks!

I am studying them and realize myself that your Church is in its faith and liturgy as sound Catholic as ours.

Therefore I am very thankful for the honor that we have met and made acquaintance at Canterbury and together took part in the consecration of the two Bishops of the venerable Anglican Church, expressing in this holy act at the same time our mutual catholicity and fellowship in the One, holy catholic and apostolic Church of Jesus Christ and His Apostles.

There have many things happened after the beginning of this century as your Church leaders made the first contact with our church in the person of Bishop Dr. Ed. Herzog of Switzerland. I think if in those days the status of your Church had been like now there would be already for many years a great bond of fellowship between our churches. Therefore we may hope that such a fellowship may be realized in our times.

I am glad to tell you that the two Iberian Churches (Spain and Portugal) in the persons of their bishops Molina and Dr. Pereira, already have asked us to realize an agreement with our Churches on the basis of full-communion like it is existing since 1931 between the Anglican Churches and our Old Catholic Churches. I suppose such an agreement might be also possible between us, although I know that the far distance might for the present such an agreement make only of theoretical significance, but nevertheless a great factor for the sake of unity. [27]

With this, Rinkel had, in the name of the communion of Old Catholic Churches, confirmed the full catholicity of the *Iglesia Filipina Independiente*. The somewhat disappointing conclusion of the first round of contact between Aglipay and Herzog 50 years earlier transformed into something that was a more satisfying encounter for the church leaders involved in the mid-twentieth century. The formal establishment of communion itself took place on 21 September 1965, when De los Reyes, Jr., and bishop Camilo Diel visited an International Old Catholics' Congress in Vienna and met there with the assembled Old Catholic episcopate.[28] Rinkel invited De los Reyes, Jr., to this meeting as follows:

> According to your letter of August 10, 1964, in which you are proposing a concordat of full Communion between your Church and the Old Catholic Churches of the Union of Utrecht, I may remember you that we intend to have our International Congress of Old Catholics in Vienna from Wednesday 22, September 1965 till Saturday 25 Sept. On the days Tuesday and Wednesday 21 and 22 Sept the Conference of Old Catholic Bishops will come together in Vienna, where the question of the concordat of full communion will be considered.
>
> We hope that it will be possible that your Church should send a representative with full authority, in the case that the Bishops' Conference might need your information for this *important* matter.
>
> I suppose that you have already received a general invitation to the Congress. With this letter I may invite your representative(s) on behalf of the Bishops' Conference.
>
> If it might not be possible for your representation to be already in Vienna at Wednesday, it will be, of course, possible to have a meeting with your representative during one of the days of the Congress itself, on 23, 24 or 25 September.
>
> The Bishops of the Intern. Conference look forward with great desire to meet your representative(s) and are praying that the proposed concordat may come into existence, and that we may thank God almighty with the words of the Psalm: Haec est dies quam fecit Dominus![29]

What had changed in the half-century between the breakdown of the correspondence between Herzog and Aglipay and the establishment of communion? It seems that two things were of the essence: (a) the introduction of a recognizably catholic statement of the faith and an appertaining kind of liturgy; (b) the recognition of the *Iglesia Filipina Independiente* by the Episcopal Church (USA) and subsequently by the various churches of the

136   P.-B. SMIT

Anglican Communion, which already were in communion with the Old Catholic Churches of the Union of Utrecht on the basis of the so-called Bonn Agreement of 1931. Of course, the one had much to do with the other: it was through Episcopal assistance that the *Iglesia Filipina Independiente* was able to restate its faith again and also to redevelop its liturgy—the ensuing documents have an undeniably Anglican flavor, therefore. All of this amounts to a different kind of negotiation of the relationship between autonomy and catholicity: the Iglesia Filipina Independiente retains its institutional autonomy yet allows itself to be influenced more strongly by other churches, which, in turn, leads to stronger ties with them. This was not without the risk of (renewed) ecclesial colonialism, yet also served to enhance the network of the church.

CONCLUSION

Conclusions on this case study can remain relatively brief. It is apparent that the anti- and postcolonial impulses that led to the establishment of the *Iglesia Filipina Independiente* also strongly influenced the manner in which this church related to other churches in ecumenical relationships. A strong emphasis on theological and ecclesial freedom is visible in particular—in the period studied here!—in the position of Gregorio Aglipay (with Isabelo de los Reyes, Sr., as a major influence). Attempts to subjugate the faith and order of the church by foreign churches, in this case, the Old Catholics, are rejected out of hand: religious independence as an expression and even a prefiguration of desired national independence are important too for this. This changes, in the context of the new and formally independent country of the Philippines, following the Second World War and in a period, in which the (American) Episcopal Church exercised considerable influence on the *Iglesia Filipina Independiente*. While retaining its institutional independence—the church never became part of the Union of Utrecht of Old Catholic Churches or, for that matter, the Anglican Communion—its identity was reconceptualized in such a manner that it could be recognized as fully catholic by Anglicans and, following on this by the Old Catholic Churches. Now, national and ecclesial independence could be combined with being church in a global catholic communion of churches.

NOTES

1. Cf. in general, Jan Visser "The Old Catholic Churches of the Union of Utrecht," *International Journal for the Study of the Christian Church* 3 (2003): 68–84; Urs von Arx, "The Old Catholic Churches of the Union of Utrecht," in *The Christian Church. An Introduction to the Major Traditions*, ed. Paul Avis (London: SPCK, 2002), 157–185; Peter-Ben Smit, *Old Catholic and Philippine Independent Ecclesiologies in History. The Catholic Church in Every Place* (Leiden: Brill, 2011), 50–69. Archival documents are kept in: Bischöflicher Archiv Bern (BABe), located in the ordinariate of the Old Catholic Church of Switzerland, and the IFI Archives, kept (when they were researched) in St. Andrew's Theological Seminary, Quezon City.

2. Cf. Dick Schoon, *Van bisschoppelijke Cleresie tot Oud-Katholieke Kerk. Bijdrage tot de geschiedenis* (2004), 18–30; Jan J. Hallebeek, "Questions of Canon Law Concerning the Election and Consecration of a Bishop for the Church of Utrecht: The Casus Resolutio of 1722," *Bijdragen* 61 (2000): 17–50.

3. Cf. in general and in comparison with other World Christian Communions, Dick Schoon, "The Union of Utrecht among the Christian World Communities: A Comparative Perspective," *Internationale Kirchliche Zeitschrift* 105 (2015): 91–103.

4. For an overview, cf. Wim H. de Boer and Peter-Ben Smit, *In necessariis unitas. Hintergründe zu den ökumenischen Beziehungen zwischen der Iglesia Filipina Independiente, den Kirchen der Anglikanischen Gemeinschaft und den Altkatholischen Kirchen der Utrechter Union* (Frankfurt: Peter Lang, 2012).

5. Cf. in general Ambrosio Manaligod, *Aglipay. Hero or Villain* (Manila: Foundation, 1977).

6. Cf. Gregorio L. Aglipay, "Nationalistic Education," *Philippine Herald*, July 6, 1923, 3; Smit, *Old Catholic and Philippine Independent Ecclesiologies in History*, 252.

7. Cf. Antje Griasch-Kirchofer, "Eduard Herzog: Katholik, Theologe, Bischof. Einführung in Person und Wirken," *Internationale Kirchliche Zeitschrift* 101 (2011): 148–155.

8. Gregorio L. Aglipay – Eduard Herzog, 30 October 1912 (BABe, AH 34, Philippinen).

9. Eduard Herzog – Gregorio L. Aglipay, 25 April 1904 (IFI Archives. OM 1.1. 1903–1910, Box 1, folder 2).

10. Eduard Herzog – Gregorio L. Aglipay, 4 June 1904 (IFI Archives. OM 1.1. 1903–1910. Box 1. folder 2).

138   P.-B. SMIT

11. International Bishops' Conference (IBC) of the Old Catholic Churches of the Union of Utrecht – Gregorio L. Aglipay, 1 September 1904 (IFI Archives. OM 1.1. 1903–1910. Box 1, folder 2).
12. IBC, 1904.
13. IBC, 1904.
14. Eduard Herzog – Gregorio L. Aglipay, 1 March 1905 (BABe, AH 85,158).
15. IBC Minutes of the meeting of 24 February 1905 (BABe. AH 34 [file Philippines]).
16. Cf. Wietse van der Velde, "The Declaration of Utrecht," *Internationale Kirchliche Zeitschrift* 105 (2015), 64–67.
17. Peter-Ben Smit and Wim H. de Boer, *"In necessariis unitas". Hintergründe zu den ökumenischen Beziehungen zwischen der "Iglesia Filipina Independiente", den Kirchen der Anglikanischen Gemeinschaft und den altkatholischen Kirchen der Utrechter Union* (Frankfurt: Lang, 2012), 135–137. – Full reference needed.
18. Smit and de Boer, *"In necessariis unitas"*, 135.
19. Smit and de Boer, *"In necessariis unitas"*, 137–138.
20. Gregorio Aglipay y Labayan, *Catequesis de la Iglesia Filipina Independiente por el Emmo. Sr. Gregorio Aglipay y Labayan, Obispo Máximo de la misma iglesia. – Aprobada por el Consejo Suprem de Obispos (no podrá ser ordenado de presbítero el que no apruebe saber esta catequesis)* (Manila, 1911).
21. Smit and de Boer, *"In necessariis unitas"*, 48.
22. Smit, *Old Catholic and Philippine Independent Ecclesiologies in History*, 315–319; Peter-Ben Smit, "The Road Towards Full Communion Between the Philippine Independent Church and The Episcopal Church," *Anglican & Episcopal History* 84, no.2 (2015): 1–45.
23. Cf. The Supreme Council of Bishops of the *Iglesia Filipina Independiente, The Filipino Missal (Book of Divine Office). The Liturgy for Holy Mass According to the Use of the Iglesia Filipina Independiente. Including the Pontifical, Ordinal and Articles of Religion* (Manila, 1961); The Supreme Council of Bishops of the *Iglesia Filipina Independiente, The Filipino Ritual* (Manila, 1961).
24. Cf. Fred Smit, "Andreas Rinkel (1889–1979)," in *Adjutorio Redemptoris. Dr. Andreas Rinkel. Aartsbisschop van Utrecht 1889–1979*, ed. W.B. van der Velde/F. Smit/P.J. Maan/M.J.IJ.W. Roosjen/J. Visser (Amersfoort: Centraal Oud-Katholiek Boekhuis, 1987), 3–197.
25. Ernst-Wilhelm Heese, ""Die Philippinische Unabhängige Kirche," *Internationale Kirchliche Zeitschrift* 54 (1964): 57–82 at 81–82.
26. Heese, "Die Philippinische Unabhängige Kirche," 81–82. German original: "2. Die Glaubenserklärung (der IFI, pbajs) ist gesund katholisch. Wir stellen fest, dass die «Tradition» nicht hinreichend erwähnt ist und dass zu wenig Nachdruck der Tatsache gegeben worden ist, dass die Ph.I.C.C. sich

7 PHILIPPINE, INDEPENDENT AND INTERNATIONAL: THE RELATIONSHIP... 139

bemüht auf die Kirche des ersten Jahrtausends und der grossen Ökumenischen Konzile zurückzugehen und dass sie die direkte und rechtmässige Fortsetzung der Alten Kirche sein will. Wir haben den Eindruck, dass diese Unterlassung auf einer wissenschaftlichen Unkenntnis beruht, weil sonst alle Glaubenselemente der ungeteilten Kirche erwähnt sind (...). 3. Es wäre besser gewesen wenn die «Filioque»-Klausel (...) ausgelassen und das Bekentnis selbst mit den Worten des ursprünglichen Glaubensbekenntnisses identifiziert worden wäre. 4. Wenn man das Sakrament der Busse ein «Bekenntnis der Sünden» nennt, so ist das nicht genau eine richtige Interpretation des Sakramentes der «metanoia» oder der «reconciliatio», da das Sündenbekenntnis nur ein Teil der Handlung ist....6. Aus historischen Darstellungen erhalten wir den Eindruck, dass die Ph.I.C.C. in ihrer liturgischen Praxis und Disziplin noch ziemlich «römisch» ist, während sie gleichzeitig theoretisch, nach ihrem Bekenntnis und Ideal, gut katholisch ist. 7. Wir glauben, dass es nichts Schwerwiegendes gibt, was die Kirche von England daran hindern könnte, die Ph.I.C.C. als eine wahre katholische Kirche zu erklären, als eine aufrichtige Zeugin des Evangeliums des Herrn und der Kirche der Apostel und der ersten zehn Jahrhunderte und mit dieser Kirche ein Konkordat über «volle kirchliche Gemeinschaft» abzuschliessen. 8. Wir möchten den Rat geben, die Kirche von England sowohl wie die Bischöfliche Kirche der USA mögen in irgendeiner Form die Beziehungen mit der Ph.I.C.C. intensivieren, damit die katholische Linie im Sinne der Alten Ökumenischen Kirche erhalten und gestärkt werde! 9. Wir sind überzeugt, dass die Ph.I.C.C., die einst von ihrem katholischen Ursprung auf den falschen Weg des Liberalismus und Unitarianismus abirrte – obwohl nicht in ihren einfachen Gläubigen – den Weg zum wahren Katholizismus zurückgefunden hat."

27. Andreas Rinkel – Isabelo de los Reyes, *The Christian Register* (Juli 1964), 8.
28. Smit and de Boer, *"In necessariis unitas"*, 113–121.
29. Andreas Rinkel – Isabelo de los Reyes, 16 June 1965 (IFI Archives (SATS), OM 1.5, Juni–Sept. 1965, Box 23).

PART II

Reappropriation, Resistance & Decolonization

CHAPTER 8

Indigenous Inculturation: A Hermeneutics of Serendipity

Antonio D. Sison CPPS

"The Philippines is in the Far East."

Far East.... I'm no longer sure when I first heard the geographical designation, but it was certainly the default cartography floating in the cultural waters I swam in as a child. The label was ubiquitous and unquestioned in Manila's urban landscape.

One day, I asked. "Far from what?" If language mirrors and shapes our perception of the world, then "Far East" ordains the asymmetric equation that my birth country is exotic and not familiar, socio-culturally backward and not fully civilized, very far indeed from the Euro-American geocultural axis that determines the rest of the world's value. As in many other academic disciplines, theology is not exempted from an intellectual cartography based on a favored center. It is fair to say that in current times, it is an issue of under-representation, not of conscious disregard. What is clear, however, are the implications of such an under-representation on the side of those who have been overlooked. For those who remain far

---

A. D. Sison CPPS (✉)
Catholic Theological Union, Chicago, IL, USA
e-mail: asison@ctu.edu

© The Author(s), under exclusive license to Springer Nature
Switzerland AG 2024
C. Lledo Gomez et al. (eds.), *500 Years of Christianity and the
Global Filipino/a*, Pathways for Ecumenical and Interreligious
Dialogue, https://doi.org/10.1007/978-3-031-47500-9_8

143

remain invisible, and their faint, distant voices easily and routinely drown in the resounding Western chorus of the proximate. Precisely because theology is contextual and perspectival, the direction of the hermeneutical current has been, by default, from the center to the edge.

Postcolonial theologians such as Laurenti Magesa of Tanzania have identified a recurrent Western "cultural possessiveness" of the Christian faith inflected in missionary history. They have called for the in-breaking of cultural viewpoints of many hues, each one deserving equal placement at the center of theological discourse. I seek to contribute to the re-direction of the flow of wisdom: theological reflection from the edge to the center.

Indigenous inculturation—"Indigenous" taken in the sense of "native to a local community"—is a departure from what appears to have been the emphasis on inculturation as a strategy employed by professional, and historically, Western, missionaries, to evangelize various cultures. It represents a postcolonial retrieval of the term's vital meaning in view of the creative and heroic efforts of Indigenous peoples who have, as artisans of their own histories and destinies, upheld the power of their own cultural genius while seeking religious synthesis. Scholars have emphasized the dialogical character of inculturation involving a two-way process of "insertion of the gospel into a particular culture" and "introduction of the culture into the gospel." This mutual assimilation was affirmed at the celebration of the fifth centenary of Christianity in the Philippines in 2021 at the Vatican.[1] Referring to the planting of the seeds of the gospel in the Philippines that began in 1521, Pope Francis proclaims: "You received the joy of the Gospel: the good news that God so loved us that he gave his Son for us...." In turn, the Philippines' Luis Antonio Cardinal Tagle responds: "The fact that the Christian faith was received by the majority of our people who gave it a Filipino character is also a gift of God...." Indeed, Filipino Indigenous inculturation is equally deserving of being celebrated as God's gift.[2]

In my work, I have chosen to use three interpretive lenses, rather like turning a prism at various angles to refract different facets of Indigenous inculturation: (1) "Hermeneutics of Suspicion"[3] to interrogate the relational asymmetries, cultural fallout, and religious implications that issued from a protracted experience of colonization; (2) "Hermeneutics of Appreciation"[4] to treasure hunt for the astonishing creativity, resilience, and tensile strength of Indigenous communities who have insisted on life though the sentence of colonial history had warranted death; and a new approach I introduce, (3) "Hermeneutics of Serendipity" to bring to light how unanticipated historical turns kindled ironic emancipatory currents that allowed for the flourishing of the Indigenous culture's creative genius in the face of colonial and postcolonial curtailment. It is this third methodological moment that I wish to draw attention to.

Derived from the Persian "Serendip," the classical name for Ceylon (now Sri Lanka), the term "serendipity" refers to "the faculty of making fortunate discoveries by chance or accident," and, also, the occurrence and instance of these discoveries.[5] As we know, serendipity has now gained wide currency as a descriptive term, from unexpected medical discoveries and scientific inventions, and even in popular culture.

In the contextual and postcolonial frame of my work, a hermeneutics of serendipity sheds light on how unanticipated turns of history kindled opportune moments that allowed for the flourishing of the Indigenous culture's creative genius notwithstanding the cruel sentence of colonial history. I understand serendipity as a conspiracy of grace; "Exodus moments" for those who have been enslaved, humiliated, and defaced by what is not-God.[6] Against insurmountable odds, the vanquished peoples were able to find unexpected creative spaces for themselves where they were afforded the chance to regain a sense of identity, dignity, and agency within the colonial crucible and its continuing trauma. Thus, grace could be found on "the edge of genius," in those fragile turns where surprising mystery and audacious creativity kiss one another.

Quiapo's Black Nazarene and the Hidden Reign of *Bathala*

With the intention of devoting deeper focus on Indigenous inculturation from a hermeneutics of serendipity, my postcolonial imagination is drawn to Quiapo's *Poong Hesus Itim na Narareno*—the Black Nazarene—and the phenomenal religious fervor in its orbit.

The Minor Basilica of the Black Nazarene, or simply, Quiapo Church, is centrally located in a busy section of old Manila, a strategic locale for a taste of the city's colonial past, and the nerve center for folk Catholic piety. Poetically, the church's original site was in Bagumbayan, present-day Luneta, where national hero José Rizal was executed.

The statue of the Black Nazarene arrived from Mexico in 1606 via the Manila-Acapulco galleon and came under the stewardship of an unnamed

Fig. 8.1 Quiapo Black Nazarene, 2014. Photograph courtesy of the author

Augustinian Recollect. In 1767, Archbishop of Manila Basilio Tomás Sancho Hernando authorized its transfer to Quiapo Church where it had since remained (Fig. 8.1). Aesthetically, the statue resembles typical Mexican *santos* of the period, and rooting further down the colonial lineage, the Catholic iconography of Spain. The special devotion to a dark-skinned Nazarene among followers who are predominantly *kayumanggi* or brown-skinned suggests a special rapport along racial lines, but this does not appear to be conclusive.[7] I propose that the unparalleled devotion to the Quiapo Black Nazarene is more than skin deep. It roots further down into the hidden regions of the Filipino psyche where the vanquished religious beliefs of a primal religion have beaten all odds, living-on organically in the rhythm of life of devotees. To validate this assertion, a trip to Quiapo is necessary for a closer look at the unique devotional practices simultaneously occurring in the church and its immediate environs.

I am inside Quiapo church one day in March. It is off-season for feasts and processions, the most significant of which falling on the first week of January leading to the feast day of the Black Nazarene on the ninth, and *Semana Santa*, particularly on Good Friday. For this first visit after years of being away as a US immigrant, I had intentionally chosen a placid period for a more attentive re-orientation and sense of space; nonetheless, devotional fervor is in the air this morning. A few devotees are penitentially walking on their knees down the center aisle to the altar—a long-held Quiapo tradition—and feeling through rosary beads on their fingers along the way. The Black Nazarene statue itself is enshrined at the center altar, a few feet above the tabernacle. I caught sight of two other life-size replicas; a few devotees had gathered around each of them, touching and hanging on to the statues prayerfully. Whether in quiet devotion on a regular day, or in a procession of millions during a major feast day, veneration and prayer by means of touch are the constant gestures of piety of the Quiapo Black Nazarene devotee.

There is good reason to argue that the practice has decisively Indigenous roots. The understanding of experience in terms of *pagdama*, or "felt experience," a sensuous perception that is naturally and firstly affective-intuitive, animates the Quiapo devotion. Filipino culture is so infused with *pagdama*, finding expression in anything from the imperative *pakiramdaman mo*, "feel what is happening," to the perceived manifestation of a departed loved one in *pagpaparamdam*, "to make one's presence felt," that De Mesa proposes the term "worldfeel" rather than "worldview" to describe the Filipino mindset.[8] The importance of *pagdama* in Filipino culture meaningfully informs our understanding of the materiality and tactility of the Quiapo Black Nazarene phenomenon; immediate contact with concrete representations of the divine is the way by which the Filipino devotee feels God's grace coming closer to home. In discussing folk Catholicism, De Mesa identifies "body language" as its main mode of communication:

> This form of religiosity, while not devoid of verbal and written language to express itself, communicates to a great extent corporeally. The physical coming together, "walking" on one's knees, lighting candles, wiping statues

148   A. D. SISON CPPS

with one's handkerchief, joining or "watching" a procession, going on a pilgrimage, are all expressions of faith in folk Catholicism. Prayer is uttered by the body in its various movements and gestures ... Words are powerful means of communication. But corporeal expressions may communicate more than words.[9]

The ancient value of *pagdama* and its material-tactile expression in the Quiapo Black Nazarene devotion open a virtual window into Filipino primal religion, where the dualistic curtain that separates the sacred from the profane was yet to be drawn back. History and anthropology from a Western perspective have often characterized the precolonial worship life in the islands as a form of "animism"; this is a term we will bypass for its condescending connotations, its tendency to undervalue Indigenous religious practices as irrational, incoherent, and superstitious.[10]

In Filipino primal religion, visible objects of nature represent levels of reality that go beyond materiality; they were inhabited by spirit beings not readily seen by the naked eye, but whose presence was felt. These nature spirits controlled the shifts in natural phenomena—fluctuations in weather, the bounty or shortfall of crop harvests, and such—and also acted upon the ebb and flow of everyday human existence. The cultural-religious schema was based on the belief in a supreme deity by the name of *Bathala*, whose divine intervention held sway in the *kapalaran* or destiny of human beings. This core belief anchored and animated the religious customs of the community so that one's plans and decisions in life rose or fell on the basis of *panalangin* or prayer that comes from *kagandahang loób*, the beauty of one's authentic inner self (as against *sama ng loob*, the debasement of one's inner self). A host of lesser nature gods and spirit beings known as *diwata* inhabited the created world alongside human beings, they lived in the celestial bodies, mountains, seas, and rain forests. For this reason, the sun, moon, and stars, as well as certain animals, trees, and rock formations, were believed to be enchanted; they were approached with reverence and wonderment. This explains why the Spaniards did not find significant built structures for worship in the archipelago as they did in their previous encounters with Mesoamerican religious culture. Neither did the island culture reflect the neighboring religious cultures of Southeast Asia such as Indonesia, Thailand, and Cambodia, with their ornate Buddhist-Hindu temple complexes. The Filipino primal godhead *Bathala* and the host of *diwata* did not require such human-made structures for their cult; the entire created world was their dwelling place, nature itself was their temple. It comes as no surprise then that the iconoclastic compulsion of the Spanish missionaries led to the wanton desecration and destruction of sacred forests and mangroves.[11]

The presence of the *diwata* was also mediated through images carved out of wood or stone known as *anito* (in lowland Luzon/Tagalog region)[12] who served as portals between the material world and the spirit world. The precolonial Filipinos believed that their departed ancestors had joined the realm of the spirits and could then be venerated as *anitos*.

It is not difficult to imagine how the Spanish Christianizing campaign found convenient analogues of the Catholic cult of the Saints in the Indigenous practice of venerating *anitos*. The Italian scholar Antonio Pigafetta, who traveled with Fernando Magallanes as his official chronicler, documents the near seamless transfiguration of an Iberian icon into a primal *anito*. In his account of the 1521 baptism of Rajah Humabon in Cebu, the statue of the *Santo Niño*—the child Jesus dressed in the finery of a European prince—so captivated the local chief's wife that she shed copious tears and begged to be baptized; she was christened as "Juana" in honor of the Castillan queen. Juana wanted the Catholic statue to replace her deities so Pigafetta presented it to her as a gift. However, an astonishing counter-phenomenon took over when the Magallanes expedition came to an end. Juana's *Santo Niño* found a niche in the pantheon of *diwatas* and assimilated with ease into primal religion so that by the time the subsequent expedition led by Miguel Lopez de Legazpi arrived 44 years later, folklore had already woven around the imported statue, essentially converting the child Jesus into a rain god.[13] The history of the *Santo Niño de Cebu* is noteworthy for shedding light on the tensile strength inherent in Indigenous Filipino religious culture—resilience in response to the allurement of a foreign religion, and incorruptibility in upholding the primal religion of the forebears.

The ability to sustain an inclusive both/and continues to animate contemporary Filipino folk Catholicism. As I had noted in another study, the Quiapo Black Nazarene devotion is a prime example of a religious double belonging.[14] While the statue and the activities surrounding its cult constitute part of the didactic, poetic, and worship life of a Catholic basilica under the aegis of the Archdiocese of Manila, the actual cultic practice as expressed in grassroots piety is descended from Indigenous cultural and religious values. We can glean further validation for this by looking into the Quiapo Church milieu.

Stepping out of the church, the street vendors positioned at the perimeter of Plaza Miranda, the open public area fronting the building, come to view. *Nazareno* replicas, rosaries of all colors and materials, scapulars, votive candles, novena booklets, and the usual religious paraphernalia associated with traditional Roman Catholic devotions are the more obvious articles available for purchase. A number of the vendors also sell para-religious articles that blur the line between officially sanctioned Catholic devotion and piety of a different sort. Known in Tagalog as *anting-anting*, these articles come in the form of amulets, pendants, humanoid figures, animal bones, and talismans, usually embossed with eclectic wordings (mostly in Latin) and symbols borrowed from Christianity; these are worn by adherents to ward off evil spirits, spells, or misfortunes. Although there are undeniable Christian elements in such articles, the *anting-anting* has its origins in primal religion. In the Filipino creation mythos, it was believed that after Bathala created the universe, he delegated human affairs to the *diwata* who were to serve as his mediators. But not all spirits were benevolent like the *diwata*; malevolent ghouls and monsters such as the horrifying *aswang* co-inhabited the world and were set to afflict human beings with all sorts of bodily and spiritual torments. To protect themselves from such attacks, ancient Filipinos kept *anting-anting* close to their persons, maintaining close physical contact with the sacred object, as a concrete means to repel real and perceived danger.

In the period of the Spanish conquest, the continued use of *anting-anting* was a form of native resistance, a way by which Filipinos asserted their sense of agency and empowerment in a subversion of the Spanish colonial hierarchy that had forcibly relegated them to the lowest rung of the sociopolitical pyramid where they were denied access to power. Rebel leaders of the Philippine revolution, notably Andres Bonifacio and the *Katipuneros*, were known to have worn *anting-anting* to protect them from the superior firepower of the Spanish forces.[15] *Anting-anting* made them feel connected to a higher power, emboldening them in the fight for freedom. Like the veneration of *anitos* that became convenient analogues of the cult of the saints, *anting-anting* analogously fit hand-in-glove into the traditional Catholic preoccupation with religious articles and relics, ultimately, liquefying the demarcation between Spanish Catholicism and Filipino primal religion.

Retracing my way to the Quiapo Church entrance, it is hard to miss the presence of elderly and middle-aged women seated on plastic stools at the edges of the nave; some praying the rosary, others, attentively conversing with individuals. These Quiapo mainstays are known as *magdarasal* or intercessors, prayer-women who listen to the everyday concerns that burden devotees, offer prayers on their behalf, and provide practical counseling when needed. Like any legitimate ministry, these services are free of charge, although "donations" left to the discretion of the devotees are welcome.

It is interesting to note that the work of the *magdarasal* has some points of overlap with the pastoral function of the ordained priesthood, and from a spatial consideration, it is the first line of shepherding available to devotees since the *magdarasal* are more accessibly positioned by the church entrance and not behind the altar like the presiding priest. In effect, the Quiapo prayer-women appear to have become alternative pastors as the ordained priests take on an ever-increasing load of sacramental assignments.

I have argued elsewhere that there is reason to posit a link between the Quiapo *magdarasal* and the ancient *babaylan*[16]—the priests or shamans of the Filipino primal religion, who, unlike the Catholic priests, were almost exclusively female (marginally, there were also priests who were male transvestites or *bayok*). The *babaylanes* served as the divinely chosen human mediators between the *diwata* and the worshipping community, who also looked up to them as wisdom figures. The priesthood of the *babaylan* had no precursor in colonial Catholicism since the ministerial role of women within the hierarchical order, that of the professed religious sisters was subordinate to the authority of the clergy; their ministries did not and could not overlap. Ultimately, the Spanish friars considered the *babaylanes* to be prime targets for Christianization. Those who eventually acquiesced to conversion were stripped of leadership roles and given a demotion; they were made to become the assistants-at-large in the parish, assigned to perform subsidiary tasks such as flower arrangements at the altar, and administrative help for processions.[17] If, as previously discussed, the ingress of colonial Catholicism had not been able to completely obliterate Filipino primal religion and its expression in folk Catholicism, could the ancient *babaylan victis*, the banished Indigenous woman-priest, not have risen as well in the form of crypto-resistance in the person of the self-ordained Quiapo *magdarasal* and her priestly ministry? Considering our fairly consistent postcolonial thesis that Spanish Catholic culture and Indigenous Filipino religious culture co-exist in a dynamic and tensive middle field, we can persuasively affirm that the Quiapo *magdarasal*, in her discretional

152 A. D. SISON CPPS

leadership and uniquely feminine priestly ministry, may well be the *babaylan rediviva*.

Finding an afterlife in grassroots piety and often undetected, primal religious expressions in the Quiapo universe are caught up in a dance of mutuality with sanctioned devotional practices. On the level of a public transcript is official Catholicism, which is framed by church teachings and doctrines as shepherded by the Philippine Church hierarchy; on the level of a hidden transcript is folk Catholicism, an Indigenous crypto-resistance that nurtures and keeps alive its own semi-autonomous rituals within the four walls of the Catholic church.

SERENDIPITY: A CONSPIRACY OF GRACE

To preach the salvific gospel of Jesus Christ to the natives so that their souls may be delivered from the clutches of Satan, this was the nucleus of the Spanish colonial mission to the Philippines, as it was in their previous expeditions in the Americas. This conviction arose from a national messianic complex where the Spaniards had appropriated for itself the image and likeness of authentic humanity; in their own eyes, they were God's new chosen people. While relativizing the arduous journey to the Philippines with a more expansive horizon, not to mention fueling missionary zeal, the audacious self-definition and conviction, for the most part, put blinders on the eyes of the colonizers. The Spaniards demonized the primal religion of the islands, refusing to acknowledge its life-giving dimensions for a possible dialogue with Christian culture. We find validation in Phelan who notes:

> Christianity was presented to the infidels as not a more perfect expression of their pagan beliefs but as something entirely new. Any resemblance between the two religions was dismissed as a diabolical conspiracy in which the devil deceived unbelievers by mimicking the rituals and beliefs of Christianity. The policy of breaking abruptly with the pagan past explains the vigor with which temples and idols were destroyed. The Spanish missionaries have been much criticized for this practice.[18]

However, Phelan qualifies his argument with a caveat—the Spanish missionaries were not modern anthropologists, thus, their indictment of "pagan beliefs" as the devil's work was consistent with their religious-cultural purview. While it is true that a synchronic critique of the Spanish

8 INDIGENOUS INCULTURATION: A HERMENEUTICS OF SERENDIPITY   153

colonial mindset would not constitute fair critical judgment of a people of their own times, I cannot help as a native informant to ask why, on the basis of the same argument, the essential principles of preaching the *evangelion*, well chronicled not just in the seminal example of Jesus Christ but also in the apostolic and Pauline traditions, were scarcely brought to bear in the case of the Spanish missions. Certainly, it was within the realm of the possible for the Spanish missionaries to draw inspiration from the open-minded and respectful dialogue with non-Christian cultures exemplified by Paul's discourse at the Areopagus (Acts 17:16-34) where he prudently built a bridge between the Christian God and the Athenians' "Unknown God." The sterling examples of Jesuit missionary Matteo Ricci (1552–1610) who tread on a similar conciliatory pathway in China, as well as his confrere Roberto de Nobili (1557–1656) in India, clearly demonstrate that a dialogical approach to culture was not a proprietary option confined to the modern mindset.

It is not unreasonable to appraise the Spanish colonizers' misplaced appropriation and monopolization of the identity of the favored "good self" that became a license for their dominance and aggression toward the Indigenous culture (inversely judged as primitive and deficient, a problem to be solved), as an internalization of their historical oppressors, the Moors, who occupied the Iberian Peninsula for eight hundred years.[19] Even in the aftermath of the *Reconquista*, the Spaniards had so thoroughly internalized their erstwhile invaders that the latter's "ghostlife" continued to operate in them; they replicated and projected the modus of militancy and antagonism from which they themselves had previously suffered.[20]

Be that as it may, are there extant resources we can turn to that may point to some Spanish attempt at cultural dialogue in the Christianizing mission to the Philippines? The *Doctrina Cristiana en Lengua Española y Tagala* ("The Christian Catechism in Spanish and Tagalog") of 1593, the first book printed in colonial Philippines, is outstanding in its effort to make basic church teaching understandable to Indigenous Filipinos. The Dominican authors and editors wrote the document in three ways: in Spanish, in the Tagalog vernacular transliterated into Roman letters, and, remarkably, in Tagalog written in the Indigenous alphabet known as *baybayin*. De Mesa has dedicated a study on the *Doctrina Cristiana*'s rendering of the Lord's Prayer, describing it as an "eloquent testimony" of the respect and appreciation of Indigenous culture by the first generation of Spanish missionaries.[21] A longer view, however, would indicate that it was also in the very hands of the Spanish missionaries that subsequent centuries would see the grievous displacement and eventual obliteration of *baybayin* in favor of the Roman text.[22] This would lead to the gradual forced extinction of the Indigenous Filipino culture's system of writing, and in a sense, its voice.

I would venture to say that if there is one group that must be given due recognition for the Indigenous/Catholic double belonging in the Philippines, it is the Filipinos themselves. The tensile strength inherent in Filipinos allowed for a double-edged response—resilience and incorruptibility—to the overtures of Christianization, ultimately raising questions as to whether the Indigenous culture was truly Christianized, or Spanish Catholic culture, "Filipinized." [23] The Indigenous response to Spanish Catholicism may be described as "sagacious," a sustained exercise of astute discernment that worked to ensure the survival and continued flourishing of primal religion in the eye of the colonial typhoon and through the post-colonial aftermath. I previously discussed how sagacity works as a necessary companion piece to serendipity; I cannot overemphasize the importance of this connection because the movement of the unexpected figured convincingly in the religious history of colonial Philippines. The fortuitous turns in the Spanish colonial mission formed an uncanny "conspiracy of grace" that incrementally set the stage for the possibility of a religious double belonging. Some of these deviations include the following:

- The Spanish settlers expected to gain full governance and control of the colony as they did in Mexico and Peru, but the geography of the Philippines, consisting of more than 7100 islands of mountains, rain forests, and coasts, extending to about 1100 miles north to south (1770 km), made consolidated Spanish oversight and control of parishes and mission outposts exceedingly difficult, if next to impossible. This offered creative spaces for Filipinos to interweave elements of Indigenous worship with Catholic practices.
- In their push to preserve Spanish ecclesiastical dominance, the friars of the eighteenth and nineteenth centuries worked to bar Indigenous Filipino clergy from leadership roles in the parish. Filipino priests were subjected to racial discrimination; they were judged to be immoral, disloyal, and intellectually inferior. As it happened, the lack of local pastors deprived the colonial mission of potential "bridge-figures" in the work of catechetical and pastoral instruction, consequently, weakening Spanish control; the very opposite of the planned objective.

8 INDIGENOUS INCULTURATION: A HERMENEUTICS OF SERENDIPITY   155

- The religious *fiesta*, the lively and colorful celebration of Catholic seasons and feast days of patron saints, was the Spanish strategy to bait resistant Filipinos to re-settle in the *cabecera* complex, the centralized town capital designed to facilitate the exercise of colonial and ecclesiastical authority over the Indigenous communities. What they had not anticipated was that the *fiesta* would serve as a semi-autonomous zone that allowed for the flourishing of *communitas*, and the liquefying of boundaries that distinguished between what was perceived as the sacred (Iberian Catholicism) and the profane (Filipino primal religion).

The desired outcome of the Spanish mission was to convert the Philippines to the true Catholic religion, and in the process, obliterate the primal religion of the Indigenous population. Serendipitously for the Filipinos, the unexpected turns worked in their favor, making room for primal religion to co-mingle with Spanish Catholicism in a double belonging. Phelan describes the providential outcome succinctly: "It meant that the Filipinos absorbed as much Catholicism as they could easily digest under prevailing conditions but not as much as the Spaniards would have wanted them to do."[24]

The notion of serendipity shares resonances with the Tagalog *Bahala na*, an expression signifying resignation of one's fortunes to fate. In its original rendering in ancient *baybayin* script, the word *Bahala* is identical with *Bathala*, the godhead of primal religion. In its fuller, original sense as *Bathala na*, the expression means entrusting one's life prospects to God. Presuming its rootedness in the core value of *kagandahang loób* (the beauty of one's authentic inner self), *Bathala na* could be understood to connote that when you sincerely put your heart and soul into an endeavor, the grace of *Bathala* will cause the cosmic forces to align in your favor in ways you do not necessarily expect.[25]

From the Filipino cultural perspective, the unexpected turns in the Spanish colonial enterprise vis-à-vis the sagacity of the Indigenous community were the conditions for *Bathala*'s conspiracy of grace. Though the facts warranted annihilation, Filipino primal religion defied all odds and flourished.

Closer to Home

In 2019, I was in Manila to participate in the overnight vigil leading to the *Traslacion,* the annual procession of the seventeenth-century icon of the Black Nazarene. The procession is one of the world's largest religious gatherings with attendance running in the millions (Fig. 8.2).

Standing among bare-footed pilgrims, young and old, the majority of them bearing the heavy cross of poverty and illness, was a humbling experience that moved me to tears. This was a gathering of the crucified peoples who came here seeking a little *more* love, a little *more* clemency, a little *more* compassion because they could no longer subsist on the scraps that fall from Jesus' table. *Mauwi sa amin ang kaharian mo,* make your Kingdom come home to us … that is the hope, that is the mission. Like a typhoon of religious fervor, the sea of pilgrims began the 20-hour procession. In this liminal interlude, the devotees claim Jesus as their own; the cross-bearing Nazarene is no longer the imported Spanish icon elevated on a marble altar in a state of inertia, he becomes the people's *Poong Hesus Itim na Nazareno,* the inculturated Savior-figure who can be touched and felt by the Filipino community of faith.

Fig. 8.2 (*Santa Santita* © 2004 Unitel Pictures)

8 INDIGENOUS INCULTURATION: A HERMENEUTICS OF SERENDIPITY 157

* The essay is based on the author's book *The Art of Indigenous Inculturation: Grace on the Edge of Genius* (Maryknoll, NY: Orbis Books, 2021)

NOTES

1. "Livestream: Pope Francis Leads Mass for 500 Years of Christianity in the Philippines." *GMA Integrated News* (March 14, 2021). Online. https://www.youtube.com/watch?v=Ev2qtrndAZo.
2. More than half-a-century ago, Vatican II's *Lumen Gentium*, Dogmatic Constitution on the Church, had already offered fertile ground from which cultural mutuality and dialogue may germinate: "Since the Kingdom of God is not of this world, the Church or People of God, in establishing that Kingdom, takes nothing from the temporal welfare of the people. On the contrary, it fosters and takes to itself, insofar as they are good, the ability, riches, and customs, in which the genius of each people expresses itself." Vatican Council II, *Lumen Gentium* 2.16. *Libreria Editrice Vaticana* (November 21, 1964). Online. www.vatican.va.
3. For a pioneering application of a hermeneutics of suspicion in theology, specifically feminist biblical scholarship, refer to Elizabeth Schussler Fiorenza, *Bread Not Stone: The Challenge of Feminist Biblical Scholarship* (Boston: Beacon Press, 1984).
4. José M. de Mesa is noted for his employment of a hermeneutics of appreciation for Filipino Theology. He asserts, "What is sorely needed is a hermeneutics of appreciation which methodologically highlights the positive in the culture." See *Why Theology Is Never Far from Home* (Manila: De La Salle University Press, 2003), 120. For fuller treatment, see Chap. 4 "A Hermeneutics of Appreciation: Approach and Methodology," 111–195.
5. Coined by eighteenth-century English political writer and publisher Horace Walpole, "serendipity" is drawn from *Peregrinaggio di Tre Giovani Figliuoli de re di Serendippo* ("The Pilgrimage of the Three Young Sons of the King of Serendip"), a collection of tales first compiled and published by Michele Tramezzino in 1555 from an Italian translation of an ancient Persian story by a certain M. Cristoforo Armeno. Theodore G. Remer, ed. *Serendipity and the Three Princes: From the Peregrinaggio of 1557* (Norman, OK: University of Oklahoma Press), 1965.
6. A suggestion that serendipity has to do with the mysterious movement of the transcendent rather than with mere happenstance can be appreciated in John Paul Lederach's work on mediation and reconciliation. Proposing "divine naiveté" as a dimension of an imaginative, serendipitous approach to peace-building, he notes, "*Divine* pointed to something transcendent,

158 A. D. SISON CPPS

unexpected, but that led toward insight and better understanding." *The Moral Imagination: The Art and Soul of Building Peace* (Oxford and New York: Oxford University Press, 2005), 115.

7. Another dark-skinned statue from the Manila-Acapulco galleon, the seventeenth-century *Nuestra Señora de la Paz y del Buen Viaje* (Our Lady of Peace and Good Voyage) enshrined in the city of Antipolo, also has a following, but nowhere near the vicinity of the devotion to the Quiapo Black Nazarene. The olive-skinned *Santo Niño de Cebu*, the statue of the child Jesus brought by the Magallanes expedition in 1565, does have a certain degree of prominence in Catholic piety, but so does the pale-skinned *Nuestra Señora del Santísimo Rosario de Manaoag* (Our Lady of the Most Holy Rosary of Manaoag), another seventeenth-century icon, whose delicate Eurasian features are etched in ivory.

8. De Mesa, *Why Theology Is Never Far from Home*, 85–86. De Mesa is careful to point out that *pagdama* does not necessarily eschew the rational-cognitive, but harmonizes with it in an "integrated sensing." See page 82.

9. De Mesa, *Why Theology Is Never Far from Home*, 82. In Quiapo, the corporeal expressions of devotion often come in the form of personal and collective sacrifice, e.g., the devout practices detailed by De Mesa. Robert J. Schreiter equates sacrifice with communication with God, of which human words often prove impoverished. "Sacrifice tries to speak where human words do not reach far enough." *In Water and in Blood: A Spirituality of Solidarity and Hope* (Maryknoll, NY: Orbis Books, 1988, 2006), 12.

10. Daryl Wilkinson offers an on-target description of the problematic connotations that bedevil the term, "…animism is an analytical operation that we do, not a type of religion that indigenous people hold to. It involves taking a non-concurrence of Western and non-Western practices as a starting point and using that dissonance, a dissonance that we call 'animism,' as a way of highlighting the presence of some not-as-yet understood difference or alterity. Animism therefore is not a shorthand for what Indigenous people are really doing, but more a statement to the effect that we don't know what they're doing, but we know we certainly wouldn't do it." "Is There Such a Thing as Animism?," *Journal of the American Academy of Religion*, vol. 85 (June 2017): 306. For Wilkinson's fuller treatment that includes a critical analysis of "new animism," the scholarly efforts to emancipate the original term from its Eurocentric, colonialist, and evolutionist moorings, see the entire article in the same, 289–311. Agbonkhianmeghe Orobator offers an incisive critical analysis of animism from an African postcolonial perspective. *Religion and Faith in Africa: Confessions of an Animist* (Maryknoll, NY: Orbis, 2018), *xviii*.

8 INDIGENOUS INCULTURATION: A HERMENEUTICS OF SERENDIPITY 159

11. John Leddy Phelan notes, "In the Philippines there were no temples to demolish. But sacred groves were cut down by zealous Spanish religious who were determined to break the magic sway such groves exercised over Filipinos." *The Hispanization of the Philippines: Spanish Aims and Filipino Responses, 1565–1700* (Madison, WI: University of Wisconsin Press, 1959, 2011), 54.

12. The Cebuano/Visayan term for a carved idol is *tao-tao,* while *anito* denotes "sacrifice." William Henry Scott, *Barangay: Sixteenth-Century Philippine Culture and Society* (Quezon City: Ateneo de Manila Press, 1994), 83, 86. To avoid confusion on the part of the reader, I have decided to use the Tagalog term *anito* as a more general appellation to refer to statues and concrete images of lowland Filipino primal religion.

13. Filipino national artist and writer-historian Nick Joaquin notes, "A ritual developed among its worshippers: a wild hopping dance to drums which, as the Pit Señor, survives to this day in the folk homage to the *Santo Niño,* as the rainmaking ritual of bathing the image survives in the fluvial procession." *Culture and History* (Pasig City: Anvil Publishing, 1988, 2004), 104–105.

14. Antonio D. Sison, "Afflictive Apparitions: The Folk Catholic Imaginary in Philippine Cinema," *Material Religion* 4, vol. 11 (December 2015): 422–442.

15. Dennis Santos Villegas, *You Shall be as Gods: Anting-Anting and the Filipino Quest for Mystical Power* (Quezon City: Vibal Foundation, 2017), 27–28.

16. Sison, "Afflictive Apparitions," 429–432.

17. Z. A. Salazar, *Ang Babaylan sa Kasaysayan ng Pilipinas* (Quezon City: Palimbagan ng Lahi, 1999), 3–4. The venerable Ignacia del Espiritu Santo, an eighteenth-century Filipina *beata* who defied the authority of the Spanish king to form a community that would flourish to be the first Indigenous religious order of women had to work surreptitiously at the margins of an androcentric, patriarchal, and colonial Catholic hierarchy. Even the likes of her could not have possibly engaged in a ministry that overlapped in the slightest with the powerful ordained priesthood, let alone positioned herself at the church frontlines. After all, Ignacia bore on her shoulders the "double crosses" of being a woman and being an *India.*

18. Phelan, *The Hispanization of the Philippines,* 53.

19. The Benedictine Abbot Juan de Salazar drew parallels between the Spanish and Hebrew peoples and asserts, "...in the law of grace the Spanish people is God's favourite and is the one which has especially succeeded to the place held by the chosen people...." He further likened the Spaniards' experience of the Moorish occupation to the Israelites' captivity in Egypt and described Philip II—the namesake of the Philippines—as a second

Solomon. *Spanish Polity* (1619) as quoted and referenced in D.A. Brading, *Mexican Phoenix: Our Lady of Guadalupe: Image and Tradition Across Five Centuries* (Cambridge: University of Cambridge Press, 2001), 33.

20. This argument aligns with Paulo Freire's diagnosis of the contradictory mindset of peoples who have experienced oppression: "They are at one and the same time themselves and the oppressor whose consciousness they have internalized." *Pedagogy of the Oppressed*, 30th-anniversary ed., trans. Myra Bergman Ramos (New York and London: Continuum, 2000), 48.

21. De Mesa, *Why Theology Is Never Far from Home*, 74–75.

22. The intuitive phonetic nuances of *baybayin* would prove to be a serious issue for Spanish ears, for this reason, the missionaries would judge the Tagalog script to be deficient in translating Christian doctrine. Vicente L. Rafael identifies the bone of contention—"the tendency of *baybayin* to suspend sense in favor of sensation." *Contracting Colonialism: Translation and Christian Conversion in Tagalog Society Under Early Spanish Rule* (Durham and London: Duke University Press, 1992, 1993), 53. To put it another way, *baybayin* was not the script to codify a worldview, rather, it was meant to serve as the written expression of a worldfeel.

23. Phelan dedicates an entire chapter to this religious-historical phenomenon, arguing: "As it happened, the Filipinos endowed certain aspects of the new religion with a ceremonial and emotional content, a special Filipino flavor, which made Catholicism in the archipelago in some respects a unique expression of their universal religion. In this process of 'Philippinizing' the major role belonged to the Filipinos. They showed themselves remarkably selective in stressing and de-emphasizing certain features of Spanish Catholicism." *The Hispanization of the Philippines,* 72.

24. Phelan, *The Hispanization of the Philippines,* 89.

25. For my discussion of *Bathala Na* in relation to the postcolonial filmmaking philosophy of Filipino national artist Kidlat Tahimik, see Antonio D. Sison, *Screening Schillebeeckx: Theology and Third Cinema in Dialogue* (New York and London: Palgrave Macmillan, 2006), 50–51.

CHAPTER 9

Decolonizing the Diaspora through the Center for Babaylan Studies

Leny M. Strobel

My name is Elenita Fe Luna Mendoza Strobel. I am Kapampangan from the Philippines. I left my homeland in 1982 and settled on Wappo, Southern Pomo, and Coast Miwok Lands. It took almost three decades to understand what settler colonialism and native genocide have done to the Land and the Peoples of the Lands I currently live in. With this realization, I acknowledge my own entanglement with this History and affirm my commitment to build relationships with the local indigenous communities so that with their permission, I may nurture and feed an indigenous future with them.

This chapter was originally published on the author's personal weblog without citations (https://lenystrobel.medium.com/decolonizing-the-diaspora-through-the-center-for-babaylan-studies-d74e4bb56616). The author hopes that this chapter with included citations in this anthology can be a rich primary resource material for decolonizing and indigenous studies in the Philippines but also can point to other resources for further research in these areas

---

L. M. Strobel (✉)
Center for Babaylan Studies, Sonoma State University, Sunnyvale, CA, USA

© The Author(s), under exclusive license to Springer Nature Switzerland AG 2024
C. Lledo Gomez et al. (eds.), *500 Years of Christianity and the Global Filipino/a*, Pathways for Ecumenical and Interreligious Dialogue, https://doi.org/10.1007/978-3-031-47500-9_9

161

162 L. M. STROBEL

I begin with this land acknowledgment because colonialism is all about the Land.[1] Dispossession of the Land led to the dispossession of our minds and bodies, our languages, our indigenous wisdom, knowledge, and practices, and especially our indigenous spirituality. This is what the violence of colonization has done to us as a people. National Artist for Literature N.V.M. Gonzalez said we developed a type of cultural Alzheimer's disease.[2] Filipino theologian Melba Maggay says we were culturally circumcised.[3] Other scholars have said we developed a split self and as a society there is now a great cultural divide between the masses and the educated elites.[4] Vicente Rafael writes of *white love*—of Filipinos falling in love with their colonizers.[5] Not only were we dispossessed of our Lands, we were also dispossessed of our innate indigenous wisdom and knowledge that sustained us for thousands of years before the colonial era.[6]

Our neocolonial educational system did not teach us to understand how colonialism works; how the modern paradigms of development and progress have tricked us into submission and we bought into the beliefs that the West, represented by the holy trinity of the International Monetary Fund (IMF), World Bank (WB), and World Trade Organization (WTO), would solve the problems of poverty, inequity and inequality, and injustice. Modernization programs via loans from the IMF and WB were poured into "developing" countries after World War II. By the 1980s the structural adjustment programs that were imposed on "third world" countries resulted in loans that the local economies could not afford to repay, sinking them deeper into debt.[7] In the Philippines, the Marcos government and succeeding leaders saw overseas Filipino workers as domestic assets that can be exported, and their remittances would shore up the homeland economy and pay the interest on these loans. Philippines is still paying for useless debts accrued during Marcos, Sr's presidency.[8]

I was in the Philippines doing research on the babaylan tradition in the early 2000s when I watched televangelist Mike Velarde of the El Shaddai movement[9] preach to his congregation at the Luneta Park. He asked everyone to wave their white handkerchiefs as if they had secured their visa to work overseas and fulfill the gospel's "great commission" (Matthew 28:16–20). He then asked those without visas yet to keep attending his church so that they may be equipped to serve God's mission as domestic workers overseas.

Framing the export of Overseas Filipino Workers as fulfilling a Christian mission may be a salve for the pain of separation and leaving loved ones, but it also bypasses structural analysis of the system of exploitation put in place by economic globalization. In this regard, the religious movement does not consider itself responsible for that need for analysis and critique. Before I left the homeland, I was working for a multinational corporation and before that, I worked for a World Bank funded project. Young and miseducated, I did not know about the development paradigm that plunged the Philippines and the global south into unpayable debts and failed infrastructure projects (for example, the Bataan Nuclear plant) and the corruption schemes that lined the pockets of Marcos and his cronies. I am from the generation who were taught instead to internalize what President McKinley said about colonizing us—that we were a people who needed to be uplifted and Christianized.[10] Missionaries and Peace Corp Volunteers were part of this civilizing project along with Hollywood movies, textbooks, and popular American culture.

Fast forward to the twenty-first century. Millions of us Filipinos left our homeland in search of jobs to feed our families. In search of opportunities to better our lives. We acquired skills to fit into the global demand for caregiving, nursing, domestic work, construction, manufacturing, and entertainment, to name a few. Rachel Parreñas, a Filipino American sociologist, calls us "the servants of globalization."[11]

By the time I arrived in the United States in 1983, the prevailing condition among Filipinos in California was marked by the stark differences between the post-1965 Filipino immigrants and the earlier Manong generation, made up of mostly single, male workers from rural areas in the Philippines. The newly arrived immigrants were educated, English speaking, and many came from the middle class and urban centers. The colonial mentality of new immigrants made them assimilate; discouraged their children from keeping their native languages; and led them to deny their ethnic roots and identities.[12]

As a newly arrived immigrant, I came to realize that my neocolonial education made me identify with the United States, but the United States didn't identify with me. Thus began my journey of understanding why, after finally arriving to live in the white man's house, I was still unhappy. I returned to school and I began to unpack, unlearn, and sought to undo the epistemic, psychic, and ontological violence of colonialism in my life.

In California, we joined a Presbyterian church and it became the site of my first experience of cultural and racial invisibility in the church. I felt "othered," exoticized, and racialized and there was no space in the mostly white, middle-class, suburban congregation for the questions I posed. I eventually left. Today, when I am asked whether I am still a Christian my response is: I am who I am today because of all that I have been in the past and that includes being raised a Methodist. I have even reclaimed and honored the Catholic faith of my mother before she converted and married my dad. And I told my father, a Methodist pastor, as he lamented my being unchurched, that I am an even better person and Christian today than I ever was. I have also taught my university students that if they choose to be Christian then they should be the best Christian they can be; be the best Muslim, be the best Buddhist, and be the best atheist they can be because at the heart of religion is the experience of wholeness, divine presence, and transcendental unity. This is what indigenous peoples mean when they talk about the sacred and holy in Nature, of God in nature. The Aetas say *Lamuwan Kata* to express this sacred wholeness.[13] The indigenous peoples on Turtle Island have many different words for this experience as well. They embody this through their relationship with the Land and all the created beings—human and non-human, visible and invisible.

Amidst this spiritual and cultural upheaval, I found the work of Virgilio Enriquez,[14] the father of Filipino indigenous psychology. His framework and his articulation of Filipino indigenous core values: *Kapwa, Pakikiramdam, Kagandahang Loob, Dangal, Paninindigan*—stirred up something deep in my soul. I listened to this stirring and followed the trail that was set before me. Although there were earlier scholars and revolutionaries who wrote about Filipino national and cultural identity, it was not until the 1970s when a Filipino indigenous psychology was articulated as a part of the movement of "indigenization from within" in the social sciences. Zeus Salazar, a contemporary of Enriquez, also created his *Pantayong Pananaw* ("for us" and "by us" perspectives) while Filipino historians forged a *Filipinolohiya*—all of these developments were part of indigenization that emerged from within the rubble of colonial constructions—the anthropologists, missionaries, linguists, historians who defined the Filipino through their own colonizing lenses. The indigenization from within discourses at first attempted to respond to these outsider perspectives and then evolved to a de-centering of the imperial gaze and focus on the assertion of a Filipino indigenous cultural identity.[15] Although diasporic identity remains a contentious and challenging issue, the assertion of a decolonized and indigenized position has taken hold in certain sectors in the diaspora led by the Center for Babaylan Studies (CfBS).

I researched the cultural identity formation of post-1965 Filipino Americans and this work turned into my doctoral dissertation that offered a framework and process of decolonization for post-1965 Filipino

Americans. I wrote, published, and started teaching at a public state university in California. Soon my first book, *Coming Full Circle*,[16] was being used as a textbook by other educators, culture-bearers, immigrants, mental health workers, and diasporic Filipinos who resonated with the framework of decolonization that I proposed. List-serves as online communities began to form to discuss this book and later to discuss the history of the babaylan tradition.

A Babaylan Studies Center and Babaylan Conferences

The babaylan has many names because there are over 170 linguistic communities in the Philippines and every community has a "babaylan" person who is recognized and acknowledged as having the power to mediate between the seen and unseen realms; is able to bring the lost soul home; propitiate the spirits; and heal the body. The work of Alicia Magos [17] in *The Enduring Ma-Aram Tradition* and Carolyn Brewer's[18] *Holy Confrontations* were key texts among others that drew my attention to the history of the babaylan along with conversations, conferences, and online discussions in the babaylan list-serve on Yahoo groups in the 1990s.

By the time the Center for Babaylan Studies was created in 2009, the decolonization path was already well paved by our ancestors, by our indigenous *kapwa*, by babaylans, by *katipuneros*, by peasant revolutionaries, by our grandmothers and grandfathers, our aunties, and uncles. But their stories were often not told or barely included in the neocolonial American patterned educational system.

In 2005, at a Filipina Women's Network Conference at New York University, Sr. Mary John Mananzan, our keynote speaker, challenged us to organize an international Babaylan conference. Between 2005 and 2009, I spent summers in the Philippines attending Babaylan Conferences and Kapwa Conferences and, together with another colleague, I brought two groups of teachers to Mindanao on Fulbright Hays Grants that immersed us in K–12 schools, indigenous communities, and schools of living tradition in Mindanao. In these sojourns, Fr. Albert Alejo, our Fulbright host, introduced us to "modern babaylans" and culture-bearers from various indigenous communities in Mindanao.

The dream of organizing an international Babaylan Conference was born in 2006 at a Kapwa Conference at the University of the Philippines in Iloilo organized by the Heritage and Arts Academies led by Kidlat Tahimik and Katrin de Guia. At the heart of this conference was the circle of indigenous elders who shared their dreams and visions for the future. The conference attendees were also encouraged to form circles and "dream" together. The handful of diasporic Filipinos from the United States gathered and the question that emerged from the gathering was: *how do we bring this gathering to the United States?* Thus, began the dream of the Center for Babaylan Studies.

In 2010, the first Babaylan Conference was held at my institution, Sonoma State University. We expected that maybe a 100 people would register. On the day of the conference, 250 attended. We presented keynote talks on Kapwa psychology,[19] indigenous healing arts, indigenous oral traditions, and culture-bearing practices among social justice, mental health, cultural arts, and political activists and practitioners. Rituals and ceremonies provided platforms for diasporic Filipinos who practiced *hilot*, traditional tattooing, *kulintang* music, and Maranao dances, among many other indigenous Filipino practices. Apo Reyna Yolanda, a babaylan from Cagayan and Celyo Rizal, and her entourage of five, attended and did ritual and ceremony with us. After the conference, Reyna Yolanda, following directions from her spirit guides, traveled to the other sites in the Bay Area, New York, and Alaska to perform rituals and offer prayers to the Lands and the peoples she visited with support from the attendees of the Babaylan Conference.

In 2011, we organized a symposium/retreat on "Decolonization as a Sacred Path" with Felipe De Leon, Jr., then Commissioner of the National Commission for Culture and the Arts (NCCA) as a key resource person. This was an invitation-only retreat to participants from the first conference to deepen our knowledge of Filipino indigenous knowledge systems and practices and to build relationships with each other that would soon form the core leadership of the Center for Babaylan Studies.

In 2008 and 2012, Filipinos from Canada and the United States attended the Kapwa Conferences at the University of the Philippines, Iloilo, and University of the Philippines, Baguio, organized by the Heritage and Arts Academies of the Philippines, led by Katrin de Guia and Kidlat Tahimik. These conferences centered on the sharing of knowledge and practices from the indigenous communities who were represented (*Cordillera, Panay Bukidnon, Talaandig, T'boli, Manobo,* and others). At these conferences, we started to build relationships with indigenous communities, elders, and youth. Many diasporic folks from the United States and Canada have been maintaining these connections since then through the Center for Babaylan Studies or through their own initiatives.

Storytelling is central to the indigenous tradition. In 2013, the second Babaylan Conference focused on the Power of Mythic Story, and we invited indigenous filmmakers Kidlat Tahimik and Kanakan Balintagos, and Grace Nono as our key resource speakers, along with the Tribal Chairman of the Federated Indians of Graton Rancheria, Greg Sarris, who is part Filipino and teller of the creation stories of the Pomo and Coast Miwok peoples, the land on which the conference was held. Our vision was to strengthen the foundation of Filipino Indigenous Knowledge Systems and Practices in the diaspora. Kapwa psychology,[20] mythic stories, dream work, rituals, and ceremony continued to shape our vision.

In 2015, we realized that we needed to address the relationship between indigenous spirituality and Christianity, and we did this at the symposium/retreat in Ohio with Fr. Albert Alejo as our keynote speaker. He talked about the apologies of the various orders of the Catholic Church to the indigenous peoples they colonized.[21] He also encouraged the attendees to nurture their indigenous spirituality even while practicing their faith traditions. At this gathering, Methodist clergyperson, Carmen Scheuerman, also gave a talk about Aeta spirituality and what she learned from the Aeta community that made her aware of the colonizing aspects of missionary work.[22] Other speakers like Natividad Delson and Grace Nono talked about how they question, reflect on, and integrate their Catholic devotion with indigenous spirituality.[23] We also supported the building of a traditional Ifugao Healing Hut led by Ifugao mombaki, Mamerto Tindongan.[24] This Ifugao Hut has since moved to Santa Fe, New Mexico, United States and is on the land under the indigenously informed stewardship of Carol Gamiao Wallace.

In 2016, the third Babaylan Conference was co-hosted by Kathara Society in the unceded Coast Salish territory in British Columbia.[25] At this conference we engaged with the native communities for the first time as we realized the importance of revitalizing indigenous traditions on lands where diasporic Filipinos are settlers. We were welcomed and hosted by the Chief of the Squamish peoples. At this conference, our invited babaylans from the Manobo tribe were possessed by spirits during a ceremony. Ifugao mombaki Mamerto Tindongan and other helpers talked with the spirits and asked for dispensation and requested the spirits to leave the conference in peace. This teachable moment was a turning point in many ways for CfBS. This is the first time that CfBS raised the question of what it means to identify not as immigrants but as settlers. Settler colonialism made us aware of the violence of native genocide and the ongoing trauma of dispossession.[26] The spirit realm, as the source of indigenous spirituality, was present and at this gathering, we recognized the need for us to learn how to integrate the seen and unseen realms.[27] We became cognizant of the violence of the civilizing processes that disconnected us from the spirit world. Looking at settler colonialism provided a different lens that felt more resonant with our decolonization practices.

In 2019, the fourth Babaylan Conference focused on the conundrums of doing indigenous work in fractured settings. We asked ourselves how we might learn from the Land and unlearn Empire; how do we reclaim our indigenous mind; how can we learn how to dwell in place; how can we develop allyship and kinship with our indigenous Kapwa on Turtle Island. Kapwa Collective, our local partners on the ground, co-hosted the conference with us in the Wahta Kanien'keha:ka Territory, also known as Toronto.[28] The theme of this gathering emerged from the critique of the use of the term "babaylan" and "indigenous" in diasporic communities as being merely symbolic and therefore further contributing to the silencing and marginalization of the living babaylans in the homeland.[29] We continue to wrestle with these "callouts" and one of our elders, Lily Mendoza, thus published a response:

> The question of what is honorable and mutually empowering in regard to relating to our Indigenous Kapwa is multilayered and complex even for our fellow Filipinos in the homeland. How much more so then for those of us in the diaspora? The work itself is fraught—one that we're having to do on other peoples' stolen land and all while we're enveloped in highly-technologized environments with only fragments of memory and extant stories from our family lineages and those of others as clues to lead us. We do what we can to learn and listen. We wrestle with the complexity. We build accountable relationships.
>
> It is crucial not to approach this sacred work with rigid missionary certainty—which kills the Indigenous Spirit in the very attempt to champion it. In reflecting on the "inevitable human problem of tribalism and the tragic results of ethnocentricity," Martin Prechtel warns us of the dangers of a preoccupation with purity. He writes, "[A] people's deep attachment to their homeland and customs is necessary, wonderful and life-giving, but should never be allowed to fuel a destructive chauvinism that excludes the rest of the world's love for its own life and land." Indigenous recovery requires Indigenous largesse of spirit in the very act of pursuing such a love.[30]

In our decade-long engagement, we sowed the seeds of decolonization and later our decolonial practices. We learned how to embody Kapwa. We are reconnecting with our ancestors and ancestral wisdom. We are learning how to dwell in place. Greg Sarris says that we can become indigenous to a place if we learn the history of the Lands and the peoples where we have settled; when we learn to live in mutual respect with all the beings that live on the Land.[31] For me as a settler, this has meant learning about the history of native genocide in California and in the US...and how this genocide connects to the colonization of my homeland.[32]

Our publications, mine and my sister's (Leny Strobel and S. Lily Mendoza), *Coming Full Circle* (2001), *Between the Homeland and the Diaspora* (2002), *Babaylan: Filipinos and the Call of the Indigenous* (2010), and *Back from the Crocodile's Belly* (2015), resonate with many readers to this day.[33] *Coming Full Circle* became a textbook in ethnic studies courses; the *Babaylan* book brought together culture-bearing and indigenous storytellers from the homeland and the United States; the *Back from the Crocodile's Belly* book, co-edited with Lily Mendoza, followed up with a focus on the importance of the indigenous paradigm in speaking back to the colonizing logic of modernity. Lily Mendoza's book, *Between the Homeland and the Diaspora*, historicizes and bridges the discourses on Filipino identity in these two places.

Today, there is a visible decolonization movement in the diaspora—in the Bay Area, New York, Los Angeles, Chicago, Toronto, and Vancouver. The use of social media by second and third-generation Filipino Americans, Filipino Canadians, and other diasporic Filipinos elsewhere who are reconnecting with their indigenous roots and ethnic heritage—is fueling the movement. Indigenous practices like *Batok, baybayin, laga* weaving, *kulintang, kali,* and martial arts, plant medicine, *hilot,* and other indigenous-inspired healing practices are flourishing. It remains to be seen whether the related social and economic entrepreneurship emerging from this cultural resurgence in the diaspora is going to be transformative in the sense of connection, engagement, and support for indigenous concerns and communities in the homeland. I am aware that it is not enough for young people in the diaspora to be interested in indigenous forms and practices although this is usually an entry point as they begin to reconnect with their Filipino heritage. Sometimes this reconnection is critiqued as nostalgic and romantic, even appropriative and extractive—and such critiques are necessary in order to deepen and sharpen our discernment as we decolonize and re-indigenize.

This is what I call the indigenous turn in our decolonization movement in the diaspora. These practices, in the form of indigenous-themed cultural productions and revival and reclamation of indigenous practices, signal a movement that points to our native brilliance and intelligence. Today social media facilitates conversations between homeland and diasporic communities; they discuss pre-colonial and indigenous beliefs; there is a growing interest in mythic storytelling and the revitalization of languages. Many are using podcasts and webinars to deepen connections and build virtual communities. But it is on the ground, in local and placed-based practices of dwelling and community building where *Kapwa* and *Ginhawa* thrive.[34]

CfBS has mindfully been working to model sustainable relationships with indigenous communities in the homeland; for decades we have nurtured our connections to the Heritage and Arts Academies of the Philippines (HAPI), Tao Foundation, Balay Patawili (Panay Bukidnon), LASIWWAI (T'boli weavers), and others. What we need at this time is to document our learnings in these collaborations and develop an archive that can be passed on to the younger generation.

CONCLUSION

The decolonization movement in the diaspora is located in the cracks of a civilization that is beginning to crumble under the weight of its own worldview that desacralized the Earth. We are struggling to make sense of the five centuries of Christianization and how this is complicit in the perpetuation of white supremacy and racism. We are recovering our indigenous spirituality that is embedded in our cultural DNA—this spirituality that comes alive as we root ourselves in Lands that were stolen by empire and where the history of genocide haunts us. We are trying to remember the indigenous roots of the Christian tradition itself. I see a younger generation of diasporic Filipinos reaching out for a sense of belonging to a homeland where the memories of the homeland are only remembered in fragments and glimpses of stories and practices. They are also wanting to learn how to be indigenous to the places where they have settled on Turtle Island. We join a global movement of spiritual refugees seeking sanctuary; learning what it means to build an indigenous future.

Fr. Albert Alejo once told me: Leny, do not worry about indigenous peoples disappearing; all it takes is for one of them to have a dream and everything becomes alive again. We are still dreaming. In articulating the aspiration to build an indigenous future, we turn to our mythic stories to inspire our creative imagination. In Herminia Coben's, *Verbal Arts of Philippine Indigenous Communities*, I was able to cull fragments of the story of *Mungan*, the first Babaylan of the *Manobo* peoples in the Agyu epic.[35] I meditated on this story and asked Spirit to tell me what the message might be for someone like me. I then wrote a piece and shared her story with other young Filipino American artists/culture-bearers and posted it on medium.com.[36] The story of Mungan has traveled outside of the homeland. Stories are alive and when they enter our bodies, we are made alive anew. Since then, her story has inspired a children's book and a dance creation (dance as medicine, dance as embodiment). I would like to close this chapter with a letter to Mungan telling of her story:

Dear Mungan,

To the people of Bukidnon, you are the first babaylan. You are the true heroine of their beloved epic, Ulaging, even though the honor goes to Agyu and his brothers.

Your husband shunned you because of your leprosy but your brothers-in-law were kind to you.

They took turns carrying you on their backs on the long journey from the sea to the mountain top of Mt. Kitanglad.

Conflict has come to the shore so your people had to flee to the mountains.

One day you told them that you didn't want to slow them down anymore.

So they built you a hut and went on their journeys, returning on occasion to bring you food and gifts.

In truth, they returned for instructions from you because you alone knew where they should go and how they can find food for their bodies and souls.

You taught them the virtue of sharing food. You told them that even if the meat is no bigger than a baby's fingernail, that they must share it.

You taught them that they can achieve immortality without first experiencing death.

You taught them that they can attain the highest state of spirituality by abstaining from material wants and sustenance.

You taught them that they will lose their fear of famine and starvation.

You taught them that their bodies will shine like gold in the end carried on a magic flying ship to the world beyond the skies.

One day, just before dawn, you began to beat your gong. Slowly at first, then building up to a rhythmic trance.

It soon became light and just before the sun rose, you looked up with amazement...

The sky in the east looked like polished metal.
You kept on beating your gong but never took your eyes off the Sun.
Gazing at it without blinking.
You were amazed that the sound of the gong now sounds like laughter and it became so loud.
When you took your gaze off the sun to look around you, all the weeds and wild plants around your hut turned to gold.
And the leprosy slowly left your body.
The Sun—source of magical power.
The blinding light heals the leprous body of the gong-playing maiden.
Your eyes became the conduit for the energy that would humanize the gong with the gift of laughter.
Having conquered disease and death, now your scabs have turned into mountain rice birds; they flew away but one of the birds returned to you with a vial of coconut oil, a gold-striped betel nut, and *pinipig* from the first harvest.
Mungan, all around you shines with golden light.
In rapture and spiritual ecstasy, your body is radiant with transcendent light.
To Lena, the first brother, you gave the first betel nut of immortality.
And as he chewed, his speech became different.
He began to speak in the words of ancient poetry.
Dear Mungan, your quest for a safe homeland for your people.
In the time of war and violence.
Your desire to lead them to paradise.
To found a new community.
To lead people in times of trouble.
Is hidden in the words of the ancient epic.
In these millennial dreams.
At the heart of it is the desire for Oneness.
People of all creeds, ethnicities belong to one extended family.
Who will attain immortality without passing thru death.
Dear Mungan,
I beseech you now to shine your light upon us.
Teach us how to gaze at the Sun without blinking.
So, too, may our bodies shine like gold.
So, too, may everything around us shine like gold.
We are your descendants in the here and now.
Flying ships carried us not quite to the world beyond the skies.
But to this continent.
Where we are tracing your steps.
Where we are building our huts.

Where we are forging Oneness.
Where we are forging Wholeness.
Shine your light upon us, Mungan.
Shine your light upon us.

The story of Mungan[37] lives among the Talaandig, Matigsalugs, Kirintekens, Ilianen-Manobo, Kulamanen, Bukidnons, Higaunon, Livunganen-Arumanen Manobo of Central, Northern, and parts of Western Mindanao. Her story lives within the bigger story of Agyu, the epic's hero. As a sacred chant, the *ulahing* is believed to be never-ending as long as there are storytellers and singers/chanters. I want to keep Mungan alive in each of us.

In 2018, I stepped down from the leadership of CfBS and continuing as an elder, I have been focusing on "walking my talk"—if becoming indigenous again means reconnecting with the Land, it has made me want to focus on learning how to dwell in place—on Wappo, Pomo, Coast Miwok lands…I am currently facilitating three small ongoing cohorts of folks who are working on apology and forgiveness, healing, and repair of the trauma caused by native genocide in California and Turtle Island. We join a growing movement around the world of decolonizing, decolonial practice, the resurgence of indigenous ways of being and knowing…in the midst of what they call the great turning, the sixth extinction …

It's all about the Land…
Decolonization is not a metaphor.[38]

NOTES

1. I learned this from Leanne Betasamosake Simpson, *As We Have Always Done: Indigenous Freedom through Radical Resistance* (Minneapolis: University of Minnesota, 2021).
2. This is an anecdote from one of our conservations. See also N.V.M. Gonzalez, *The Novel of Justice: Selected Essays (1968-1994)* (Mandaluyong City, Philippines: Anvil Publishing, 2016).
3. Melba Maggay, *A Clash of Cultures: Early American Protestant Missions and Filipino Religious* Consciousness (Mandaluyong City, Philippines: Anvil Publishing, 2011).
4. Cf. Leny Mendoza Strobel, "A Personal Story: Becoming a Split Filipina Subject," *Amerasia Journal* 19, no. 3 (1993): 117–30.

5. Vicente Rafael, *White Love and Other Events in Philippine History* (Durham: Duke University Press, 2000).
6. For further discussion, please see Leny Mendoza Strobel, ed., *Babaylans: Filipinos and the Call of the Indigenous* (Santa Rosa, California: Center for Babaylan Studies, 2010); S. Lily Mendoza and Leny Mendoza Strobel, eds., *Back from the ∆Crocodile's Belly: Philippine Babaylan Studies and the Struggle for Indigenous Memory* (Manila, Philippines: University of Santo Toman Publishing House, 2015).
7. Eric Toussaint, "The World Bank and the Philippines", *Committee for the Abolition of Illegitimate Debt* Series: 1944-2020, 76 Years of interference from the World Bank and the IMF (Part 11) (17 April, 2020), https://www.cadtm.org/The-World-Bank-and-the-Philippines
8. Eduardo C. Tadem, "Philippines: The Marcos debt", *Committee for the Abolition of Illegitimate Debt* (5 November 2018), https://www.cadtm.org/Philippines-The-Marcos-debt
9. http://www.seasite.niu.edu/tagalog/modules/modules/philippinereligions/el_shaddai_profile.htm
10. See Mckinley in Mendoza, "Back from the Crocodile's Belly" in this anthology.
11. Rhacel Salazar Parreñas, *Servants of Globalization: Migration and Domestic Work*, 2nd ed. (California: Stanford University Press, 2015).
12. On colonial mentality, see Cristina Lledo Gomez, "Bangon na, Pinays Rise Up" in this anthology.
13. Methodist Pastor Carmen Schueurman, a Kapampangan, works with the Aeta congregation. She taught us about Aeta spirituality at the 2015 CfBS Symposium/Retreat on Indigenous Spirituality and Christianity held in Ohio, United States. To learn more about the Aetas and their spirituality, see Rudolf Cymorr Kirby Martinez, "The Health Ritual of "Pag-aanito" among the Aetas of Nabuclod, Pampanga, Philippines, *Journal of Health and Caring Sciences* 1, no. 1 (2019): 41–47
14. Cf. Virgilio Enriquez, *From Colonial to Liberation Psychology: The Philippine Experience* (Diliman, Philippines: University of the Philippines Press, 2008) and other works by Enriquez.
15. For the development of *Sikolohiyang Pilipino*—from Filipino values determined from a colonial gaze to values reinterpreted out of a resistance to colonialism, cf. Narcisa Paredes-Canilao and Maria Ana Babaran-Diaz, "Sikolohiyang Pilipino: 50 Years of Critical Emancipatory Social Science in the Philippines (*Sikolohiyang Pilipino: 50 Taon ng Kritikal at Mapagpalayang Agham Panlipunan sa Pilipinas*), in *Handbuk ng Sikolohiyang Pilipino (Handbook of Filipino Psychology)* Bolyum 1: Perspektibo at Metodolohiya (Vol 1: Perspectives and Methodology) ed.

Rogelia Pe-Pua (Diliman, Quezon City: The University of the Philippines Press, 2018), 200–15.

16. Leny Mendoza Strobel, *Coming Full Circle: The Process of Decolonization Among Post-1965 Filipino Americans* (Quezon City, Philippines: Giraffe Books, 2001).

17. Alicia Magos, *The Enduring Ma-Aram Tradition: an Ethnography of a Kinaray-a village in Antique* (Quezon City, Philippines: New Day Publishers, 1992).

18. Carolyn Brewer discusses the process of extermination of the Babaylans in the first 100 years of colonization. Cf. Carolyn Brewer, *Holy Confrontation: Religion, Gender and Sexuality in the Philippines 1521-1685* (Institute of Women's Studies, St. Scholastica's, Philippines, 2001).

19. Katrin De Guia, *Kapwa: The Self in the Other: Worldviews and Lifestyles of Filipino Culture-bearers* (Pasig City, Philippines: Anvil Publishing, 2005).

20. Cf. Virgilio G. Enriquez, "Sikolohiyang Pilipino: Perspektibo at Direksyon (Filipino Psychology: Perspectives and Direction)" in *Handbuk ng Sikolohiyang Pilipino* Bolyum 1, edited by Pe-Pua, 19–31.

21. For Albert Alejo's recent discussion on church apologies to indigenous peoples, go to the web conference recording of *500 Years of Christianity and the Global Filipin@: Postcolonial Perspectives* at the Berkeley Center for Religion, Peace & World Affairs, Georgetown University (Feb 8-9, 2022), https://berkleycenter.georgetown.edu/events/500-years-of-christianity-and-the-global-filipin

22. To learn more about the Aetas and their spirituality, cf. Martinez, "The Health Ritual of "Pag-aanito" among the Aetas of Nabuclod.

23. For more on Natividad Delson, cf. Lisa Suguitan Melnick, "A Healer's Path Comes Not By Chance" (March 14, 2016), https://www.positively-filipino.com/magazine/a-healers-path-comes-not-by-chance. For Grace Nono, cf. Karina Lagdameo-Santillan, "The Three faces of Grace Nono: Filipina performing artist-ethnomusicologist-culture facilitator" (July 3, 2021), https://www.pressenza.com/2021/03/the-three-faces-of-grace-nono-filipina-performing-artist-ethnomusicologist-culture-facilitator/

24. On Mamerto Tindongan and his sculptures, cf. https://mamertotindongan.wordpress.com/about/

25. https://www.katharasociety.org/

26. On settler colonialism, cf. Patrick Wolfe, "Settler colonialism and the elimination of the native," *Journal of Genocide Research* 8, no. 4 (2006): 387-409; Patrick Wolfe, *Settler Colonialism* (New York: Continuum, 1999); and Edward Cavanagh, ed., *The Routledge Handbook of the History of Settler Colonialism* (Oxfordshire, England, UK: Routledge, 2020).

27. For more on the transpersonal worldview of the Filipino, that is the cultural acceptance of the unseen world, even after attempts by colonizers to

demonize and denigrate this cultural belief, cf. Jaime C. Bulatao S.J., "Filipino Transpersonal World View", in *Handbuk ng Sikolohiyang Pilipino (Handbook of Filipino Psychology)* Bolyum 2: Gamit (Vol 2: Application) edited by Rogelia Pe-Pua (Diliman, Quezon City: The University of the Philippines Press, 2019), 43–47.

28. For more on the *Kapwa Collective*, cf. *https://kapwacollective.tumblr.com/*
29. On the dangers of decolonizing from urban settings while unintentionally silencing the voices of Babaylans on the ground, see Grace Nono, *Babaylan Sing Back: Philippine Shamans and Voice, Gender, and Place* (Ithaca, New York: Cornell University Press, 2021). For a brief summary of this complexity, cf. in this anthology, Cristina Lledo Gomez, "Bangon na: Pinays Rise Up."
30. S. Lily Mendoza, *On "Filipinos" and the Question of the "Indigenous"* (Nov 22, 2020), https://mendoza-91197.medium.com/on-filipinos-and-the-question-of-the-indigenous-27ccdf96c321. For the quote from Martin Prechtel, cf. Martín Prechtel, *Rescuing the Light: Quotes from the Oral Teachings of Martín Prechtel* (Berkeley, California: North Atlantic Books, 2021).
31. Greg Sarris' keynote talk at the 2016 Babaylan Conference: https://www.youtube.com/watch?v=EU2n-5_JueE
32. The United States' formal colonization of the Philippines began after the Indian Wars and many soldiers were deployed to the Philippines in the aftermath.
33. Strobel, *Coming Full Circle*; Strobel, ed., *Babaylans*; Mendoza and Strobel, eds., *Back from the Crocodile's Belly*; S. Lily Mendoza, *Between the Homeland and the Diaspora: the Politics of Theorizing Filipino and Filipino American Identities: a Second Look at the Post Structuralism-Indigenization Debates* (New York: Routledge, 2002).
34. More recently I have written (with Professors Violeta Bautista and Elizabeth Marcelino of UP Psychology Dept) about Ginhawa as the Filipino concept of wholeness and wellbeing. Cf. Leny Strobel, *GINHAWA/ BREATH: Wholeness and Wellness in the Filipino and Filipino American Experience* (Oct 11, 2021), https://lenystrobel.medium.com/ ginhawa-breath-wholeness-and-wellness-in-the-filipino%C2%B9-and-filipino-american-experience-e4346b2164f8
35. Herminia Menez Coben, *Verbal Arts in Philippine Indigenous Communities: Poetics, Society, and History* (Manila; Ateneo De Manila University Press, 2010).
36. Leny Strobel, "Mungan: The first babaylan," (Jan 1, 2020), https://lenys-trobel.medium.com/mungan-the-first-babaylan-6cd70bdfa1bf

37. I culled this version of the story from the work of Herminia Coben in Coben, *Verbal Arts in Philippine Indigenous Communities.*
38. Eve Tuck and K. Wayne Yang, "Decolonization is not a metaphor," *Decolonization: Indigeneity, Education & Society* 1, no. 1 (2012): 1–40. See also Melissa Spin, https://radicaldiscipleship.net/2015/05/28/unmothered-in-halves-from-the-center-of-babaylan-studies-conference/—Melissa Sipin.

CHAPTER 10

Back from the Crocodile's Belly: Christian Formation Meets Indigenous Resurrection Redux

S. Lily Mendoza

PERTURBATIONS

It was the late 1970s and I was in the heat of my Christian missionary zeal. My experience of becoming "born-again" in my first year in college had all the marks of radical conversion: a new worldview, a different motivation for living, and a new sense of identity and destiny as a "child of God." Not only did it have the effect of turning my whole life around, it also gave me the sense of having figured out life and the universe, much like finding the

---

An earlier version of this chapter was published in *HTS Theologiese Studies/ Theological Studies*. Vol 73 no3 (2017), a4660. https://doi.org/10.4102/hts. v73i3.4660

S. L. Mendoza (✉)
Oakland University, Rochester, MI, USA

Center for Babaylan Studies, Sunnyvale, California, USA
e-mail: mendoza@oakland.edu

© The Author(s), under exclusive license to Springer Nature Switzerland AG 2024
C. Lledo Gomez et al. (eds.), *500 Years of Christianity and the Global Filipino/a*, Pathways for Ecumenical and Interreligious Dialogue, https://doi.org/10.1007/978-3-031-47500-9_10

180 S. L. MENDOZA

Holy Grail. Or so I thought. One day, to my utter disbelief and consternation, I got word of a former nun—then an up-and-coming scholar/anthropologist—purportedly having "left the faith" and having become a "non-believer." "She's turned pagan" was the report—after immersing herself in a tribe in the Northern Philippines that she had been studying.

I know I should have been curious, but my own measly exposure to native practice offered little motivation. In one *cañao* ceremony[1] that I once witnessed among the mountain peoples of the Cordilleras—one involving the ritual slaughter of a pig, a priest-like figure in colorful woven g-string, head gear, and tooth and bone necklace adornment uttering strange incantations, along with the rhythmic dancing to the beat of gongs—what came up for me were hair-raising conjurations of the demonic and of unclean spirits—things we Christians were taught never to dabble in. (I forget now the occasion of why I was there in the first place, but I made sure to sit as close to the outer edge of the circle as possible and not partake of the sacrificed meat, fearing spiritual contamination.) Though perturbed by news of the ex-nun/scholar turning "pagan," the certainty of my well-(in)formed "armor" of Christian apologetics kept me from probing further. After all, when you've already found the Truth (truth with a capital "T"), what else is there to know? In my mind, the only way to explain such anomalous turning is that "she's gone off the deep end"—much like the sort of "going native" phenomenon so well-documented in the anthropological literature. Little did I know that, decades later, the same would be said of me: "Lily has gone off the deep end!"

When the European colonists came to the Americas, one of the challenges they had to face was the phenomenon of defections among the ranks of the army soldiers to the native communities. Throughout the seventeenth through to the nineteenth centuries, American historian David Stannard recounts how it is that "while almost no Indians voluntarily lived among the colonists, the number of whites who ran off to live with the Indians was a problem often remarked upon,"[2] belying Thomas Paine's lament that "[I]t is always possible to go from the natural to the civilized state, but it is never possible to go from the civilized to the natural state."[3] The phenomenon of hundreds of ("civilized") British army soldiers choosing to stay and live with the "pagan" native communities whom they were supposed to vanquish so worried the early British settlers (Benjamin Franklin, among them) that they criminalized such by instituting court martial for anyone caught defecting.

Christian Formation and Root Disconnection

In a 2013 book I co-edited, titled, *Back from the Crocodile's Belly: Philippine Babaylan Studies and the Struggle for Indigenous Memory*, tracking some of this perturbation in my own life, I wrote:

> A story is told that when the Spaniards (who colonized the Philippine islands beginning in the 16th century) began to understand the power and potency of the babaylan,[4] they so feared the latter's spiritual prowess that they not only killed many of them but in some instances, fed them to crocodiles to ensure their total annihilation. While appearing in the archive primarily in connection with a 1663 babaylan uprising in a Visayan town (where the corpses of a babaylan charismatic rebel leader and his followers were impaled on bamboo stakes and deliberately placed on the mouth of a river to be eaten by crocodiles), the story captures a broad truth: colonial violence did consume indigenous culture (the 2001 account of religious historian Carolyn Brewer details the systematic demonization of these indigenous healers and their ostracism and social "dismemberment" as brujas or witches).

> The colonial enterprise was indeed a ravenous maw. Yet, the babaylan tradition never really died; it remained alive inside the colonial religious infrastructure. Across the centuries, its whispers and ache, its raw force and quiet upwellings, continue to speak.[5]

I had not known of this spiritual healing tradition among the indigenous peoples in my home province of Pampanga, Central Luzon, Philippines where I grew up except as "the work of the devil and of evil spirits," and most of their healing work, as based on nothing more than superstitious belief. After all, I grew up a pastor's kid, my father being one of the first converts to Protestant Methodism brought over by the American missionaries as part of their so-called civilizing mission at the turn of the twentieth century.

Childhood memories were marked with our family labeled as "unusual" for being Protestants in a predominantly Catholic country. Although our mother was raised Catholic, she dutifully converted and became the church organist of our local Methodist church upon marrying our father. For us, it meant being inured to a lot of "wrong belief," or so it seemed— the idolizing of saints (particularly during town *fiestas* where elaborate processions were held in their honor), the fanatical self-flagellation of devotees during Holy Week, the veneration of Mother Mary, the belief in purgatory, and what we regarded as a host of "superstitious" beliefs that continued to thrive under the veneer of Catholicism. In all of this, the feeling of having a "leg up" over our Catholic kin came at a price: our exclusion from many community happenings which looked like so much fun, if not fearsomely idolatrous, irrational, and, at best, misguided from where we sat in our self-righteous pedestal. Embedded in a mostly Catholic neighborhood, what served as our family's alternative community was the local United Methodist church. We spent most of our community life in church: in Sunday School, worship service, choir rehearsals, Methodist Youth Fellowship meetings, etc.

By the time I attended college, I became a "born-again Christian" through the witness of a local chapter of the Inter-Varsity Christian Fellowship (IVCF) on campus, an Oxford-originated student movement known for its well-reasoned, highly intellectual approach to Christian discipleship and evangelism. My involvement became life-transforming. Given my tenacious left-brain orientation, I devoured Christian apologetics, sat in biblical hermeneutics classes at the Asian Theological Seminary and the Alliance Biblical Seminary, and immersed myself in biblical studies and discussion groups and submitted to the tutelage of brilliant mentors and elders. I subsequently became part of the original cohort that founded the Institute for Studies for Asian Church and Culture (ISACC)—a progressive Christian organization aiming for a faithful incarnation of the gospel within the Asian context led by the renowned Christian writer and social anthropologist, Melba P. Maggay. For more than three decades, discipling the *intelligentsia* for Christ became my life's great adventure, leading a group of brilliant interdisciplinary scholars and doctoral students in biblical integration while working as a researcher/writer at the University of the Philippines.

But while I was good at what I did and deemed my life—as a clandestine missionary among the *intelligentsia*—full of meaning and purpose, unbeknownst to many, I harbored a nagging sense of failure, of somehow not "measuring up" regardless of my earnestness, that no amount of preaching of God's unconditional love could assuage. My prayer journal bore witness to the struggle, recording memorized passages such as that in Isaiah 42:3: "A bruised reed he will not break; a dimly burning wick he will not quench" or in 2 Corinthians 12:9: "My grace is sufficient for you, for my power is made perfect in weakness" etc., and yet, the confounding torment persisted, my journal pages hemorrhaging with agonizing morbid introspection, constant groveling, and asking for forgiveness. The mystery of why (despite my conscious embrace of the biblical teaching of God's unconditional love) I could not feel whole inside would haunt me throughout my years of ardent missionizing.

ROOT ENCOUNTER: AN INDIGENOUS AWAKENING

It was not until a graduate course in the humanities, titled, "The Image of the Filipino in the Arts," that I would find the key to my mysterious self-sabotaging syndrome (yes, that was what it was—a self-sabotaging affliction, much like a gardener's constant surveillance of a plant's progress by digging it up by its roots to see how it is doing!). The class was taught by an ethnomusicology professor who conducted first-hand research into the arts of our ethnolinguistic communities that were relatively less penetrated by colonization, missionization, and modern development and that still retained much of their land-based cultures and traditions. In the class, we were introduced to these indigenous communities' intricate weaving designs, the wild vibrant colors of their textiles, their basketry, dances, songs, chants, and epic oral narrations—and what these expressed in terms of a different way of being in the world. For the first time, I encountered the supple world of non-individualistic interconnectedness, the delicate sensitivity of *kapwa* (shared being), the generosity of community, the lack of divide between the material and the spirit world, the openness of *loob* (inner being), the gracious receiving of gifts of beauty and creativity from the other world through dreams, visions, and the power of ritual.

I recall coming out of every class session bawling my heart out, walking back to my dorm room in tears, not knowing what it was that hit me from all the innocent descriptions of those indigenous works of art, overcome by very powerful emotions. Only later would I come to understand the meaning of those tears, that they were tears of recognition. Here at last was a different mirror held up to me. The Brazilian educator Paolo Freire once remarked in an interview that when all the authoritative representations around you have nothing to do with your reality, it is like looking into a mirror and finding no one.[6] And sitting in that class and being introduced for the first time to the unique ways of being of our indigenous peoples, talked about not in a degrading, primitivizing, and insulting way, but in recognition of their true beauty, nobility, and grace, I saw myself. No longer would the intuitive world that I sensed I had always shared with the creators of those works of art but had been compelled to repress in favor of the purportedly superior world of the colonial masters, appear in my eyes mangled and distorted. Here it was—revealed to me in all its stark beauty, calling up from within me my own beauty. At last, I was no longer the ugly bastard child of the West, an American wannabe. In that first time encounter with the true beauty of our people, I was birthed anew, welcomed home as it were and told, it is okay to be who you are: a *Pinay*, a *Kapampangan*, brown-skinned, a natural groupie, with a tongue made for *Kapampangan*-speaking, not English-speaking. *Malagu ka.* You are beautiful. Since then, in both my scholarship and personal life, I committed to learning all I can about indigenous lifeways and, with the help of teachers, to recovering my own indigenous soul. And the more I learned, the deeper I fell in love.

Reprising History: US Adventurism in the Philippines

But to backtrack a little and provide a fuller context to the significance of this transformative moment, I need to reprise briefly the history of relations between the Philippines and the United States (where I now reside). Unbeknownst to many, the Philippines occupies a central place in the history of the United States in that it marked the latter's initial entry into the race to superpower-dom. For to become a superpower, what it took was the seizing and takeover of territories for the purpose of extracting resources, enlarging one's market share, and projecting economic and military might abroad. In the year 1898, the Philippines had just declared itself a free and independent republic after fighting a war of liberation from close to 350 years of Spanish rule. It was also the moment when the United States, in a bid to join the fray for superpower land grabs, made the fateful decision to seize the fledgling republic for its own colonial possession, inventing as justification the mythic narratives of Benevolent Assimilation, White Man's Burden, and Manifest Destiny[7] to reconcile its projected self-image of being a freedom loving nation (having just fought its own war of independence) with its coveted aspiration of becoming an Empire.

No other piece of official proclamation is more emblematic of the ruses of the imperial mind than the speech of then President William McKinley to a Methodist delegation, justifying his decision to annex the Philippines:

> I would like to say just a word about the Philippine business... The truth is I didn't want the Philippines, and when they came to us, as a gift from the gods, I did not know what to do with them... I thought at first we would

take only Manila; then Luzon; then the other islands perhaps also. I walked the floor of the White House night after night until midnight; and... I went down on my knees and prayed Almighty God for light and guidance more than one night. And one night it came to me this way:... (1) that we could not give them back to Spain—that would be cowardly and dishonorable; (2) that we could not turn them over to France and Germany...—that would be bad business... (3) that we could not leave them to themselves—they were unfit for self-government ...; and (4) that there was nothing left for us to do but to take them all, and to educate the Filipinos, and uplift, civilize and Christianize them... And then I went to bed, and went to sleep, and slept soundly, and the next morning I sent for the chief engineer of the War Department, and I told him to put the Philippines on the map of the United States, and there they are, and there they will stay while I am President![8]

Spain, at that point, unable to countenance the prospect of defeat at the hands of "mere *Indios*," in a face-saving move, decided to strike up a deal with the United States in an 1898 Treaty drawn up in Paris that would have the two powers hold a mock battle, by the end of which, Spain was to cede the Philippines to the United States for the price of $20 million.[9] The deal done, the United States then proceeded to invade the Philippines in early 1899, leaving in its wake the massacre of half a million to a million Filipinos, the commission of torture and other numerous war crimes and atrocities, the burning and destruction of whole villages, and the annihilation of the country's infrastructure.[10] By 1902, three years after the fighting commenced between the United States and the Philippines, the former would declare victory, but ten years into its formal occupation of the islands, the United States would continue to face protracted guerrilla resistance by determined Filipino revolutionaries. It was only with the arrival of what Elliott calls, "the second army of occupation"[11] (i.e., the army of US civilian administrators, the Thomasite teachers, the Protestant missionaries, and American Peace Corps Volunteers) that the conquest of the Philippine islands was effectively secured through the ensuing ideological subjugation of the populace.

Brief as the United States's formal occupation may have been (half a century) compared to Spain's protracted regime (of over three centuries), American colonialism in the end appears to have marked the Filipino psyche in far more lasting and insidious ways. And that is because Spanish education was mostly a haphazard affair concerned primarily with catechetical instruction, whereas American schooling was systematic and efficient, inscribing the imperial, white supremacist ideology within the

186   S. L. MENDOZA

institution's very instruments of knowing so that anyone run through the system could not but be, as nationalist writer Renato Constantino put it, "mis-educated."[12]

CONQUEST AND THE CHRISTIANIZING MISSION[13]

The unfolding of this history in my own awareness happened quite belatedly. As a Christian convert, for the longest time, I was a Filipino only by sheer geographic accident; in terms of worldview, I took pride in being "non-culture-bound," allied with the transcendent Truth of God-in-Christ that was purportedly unchanging, eternal, and true for all times, peoples, and places. Within such reckoning, any documenting of the brutality of US hegemony in our country—accomplished hand-in-glove with a Christianizing mission—ended up being soft-pedaled, if not altogether denied, as being "expedient" within God's sovereign plan in the world for the Philippines. And who could quarrel with God?

As it turns out, it is this suppressed history that I realized lay at the root of my self-sabotaging pathology—what postcolonial scholar Gayatri Spivak terms "epistemic violence," the trauma visited upon a people's psyche when their sense of themselves and their world is exploded through denigration, demonization, delegitimation, or simply, disallowance.[14] As I delved further into this history, I learned that this ideology, presuming white racial superiority, pretty much wore the garb of Christian religion. Europe's supremacist identity, after all, is—historically—Christian-derived, and its genocidal settling of the so-called New World, justified as "God-ordained," sanctioned by the Christian "Doctrine of Discovery".[15] Under the sway of this racist colonial ideology, albeit now sanitized in the seemingly more race-neutral discourse of "modernity" and "progress," I grew up believing that Europe and the West held the status they did in the world because of some inherent superiority they possessed—either that, or for one reason or another, they were peculiarly blessed by God to rule the world, and to strive to be like them was the only way forward for "backward" countries such as ours.

In church and in the schools, we learned all about this strange other world—one "far more advanced," "more developed," and in every way "better" than the world we Filipinos inhabited. Indeed, our entire educational system was oriented toward that other world. We came to know ourselves primarily via the view from the outside. We were told who we were and what we were like, by outsiders who presumed to know us better than we knew ourselves. Absent knowledge of the subtle codes of communally inflected relational protocols, they innocently (sanctimoniously) preached (and imposed) their own individualistic cultural norms: "Never rely on others; it's a sign of weakness." "Learn to stand on your own two feet." "Let your 'yes' be a 'yes' and your 'no,' be a 'no'; don't be a liar." "This is a duplicitous culture; people never mean what they say and say what they mean." "Filipinos can never be leaders; they're never on time." "Filipinos are lazy; they are too much predisposed to contentment." Thus were culturally redeeming values and practices (such as "*kapwa*," "*pakikiramdam*," "*bayanihan*," and "*kagandahang loob*") worked out communally over millennia of living together on the land constantly misperceived and judged ethnocentrically by outsiders as in fact signs of a wimpy, weak, and dependent Filipino character.[16]

In church, the hymns we sang extolled God's eternal faithfulness all through summer, winter, springtime, and autumn, making one wonder whether having only "dry" and "wet" seasons somehow took away from God's watchfulness over these tropical islands. In science classes, we were taught not to believe in ghosts—and, dutifully, we did not; we were just afraid of them. As Christians, we were made to shun "superstitious" beliefs and the veneration of *anitos* or spirits in nature. I recall an esteemed Christian mentor of mine saying with pride in a bible study on Genesis that it is only within Christianity that science could have possibly flourished because, for the first time, people who formerly believed that spirit beings resided in nature (and were, therefore, wary to explore, dissect, investigate, and experiment with impunity) now understand that spirits do not reside in trees, rocks, or animals and that the true God is actually transcendent, and that his creation (gendering intended) is given to us humans to "manage," exercise dominion over, and use to his glory.[17] No wonder Francis Bacon, the father of modern science, would encourage boldly the torture and enslavement of Nature, urging that she be put on a rack (similar to the one they used in the Middle Ages to torture so-called "witches") to make her yield her secrets.[18]

The internalization of this colonial, nature-dominating worldview is described by one Filipino scholar thus:

> The moment we began to view ourselves through Western eyes, what we held sacred suddenly became worthless, our virtues were turned into vices, our strengths turned into weaknesses, and our triumphs into failures. We could no longer be proud of anything truly our own and began to regard

188   S. L. MENDOZA

anything native as primitive and undeveloped. Anything indigenous became a source of embarrassment and uneasiness.[19]

THE GREAT UNRAVELING

My sojourn to the United States, not by choice but under duress, brought other realizations. One is that the much-touted American Dream that at one point, I must admit, also captivated my imagination, is really a nightmare—built on the massacre and annihilation of 95% of an estimated 100 million native people living up and down the Americas prior to Columbus' incursion into the so-called New World in 1492, the subsequent takeover of these native peoples' territories through treachery and deceit if not outright theft, and, the massacre of approximately between 30 and 60 million Africans in the process of enslaving the 12 million who survived the enterprise, whose unpaid labor (an estimated equivalent amount today as anywhere between one and five trillion dollars) virtually produced much of the country's enormous wealth and infrastructure.[20] Wealth, I would find out, is never an autonomous term but a relative one. On a limited planet, its singular condition of possibility is the violent appropriation of Nature's resources as well as that of other people's labor and surplus product. That is, the wealth creation that alone makes modern "progress" possible, according to writer and indigenous Mayan-inspired teacher Martin Prechtel, would not have been achievable without a massive regime of coercion, enslavement of other human beings, living matter (such as plants and animals), and the turning of so-called inert substances (minerals and metals) into laboring machines.[21] Notice the paradigm shift from a relationship (among indigenous peoples) with Nature as Mother, where you take nothing from Her as your sacred life source without giving something back to modern Christian culture's view of nature as nothing more than "resource," dead matter to do with as we please. Prechtel tells of his experience among the Mayans (those that did not go the imperial route) whose spiritual economy of the village required that you continuously give gifts back to that which gives you life. He writes:

> A knife, for instance, is a very minimal, almost primitive tool to people in a modern industrial society. But for the Mayan people, the spiritual debt that must be paid for the creation of such a tool is great. To start with, the person who is going to make the knife has to build a fire hot enough to produce coals. To pay for that, he's got to give an [offering] to the fuel, to the fire....

Once the fire is hot enough, the knife maker must smelt the iron ore out of the rock. ... What's left over represents the debt, the hollowness that's been carved out of the universe by human ingenuity, and so must be refilled with human ingenuity. A ritual gift equal to the amount that was removed from the other world has to be put back to make up for the wound caused to the divine...

There is a deity to be fed for each part of the procedure. When the knife is finished, it is called the "tooth of earth." It will cut wood, meat, and plants. If the necessary [offerings] have been ignored in the name of rationalism, literalism, and human superiority, it will cut humans instead.[22]

He concludes:

All of those ritual gifts make the knife enormously "expensive," and make the process quite involved and time-consuming. The need for ritual [offering for the debt incurred in taking anything from nature] makes some things too spiritually expensive to bother with. That's why the Mayans didn't invent space shuttles or shopping malls or backhoes [not because they can't]. They live as they do not because it's a romantic way to live—it's not; it's enormously hard—but because it works.[23]

And indeed, this premodern paradigm (for lack of a better word), also shared by our indigenous cultures in the Philippines, has been working so well for our human ancestors for hundreds of thousands of years that they have not seen the need to fundamentally change it. Theirs is a circular loop of reciprocal gift-giving and generosity that has effectively preserved the balance of life and honored the holy in nature. Death itself is simply part of that cycle of giving and receiving, of feeding and someday becoming food for others. Immortality is not an aspiration; it is imperial. With the advent of domestication, the radical shift from hunting and gathering (living on Nature's generosity) to settled agriculture (requiring the re-engineering of nature toward serving strictly human needs), and the consequent accumulation of surplus product and the linear invention of time, a new logic of progress, human specialness, unbridled taking without giving back (because we can) and unrelenting competition for more and more and more was introduced into life on the planet. Thereafter, the new imperative of conquest, hierarchy, and domination began to spread and take root and, horrifyingly, has now become the default condition of all of us modern humans.[24]

190 S. L. MENDOZA

A new definition of human *being* then began to be concocted in service of the conquering syndrome. Enshrined in the language of liberalism and justified by the Christian doctrine of stewardship, work, and striving "for the glory of God," "full humanity" now demanded exhibition of a rationality that excluded feelings, passions, and intuition; a competitive resolve to accumulate wealth at all costs; a focus on material comfort and mastery of nature; an individualistic orientation not beholden to relationships of interdependency; and finally, a possessive, acquisitive drive committed to private ownership.[25] And given that indigenous peoples lived by a set of values tangential if not opposite to these, they did not qualify as human beings and therefore could be dispossessed of their land, territories, and resources with impunity.

The arbitrary naturalization and universalization of this "liberal" (and I would say, supposedly "Christian") understanding of what it means to be a human being took a very long time to normalize, reaching its zenith only in the last 200 years of industrial civilization, and not without resistance from indigenous peoples around the globe. And already, it has wreaked such havoc on the planet as to make the prospect of collapse—and not just economic, but ecological and civilizational—a very real worry and concern (at least among those with access to alternative media).

Indigenous (Re)turnings

It is not my aim in this chapter to speak exclusively about this modern Holocaust scenario; instead, I also wanted to speak of what, in my encounter with the indigenous world of my ancestors, I have come to love and become energized by, bearing witness to a vibrancy and resurgence not only in out of the way places around the world where indigenous peoples still live, but also in the hearts of modern humans hungering for a different vision of how to live in our severely wounded and suffering planet. In what little space remains, I wish to share some of these learnings beginning with those gleaned from the work of a Jesuit priest anthropologist friend of mine, Fr. Albert Alejo, whose own understanding of Christian missions has been radically altered by his long-standing commitment and ongoing relationships with indigenous peoples in Southern Philippines where he taught for years at the Ateneo de Davao University. In an article he wrote on popular spirituality, he defines the phenomenon primarily as an expressive form of "cultural energy." Alejo tells of one tradition in his home province in Obando, Bulacan where "people would offer dances especially those who ask for a child."[26] He notes that one can also ask for a partner in life; however, if one does not know the appropriate dance steps, a child might be given instead. The town fiesta where the fertility dance is performed lasts for three days. He tells the story that once, when he was in high school actively promoting the cultural event as a tourist attraction, he was with a major media outlet trying to document the event and taking photographs when he was moved to leave the ranks of spectators and join the procession instead. He reports:

> In the beginning, I was too shy to move. But I saw couples wanting to get children. In the beginning they were also shy. But as we processed, we were all put in a trance. Something happened, something moved us through the body that also moved us through the community and through the color and the sounds. We were touched. And I said to myself, now I understand why this thing will not die. There is something immortal in this practice. There is something spiritual here. I wonder whether the many people, including the priests who had worked in Obando really understood it.[27]

Given the power of what he just experienced, he puzzled at the glaring absence of any reference to such practices of popular spirituality in religious textbooks. Observing the same sad fate about another region's devotions, he writes:

> When Our Lady of Peñafrancia is processed, the whole Naga City comes alive in a colorful devotion. And yet, nothing of this spirit occupies a page in our religious instruction. In the seminary, we mouth all this rationalist Cogito, I think therefore I am. But there could be other approaches to existence: I dance, therefore I am. We dance, therefore, we collectively exist and live as Christians. We wear colorful hats, therefore, we are alive in our faith. We shake our bodies, we sweat, and we feel the hurt and we feel the healing, and that is how we experience the Divine. My mother would always tell me, when you come back here, please bring lana or oil for my aching back, [one that is blessed], etc. Many of us have been healed in this kind of spirituality but we have been de-inculturated by our own convents or seminary, by our formators and formation programs. Some people say they do not understand Filipinos who, in their physical fatigue, still insist on walking on their knees when they pray. Why do they impose physical hardship on their bodies? I suggest this is explained by realizing that even their language is [a] bodily language. The body is a language... Their life is the life of their body. Their happiness, fatigue and rest is their body...That is their language. That is how they communicate.[28]

192   S. L. MENDOZA

At the launch of our book, *Back from the Crocodile's Belly*, I remarked as well on the lack of bifurcation in our indigenous cultures between the sacred and the profane, and between what we normally think of as "good" and "evil." I noted, for example, the dual signification of the crocodile in popular discourse as, on the one hand, a devouring and insatiable beast (and even now used in editorial cartoons and protest rallies to symbolize the obscene greed as in the pork barrel scandals rife in our homeland) and, on the other hand, our reference to it in *Back from the Crocodile's Belly*, as in fact, the Crocodile god—fit to receive and be given offerings and our task as that of taking up the sacred work of singing and storying the fragments of indigenous memory back into remembrance and wholeness, of coaxing the Crocodile god to give up the pieces of the bodies of the *babaylan* healers he has swallowed in exchange for our offerings of grief, beauty, and eloquence.[29] Here, the representation of the Crocodile as both a devouring god and a life-giving resurrection womb calls to mind the figure of Mama Drago, resonant in Scythian myths, as well as Celtic, and other ancient Indo-European cultures, as being in fact a figure of the Earth Mother, the source of all life, ungrudgingly supplying her children with nourishment and abundance provided she is fed, in turn, by her children's offerings of human ingenuity with grief and remembrance. But the same nurturing Mother becomes a hungry devouring beast when denied her due (as we witness today in the denying of her waters in drought, or in the similar withdrawing of fertility from her soils, or her thundering response to human expansionist folly in the catastrophic floodings, tornados, and forest fires that increasingly have become the norm across the globe). Similarly, indigenous cultures believe that ancestors, too, become hungry ghosts when not fed offerings of grief, beauty, and eloquence, for, as writer Martin Prechtel notes, unlike our more distant and intact forebears, "our [more recent] ancestors weren't necessarily very smart. In many cases, they are the ones who left us this mess. Some of them were great, but others had huge prejudices."[30] Thus, we feed and heal them with our offerings, lest they remain hungry ghosts, unable to take their rightful place as ancestors, causing us to live out their prejudices in our lifetime, and creating cultures ridden with depression, violence, and despair.

The beauty I see in this way of reckoning is that rather than the constant separation of good versus evil and the search for purification via religions of exorcism and demonization, we witness instead relationships of mutuality and honoring, of giving and receiving, of offering to the Other

10 BACK FROM THE CROCODILE'S BELLY: CHRISTIAN FORMATION MEETS... 193

World what is its due and receiving from it with abundant gratitude. As Alejo writes, remarking on the evangelical practice of a small group of believers at the back of their Jesuit house of constantly exorcizing and rebuking devils every weekend at their worship services:

> In contrast, I have witnessed many tribal rituals. In the mountains, there are also many spirits, some benevolent, some malicious, and some simply hungry. What do the tribal baylans do? In different forms, in different ways, they would reserve some food for the malignant spirits. "There is food for you here. Please don't bother us because we are going to have a special event. Please, do not go beyond this line." This "pasintabi" [respectfully asking for permission] has many names in different ethnic groups. The idea is that we negotiate with the spirits. We don't shout at them. We don't rebuke them. I think that, in general, that is a better way to deal with spirits.[31]

For me, this journey of allowing myself to be taught by the spirit of our ancestors has been both humbling and exhilarating beginning with that moment of epiphany in the humanities classroom. In my other academic writings, I have begun to refer to it as "a love story."[32] For, as we wrote in our Crocodile book, "It is not enough to see and grieve what is wrong in the world; one needs also to fall in love."[33] Indeed, discovering the world of our ancestors—"before the invention of violent hierarchies and the beauty-killing empires, machines, markets, standing armies, corporations, and governments that now threaten our world"[34]—is like being born anew into a new world. A world full of wonder, mystery, and so much more humanity, so different from the depressing one we live in today that is filled with hungry ghosts, unmourned dead, and medicated casualties of modern civilization.

In summarizing his reflections on popular spirituality (and I am appropriating the term loosely here as a kind of spirituality that still retains the memory of an older, more anciently indigenous spirituality), Father Alejo concludes that this kind of spirituality is not a rejection of other ways of practising spirituality; it is simply:

> an expression of a particular way of being human, a particular way of connecting to the Divine. It is the energy to be themselves [a way of celebrating who they are]. It is a spirituality of the body not of abstracted essence of the spirit. It is a spirituality of the many, not of the soloist individual. It is a spirituality of celebration, and never of denial of the self or of the world. It is also a spirituality of [meaning and] negotiation, not of [dogma or doctrine].[35]

194   S. L. MENDOZA

In the olden days when my life's purpose as a Christian was about "bringing everyone to the fold under the banner of Christ," whenever I encountered anyone of a different faith, no matter my attempts at dialogue, cultural sensitivity, or compassionate opening to the "truths" of other practices or traditions, in the end, I always had the trump card up my sleeve. As a Filipino thinker, scholar, and Christian writer, Melba Maggay cannot help but conclude even after her excellently nuanced analysis of the cultural faux pas of the early Protestant missionaries in the Philippines in her book, *A Clash of Cultures*, that

> [w]e need to wrestle with our own culture at its point of greatest power and peril *if we are to bring it under the light of Christ. Only then can we presume to say something about the uniqueness and superiority of Christ to the great cultures around us.*[36] (emphasis added)

Meaning: cut through the "smoke and mirrors"—the goal in devoting all that effort to understanding the indigenous culture was finally, simply one more time, more effectively to bring Filipinos under the supposedly "superior" sign of Christ. For much of my adult life, I was myself the articulator of this supposed supremacy that ironically was ultimately also doing damage to me. And for more than 20 years now, my work has been to pursue relentlessly the grip of that superiority on my own soul and its reach into the culture of my people in order to undo its damaging denigration and recover a much bigger and more indigenous sense of God and spirit in my life.[37]

So, now I ask continually: What if, as Christians, we were to humbly lay down the trump card—no matter if doing so may feel like "going off the deep end"—and take genuine curiosity in others not just for the purpose of better missionizing them, but to learn from what they have to teach us from their own truths? Are we willing to let our Christian story take its place as only one—worthy as it is—among many other true stories in a posture of mutual giving and co-creation of a future we can all share?

Andrew Walls, leading British historian of Christian missions, may have uncannily given us a hint on precisely the kind of humility needed for such a gesture of divestment.[38] In his interpretation of the word "primal" (as it pertains to "first" or "land-based/land-taught" peoples) he strips the word of its evolutionary connotations and notes:

[T]he word "primal" is not a euphemism for "primitive"... The word help-fully underlines two features of the religions of the peoples indicated: *their historical anteriority and their basic, elemental status in human experiences. All other faiths are subsequent and represent, as it were, second thoughts...*[39]

Could it be that all this time, that is what we have been doing—majoring on second thoughts (!)? And that it's now high time to listen and learn again from those who, against all odds, have remained rooted in that primal revelation that is the Earth herself, the ultimate source of wisdom?

It is time to take the plunge...

NOTES

1. A festival or ceremony of tribal peoples in Northern Philippines involving the ritual slaughter of a pig, chicken, or other animal as a thanksgiving offering to the deities, *anitos* (nature spirits), and departed ancestors for protecting and watching over their land.
2. David Stannard, *American Holocaust: The Conquest of the New World* (New York: Oxford University Press, 1992), 103.
3. Thomas Paine, *The complete writings of Thomas Paine*, Vol. 2 (New York, NY: The Citadel Press,1895), 402.
4. The term "babaylan" refers to the indigenous healing tradition that among our various tribes in the Philippines is known by the differing names of *mumbaki, dawac, ma-aram, catalonan, beliyan, balyan, baylan, patutunong*, etc.
5. Mendoza & Strobel (eds.), *Back from the crocodile's belly*, 13–14.
6. The interview is one I remember viewing on YouTube, but is now no longer available.
7. Cf. Reginald Horsman, *Race and manifest destiny: Origins of American racial Anglo-Saxonism* (Cambridge, MA: Harvard University Press, 1981); Winthrop D. Jordan, *The white man's burden: Historical origins of racism in the United States* (New York, NY: Oxford University Press, 1974); Stuart C. Miller, *"Benevolent assimilation": The American conquest of the Philippines, 1899–1903* (New Haven, CT: Yale University Press, 1982).
8. Daniel B. Schirmer & Stephen R. Shalom (eds.), *The Philippines Reader: A History of Colonialism, Neocolonialism, Dictatorship, and Resistance* (Boston: South End Press, 1987), 22–23.
9. Theodore S. Gonzalves, "The Mock Battle that Ended the Spanish-American War," *National Museum of American History* (December 18,

2018) viewed July 11. 2023, from https://americanhistory.si.edu/blog/mock-battle

10. Cf. Pennee Bender (Producer, Screenwriter, Director), Joshua Brown (Director), Andrea Ades Vasquez (Director), *Savage Acts: Wars, Fairs, and Empire 1898–1904* (2006) New York, NY: American Social History Project, viewed July 11, 2023, from https://vimeo.com/299901299

11. Charles B. Elliott, *The Philippines* (Ann Arbor, Michigan: University of Michigan Library, 2005), 229.

12. Renato Constantino, "The miseducation of the Filipino," in C. N. Lumbera & T. Gimenez-Maceda (eds.), *Rediscovery: Essays in Philippine life and culture* (Quezon City: Department of English, Ateneo de Manila and National Book Store, Inc., 1977), 125–145.

13. Some parts of this section may be found in S. Lily Mendoza, "Tears in the archive: Creating memory to survive and contest empire," in R. Lustig & J. Koester, (eds.), *Among US: Essays on identity, belonging, and intercultural competence*, rev. ed., (Boston: Pearson, 2005/2006), 233–245.

14. Gayatri C. Spivak, "Can the subaltern speak?", in Cary Nelson & Lawrence Grossberg (eds.), *Marxism and the interpretation of culture* (Champaign, IL: University of Illinois Press, 1988), 271–313.

15. Robert J. Miller, *Native America, discovered and conquered: Thomas Jefferson, Lewis & Clark, and Manifest Destiny*, (Westport, Connecticut, USA: Praeger Publishers, 2006); Robert J. Miller, Jacinta Ruru, Larissa Behrendt, & Tracey Lindberg, *Discovering indigenous lands: The Doctrine of Discovery in the English colonies* (Oxford: Oxford University Press, 2012); Lindsay G. Robertson, *Conquest by law: How the discovery of America dispossessed indigenous peoples of their land* (New York, NY: Oxford University Press, 2005); Steven Newcomb, *Pagans in the Promised Land: Decoding the Doctrine of Discovery* (Golden, CO: Fulcrum Publishing, 2008).

16. On the colonial misinterpretation of Filipino cultural values and their reinterpretation by Filipino psychologists, birthing a distinctive Filipino psychology, *Sikolohiyang Pilipino*, see "Sikolohiyang Pilipino: Beginnings, institutionalization and pioneering gains" in S. Lily Mendoza, "Theoretical Advances in the Discourse of Indigenization," in Rogelia Pe-Pua (ed.), *Handbuk ng Sikolohiyang Pilipino (Handbook of Filipino Psychology)* Bolyum 1: Perspektibo at Metodolohiya (Vol 1: Perspectives and Methodology) (Diliman, Quezon City: The University of the Philippines, 2018), 252–86 at 252–62. For an understanding of Filipino cultural values based on the core concept of "kapwa," see Virgilio G. Enriquez, *Kapwa: A Core Concept in Filipino Psychology* (Kapwa Isang Buod na Konsepto sa Skilophiyang Panlipunang Pilipino), in Pe-Pua, *Handbuk ng Sikolohiyang Pilipino*.

17. On the Filipino transpersonal worldview (belief in the spirits or anitos and in trees, rivers, and nature) which was demonized by the colonizer and yet remains in the consciousness of many Filipinos today, see Jaime C. Bulatao, SJ "Filipino Transpersonal World View (Ang Trasnpersonal na Pananaw sa Mundo ng mga Pilipino)", Rogelia Pe-Pua (ed.), *Handbuk ng Sikolohiyang Pilipino (Handbook of Filipino Psychology)* Bolyum 2: Gamit (Volume 2: Application) (Diliman, Quezon City: The University of the Philippines, 2019), 43–47

18. Cf. nuanced discussion of the debate around the attributed quote in Merchant, Carolyn. "The scientific revolution and the death of nature." *Isis* 97.3 (2006): 513–533.

19. De Leon in Grace Nono, *Song of the babaylan: Living voices, medicines, spiritualities of Philippine ritualist-oralist-healers* (Quezon City, Philippines: Institute of Spirituality in Asia, 2013), 27.

20. Cf. Stannard, David. *American Holocaust: The Conquest of the New World* (New York, NY: Oxford University Press, (1992). ftnt 9, 317

21. Cf. Prechtel in Derrick Jensen, "Saving the indigenous soul: An interview with Martin Prechtel," *The sun magazine* (2001), viewed 8 May 2017, from *http://thesunmagazine.org/issues/304/saving_the_indigenous_soul*

22. Prechtel in Jensen (2001).

23. Prechtel in Jensen (2001).

24. Cf. Larry Rasmussen, *Earth, community, earth ethics* (Geneva: WCC Publications, 1996); Daniel Quinn, *Ishmael* (New York, NY: Bantam Books, 1992/ 1995, 1996); Paul Shepard, "A Post-Historic Primitivism," in J. Gowdy, (ed.), *Limited wants, unlimited means* (Washington, D.C.: Island Press,1998), 281–328; Paul, Shepard, *The tender carnivore and the sacred game.* (Athens, GA: The University of Georgia Press, 1973/1998); Paul Shepard, *Nature and madness* (Athens, GA: The University of Georgia Press, 1982/1998): Spencer Wells, *Pandora's Seed: The unforeseen cost of civilization* (NY: Random House, 2010); John Zerzan (ed.), *Against civilization* (Los Angeles: Feral House, 2005).

25. S. Lily Mendoza, "Savage representations in the discourse of modernity: Liberal ideology and the impossibility of nativist longing," *Decolonization, Indigenization, Education, and Society*, 2(1) (2013): 1–19; Bhikhu Parekh, "Liberalism and colonialism: A critique of Locke & Mill," in Jan N. Pieterse & Bhikhu Parekh (eds.), *Decolonization of imagination: Culture, knowledge and power* (London: Zed Books, 1995), 81–98.

26. Albert Alejo, "Popular spirituality as cultural energy," in *Lecture series 3 on spirituality: Context and expressions of Filipino spirituality* (Manila: Center for Spirituality, 2004), 33–52 at 34.

27. Alejo, "Popular spirituality as cultural energy," 35.

28. Alejo, "Popular spirituality as cultural energy," 39.

29. Mendoza & Strobel (eds.), *Back from the crocodile's belly*.
30. Prechtel in Jensen (2001).
31. Alejo, "Popular spirituality as cultural energy," 45.
32. S. Lily Mendoza, "Out of modernity into deep ancestry: A love story," in K. Sorrels & S. Sekimoto (eds.), *Globalizing intercultural communication* (Thousand Oaks, CA: Sage, 2016), pp. 44–55.
33. Mendoza & Strobel, *Back from the crocodile's belly*, 8.
34. Mendoza & Strobel, *Back from the crocodile's belly*, ii.
35. Alejo, "Popular spirituality as cultural energy," 46.
36. Melba P. Maggay, *A clash of cultures: Early American Protestant missions and Filipino religious consciousness* (Manila: Anvil Publishing, Inc. for De La Salle University, 2011), 198.
37. See within this volume the chapter by Lledo Gomez regarding colonial oppression of Filipinos resulting in colonial mentality, in Cristina Lledo Gomez, "Bangon Na. Pinays Rise up".
38. Andrew Walls, *Missionary Movement in Christian History: Studies in the Transmission of Faith* (Maryknoll, NY: Orbis Books, 1996).
39. Walls, *Missionary Movement in Christian History*, 120–121.

CHAPTER 11

The Ygollotes' Pudong and the Insurrection of the Reeds In the Post-Human Commune

Ferdinand Anno

The "post-human" in critical theory is mainly understood in relation to artificial intelligence and the technopoly.[1] Here, I use the idea of the post-human commune in terms of its ecological sense, and in relation to the politics of negating the anthropocentrism of our eschatological imagination.[2]

In April 2021, President Rodrigo Duterte lifted the nine-year-old ban on new mining deals and moved for the revival of the Marcos-era Chico River Basin Development Project in the Cordillera region.[3] This included the commencement of the Gened 1 and 2 hydroelectric power projects in the Apayao-Abulug river in the northern part of the region. In December 2022, at the twilight of his presidency, Duterte included the lifting of the ban on open-pit mining.[4] These all happened during the Covid-19 global pandemic which continues to exist in its different manifestations to this day, setting a "new normal" for the world. It is these developments under the "new normal" regime that serves as the immediate context of my desire to resurface the *Pudong* rite of the Ygollotes of Gran Cordillera and

---

F. Anno (✉)
Union Christian College, San Fernando, La Union, Philippines

© The Author(s), under exclusive license to Springer Nature Switzerland AG 2024
C. Lledo Gomez et al. (eds.), *500 Years of Christianity and the Global Filipino/a*, Pathways for Ecumenical and Interreligious Dialogue, https://doi.org/10.1007/978-3-031-47500-9_11

to communicate what it may say about Christianity's *leitourgi*-cal witnessing in the contemporary world.

THE *PUDONG*

The *Pudong* is a bundle of reed sticks with knotted ends that most of us in the mountain region install in places where we gather for a ritual event. The installation could also be positioned at the entrance and walkways of a village. The *Pudong* provides assurance that all dwellings and the people they shelter are under divine protection. The *Pudong* assures that no property or persons will be trespassed and violated throughout the gathering. Those who infringe on the boundaries set by the *Pudong* would consequently suffer the wrath of the spirits.[5] There are numerous rites within the mountain region that are closely linked to the Pudong. Each of these rites serves to highlight the *Pudong*'s role as a sacred practice that designates specific days and spaces as hallowed. It calls for the cessation of work, including the exploitation of the earth, and serves as a reminder to the community about the importance of living together harmoniously (known as *sinpangili*). Furthermore, the *Pudong* serves as a declaration of comprehensive rest for all beings and objects and acts as a ritual of communion with ancestral and/or nature spirits.[6]

THE *PUDONG* RITE

What does it mean when an Igorot plants the *Pudong* on the ground? Is the ritual unconnected to the clear and present danger facing our planet? Whenever Igorots gather as a community, they make it a point to plant or install a *Pudong* prominently in the vicinity of the gathering or the entrance of the village for people to take notice. On occasions like our rest days, this comes with the announcement of the commencement of the Sabbath. The planting of the *Pudong* is accompanied by prayers bidding everyone, both seen and unseen, to look after the houses, gardens, swidden farms, livestock, properties, and all that the villagers leave for the gathering. Among the Ibalois of southern Benguet, the Pudong sticks are planted like a gateway through which the ancestral spirits come by to commune with the living. It is this communion of the living, the ancestral spirits, the earth, and all that dwell therein that calls on all people and every living being to observe a solemn pause from whatever activity or work they are doing. When the *Pudong* is standing, the whole earth and all of life rest. In light of this brief description of the Pudong and its significance for my people, the Igorots, I propose five theses below, which I argue can assist in the formation of an ecumenical/inter-faith spirituality of resistance in light of the continuing reality of development aggression in the Philippines, and in particular, the Gran Cordillera Central. In addition, it can help develop a spirituality that is desperately needed to heal and care for our damaged earth and its living beings, a damage that derives from a colonial Christian approach.

Thesis One: When *We Plant the Pudong*, We Call on People to Be a Community Again

The Pudong signals a movement from separation to communion. When knotted and stuck on the ground, the *Pudong* calls on the people to come together as a *sinpangili* (one nation), a community where social differentiation is suspended. The ritual action/object declares that the community bond is stronger than the enticements of "correct religion," money, and power and that indigenous communities can be united in solidarity in upholding their rights to their ancestral lands and self-determination. The contemporary politics of development divide. Using patronage politics, the developmental dispensation breeds its partisans from among the indigenous populations, marginalizes the voices of many, and tries to undermine indigenous political processes.

Moreover, Igorots believe that the *Pudong* is a gateway through which ancestral spirits come by to commune with the living. What this means is the expansion of the natives' communal self-understanding. In this ritual, all creatures are reminded of their sharing of the land and this life with ancestral spirits and that the living must relate with them in filial reverence.

Under the guise of Christianization, the colonial government and missionary organizations have become aggressive in their cultural re-engineering programs designed to destroy the communities' resistance. These included Christian religious education, spiritual formation, and allied programs aimed at erasing the Igorot's indigenous memory and identity. Together with the establishment of a public education system, Christianization became the proverbial Trojan Horse employed to help disorient the natives away from their indigeneity and spirituality toward submission to a new colonial identity, a "Euro-Christian" cosmology and way of life. Today, missionary conquests[7] continue mainly through the evangelization work of free evangelical churches; this time, they have been joined by big business and government agencies like the National Commission on Indigenous Peoples (NCIP) and the National Task Force to End Local Communist Armed Conflict (NTF-ELCAC). Together, these groups put up cultural and political barriers to foil the attempts of organized Igorot groups to come together in a pan-Cordilleran *sinpangili* (united community/one nation) in defense of the Igorot homeland.[8] Practiced almost everywhere in the mountain region, the planting of the *Pudong* reminds us that the *Kaigorotan* is one and our security lies not in those whose agenda is to sever our culto-spiritual relationship with the earth but in the religious and proper observance of the rites of radical connectivity with the earth.

Thesis Two: When We Plant the *Pudong*, We Declare the Land and All That Dwell Therein as Holy

When colonial Christianity entered the Philippines and declared that *Kabunian* was not in charge anymore and that "the One True God" of Christianity was the only one who was holy, owned everything, and known only through the Christian faith, everything and everyone in the lands of the Philippines became disenchanted and desacralized. The land effectively became a mere resource for humanity to exploit, for the latter's "flourishing." More directly, I argue that Christianity's radical monotheism contributed to the eventual rape of Gran Cordillera.[9]

When we declare things as holy, we stand in awe of them. We are duty-bound to be reverential about and toward them. We preserve them in their pristine form, as we have found them, as much as possible. We protect them. We live in harmony with them, celebrating their power, and feasting around them as they provide their good graces and blessings. At the same time, we also seek restitution and balance with them whenever we offend them. This is what the planting of the Pudong is about: it declares the land and all that dwell within it as holy. This has implications—for our relationship with the land and all of its living beings and accordingly governs our behavior toward them. The opposite then of the desacralization of the land and its creatures is the planting of the *Pudong*. The planting reinscribes and reinforces the holiness that belongs and has always belonged to the land and its creatures but was forgotten with the advent of the Christian colonial approach (singularly focused on the "One True God" from the touted "one true religion"). Replanting the *Pudong* throughout the land is a reminder we need, to see the sacrality of all that surrounds us and thus the respect demanded toward them, because of their sacrality. This leads me to my third thesis.

THESIS THREE: WHEN WE PLANT THE PUDONG WE "RE-SACRALIZE" THE PROFANED EARTH

To the Igorot, the land is inherently sacred, and ritual performances like the Pudong are occasions for the public affirmation of this reality. The act of planting the *Pudong* reclaims and celebrates the existence of a cultic relationship between the earth and her tillers, a mutuality designed to sustain life and, insofar as local priests or shamans are concerned, a relationship designed in the mind of divinity.

The current neo-liberal order relies heavily on the wanton exploitation of the earth and its resources. Thus big corporations, bureaucrats, and their cultural agents must "manufacture people's consent" [10] by all means, including fascist repression and militarization. Cultural agencies, including religious groups, are being co-opted in this social project of manufacturing consent and softening people's resistance. Christian revivalism, with its American frontier "this-world-is-not-my-home" gospel, has been negating and disenchanting the non-human environment while, at the same time, with a stroke of genius, tapping into indigenous peoples' primal spirituality to sell itself as a religious alternative. [11]

What the *Pudong* ritual declares is the faith affirmation that the earth is not simply anyone's property to trespass and exploit as one pleases; it manifests as living and pulsating the faith affirmation that the earth is the core of the sacred realm or the "*Kabunian*" reality. [12] The mountains, to use Hebraic scriptural language, are "where bushes burn." They reveal the face of divinity and they call for sandals to be removed. Similarly, the *Pudong* cries out, "Stay off the sacred!"

THESIS FOUR: THE *PUDONG* RITUAL CALLS FOR A JUBILEE FOR THE EARTH AND ALL THAT DWELL WITHIN

In Igorot cosmology, the land is a living creative organism that shares the biological characteristics of other living creatures. If the human, the water buffalo, and other work animals tire, so does the land. The earth needs to rest, and so do its tillers. Even the gods and spirits need rest. In other words, the *Pudong* calls for the relief of the land and all that dwell within. In the case of the Northern Kankanaey's or the Y-Bontoc's *Tengao* or the Itneg/Tingguian's *ubaya*, the planting of the *Pudong* signals the beginning of the sabbath for everyone and every creature.[13] The call to rest is so thorough that no one is allowed entry to or exit from the village throughout the *Tengao*. This is *cultus*. That is, mutual care, at its highest symbolic form. The Igorots' reason for being takes its cues from the people's *cultus*. The *tengao* calls for the resting of the land. It is incumbent upon the tiller to ensure that the land is at rest. This is the Igorot's part in its cultic relationship with the land. The *Pudong* serves to remind the Igorot tillers of their part in the covenant.

The whole Gran Cordillera chain of mountains is already partitioned by applications from multinational corporations involved in large-scale mining, logging, hydroelectric, coal, geothermal, pharmaceutical, and other extractive industries. The Mining Act of 1995 further intensified development aggression leaving the mountains and their tillers needing a real experience of rest.

One story among the Amburayan Kankanaeys, also known as Bago-Igorots, says that the continuous denuding of their mountain abodes made the gods and spirits flee, leaving their balding mountains devoid of divine presence.[14] As a result, the lands and communities living under the shadows of these mountains have been left unprotected by the gods and spirits. This state of abandonment effectively sentenced the *papattayan*s of the foothills (sacrificial altars) to their death. When the gods and the spirits have flown, the altars lay idle and the religion and culture surrounding them die.

To the Igorot, the planting of the *Pudong* is as potent a ritual as the missionary *conquistador*s' ritual of cross-planting. If the latter ritual meant the subjugation of the land and its people, the first sought to reaffirm the integrity and freedom of the land, water, sky, and people. However, if the Christian cross speaks of how God touched the ground so that the whole of creation may live life to the full, the *Pudong* participates in the mystery of that "old rugged cross" in its calling on the villages to touch the ground more intentionally and know that the earth is holy ground. Long uprooted from our Adamic selves, we need to touch the ground, remove our shoes and sandals, and see God again in the burning bush.

THESIS FIVE: THE PLANTING OF THE *PUDONG* SIGNALS THE INSURRECTION OF LUMAUIG'S REEDS

The Ygollotes of the Cordillera mountain region include the Ifugao. The Ifugao tells of a story that in the beginning, when the world was all thickets and marshes ruled by ugly monsters and hideous beasts, Lumauig descended from the sky into the valleys and plains and gathered all the reeds (*Pudong*) that were trampled upon by the beasts.[15] He broke the reeds into several halves and scattered them all over the world. Then Lumauig went up to the top of Mount Polis and cried in a loud and powerful voice that reverberated throughout the earth, "Rise and speak!" The reeds became people, and thereafter, were the peopling of the earth.[16]

There is a political theological continuum between the *Pudong* rite and the insurrection of the reeds. When pushed to its logical limit, the *Pudong*'s call for resting all life is an invitation to conversion or to re-living the moment of the reeds' breaking and their consequent release. Colonialism, Christianization, and the "Capitalocene"[17] have reduced the native into wilting reeds. The *Pudong* rite, planted in the mountain range where Mt. Polis[18] is, can call to mind that reeds became people in their rising and speaking truth to power. In the lowlands, Philippine Christianity redeemed itself when it sprang and rose "from below"[19]—from the same ground where the first Christian cross was planted. Similarly, the planting of the *Pudong* signals the rising of the native, the cultic partners to the earth, and gives witness to the gospel of the old rugged cross in a strange "tongue."

This story of the peopling of the earth indigenous to the Ifugao-Igorot is often revisited by some organized communities that see its relevance to the need for the Ygollotes to rise and speak against colonial aggression from the state, big business, and religious organizations hostile to their earth-based spiritualities.[20] Christianity can re-discover in both the *Pudong* rite and narrative an anthropological construct more in tune with the eco-centric and egalitarian imagination of the Christian scriptures than the anthropocentric and androcentric cosmologies of imperial Christianity.

CONCLUSION

Having laid out my five theses on the *Pudong's* significance for forming an eco-spirituality of resistance this essay proposes that our reflections during the continuing commemoration of the five hundredth year of Christianity in the Philippines should include the following: First, Christianization's contribution to the marginalization of indigenous peoples, their spiritualities, and their ecocentric ways of living; second, Christianization's contribution to the desecration and plunder of indigenous peoples' ancestral lands; third, Christianization or Christianity's necessary change of role into becoming partners with and companions to indigenous peoples in their continuing struggle for national identity, self-determination, and as the guardians of the earth's last frontiers; And last, the opportunity of Christianity and the whole world to learn from the *Pudong* rite—it can teach and inform us all about the continuing decolonization and contextualization of our *leitourgia* or our public work as faith communities supposedly committed to the transformation of our world into the reign of God, a world where there is room for all, especially the most vulnerable and marginalized.

NOTES

1. As described and defined by Neil Postman in Neil Postman, *Technopoly: The Surrender of Culture to Technology* (New York: Vintage Books, 1992) and his other writings such as *Conscientious Objections: Stirring up Trouble about Language, Technology, and Education* (New York: Vintage Books, 1992) and Postman et.al., *Where Do We Go from Here? The Quest for Narratives in a Technological Society* (Vancouver: Regent College, 2000).
2. This cosmo-vision is espoused and depicted in various traditions like the Judaeo-Christian scriptures, East Asian visual arts, Celtic and naturalist mystics, Franciscan communities, and indigenous religious traditions among others.
3. See Karl Ocampo, Leila Salaverria, and Nestor Corrales, "Duterte lifts 9-year ban on new mining deals," *Inquirer.Net,* April 16, 2021. https://newsinfo.inquirer.net/1419780/duterte-lifts-9-year-ban-on-new-mining-deals.
4. See Enrico dela Cruz and Ed Davis, "Philippines ends open pit mining ban to reinvigorate industry," *Reuters, December 28, 2021,* https://www.reuters.com/business/environment/philippines-lifts-four-year-old-ban-open-pit-mining-2021-12-28/.

11 THE YGOLLOTES' PUDONG AND THE INSURRECTION OF THE REEDS... 207

5. Carmencita Cawed, *The Culture of the Bontoc Igorots* (Manila: MCS Enterprises, 1972), 32.

6. See Ferdinand Anno, "On Earth as in Heaven: The Earth in the Pudong Leitourgia of the Post Human Commune," *Decolonizing Ecotheology: Indigenous and Subaltern Challenges*, eds. S. L, Mendoza & G. Zachariah (Oregon: Pickwick Publications, 2022), 77–92.

7. So named by Tinker in the North American context. See George Tinker, *Missionary Conquest: The Gospel and Native American Cultural Genocide* (Fortress Press, 1993).

8. The pan-Cordilleran project, or the idea of "Kaigorotan" (the various ethno-linguistic groups in the Cordillera region as one nation) pushed by various indigenous groups to collectively resist development aggression has been, lately, labeled by officials of the NCIP as "Communistic." See https://www.facebook.com/manja.bayang/videos/10157881250706899/

9. The Gran Cordillera is a mineral-rich mountain region located in the northern-central part of the island of Luzon, covering an area of approximately 8700 square miles. It is home to a diverse array of indigenous communities, including the Ibaloi, Kankanaey, Ifugao, Bontoc, Kalinga, Isneg, and Itneg ethno-linguistic groups.

10. Noam Chomsky, *Letters from Lexington: Reflections on Propaganda* (Boulder, Colorado: Paradigm Publishers 2004), 13.

11. Harvey Cox, *Fire from Heaven: The Rise of Pentecostal Spirituality and the Reshaping of Religion in the Twenty-First Century* (London: Cassel, 1996).

12. William Henry Scott, *On the Cordillera, A Look at the Peoples and Cultures of the Mountain Province* (Manila: MCS Enterprises, 1966), 142.

13. The Tengao and Ubaya are rest days that the Ygollotes of the Cordillera, particularly the Kankanaeys, Bontocs,and Itnegs, regularly observe. During these rest days, the Pudong rite is prominently practiced, albeit with variations in its methods, expressions, and interpretations.

14. Florentino Hornedo, *The Favor of the Gods: Essays in Filipino Religious Thought and Behavior* (Manila: University of Sto. Tomas Publishing House, 2001).

15. *Lumauig* is the other name for divinity among the scripture-less Ygollotes. Christian missionaries often import their Trinitarian thinking into indigenous "god-talk" and interpret *Lumauig* as the incarnation or the son of *Kabunian* (and *Kabigat*, another name associated with the realm of divinity, as the third person of the Trinity) See Howard Wilson Widdoes, *Autobiography of Howard Wilson Widdoes* (United Theological Seminary, Ohio: The Center for the Study of Evangelical United Brethren History, 1987), 297–298, and M. Walley, *The Story of the Bago*, an unpublished MA thesis submitted to the graduate faculty of Osias Educational Foundation,

Philippines. On the Bago Igorot people, see my essays—Ferdinand Anno, *Bago Origins: The Tale of Two Sapo* (Union Theological Seminary, 2014), https://www.academia.edu/8117784/BAGO_ORIGINS_The_Tale_of_Two_Sapo, and Ferdinand Ammang Anno, *Of Sintatako, Tongtongan, Bengas, and Papatayan: The Bago Igorot and the New World* (Dasmariñas, Philippines: Center for the Arts, Liturgy and Music, Union Theological Seminary), https://www.academia.edu/8117867/Of_Tongtongan_Begnas_and_Papatayan_The_Bago_Igorot_and_the_New_World.

16. F. Landa Jocano, *Myths and Legends of the Early Filipinos* (Quezon City, Philippines: Alemar-Phoenix Publishers, 1971).

17. The term "Capitalocene" focuses on the ways in which capitalism has shaped and transformed the environment, exploiting nature and labor for the sake of capital accumulation. It highlights the interconnectedness of capitalism, colonialism, and environmental exploitation. On the coinage of the word, see Jason W. Moore, *Anthropocene or Capitalocene? Nature, History, and the Crisis of Capitalism* (Oakland, CA: PM Press, 2016).

18. Mt. Polis is prominently featured in the Ifugao myth recounting the origins of humanity. According to the myth, Lumauig, the god of the mountains, selected Mt. Polis as the sacred site where he summoned the reeds that he had shattered into halves and dispersed across the earth to rise and speak. Their ascent signaled the birth of humankind. For more details, refer to Jocano's work, *Myths and Legends of the Early Filipinos.*

19. Reynaldo Ileto, *Pasyon and Revolution: Popular Movements in the Philippines, 1840–1910* (Quezon City: Ateneo de Manila University Press, 1979).

20. Ferdinand Anno, "Indigenous Theology, Sources and Resources: Perspectives from the Philippines," *The Ecumenical Review* 62:4 Wiley (2010): 371-378, 371-72.

CHAPTER 12

Introducing Jeepney Hermeneutics: Reading the Bible as Canaanites

Revelation Enriquez Velunta

Two empires meet (Jesus and the centurion); and curiously enough, they are pleased with one another.[1]

While doing his rounds Jesus finds St. Peter, at the pearly gates, looking worn out and very, very tired. "Rocky," he says to his friend, "why don't you take a break. I'll handle the processing for you." "Thanks, Jesse," Peter replies with glee and leaves with his rooster. Jesus takes over and as he looks down the long line of people being processed, he notices an old man who looks very, very familiar. Jesus felt he knew the old man.

This essay draws from at least three sources: the Matthew Chapter of Velunta's Ph.D. dissertation, *Reading the Bible inside a Jeepney* (Vanderbilt University) published with the same title in 2017; a paper presented at the Mission in the Context of Empire Consultation in Bethlehem, Palestine, October-November 2015; and from pages of Daniel Patte, Monya A. Stubbs, Justin Ukpong, and Revelation Velunta, *The Gospel of Matthew: A Contextual Introduction for Group Study* (Nashville: Abingdon, 2003), 137-151.

R. E. Velunta (✉)
Union Theological Seminary, Dasmariñas, Cavite, Philippines

© The Author(s), under exclusive license to Springer Nature Switzerland AG 2024
C. Lledo Gomez et al. (eds.), *500 Years of Christianity and the Global Filipino/a*, Pathways for Ecumenical and Interreligious Dialogue, https://doi.org/10.1007/978-3-031-47500-9_12

209

Eventually, he was face to face with the old man. Jesus asks, "Sir, what did you do when you were back on earth?" "I was a carpenter," the old man replied. The reply got Jesus very excited. "What made your life very special then?" he continued. "I had a very special son," was the reply. A carpenter who had a special son? This got Jesus more excited! "What can you tell me about your son?" Jesus drew closer as he asked. "Nails and wood!" the carpenter answered. "Nails and wood?" Jesus was beyond ecstatic. He blurts out, "Father?" The old man responds, very surprised, "Pinocchio?"

Diversity is a gift. Difference is a fundamental fact of life. God created everyone and everything different. No two people are exactly alike. No two fingerprints are exactly alike. The same goes with experiences. No two people in any gathering is alike. Plurality is God's gift. *Father and son, nails, and wood do not always point to Jesus. They can also point to Pinocchio.*

Unity is grounded on difference! If we thought, spoke, prayed, did everything in the same way, we would not be here today. My youngest son when he was five, agreeing with my point about the gift of diversity, quipped: "You're right, *Tatay* (Father)! Because if everyone looked like you, the world would be a creepy place."

There is always more than one way of doing things. There is always more than one way of reading any text. Actually, there is legion. Interpretation is always particular and perspectival. Good news is always relative. When David killed Goliath, it was good news to the Israelites, bad news to Philistines (1 Samuel 17), and tragic news to Goliath's mother even if we do not hear her voice in the biblical text!

JEEPS AND JEEPNEYS

Difference has never been the world's problem. Our collective problems, woes, and pains arise when we force a single truth upon a plural world. We have a name for this structural and systemic violence: imperialism. The World Communion of Reformed Churches (formerly the World Alliance) in its 2006 Manila Declaration pronounced:

> The first one thousand years of Christianity was one millennium of war and destruction in the name of Jesus Christ. And those "civilizing missions" have not stopped. Even today, the most oppressive and dehumanizing societies are led by "Christian" centurions who have no qualms maiming and destroying those who are not "one of them."

Western Christianity has been closely related to empire since Roman days. Since then it has spread throughout the world, and now it is being used to provide ideological legitimization for today's empire. Globalized Christendom and the 'crusades' it embark upon today are symbiotically intertwined with global capital and the power of the global empire. In its triumphalistic pursuits, it discounts if not condemns all other religious faiths and cultures. The indigenous religions of many communities are destroyed and Islam is vilified.

The convergence of Christian religion with Western modernity has destroyed the religious and cultural life of peoples and their communities throughout the world. The powers and principalities of the global market and empire are being baptized by these theological distortions of 'Christianity', which promote religious conflicts and bigotry globally.

The Christian religion of empire treats others as 'gentiles' to be conquered, as the 'evil empire' to be destroyed, or as the 'axis of evil' to be eradicated from the earth. The empire claims that the 'goodness' of the empire must overcome these 'evils'. Its false messianic spirit is imbued with the demonic.

These false claims destroy the integrity of faiths, and radically erode the identity of Christian faith in Jesus Christ. As the spirit of empire penetrates souls, the power of global empire possesses the bodies of all living beings. Lord of its domain, it builds temples for the global market to serve Profit (Mammon).

The empire uses 'democracy' as an umbrella term for the kind of political regime that it would like to see installed all over the world. Bringing democracy to countries that do not yet have it is claimed as the defining purpose of US foreign policy. For the US, democracies abroad are regimes that support or follow its dictates.[2]

Imperialism is forcing a single truth upon a plural world. And it is, by whatever name, primarily a textual project. The Bible remains imperialism's most effective text. Biblical interpretation in many Asian countries continues to privilege the centers of power within, behind, and in front of the text. Biblical studies, particularly in the Philippines, remain a stronghold of colonial scholarship especially among Protestant churches. Denominations refuse to become autonomous and continue to depend on their mother institutions in the United States, Europe, or elsewhere in the so-called First World in the past century or the Global North these days. Church buildings and institutions are named after benevolent foreign church leaders and missionaries. Many seminaries (protestant and evangelical, less so in Catholic seminaries) continue to depend heavily on foreign teachers (who are usually paid in dollars by foreign boards) than natives (who are usually paid in the local currency and, oftentimes, significantly below the living wage). Libraries are filled with books written by European and American scholars and continue to receive donations of old throw-away books from these continents where most of the funding for colonial Christianizing mission are based. Traditional historical-critical methods remain the key reading paradigm. Establishing what the Bible meant in the past is the required, the correct, and the first step toward discerning what it means today. Carlos Abesamis, a Filipino Jesuit, one of the founders of EATWOT (Ecumenical Association of Third World Theologians) and a biblical scholar, remarked that nothing is the matter with foreigners doing foreign theology (for themselves). The issue is that Filipino theology is a photocopy of Euro-American theology.[3] It is not uncommon to hear the work of many Third-World or southern and minority scholars described as "interesting" while the work of a lot of European-American, mostly male, scholars described as "scholarly." Kwok Pui-lan in many of our conversations have repeatedly asked: "Why do we accept the work of less than 1% of the one-third of the world's male population, the European-American third, as normative for all?"

But the reality is this: no two interpretations are exactly alike. Those of us who engage the biblical writings know that, right now, there are over 5700 manuscripts of the New Testament in Greek. And no two are exactly alike. Hermeneutics is plural.

The wealth of diverse interpretations in the former colonies in Asia can be summarized into three categories: those that locate meaning in the "world behind texts," those that locate meaning in the "world of or in the texts," and those that locate meaning in the "world in front of the texts."[4] Those interpretations that fall under the first category presuppose that scripture serves a referential function, the text is a "window" to a privileged past—to Israel, to the historical Jesus, to the Gospel writers and their intentions, to the early Christian communities, etc.—that could be recovered. Interpretation is, therefore, aimed at first establishing what the text meant in order to arrive at what it means for today. The task of the interpreter is to recover meaning from behind the text to the historical setting from which it came. Traditional historical-critical methods like source,[5] form,[6] and redaction criticism[7] would fall under this category.

The second category of interpretations employ "closed reading" focused on plot, characters, setting, discourse, structure, implied authors, and implied readers in order to get at "what is in the text." If the first category privileged the past that the text referred to as the source of meaning, the second category privileges the text itself. This second category would include most literary methods like narrative,[8] structural,[9] and rhetorical criticism.[10] In such cases interpreters presuppose scripture as "story," a text that "has life all of its own." And this "living" text is able to create or conjure communities of readers/hearers.

The third category would include readings that privilege social location.[11] This means that this category is not located in the past or in the text, but in parts of the text that point "beyond the text" or "in front of the text": its rhetorical features as well as all the signs of ideological tensions, whether these are socio-economic, political, cultural, religious tensions that are recognizable, despite the fact that the text seeks to suppress them, for instance, by *marginalizing* characters, institutions, or events that manifest these tensions. These rhetorical features and ideological tensions are textual features that point "beyond the text," in the sense that they are recognizable by the ways in which they powerfully affect readers in situations similar to those suppressed by the text. Thus, these "in front of the text" textual features are most directly recognizable when they are activated by present-day readers. After all, interpretations are, as Mark Taylor puts it, "constructs of socially located flesh-and-blood readers."[12] Scripture then serves as a "mirror" that helps inform—*not define*—concrete life settings. Most advocacy approaches—liberationist,[13] feminist,[14] womanist,[15] reader-response criticism,[16] cultural,[17] postcolonial studies,[18] and queer[19]—would fall under this category.

My proposal, as an example of a "reading in front of texts" takes into account the primary role of culture and socio-political context in interpretations of the Bible, and in the process, elucidates dimensions of the text that otherwise would remain hidden. Simply put, I am a Filipino and this project is a Filipino reading of the Bible; in this particular instance, a specific pericope from Matthew. It is akin to Delores Williams's argument, in *Sisters in the Wilderness,* that her construction of Christian theology or god-talk is informed by the statement: "I am a black WOMAN."[20] More specifically my proposal shows how Filipino perspectives generated in resistance to imperialism and colonialism highlight certain aspects of the biblical texts and of their historical contexts that remain hidden when they are read from European-American perspectives.

What I am proposing is another "Canaanite" reading[21] that I am offering as a contribution to the developing archive of resistance and liberation discourses from the Third World and Fourth World or the so-called Global

South; a reading aimed to disrupt and challenge the hegemony of Western scholarship in biblical studies, especially in plural Asia. Most people do not know that the American occupation of the Philippines sent over one million Filipinos to heaven.[22] Most people do not know that the Americans designated Mindanao, the richest part of the country where Moros and indigenous peoples lived, the Land of Promise. Most people do not know that the occupation forces called the natives "niggers," "injuns," "heathens," "pagans," "tail-less brown monkeys," and "Canaanites" (especially the inhabitants of the Land of Promise!).

R.S. Sugirtharajah rightly argues that historical-critical methods were not only colonial in the sense that they displaced the norms and practices of our indigenous reading methods, but in that they were used to justify the superiority of Christian texts and to undermine the sacred writings of others. These methods are colonial because they insist that the right reading is mediated through the "proper" use of historical-critical tools alone. He laments, "Look at the opening of George Strecker's *The Sermon on the Mount: An Exegetical Commentary* (1988): 'No proper exegesis of the Sermon on the Mount can ignore the research of more than two hundred years of historical-critical research into the New Testament.'"[23]

Kwok Pui-lan, in another conversation, has argued that in theological education, a large part of the curriculum has been the study of the lives and thoughts of white, male, Euro-American theologians, to the exclusion of many other voices. More importantly, the theologies done by these people are considered normative, which set the standards and parameters of what "theology" should be.

Musa Dube reminds us that when it comes to the connection of the Bible, its readers, and its institutions to Western imperialism, there is no call for special pleading.[24] Laura Donaldson asks:

> What civilization invented the most brutal system of conquest and exploitation the world has ever known? Christian. Who made slavery the basis for capitalist expansion? Christians. What religion has been the most responsible for the genocide of aboriginal peoples? Christianity. In my view, the Christian church has a much more substantial record of pure evil than any final good.[25]

Canaan Banana posits that the Bible is an important book of the church and that it includes liberating messages; nevertheless, there remains the sense in which, unless one embraces the Christian concept of God, one is not fully a person of God.[26] Mary John Mananzan in many of her lectures has pointed out that the Bible, in spite of all the reinterpretations, remains a book written from a patriarchal, dominator, imperial perspective and thus must be used to inform and not define life and its struggles.

Robert Allen Warrior's essay, "Canaanites, Cowboys, and Indians,"[27] argues that the liberationist picture of Yahweh is incomplete. In the conquest narratives, Yahweh the liberator becomes Yahweh the conqueror. Warrior rightly points out that the obvious characters in the Exodus and Conquest narratives, for Native Americans to identify with, are the Canaanites, the people who already lived in the Promise Land. He also argues "that the Canaanites should be the center of theological reflection and political action. They are the last remaining ignored voice in the text, except perhaps for the land itself."[28] The conquest stories, for Warrior, with all their violence and injustice must be taken seriously by those who believe in the God of the Old Testament. Unfortunately, biblical critics rarely mention these texts and when they do, Warrior points out, they express little concern for the indigenes and their rights as human beings and as nations. Especially ignored are the passages where Yahweh tells the Israelites to mercilessly annihilate the indigenous population. Warrior then notes that oppressive narratives of conquest, anti-Semitism, sexism, heterosexism, imperialism, and racism remain in the canonized text.[29]

How, then, does one do a de-colonizing reading of an imperializing text?[30] In other words, how does one read the Bible without perpetuating the self-serving paradigm of constructing one group, one race, one gender, one people as superior to another?[31] How do Asian Christians overcome the alienation they feel as they try to relate the biblical world, colonial Christianity, and their own reality?[32]

When America claims privilege as the new Israel, how does a people, pacified by the veterans of the genocide of the Native Peoples, read the Bible as a Canaanite? I suggest reading the Bible inside a jeepney. "Reading the Bible Inside a Jeepney" begins with one's view of the Bible. Traditional roles of scripture are problematic, when they involve submission to the text or, more exactly, defining the authority of the text in terms of moral prescriptions or visions (ideologies, religious views, etc.) that it posits or carries. Many Asian Bible interpreters—mimicking their Western teachers—begin with the theological affirmation, explicit or not, that the Bible is "God's Word" and that it offers access to the Complete and Final Revelation of the One True God, Jesus Christ. Jeepney hermeneutics presupposes that the Bible is an American military jeep, a sword, an imperializing text—a dangerous text, as demonstrated throughout history by the many horrendous crimes committed in its name, especially among peoples and nations constructed as "Canaanites." Jeepney hermeneutics is about beating swords into plowshares.

The US Army back in 1940 required an all-terrain reconnaissance, go-anywhere, vehicle that seated three and had a mount for a 30-caliber machine gun. Anyone who has been to the Philippines knows that Filipinos have turned this military vehicle into a sort of mini-bus that can accommodate up to 20 people. Or more, including animals. There are those who look at a jeepney and call it Frankenstein's monster. There are others who see it as a "Filipino home on wheels," complete with an altar. The military jeep was, and still is, a sort of imperializing text. A jeepney resists this text.

Reading Matthew inside a Jeepney

Interpretation, by definition, is always perspectival and particular. I would like to take the Gospel of Matthew as an example for my proposed decolonizing reading. This interpretation of Matthew as an imperializing text presupposes the reality of an empire (the Roman Empire—the contemporary empire perceived as a reality by the biblical colonized people) as a backdrop to the construction of the narrative. Many Filipinos employ a similar assumption when engaging Filipino resistance literature, for example, Jose Rizal's *Noli Me Tangere* and *El Filibusterismo*, Francisco Baltazar's *Florante at Laura*, and Carlos Bulosan's *America Is in the Heart*. This interpretation does not equate the Gospel of Matthew with historical facts. What it does is argue that the Gospel is constructed and framed by a particular historical setting, in this case the Roman imperial occupation.[33] Anticolonialist, Franz Fanon, and educator, Paolo Freire, show that dynamics leading to literary production exist not only between the colonizer and the colonized, but also between various interest groups of the colonized, some of which try to gain power to define national cultural identity, as well as to compete for the attention of their collective oppressor. The interpretation below argues that Matthew is not rejecting Roman imperialism, but seeking its favor, or at least condoning it.[34]

This interpretation also presupposes resistance, as reflected in what activist Salud Algabre and historian Reynaldo Ileto call "little traditions."[35] Algabre and Ileto memorialize all those resistance fighters who have been victimized by the violence of institutionalized forgetting, a fate most of the unnamed children in Matthew share.

Matthew, Empire, and the Pais

Musa Dube[36] posits the following questions in order to measure whether Matthew's Gospel is an imperializing text: "1. Does this text have a clear stance against the political imperialism of its time? 2. Does this text encourage travel to distant and inhabited lands, and if so, how does it justify itself? 3. How does this text construct difference: Is there dialogue and mutual interdependence, or condemnation and replacement of all that is foreign? 4. Does this text employ gender representations to construct relationships of subordination and domination?"[37]

Using these questions to analyze Matthew and its effects upon its readers, Dube concludes that the author's stance toward the imperial powers presents imperial rule and its agents as holy and acceptable.[38] Matthew's Jesus is politically un-subversive and encourages travel to distant and inhabited lands.[39] Matthew's positive presentation of the Empire and the decision to take the word to the nations (Matt. 28:16-20) is born within and as a result of stiff competition for power over the crowds (Israel) and the favor of the Empire.[40] Matthew's mission to the nations embodies imperialistic values and strategies. Matthew does not seek relationships of liberating interdependence among nations, cultures, and genders. Rather, this Gospel upholds the superiority of some races and relegates other races to inferiority. Matthew represents gender relationships as relationships of subordination and domination by featuring the Canaanite woman (15:21-28)[41] and the centurion (8:5-13) in contrasting stories, which foreshadows the mission to the nations. The Canaanite is described and likened to a "little bitch" or a dog (15:26-27) while no one in Israel has faith greater than the centurion's (8:10). Matthew's presentation of Pilate, his wife, and the Roman soldiers at the trial, death, and resurrection of Jesus show a clear-cut pro-empire position (27:1–28:15).

The encounter between the centurion and Jesus, according to Dube, particularly highlights Matthew's stance toward the Empire.[42] Both men are presented as having authority to effect things simply by the power of their words (Matt. 8:8-9). The comparison of Jesus' authority with that of the centurion's has the effect of sanctifying the imperial power. Jesus pronounces the centurion's faith greater than the faith of everyone in Israel (Matt. 8:10), a statement that contrasts the imperial agent with the colonized and exalts his righteousness above theirs. The passage casts imperial officials as holier and predicts that they, and other groups, will have more power (in the kingdom of Heaven). Such characterization not only disguises what imperial agents represent—institutions of exploitation and oppression—but also pronounces imperialism holy and acceptable. A quick survey of the history of the interpretation of Matthew and centuries of Western colonization—euphemistically called "civilizing missions"—in Asia, Africa, and Latin America shows that most interpreters followed the Gospel's imperial rhetoric.

The centurion is to Matthew as the 30-caliber machine gun mount is to the military jeep. To read Matthew inside a jeepney is to celebrate the fact that the first thing Filipinos did in their transformation of the military jeep was to rid it of that machine gun mount. To read Matthew inside a jeepney is to affirm the reality that weapons of mass destruction (military jeeps) can be transformed into Filipino homes on wheels (public utility jeepneys). To read Matthew inside a jeepney is to argue that a three-seater, when its boundaries and walls are stretched and transgressed, can accommodate 20 or more people!

To read Matthew inside a jeepney is to remove our gaze from the centurion—and even Jesus, who mimics the centurion—and rather focus our gaze on someone else within the text. I suggest focusing our attention on the servant (*pais* in Greek) of 8:5-13.

The *pais*, whether translated son, daughter, girl, boy, servant, slave, or sex slave, is a child. He or she serves to remind flesh and blood readers that the reality of empire—in varying forms and degrees—is experienced by children and by those who are treated as children. Political sociologist Ashis Nandy draws attention to the way the colonized are viewed as children by the colonizers.[43] Fred Atkinson, the first American General Superintendent of Education in the Philippines, inaugurated more than a century of racist public education in the islands when he remarked that "the Filipino people, taken as a body, are children and childlike, do not know what is best for them. ... By the very fact of our superiority of civilization and our greater capacity for industrial activity we are bound to exercise over them a profound social influence."[44]

The *pais* reminds flesh and blood readers that children's oppression—of varying forms and degrees—is written in the text because, despite the rhetoric that God's reign is for children (Matt. 19:14), no child is ever named—except Jesus—or is given a voice in the Gospel—except Herodias's daughter, who says what her mother tells her to say. Like the Canaanite woman's daughter (15:21-28) and the *pais*, Herodias's daughter serves only as a medium through which competing discourses present their claims. The girl falls prey to manipulation by her mother and by Herod. We don't even get to hear the cries of the children who are massacred in 2:18, only their mothers' cries. Children are the primary victims of Matthew's "culture of silence."

Look at how the *pais* is described in Greek: *ho pais mou*, "the servant who is mine" (8:6). That child's body is under somebody else's control—whether it's his father, his owner, or, like Rosario Baluyot, her pedophile.[45]

The centurion's act on the *pais*'s behalf emphasizes the latter's marginalization. As far as Matthew is concerned, the *pais* cannot speak or seek his own healing. Yet, because that child is "paralyzed," albeit momentarily, he also paralyzes his owner, who must seek help from Jesus. The child also interrupts the goings and the comings of the centurion's soldiers, since the centurion is not with them to give them orders (Matt. 8:9). Thus, with his paralysis, the child also interrupts the imperial expansion. Throughout the Gospel, characters come and go, borders are crossed: magi from the East come seeking the king of the Jews (2:1-12); Joseph and his family flee into Egypt (2:13-15); Herod sends his death squads to Bethlehem to murder children (2:16-18); Joseph and his family go to Nazareth, from Egypt (2:19-23); Jesus goes to John the baptizer and is led by the Spirit into the wilderness (3:1-4:11); Jesus leaves Nazareth and makes his home in Capernaum (4:12); the centurion comes to Jesus and the latter is convinced of the imperial authority that effects goings and comings, travel to distant lands, and control at a distance (8:5-13). The disciples are systematically prepared for their commissioning (10:1-42); the Canaanite woman comes to Jesus (15:21-28); the heavy-laden come to Jesus (11:28). Jesus eventually sends out his disciples (28:16-20). Everyone in the story moves, except the *pais* in Matthew 8:5-13. Yes, even for a brief moment, the *pais* revels in the space her paralysis brings. For about eight short verses in the very long 28 chapters of the Gospel of Matthew, the *pais* is free of the centurion. The colonized is free of her colonizer.

Conclusion: Jeepneys and Today's Pais[46]

Tens of millions from the Third World or southern countries, majority of whom are women, are the global servants of late capitalism. They find themselves squatters, informal settlers, or internal refugees, militarized, displaced, and dispossessed, in their own homelands, as trans-nationals wreak havoc in the name of profit, globalization, and development. Many of those who have opted for "The Land of Opportunity"—the United States—find themselves treated as second-class citizens, as illegal immigrants, or, worse, as terrorists! Hundreds of thousands of our children, many of them are girls, victims of human trafficking, prostitution rings, and cyber-sex syndicates. The Philippines is one of the top countries where physical and online sexual exploitation of children happen and the COVID-19 pandemic has worsened it.[47] Over 800 million women spend up to 20 hours each day looking for water. Tragically, there are more WIFI hotspots in the world today than toilets. Yet despite all these dehumanizing conditions and oppressive structures that prey on the powerless and the marginalized, the *pais*, today's *paides* (plural of *pais*) have always resisted. This is why mortar shells have become church bells; why M-16 and AK-47 rifle barrels have become flutes; why implements of war have become peace bells; why Israeli-made tear gas canisters have been used as Palestinian flower pots; why jeeps have been transformed into jeepneys in the Philippines. Swords can be turned into plowshares and spears into pruning hooks.

The jeepney serves as an excellent symbol of resistance and decolonization.[48] Now, because of the Gospel of Matthew, we have another symbol, the *pais* who disrupts imperial progress, even if only briefly, in the Gospel of Matthew. The *pais* was alone in the Matthean narrative of imperial expansion. Those of us who have seen the *pais'* plight and who are involved in the struggles—for land, for liberty, for peace based on justice, for wholeness of life for all—in the name of today's *paides* are legion. The *pais* resists. The *pais* persists. The *pais* is Filipino!

NOTES

1. Fritz Kunkel, *Creation Continues: A Psychological Interpretation of Matthew* (New Jersey: Paulist, 1989), 120-121.
2. An Ecumenical Faith Stance Against Global Empire for A Liberated Earth Community available at http://www.peaceforlife.org/resources/statement/partners/325-an-ecumenical-faith-stance-against-global-empire-for-a-liberated-earth-community, accessed 5 October 2015.
3. Carlos Abesamis, *What is Inside the Wooden Bowl?* (Quezon City: Socio-Pastoral Institute, 1997), 23, 33.
4. For an elaboration of the various worlds of the text in connection with biblical interpretation, see Sandra M. Schneiders, *The Revelatory Text: Interpreting the New Testament as Sacred Scripture*, 2nd ed. (Collegeville, MN: Liturgical Press, 1999).
5. See, for example, Camille Focant, ed., *The Synoptic Gospels: Source Criticism and the New Literary Criticism* (Leuven: Peeters Publishers, 1993); Olegs Andrejevs, *Apocalypticism in the Synoptic Sayings Source: A Reassessment of Q's Stratigraphy*, Wissenschaftliche Untersuchungen Zum Neuen Testament. 2. Reihe 499 (Tübingen: Mohr Siebeck, 2019).
6. See, for instance, Edgar V. MacKnight, *What Is Form Criticism?*, Guides to Biblical Scholarship. New Testament Series (Philadelphia, PA: Fortress, 1971); Marvin A. Sweeney and Ehud Ben Zvi, *The Changing Face of Form Criticism for the Twenty-First Century* (Grand Rapids, MI: Eerdmans, 2003.

7. See, for example, Norman Perrin, *What Is Redaction Criticism?*, Reprinted (London: SPCK, 1976); Sweeney and Ben Zvi, *Changing Face*; Jakub Slawik, "Exegesis of the Book of Isaiah 61:1–11: Redaction Criticism and Inquiry into the Identity of the Prophet Known as Trito-Isaiah," *Collectanea Theologica* 90, no. 5 (2021): 241–93, https://doi.org/10.21697/ct.2020.90.5.11

8. See, for example, Mark Allan Powell, *What Is Narrative Criticism?*, Guides to Biblical Scholarship. New Testament Series (Minneapolis, MN: Fortress, 1990); Ma. Marilou S. Ibita, "Including the Hungry Adelphoi: Exploring Pauline Points of View in 1 Corinthians 11:17-34," in *By Bread Alone: The Bible through the Eyes of the Hungry*, ed. Sheila E. McGinn, Lai Ling Elizabeth Ngan, and Ahida Calderon Pilarski (Fortress Press, 2014), 159–84.

9. See, for instance, Daniel Patte, *Structural Exegesis for New Testament Critics*, Guides to Biblical Scholarship. New Testament Series (Minneapolis, MN: Fortress, 1990); Vincent A. Pizzuto, "The Structural Elegance of Matthew 1-2: A Chiastic Proposal," *The Catholic Biblical Quarterly* 74, no. 4 (2012): 712–37.

10. See, for example, Phyllis Trible, *Rhetorical Criticism: Context, Method, and the Book of Jonah.*, Guides to Biblical Scholarship. Old Testament Series (Minneapolis: Fortress, 1994); Stanley E. Porter and Bryan R. Dyer, *Paul and Ancient Rhetoric: Theory and Practice in the Hellenistic Context* (Cambridge: University Press, 2016).

11. See, for example, Fernando F. Segovia and Mary Ann Tolbert, *Reading from This Place: Volume 2. Social Location and Biblical Interpretation in Global Perspective* (Minneapolis, MN: Augsburg Fortress, 1995).

12. He shared this during a seminar at the SBL-AAR meeting in Orlando, Florida, November 1998.

13. See, for instance, Norman K. Gottwald, *The Bible and Liberation: Political and Social Hermeneutics*, Rev. ed. (Maryknoll: Orbis Books, 1983); Ndikho Mtshiselwa, "In Chains, yet Prophetic! An African Liberationist Reading of the Portrait of Paul in Acts 27," *HTS Teologiese Studies / Theological Studies* 71, no. 1 (2015): 1–9, https://doi.org/10.4102/hts.v71i1.2746

14. See Carol Newsom and Sharon H. Ringe, eds., *The Women's Bible Commentary.* (London: SPCK, 1994); Elisabeth Schüssler Fiorenza, *Searching the Scriptures. 1: A Feminist Introduction* (London: SCM, 1994); Athalya Brenner and Carole Fontaine, eds., *A Feminist Companion to Reading the Bible: Approaches, Methods and Strategies*, The Feminist Companion to the Bible (Sheffield: academic press, 1997); Susanne Scholz, ed., *The Oxford Handbook of Feminist Approaches to the Hebrew Bible*, Oxford Handbooks (Oxford: University Press, 2021).

15. See, for instance, Delores S. Williams, *Sisters in the Wilderness: The Challenge of Womanist God-Talk* (Orbis Books, 1993); Mitzi Smith, "Paul, Timothy, and the Respectability Politics of Race: A Womanist Inter(Con) Textual Reading of Acts 16:1–5," *Religions* 10, no. 3 (2019): 190-, https://doi.org/10.3390/rel10030190

16. See, for instance, Jane P. Tompkins, *Reader-Response Criticism: From Formalism to Post-Structuralism.* (Baltimore, MD: Johns Hopkins University Press, 1980); Robert M. Fowler, *Let the Reader Understand: Reader-Response Criticism and the Gospel of Mark* (Minneapolis, MN: Fortress, 1991).

17. See Brian K. Blount, *Cultural Interpretation: Reorienting New Testament Criticism* (Minneapolis, MN: Fortress, 1995); Lizette Tapia-Raquel, "The Gospel According to Lualhati Bautista" (Southeast Asia Graduate School of Theology, 2010); Ma. Marilou S. Ibita, "A Conversation with the Story of the Lord's Supper in Corinth (1 Cor 11:17-34): Engaging the Scripture Text and the Filipino Christians' Context," in *1 and 2 Corinthians: Texts @ Contexts Series*, ed. Yung Suk Kim (Minneapolis, MN: Fortress Press, 2013), 97–114.

18. Fernando F. Segovia, "Postcolonial Criticism and the Gospel of Matthew," in *Methods for Matthew*, ed. Mark Allan Powell (New York, NY: Cambridge University Press, 2009); Musa W. Dube, *Postcolonial Feminist Interpretation of the Bible* (Saint Louis, MS: Chalice Press, 2000); See, for example, R.S. Sugirtharajah, *The Bible and Asia: From the Pre-Christian Era to the Postcolonial Age* (Cambridge, MA: Harvard University Press, 2013); R.S. Sugirtharajah, *Exploring Postcolonial Biblical Criticism: History, Method, Practice* (Chichester, West Sussex, UK ; Malden, MA: Wiley-Blackwell, 2012); Pui-lan Kwok, "Elisabeth Schüssler Fiorenza and Postcolonial Studies," *Journal of Feminist Studies in Religion* 25, no. 1 (2009): 191–97, https://doi.org/10.2979/FSR.2009.25.1.191

19. See Theodore W. Jennings, *Jacob's Wound: Homoerotic Narrative in the Literature of Ancient Israel* (New York, NY: Continuum, 2005); Marcella Althaus-Reid, *Indecent Theology: Theological Perversions in Sex, Gender and Politics* (New York, NY: Routledge, 2001); Deryn Guest et al., eds., *The Queer Bible Commentary* (London: SCM Press, 2006); Ken Stone, ed., *Queer Commentary and the Hebrew Bible*, Journal for the Study of the Old Testament. Supplement Series 334 (Sheffield: Sheffield Academic Press, 2001).

20. Delores S. Williams, *Sisters in the wilderness: the challenge of womanist God-talk* (Maryknoll, NY: Orbis, 1993).

21. For one of the most comprehensive collections of "Canaanite Readings," see Laura E. Donaldson, *Postcolonialism and Scriptural Reading*, Semeia : An Experimental Journal for Biblical Criticism 75 (Atlanta: Society of Biblical Literature, 1996); James Treat, *Native and Christian: Indigenous*

Voices on Religious Identity in the United States and Canada (New York, NY: Routledge, 2012).

22. See Read E. San Juan, *An African American Soldier in the Philippine Revolution.* Available at http://clogic.eserver.org/2009/SanJuan.pdf, accessed October 15, 2015.

23. Georg Strecker, *The Sermon on the Mount: An Exegetical Commentary,* Trans. O.C. Dean, Jr. (Nashville: Abingdon, 1988), 11.

24. Dube, *Postcolonial Feminist Interpretation,* 14.

25. Laura E Donaldson, "Postcolonialism and Biblical Reading: An Introduction," *Semeia* 75 (1996): 7.

26. Dube, *Postcolonial Feminist Interpretation,* 15.

27. See Robert Allen Warrior, "Canaanites, Cowboys, and Indians: Deliverance, Conquest and Liberation," in *Native and Christian: Indigenous Voices on Religious Identity in the United States and Canada,* ed. James Treat (New York, NY: Routledge, 2012), 93–104.

28. Warrior, "Canaanites, Cowboys, and Indians: Deliverance, Conquest and Liberation," 98.

29. See Warrior, "Canaanites, Cowboys, and Indians: Deliverance, Conquest and Liberation," 102.

30. See, for instance, Fernando F. Segovia, *Decolonizing Biblical Studies: A View from the Margins* (Maryknoll, NY: Orbis Books, 2000); Mark G. Brett, *Decolonizing God: The Bible in the Tides of Empire*, The Bible in the Modern World 16 (Sheffield: Phoenix Press, 2009).

31. See, for example the discussion in Adele Reinhartz, "The Hermeneutics of Chutzpah: A Disquisition on the Value/s of 'Critical Investigation of the Bible,'" *Journal of Biblical Literature* 140, no. 1 (2021): 8–30.

32. See, for instance, Ma. Marilou S. Ibita, "Exploring the (In)Visibility of the Christ-Believers' 'Trans-Ethnicity': A Lowland Filipina Catholic's Perspective," in Ethnicity, Race, Religion: Identities and Ideologies in Early Jewish and Christian Texts, and in Modern Biblical Interpretation, ed. Katherine M. Hockey and David G. Horrell (London: T&T CLARK, 2018), 183–201.

33. The Gospel of Matthew is a narrative discourse constructed against the backdrop of Roman imperial occupation. Most interpreters of the Gospel prior to the year 2000 disregard the shadow of empire in their readings.

34. For readings that situate Matthew as against the Roman Empire, see Warren Carter, *Matthew and Empire: Initial Explorations* (Harrisburg: Trinity Press International, 2001); Warren Carter, "Resisting and Imitating the Empire: Imperial Paradigms in Two Matthean Parables," *Interpretation (Richmond)* 56, no. 3 (2002): 260–72, https://doi.org/10.1177/002096430005600303; John Kenneth Riches and David C. Sim, *The Gospel of Matthew in Its Roman Imperial Context* (London: T & T Clark International, 2005).

35. This is discussed thoroughly in Reynaldo Clemena Ileto, *Pasyon and Revolution: Popular Movements in the Philippines 1840-1910* (Manila: Ateneo de Manila Press, 1979).

36. Dube, *Postcolonial Feminist Interpretation*, 14.

37. See Dube, *Postcolonial Feminist Interpretation*, 57.

38. See Dube, *Postcolonial Feminist Interpretation*, 132, 140, 154, 168, and 171.

39. For a representation of Jesus as against the empire, see the abovementioned works of Carter and the contributions in the book of Riches and Sim.

40. See Dube, *Postcolonial Feminist Interpretation*, 137-138.

41. See Dube, *Postcolonial Feminist Interpretation*, 127-195. For a recent and empowered reading of the Canaanite woman in the Philippine context, see M. Ibita and M.S. Ibita, "Choosetochallenge: Covid-19, Community Research, and the Canaanite Woman," *Acta Theologica* 43, no. suppl 35 (2023): 180–99, https://doi.org/10.38140/at.v35i1.6375

42. See Dube, *Postcolonial Feminist Interpretation*, 131-132.

43. See Leela Gandhi, *Postcolonial Theory: A Critical Introduction* (Edinburgh: Edinburgh University Press, 1998), 32.

44. Daniel B. Schirmer and Stephen Rosskamm Shalom, eds., *The Philippines Reader: A History of Colonialism, Neocolonialism, Dictatorship, and Resistance* (South End Press, 1987), 44.

45. Rosario Baluyot was a 12-year-old prostitute in Olongapo City. A Swiss doctor who came as a tourist to the Philippines used her and inserted a vibrator into her vagina. The vibrator broke in half, and one-half remained inside her. After some weeks she began to have stomach pains. When she was examined, the rusting object was found inside her. She died of infection. For more details, see Fritzie Rodriguez, "Remembering the rape of Rosario Baluyot," available from https://www.rappler.com/voices/ispeak/60590-rosario-baluyot-philippines-rape/ (accessed July 25, 2023).

46. For a fuller discussion, see Revelation Velunta, "The Ho Pais Mou of Matthew 8:5-13: Contesting the Interpretations in the Name of Present-Day Paides," *Bulletin for Contextual Theology*, Vol 7.2 (June 2000): 25-32.

47. See Commission on Human Rights, "Statement of the Commission on Human Rights on the Preliminary Findings of the Un Special Rapporteur on the Sale and Sexual Exploitation of Children," December 22, 2022, https://chr.gov.ph/statement-of-the-commission-on-human-rights-on-the-preliminary-findings-of-the-un-special-rapporteur-on-the-sale-and-sexual-exploitation-of-children/. For a related discussion, see also the contribution of Cristina Lledo-Gomez in this book entitled "*Bangon Na*, Pinays Rise Up: Reclaiming Pinay Power Dismantled by a Christian Colonial Past."

48. However, the jeepney itself is in danger of being phased out by December 31, 2023 in the Philippines in view of a Public Utility Vehicle Modernization Program or the Department of Transportation Order No. 2017-011 contested by jeepney drivers themselves. For more information, see Teodoro C. Mendoza, "UP CIDS Discussion Paper Series 2021-02: Addressing the 'Blind Side' of the Government's Jeepney 'Modernization' Program," in University of the Philippines Center for Integrative and Development Studies, 2021, https://cids.up.edu.ph/discussion_paper/up-cids-discussion-paper-series-2021-02-addressing-the-blind-side-of-the-governments-jeepney-modernization-program/

CHAPTER 13

Inang Diyos, Inang Bayan: The Virgin Mary and Filipino Identity

Jamina Vesta M. Jugo

A Mary for Filipinos?

My grandmother once dreamed of standing onshore as a big, white boat approached. It was a beautiful boat. She was overcome by an urge to jump aboard, even though she knew she might miss and drown in the choppy water. She also had a sensation of pain in her chest; she felt that it would go away if she managed to board the boat. Just as she was about to attempt the leap, a giant woman dressed in traditional Ifugao garb appeared. She picked my grandmother up by the shoulders and put her down further inland. "Dito ka (You stay here)," said the woman, as the boat sailed away. That was when my grandmother woke up—out of breath, but her chest pain suddenly gone. She told me that she was convinced that she had narrowly missed having a heart attack. The Virgin Mary had visited her in the form of an Igorot woman to ensure that she would not die before her time.

J. V. M. Jugo (✉)
European Studies Program, Ateneo de Manila, Quezon City, Philippines
e-mail: jjugo@ateneo.edu

© The Author(s), under exclusive license to Springer Nature Switzerland AG 2024
C. Lledo Gomez et al. (eds.), *500 Years of Christianity and the Global Filipino/a*, Pathways for Ecumenical and Interreligious Dialogue, https://doi.org/10.1007/978-3-031-47500-9_13

227

My late grandmother was ardently devoted to the Virgin Mary, even after she had converted to an Evangelical congregation that (officially) frowns on saints and Marianism. It makes sense that she would consider this dream a Marian intervention. What makes less immediate sense is her envisioning of the Virgin Mary as Ifugao. My grandmother was not Ifugao. Actually, she was an Ilonggo-speaking,[1] light-skinned, Spanish-Filipina *mestiza* from Bacolod—practically as far away as one can get from being Ifugao while still being some kind of Filipino. She had also grown up around conventional images of the Virgin Mary depicting her as Caucasian. "Brown" images such as Our Lady of Piat (Cagayan, Philippines) were the exception, as, indeed, they still are in the Philippines. Yet the Virgin appeared to her in skin and clothes that could be nothing other than Filipino: not broadly Asian, not Hispanic, but explicitly and plausibly only Filipino. Mary, as the more approachable face of the divine, would reflect a devotee's personal context, and for many believers like my grandmother, that context constantly foregrounds Filipino identity. This was how my grandmother became sure that the Virgin Mary had come specifically to visit and intervene for *her*. God has no nationality, but Mary and her son Jesus can.[2]

I present this anecdote as emblematic of how many Filipinos see the Virgin Mary as having a special connection to *Filipino* Catholics, and not simply belonging to world Catholicism.[3] While Philippine provinces and municipalities might have their own patron saint (which in some cases is an aspect of the Virgin Mary), the Virgin Mary herself can be seen as the patron saint of the whole country and/or all Filipinos.[4] As Deirdre de la Cruz argues, these various aspects of Mary allow for local specificity while helping to forge a "Filipino universal" that unites all the country's Catholics.[5]

In May 2020, the Philippine Catholic bishops jointly commemorated the Philippines to the Immaculate Heart of Mary on the feast day of Our Lady of Fatima.[6] Considering this period was during the height of the global Coronavirus pandemic, and that the Philippines was suffering proportionally more casualties than its neighbors, the consecration could hardly have come at a more emblematic time. Ceremonies like this one institutionalize narratives binding Mary to the Philippines as the country's mother, whose care is heightened in times of great suffering.

Filipino Catholicism's especially strong Marianism is traced back to the early years of Christianization. Spanish clerics must have recognized that Christianity would take root in the Philippines only if it could somehow tame and absorb local matriarchal traditions.[7] Thus, mother goddesses were subsumed into the figure of the Virgin Mary. As for indigenous women themselves, they were compensated for the loss of their egalitarian status through Marian narratives glorifying selfless, de-sexualized domesticity.[8] The female (or sometimes queer male) shamans called *babaylan* or *catalonan*, however, would not be given space in this new order.[9] They were to be demonized as witches, only for their legend to be resurrected in post-independence times as symbols of feminism, gender diversity, and re-indigenization.[10]

Marianism as deployed in lived religion can dignify the lives of people in marginalized positions, especially those who identify as women and/or are in subservient positions—which are, of course, often the same thing.[11] Influence and moral authority, the forms of power most often attributed to women, can have very real impact when women are able to invoke Mary, embodying her through their own motherhood.[12] Marianism can discourage believers from bracketing stereotypically feminine, domestic stories from heroic, messianic narratives that are still mostly presented as the province of men.[13] The figures of Mary and Jesus in the Philippines still tend to conform to conservative gender roles, but at least they are inextricably bound together in one story.

On the other hand, Marianism can function as a vehicle for internalized misogyny, convincing women to adopt domesticated, subservient roles. If a woman has talent and/or power, she should use it entirely in the service of others, especially family.[14] When set against the figure of the whore, the resulting dichotomy pits "good" women against "bad" women. Marianism may present the Virgin Mary as an impossible ideal that traps families in abusive dynamics.[15] Benevolent sexism as sacred ideal is harder to detect, much less outright rebel against.[16]

Indeed, Marian ideals affect both men and women, Marianismo in Latino/Latine cultures, as pointed out by Stevens, is the feminine twin to machismo.[17] Both attitudes help to perpetuate each other.[18] Machismo pressures men to project dominance, often to the extent of endangering themselves and others.[19] Marianismo pressures women to model themselves on a sacrificial view of the Virgin Mary.[20] Women are supposed to be both wives and mothers to men, gently wielding their (supposed) spiritual/moral superiority in order to keep families together and enforce sexual boundaries.[21] Men are considered less capable of doing so themselves.[22] Of course, this encourages the condoning of domestic abuse, and/or victim blaming in cases of sexual assault.[23]

230 J. V. M. JUGO

All these negative tendencies have been spotted in Filipino society by feminist scholars and activists.[24] The Marian connection does not appear to have been made as explicitly, however—at least not in popular discourses. This is one instance where Filipinos might do well to look at other cultures with similar experiences, in this case with Hispanic Catholicism. Interrogating Latine Marianismo might help Filipinos to recognize similar patterns in their own Marianism and look for healthier means of living out their values. Stevens' initial concept has been critiqued and expanded upon in the intervening decades, especially with regard to differences between socio-economic classes.[25] Hence, analyses of Marianismo have become more complex over time, and Filipino Catholics may offer a valuable contribution to the ongoing discussion.

IMPERIALISM, COLORISM, NATIONALISM

Marianism lies at the heart of the Philippines' historical ties to Spain, and, later, to the gradual emergence of its national consciousness. Marianism was and is a vehicle for the inculturation of Roman Catholicism, blending Christian traditions with pre-colonial beliefs in mother goddesses and female guardian spirits.[26] That said, the acceptance of Marianism on the islands was far from passive. As Ileto has famously shown, Spanish Catholicism met the vibrant traditions and creativity of local populations.[27] The mother-son bond between Mary and Jesus resonated with pre-existing matriarchal traditions, resulting in the highlighting of this aspect of the Christ story, as compared to Catholicism in other parts of the world.[28] Pre-colonial mother or guardian goddesses live on through the Virgin Mary, as epitomized by the guardian goddess of Mt. Makiling being now known as Mariang Makiling.[29] The names and surrounding mythology of these pre-European goddesses are lost, or largely unknown outside indigenous communities and academia.[30] A lack of direct knowledge about Spanish Catholic traditions also hinders understanding Marianism's inculturation and indigenization in the Philippines.

The blending of traditions is perhaps more obvious in some Chinese-Filipino Marian devotions, which fuse the Virgin Mary with Kwan Yin or Guanyin, the deity usually described in English as the Goddess of Mercy.[31] That said, the blending of traditions found in Filipino Marianism might elide the violence that accompanied colonization and Christianization—as does the term "inculturation" itself.

Aesthetics and empire go together to a considerable degree. The conventional image of the Virgin Mary in Filipino paintings and sculptures is decidedly Caucasian, with fair skin, a high and narrow nose, and light or blond curls.[32] Black Madonnas, therefore, have a special if not necessarily unique significance in Filipino Catholicism.[33] In the Philippines, as perhaps in many other societies where the majority of the population would identify as non-white, a dark-skinned Madonna validates the status of being a person of color.[34] The reader may notice parallels to another New World Black Madonna, specifically La Guadalupana of Mexico.[35] La Guadalupana's dark skin, and the legend of the image appearing on the apron of an indigenous man named Juan Diego to prove the authenticity of his Marian visions to skeptical Spanish priests, validates indigenous identity in the face of Eurocentrism.[36] La Guadalupana shows that the faith of indigenous people is just as genuine as, if not more so than, that of the missionaries who came to supposedly civilize them.[37]

The closest figure to La Guadalupana in the Philippines is likely to be Our Lady of Guidance, currently housed in Ermita Church in Old Manila. Of ambiguous origin, she is made of molave wood, which suggests she might have been carved in the Philippines in the earliest years of Christianization. A popular legend is that Spanish soldiers found indigenous Filipinos worshiping her in a shrine decorated with pandan leaves—a feature of devotion to her to this day. The combination of Catholic statuary and native rites places syncretism at the root of Our Lady of Guidance's legend. Her vestments echo this narrative, being a combination of a Spanish-style mantle and an indigenous tapis skirt. In this way, she is rather different from La Guadalupana. If the Mexican image suggests a somewhat defiant anti-colonial Mexican identity, Our Lady of Guidance posits a gentler inculturation of Marianism blended with precolonial mother goddess worship.

Of course, this is not to say that anti-colonial or even revolutionary Marianism is absent from the Philippines. The Virgin of Balintawak is known to Filipino Catholics but is less popular among them than in the Aglipayan community. A detailed, influential account of this apparition is found in the so-called *Novenario*, one of the foundational texts of Aglipayanism.[38] The Aglipayan Church, which its founder, Gregorio Aglipay, officially separated from the Catholic Church in 1902, is an explicitly revolutionary movement. It is doctrinally and ritually similar to Catholicism but was created to give Filipinos a religious structure free from both Spanish and American control. Given the fusion of religious and secular power in Philippine politics—a state of affairs that persists to this day—indigenous Churches were very much about movements for self-rule.[39]

The Balintawak story centers on leaders and troops from the Katipunan pro-independence revolutionary army hiding in the area's mountains.[40] The fighters were planning to descend to Manila, but the Virgin appeared to an unnamed Katipunero in a dream, warning them to be careful.[41] The army decided to remain in the mountains.[42] This turned out to be a good decision, as the Spanish authorities suddenly clamped down on Katipunan agents in Manila.[43] A few were arrested, but the overwhelming majority remained at large in Balintawak.[44] The Marian apparition is supposed to have saved the Revolution—at least for the moment.

The *Novenario* story is considered the first instance of the Virgin Mary being explicitly identified with *Inang Bayan*—Mother Country or Mother of the Nation.[45] Formerly looking to Spain as their Mother Country, Filipinos now nurtured a national consciousness fusing patriotism and religion.[46] I argue, however, for a narrative interpretation that is rather different from the replacement of one mother figure by another, especially since it is less likely that many Filipinos beyond elite or *ilustrado* circles looked to Spain as their Mother Country.

As *Inang Bayan*, the Virgin of Balintawak (Quezon City, Metro Manila, Philippines) is still arguably compatible with patriarchal expectations for Filipino mothers in difficult marital situations. "Traditional" Filipino mothers are expected to smooth over conflicts, perhaps endure abuses from their husbands in order to ensure family togetherness. However, a good mother also knows when this abuse becomes untenable, especially when directed at her offspring. Putting her children's welfare first, she leaves or expels her husband, even in the face of opposition from him and/or the community. The Virgin of Balintawak, therefore, asserts herself as the mother of the nascent Filipino nation, or, in a sense, as the Philippines itself. As for Spain, it is not the Mother Country, nor even the former Mother Country, but an abusive father figure whose authority can and must be overthrown.

As such, the Virgin of Balintawak does not necessarily present a separate or oppositional story to the more pro-colonial Marys preceding her—she and her Son still have white faces while wearing their Filipino garb.[47] She is one aspect of a highly complex maternal figure. This figure helps devotees survive an abusive status quo, but often in a way compatible with perpetuating said abusive order. At critical junctures, however, she supports her children in leaving situations where abuse is no longer bearable. Marianism of this type can fuel nigh-miraculous waves of social uprising, but we may also ask whether it really overturns dominant narratives. Does the Virgin of Balintawak reject abuse in principle, or does she appear when abuse is too excessive to be borne, and it is finally acceptable to change the situation?

Mary and Overseas Filipin@ Workers (OFW's)

Besides providing the ur-example of maternal sacrifice, Mary's story often has special resonance for overseas Filipin@ workers (OFW's) and their families. On the one hand, Filipina mothers who work overseas to send remittances home to their families may see themselves in Mary's sacrifice and heroic example of motherhood.[48] I would also argue that mothers of faraway OFW's may feel connected to the story of a woman whose child must leave home on a potentially dangerous journey for the greater good of family and community. The material uplifting of the family through the mother's or child's remittances is a micro-level form of (limited) salvation/redemption.

Collantes points out that Marian images of self-sacrificial, maternal care are core to the marketing of Filipinas as ideal care workers on the international job market.[49] Certain higher-prestige sub-sectors of this transnational market—for instance, as registered nurses in countries that recognize their university qualifications—Filipinas can also command higher pay and greater job security. However, this does not necessarily equate to comfort and safety. The disproportionately high rates at which migrant Filipino health workers—of all genders—became ill and died during the Coronavirus pandemic, in comparison to their native-born co-workers,[50] grimly underlined the sacrificial and even martyrological dimensions of this type of work.[51] On the other hand, growing consciousness of the need for foreign—not least Filipina—health workers to serve the aging populations of the Global North highlights the redemptive and heroic potential of Marianism: Filipinas' paid care work will save their patients and, by extension, their host societies, as well as their own families back home.[52]

Marian narratives also provide models for navigating transnational intimacy—unfortunately, often to the effect of reinforcing sexual double standards. Patriarchal sexual norms in the Philippines demand that a woman remain a virgin until marriage, and remain sexually faithful to her husband even if he should stray[53]—exactly what some men are more likely to do when their wives are abroad.[54] OFW women themselves must negotiate a potentially hostile cultural environment overseas, where they are often stereotyped as prostitutes, mail-order brides, or sexually available domestic workers.[55] It is one side of the overall hyper-sexualization of Asian women in a Eurocentric world.[56] Certainly, this is not to let Filipino society off the hook, so to speak, given its tendencies to promote rape culture[57] and the sexualization of children of all genders. However, in a decolonizing analysis, we must account for how global economic inequality and geopolitics lead to intersectional forms of racialized and sexualized violence, which some Global South women attempt to deal with by leaning on Marianism.

The flexibility of Marian narratives is why they continue to hold sway for Filipinos in the face of such drastic cultural shifts as mass labor migration[58] and, more recently, the onset of all-encompassing communication technology and/or social media.[59] Such forces might initially seem to break down traditional family structures and encourage women to form ties with geographically far-off areas. This turns out to be far from the case, at least for many Filipina mothers.[60] Cellphones offer women yet more opportunities—or demands—to fulfill their traditional role of providing the bulk of care work and emotional labor for their families.[61] As mobile banking functions become more advanced, the cellphone also becomes the mechanism for exerting financial power. In the case of mothers who are migrant workers, they can serve as the vessel for the everyday miracle known as remittances.

Soriano, Lim, and Rivera-Sanchez dissect this narrative in their analysis of the portrayal of Filipina mothers in telecommunications advertising, cannily titling their article "The Virgin Mary With the Mobile Phone."[62] Mothers are almost always shown using cellphones in their capacity as family caregivers: staying up-to-date on children's welfare, managing household expenses, etc.[63] Absent are depictions of mothers using their phones to arrange some leisure activities for themselves, or maintain relationships with other people, such as old friends and classmates, beyond their families.[64] Even the husbands in such advertisements are likely to see them as all-giving, sexless carers rather than genuine romantic partners.[65]

Just like OFW's themselves are purported to be, the Marian narrative interwoven into the prototypical OFW story is resilient and adaptable. (Post-)Modern technological advances, far from attenuating Marian narratives, more often facilitate their expansion across time and space.

Marianism and Women Political Leaders

Marian hyper-emphasis on women's maternal role might seem to militate against their political participation. However, anyone with a cursory knowledge of Philippine history or current events would remember that the Philippines has already had two female Presidents.[66] Top alternate contenders for the 2016 and 2022 Presidential elections also happened to be women: Grace Poe and Ma. Leonor "Leni" Robredo, respectively. This is neither an irony nor a contradiction. It is the highest-profile manifestation of a specifically Filipino political Marianism. Women's power on the political scene is acceptable insofar as it can be framed as maternal. Even better when this includes specifically Marian elements like sacrifice and/or enmeshment with the story of a martyred male Messiah.

Indeed, it seems that maternal/Marian elements are *necessary* for the legitimation of women's heroism in post-independence Philippines. Such conceptual constraints are in large part a legacy of national memory. Studies of national memory in countries like Poland[67] and Mexico,[68] as well as the Philippines, show how foundational narratives can exert decisive influence on acceptability of public/political roles for women in the present. When non-domestic or explicitly martial forms of female heroism are forgotten, present-day women will have greater difficulty taking on such roles themselves.

Doran presents a detailed analysis of revolutionary women in Philippine national memory.[69] Overtly maternal figures like Teodora Alonso, the mother of Jose Rizal, or Tandang Sora, who frequently assisted and sheltered the Katipunan, are more likely to rise to prominence.[70] However, women who led or participated in combat, such as Trinidad Perez Tecson, will have their battle experience downplayed, instead of remembered as caring for sick fighters.[71] These more maternal elements are not outright lies—Tecson did indeed care for her ill and injured comrades.[72] However, they tend to be centered at the expense of less conventionally feminine or maternal biographical elements that would render these historical figures more multi-faceted.[73]

Nevertheless, women who fight like men have become enshrined in the national memory. Gabriela Silang is perhaps the most famous female warrior in Philippine history. Her story will be analyzed here as the exception that proves the rule. Gabriela is numbered in the pantheon of national heroes even though, like fellow national hero Lapu-Lapu, she did not fight under the banner of Filipino nationhood. At the time of her armed

236   J. V. M. JUGO

struggle (1762-63), Filipino identity did not exist in a form recognizable today. Uprisings tended to happen in the name of a tribe or nation—in this case, the Ilocanos.

Gabriela Silang became an anti-colonial *generala* after her husband, Diego Silang, the original leader, was betrayed and assassinated by a spy in the pay of Spanish authorities.[74] Gabriela would be a thorn in the side of the Spanish Crown until she was eventually captured and hanged with some of her troops.[75] The Silangs' revolution is recognized as one of the first anticolonial uprisings by Hispanized Filipinos—rather remarkable since Gabriela only led the Ilocano rebellion for four brief months before her own death.[76]

Stereotypically feminine care work is notably absent from Gabriela Silang's narrative. The emphasis is on her physical courage and ability to command men. No portraits of Silang remain from her lifetime. However, the equestrian monument erected in her honor at the Ayala Triangle gives a fairly good notion of her portrayal in national memory. Hair streaming, swerving her horse in a complicated maneuver, bolo raised high, this Gabriela is very much a heroine of the battlefield. Brow furrowed and mouth wide open to shout orders or battle cries, she exudes fierce dynamism rather than calm domesticity.

Gabriela Silang's legacy takes a more explicit form in modern Philippine politics through the country's main feminist party, which named itself after her. Founded in 1984, the party's full name is General Assembly Binding Women for Reforms, Integrity, Equality, Leadership, and Action—hence GABRIELA.[77] The somewhat forced acronym shows just how determined the Party was to invoke Gabriela Silang's story—or legend—as their own model for feminist, anti-imperialist Filipino womanhood.

More commonly, today's women leaders may legitimate their power in spaces ranging up to the national political arena by embodying the archetype of the Virgin Mary. Supporters of women leaders might legitimate a woman's power by presenting her as an embodiment of this archetype, regardless of the woman's own wishes and strategies for self-presentation. Widows following martyred husbands into high-profile politics are a common trope in more recent Philippine history, with Corazon Aquino being the archetypical example.

Such a woman's motivation, per patriarchal ideals, is private devotion to her husband and his life mission, rather than a personal desire for leadership. Private devotion, therefore, allows crossover into the public sphere. Widowhood also creates stronger parallels to Marian narratives, by casting the dead husband as Christ to the woman's Mary. In a manner of speaking, the martyred husband is resurrected in the form of his widow, who becomes (more) politically active in order to continue his mission. This pseudo-incestuous formula fusing the assassinated spouse with the martyred Messianic son is in keeping with Filipino-lived Catholicism. Filipinos, especially older ones, often refer to the sacred mother-son pair as "Mama Mary" and "Papa Jesus." Mary is always the mother, but Christ seems to blur the lines between father and older brother for Filipinos.

Aquino implicitly leaned on Marian tropes of moral purity and mercy to forestall predictable criticisms about her leadership. One of her most famous quotes states, "I concede I cannot match Mr. Marcos when it comes to experience. I admit that I have no experience in cheating, stealing, lying or assassinating political opponents."[78] Once she was President, however, some of the very qualities that drew the public to her—respect for human rights, non-violence, and maternal mercy—seemed to anger some of the very soldiers who deserted Marcos to support her movement.[79] She was considered "weak" against both communism and against the more power-hungry men of her own family.[80]

My own personal experience as a volunteer for the Robredo campaign comes into play in my analysis, as I was direct witness to the shaping of Marian narratives and was one of those who attempted to push back against them when I deemed them excessive. Robredo's public feminism generally perpetuated traditional Catholic tropes of motherhood. It directly opposed what Parmanand terms the punitive, "Macho Messiah" narratives of Dutertism, which posited Duterte and his allies as strict patriarchs who were willing to use violent or even deadly force against the most recalcitrant of their child-citizens.[81] A gendered discourse positing a feminized, Marian respect for human rights versus a harsh, masculine law-and-order approach had already pervaded the Philippine landscape by this point.[82] One of its most explicit representations had appeared as early as 2016, in Raffy Lerma's famous portrait of Jennilyn Olayres holding the corpse of her partner, tricycle driver Michael Siaron, one of the thousands slain by police and vigilantes during the Duterte administration's War on Drugs.[83] Lerma titled his photograph "La Pieta."[84] Whether or not she intended it, Robredo took on these gendered codes by choosing to lean her campaign on an expanded form of maternal authority.

Lacking large donors and dynastic wealth, Robredo's campaign often had to draw from the resources of volunteers. In giving of their own money and time, the volunteers themselves—who were most often women—became sacrificial mother figures. These tropes were extended into the conduct of Leni's overall campaign. Robredo's supporters were exhorted to turn the other cheek in the face of consistent online and offline attacks. The Robredo campaign thus fell back on a politics of respectability that played right into the hands of pro-Marcos populists, who accused it of elitism and of weakness against enemies of state and society. Though Robredo was more liberal, pro-poor, and experienced in public service than Corazon Aquino, some opponents—not least Marcos' sister, Governor Imee Marcos—claimed she had the same weakness as her predecessor in leadership, that is being a "housewife" like Aquino.

A Marian maternalism and Inang Bayan imagery pervaded Robredo's campaign—with the twist that she was a modern, professional woman with a successful career as a human rights lawyer and effective plans for the nation's future. This angle was not a complete departure from more traditional Marian/maternal tropes—a good mother is also supposed to be a competent household manager. If the nation is portrayed as one big family or home, a woman can take the lead if she can present herself as its rightful mother.

Future Marian Narratives?

When is Marianism liberatory, honoring the struggles of people whose stories might otherwise be devalued and forgotten? When is it unitive, bringing disparate people and groups into a larger kinship community? On the other hand, when does Marianism have a merely palliative effect, encouraging Filipinos, especially girls and women, to endure suffering even when there are feasible means of liberating themselves and others?

Some critiques call for the abandonment of Marianism altogether, particularly from those who consider Marianism and the (excessive) adoration of saints to be a type of idolatry or accidental polytheism. Rapid growth of Protestant congregations in the Philippines and the Philippine diaspora will likely amplify such criticisms against a distinctly Catholic mode of worship.

However, critiques can come from within communities of Marian devotion. Filipinas can point out and try to dismantle oppressive uses of Marianism precisely because of their Marian devotion, which they wish to be channeled in healthy, liberating ways. Academic articulations of these critiques are more common among women and feminist scholars, not least theologian and activist Sister Mary John Mananzan.[85] Many Filipinas are still convinced that their value is tied to sexual purity, and to being a "good" wife and mother.[86]

The self-sacrificing maternal role is accompanied by family set-ups that uphold the mother as the ultimate moral authority—at least within the home. Her perpetual sacrifice is a debt that her offspring must always carry, but can never truly repay. Absolute obedience and devotion to their mothers, even if these mothers have failings of their own (as do all human beings), and excessive filial piety hinder individual maturation. In psycho-social terms, this tends to produce adults with weak egos and emotional regulation—exactly the type of people who might perpetuate, condone, or fall into abuse dynamics throughout life. Generational trauma is cyclical and requires deep interrogation of whether the love we give is truly supportive and healthy. On the much more positive side, we can also argue that, when sacrifice and suffering are less dominant in Filipina mothers' ideal narratives, their freedom need not come at the expense of the people who depend on them. A self-respecting and self-actualized mother is better able to respect and encourage her children's individuation. The liberation of Filipina mothers enables that of their children, as well.

On a wider community or national level, political Marianism is associated with a flawed status quo. So desperate are some Filipinos for change that they will turn to violent, counterfactual Messianism. Does this mean it is time to leave Marianism behind? Or might there be underexplored ways to channel Marianism for liberating purposes?

Filipinos might look to the Assumption, wherein Mary ascends bodily to Heaven. If Mary herself can represent Filipinas and/or the Philippines, then perhaps this story points toward the transcendence of destructive social cycles, ascending to a healthier and freer state of being. This could open up much-needed discussions about what a "higher state" in the Philippines, or a healthier Filipino society, would actually look like. This might be a way out of what I have elsewhere called "The *Noli* trap," where analysts and artists point out problems, but for whatever reason do not (yet) offer clear alternatives or solutions.[87] That said, there are major drawbacks to a narrative that aims to manifest Heaven on Earth, not least the possibility of pursuing unfeasible, unworldly strategies. If Filipinos have such difficulty manifesting Easter, does it make sense to expect them to imagine Heaven?

Another possibility, which I argue is both more obvious and more fraught, is to reconsider Mary's role in Paschal and Easter narratives. Filipino Catholic religiosity, especially in the so-called folk versions, tends to emphasize the Passion/Good Friday and sideline Easter.[88] It is argued that this tendency reflects the national context of post-colonialism/neo-imperialism and severe social inequality.[89] The Philippines, and particularly its poor, have not yet experienced their own Easter; they seem to remain in the Passion stage. On the other hand, one can also argue that these tendencies encourage Filipinos to stay stuck in cycles of oppression. It becomes harder to recognize possible roads to liberation, especially when those deviate from the beaten path. Those who do not recognize or proclaim the Good News—or at least its incipient/potential arrival—must remain in Purgatory.

Though not necessarily phrased in religious terms, this Passion-oriented mentality faces growing critiques. Outcries against the romanticization of poverty are increasingly common.[90] Resilience, a much-touted Filipino survival trait, is not immune from critique, either.[91] Officials can use the concept of resilience to avoid accountability, perhaps most clearly in post-disaster contexts.[92] Instead of upholding their duty to provide honest and competent support for recovering populations, they pass their responsibilities back to these "heroic" grassroots communities.[93] The community's Paschal trials become indefinitely protracted, as it is forced to implement a recovery program out of its own depleted resources.

Even as Filipinos seem to have difficulty letting go of unhealthy narratives, there is also a clear sense of dissatisfaction with mainline historical discourses. It is no coincidence that the decline of institutional Church power in the Philippines is accompanied by the declining effectivity of political Marian narratives. I claim that staunch Church opposition to the Reproductive Health Bill can be interpreted as a demand that Filipinas do their utmost to be sacrificing mothers, regardless of the damage done to them and their families by giving up effective family planning options. Citizens' frustration with this politicking undermined the Church's moral authority, paving the way for Duterte and his allies, who could more easily flout the Church's anti-dictatorial People Power narratives.[94] Leni Robredo took on all this baggage when she decided to ally with the Church for the 2022 elections. The alliance is compatible with the Marian narrative of her own campaign, but might have done more harm than good to her political prospects. No surprise that, contrary to the wishes of some of her more liberal supporters, Robredo did not promise to finally legalize divorce in the Philippines. Instead, she advocated for improved annulment procedures: a position that would be more in line with the wishes of her Church allies. This provided more fuel for opponents' conflation of Robredo's movement with that of Corazon Aquino, despite the latter being much more conservative.

At the same time, the growth of political non-mainline Protestantism in the Philippines is directly tied to the rise of the macho, violent narratives of Dutertism. Such narratives valorize an authoritarianism that aims to brutally eradicate both crime and political opposition: a distorted vision of the Christ who brings not peace, but the sword. Society sacrifices its undesirables—and sometimes a number of innocents tallied as "collateral damage"—in order to bring about the New Kingdom. Some of Duterte's most reliable supporters are Philippine Pentecostal and Evangelical Churches like Iglesia ni Cristo, which has bloc-voted in his favor. Of course, this is not to say that political Protestantism is necessarily destructive or violent. Nevertheless, the form it takes in the Philippines allies with both the imagery and campaign machinery of dictatorship. A macho Messianism appears to have won the day for the moment, but Marianism still fitfully deployed by the liberal opposition. It might be that, if the liberal opposition adapts to the situation and (hopefully) improves its strategies, its Marianism will evolve, as well.

One potential path forward starts with remembering that the Passion is ultimately supposed to pave the way for Easter. Christ's suffering does not find its full meaning without Resurrection. Mary's son is not just the Christ who is crucified, but the Christ who rises again. Mary herself is not just a suffering mother or the mother of a suffering son, but an agent for community or world redemption.

What, then, are the building blocks of this more Easter-centric version of Mary's role?

Scripture offers little in the way of suggestion. The canonical Gospels show Mary playing a prominent role during the Passion, especially at the foot of the Cross. Her presence at the Pentecost is canonical, but highlighted neither in Scripture nor Filipino Catholic tradition. Mainstream Catholic iconography generally reinforces this understanding. Versions of the Pieta are mainstays of Catholic imagery all over the world. The Annunciation, Nativity, and Assumption are also common motifs in art.

However, Scripture has never been Catholicism's only source of story and tradition. A less well-known practice called the *Salubong* dramatizes a non-canonical reunion of Christ and Mary after the Resurrection. This particular extrapolation of Gospel is not unique to the Philippines,[95] but there is no authoritative explanation of how Salubong started, or how the story entered Philippine Catholicism. At the Salubong, a statue of Christ and one of Mary start off in separate locations, and then meet in a third location as the two processions merge into one. In some communities, the statues are veiled, and at their "meeting" a local child dressed as an angel unveils the statues, allowing mother and son to face each other. Not only does this ritual concretize Easter, but it also gestures at the special role of the young in announcing and facilitating the community's salvation. The Salubong, like many Easter Sunday practices, is vastly overshadowed by Good Friday rituals in the Philippines. It may be time to explore the potential of this tradition further.

Of course, Filipinos might delve deeper into Mary's Magnificat, from the Book of Luke (Luke 1:46-55). The song, with its talk of striking down the mighty, uplifting the weak, and feeding the hungry, has an inescapable political, even revolutionary, meaning—not least in the Philippines, where wealth gaps and food insecurity are pressing problems. However, it is hardly known outside Filipino theological circles. Perhaps Filipino theologians, especially feminist theologians, could play a role in exploring and popularizing political meanings of the Magnificat. Perhaps the realm of arts and culture can play a role: a musical play about Mary and Jesus, actually titled *Magnificat*, has proved fairly successful. With music by Ryan Cayabyab, it stands in the realm of high rather than popular culture, but may prefigure deeper explorations of Mary's Scriptural role.

However, I argue that Mary and Marianism can be relevant and constructive for Filipinos and Philippine politics. As much as Filipino Catholics love Mary, or perhaps because of that devotion, we have been doing her a disservice by deploying her story in such limited ways. A living, future-oriented Marianism can and should go past the dominant Marian narratives to discover more angles that can promote the liberation of the Philippines and its women.

Notes

1. My grandmother was quad-lingual. Besides Ilonggo, she was fluent and enjoyed reading in both English and Tagalog, and could speak at least some Spanish. She was proud of her facility with languages, and I believe she would have liked to have it noted here.
2. Jeane C. Peracullo, "Maria Clara in the Twenty-First Century: The Uneasy Discourse Between the Cult of the Virgin Mary and Filipino Women's Lived Realities" *Religious Studies and Theology* 36, no.2 (2017): 139–54 at 149.

13 INANG DIYOS, INANG BAYAN: THE VIRGIN MARY AND FILIPINO IDENTITY   243

3. Niels Mulder, "Localization and Philippine Catholicism" *Philippine Studies* 40, no. 2 (1992): 240–54 at 248.

4. Mulder, "Localization and Philippine Catholicism", 248.

5. Deirdre De La Cruz, *Mother Figured: Marian Apparitions and the Making of a Filipino Universal* (Chicago and London: the University of Chicago Press, 2015).

6. Ferdinand Patinio, "Bishops to lead consecration of PH to Mary on May 13", *Philippine News Agency,* May 12, 2020, https://www.pna.gov.ph/articles/1102641#

7. Mulder, "Localization and Philippine Catholicism", 241.

8. Rae Sanchez, "Disrupting Disruptions: Charting and Challenging Notions of Gender in Philippine Feminist Theologizing." *Feminist Theology* 30, no. 3 (2022): 332–52 at 341.

9. Sanchez, "Disrupting Disruptions", 345.

10. Sanchez, "Disrupting Disruptions", 341.

11. Pedro S. Archútegui, "The Mother of Jesus," *Philippine Studies* 22 (1974), 234.

12. Cheryll Ruth R. Soriano, Sun Sun Lim, and Milagros Rivera-Sanchez, "The Virgin Mary with a Mobile Phone: Ideologies of Mothering and Technology Consumption in Philippine Television Advertisements," *Communication, Culture & Critique* 8 no.1 (2014): 1–19 at 10–11.

13. Archútegui, "The Mother of Jesus", 234.

14. Peracullo, "Maria Clara in the Twenty-First Century," 139-140.

15. Evelyn P. Stevens, "Machismo and Marianismo," *Society* 10 (1973): 56-73.

16. CF. Cristina Lledo Gomez, "Bangon na, Pinays Rise Up", in this anthology for an explanation of benevolent sexism and the use of Mary to promote this type of sexism in the Catholic faith.

17. Stevens, "Machismo and Marianismo."

18. Stevens, "Machismo and Marianismo."

19. Stevens, "Machismo and Marianismo," 57–59.

20. Stevens, "Machismo and Marianismo," 57–59.

21. Linda Castillo, Flor V. Perez, Rosalinda Castillo, and Mona R. Ghosheh, "Construction and Initial Validation of the Marianismo Beliefs Scale," *Counseling Psychology Quarterly* 23, no. 2 (2010): 163–75.

22. Castillo et al., "Construction and Initial Validation of the Marianismo Beliefs Scale."

23. Castillo et al., "Construction and Initial Validation of the Marianismo Beliefs Scale."

24. Peracullo, "Maria Clara in the Twenty-First Century."

25. Tracy Bachrach Ehlers, "Debunking Marianismo: Economic Vulnerability and Survival Strategies Among Guatemalan Housewives," *Ethnology* 30, no. 1(1991): 1-16; Gloria González-López and Matthew C. Gutmann,

244   J. V. M. JUGO

"Machismo," pp. 1328-30, in *New Dictionary of the History of Ideas*, edited by Maryanne Cline Horowitz (editor-in-chief) (Detroit, New York, etc.: Thomson Gale, 2005), 1329.

26. Mulder, "Localization and Philippine Catholicism," 341.
27. Reynaldo Clemeño Ileto, *Pasyon and Revoution: Popular Movements in the Philippines, 1840-1910* (Quezon City: Ateneo de Manila University Press, 1979).
28. Ileto, *Pasyon and Revoution*.
29. Resil B. Mojares, "Stalking the Virgin: The Genealogy of the Cebuano Virgin of Guadalupe," *Philippine Quarterly of Culture and Society* 30, no. 1 (2002): 138-71 at 144.
30. Mojares, "Stalking the Virgin," 144.
31. Aristotle C. Dy, "The Virgin Mary as Mazu or Guanyin: The Syncretic Nature of Chinese Religion in the Philippines," *Philippine Sociological Review* 62 (2014): 41–63.
32. Peracullo, "Maria Clara in the Twenty-First Century," 145.
33. Mojares, "Stalking the Virgin."
34. Mojares, "Stalking the Virgin."
35. Mojares, "Stalking the Virgin."
36. Mojares, "Stalking the Virgin," 161.
37. Mojares, "Stalking the Virgin," 161.
38. Peter-Ben Smit, "Legitimizing Context: The Literary and Theological Function of Mary and Mariology in Aglipay's *Novenario de la Patria*," *Philippiniana Sacra* 55, no. 165 (2020): 239–64.
39. See in this anthology Eleuterio J. Revollido, "An Independent Catholic, Nationalist People's Movement – The Iglesia Filipina Independiente (Philippine Independent Church)."
40. Smit, "Legitimizing Context," 244.
41. Smit, "Legitimizing Context," 244.
42. Smit, "Legitimizing Context," 244.
43. Smit, "Legitimizing Context," 244.
44. Smit, "Legitimizing Context," 244.
45. Smit, "Legitimizing Context," 243.
46. Smit, "Legitimizing Context," 243.
47. Smit, "Legitimizing Context," 251.
48. Pei-Chia Lan, "Maid or Madam? Filipina Migrant Workers and the Continuity of Domestic Labor," *Gender and Society* 17.2 (2003): 187—208 at 196.
49. Christianne F. Collantes, "Reproductive Dilemmas, Labour and Remittances," *South East Asia Research* 24, no. 1 (2016): 77–97 at 86.
50. Readers may already have recognized this phenomenon as a prime example of systemic racism and xenophobia. Filipino nurses often felt they had less

capacity to refuse high-risk shifts or pressure employers for access to PPE, due to a combination of racist workplace hierarchies and fears about losing their jobs and visas. Cf. Catherine E. Shoichet, "Covid-19 is Taking a Devastating Toll on Filipino American Nurses," *CNN* December 11, 2020, https://edition.cnn.com/2020/11/24/health/filipino-nurse-deaths/index.html# and Aasma Day, "Why So Many Filipino Health Workers are Dying of Covid-19," *Huffington Post* April 12, 2021https://www.huffingtonpost.co.uk/entry/filipino-health-workers-coronavirus-nhs_uk_606f133fc5b6865cd299ff05. Crowded housing and stress among this professional community worsened the spread of the virus. In Day, 2021.

51. In Shoichet, 2020 and Day, 2021.
52. Collantes, "Reproductive Dilemmas, Labour and Remittances," 86.
53. Eric Julian Manalastas and Clarissa C. David, "Valuation of Women's Virginity in the Philippines," *Asian Women* 34, no. 1 (2018): 23–48 at 27.
54. Lan (2003), 193.
55. Lan (2003), 202.
56. Lan (2003), 202.
57. Jose Felix Falgui, Emmanuel B. Parreño, and Christopher F. Sasot, "Defenders Defending Duterte: Positioning Analysis of Apologists' Defenses of Former Philippine President Rodrigo Roa Duterte in the Context of Making Rape Jokes," *Journal of Namibian Studies* 34, no.2 (2023): 273—92.
58. Peracullo, "Maria Clara in the Twenty-First Century," 140–41.
59. Cheryl Ruth R. Soriano, Sun Sun Lim, and Milagros Rivera-Sanchez, "The Virgin Mary with a Mobile Phone: Ideologies of Mothering and Technology Consumption in Philippine Television Advertisements", *Communication, Culture & Critique* 8, no. 1 (2015):1–19.
60. Soriano et al., "The Virgin Mary with a Mobile Phone," 2.
61. Soriano et al., "The Virgin Mary with a Mobile Phone," 2.
62. Soriano et al., "The Virgin Mary with a Mobile Phone."
63. Soriano et al., "The Virgin Mary with a Mobile Phone," 8–9.
64. Soriano et al., "The Virgin Mary with a Mobile Phone," 8–9.
65. Soriano et al., "The Virgin Mary with a Mobile Phone," 12.
66. Peracullo, "Maria Clara in the Twenty-First Century," 141.
67. M. Grabowska, "Bringing the Second World In: Conservative Revolution(s), Socialist Legacies, and Transnational Silences in the Trajectories of Polish Feminism," *Signs: Journal of Women in Culture and Society* 37, no.2 (2012): 385–411.
68. Carlos Monsiváis, "When Gender Can't Be Seen Amid the Symbols: Women and the Mexican Revolution," 1–20, In *Sex in Revolution: Gender, Politics, and Power in Modern Mexico*, ed. Mary Kay Vaughan, Gabriela

246   J. V. M. JUGO

Cano, and Jocelyn H. Olcott (Durham, North Carolina: Duke University Press, 2006).

69. Christine Doran, "Women in the Philippine Revolution," *Philippine Studies* 6, no.3 (1998): 361–75.

70. Doran, "Women in the Philippine Revolution," 364–65.

71. Doran, "Women in the Philippine Revolution," 357.

72. Doran, "Women in the Philippine Revolution," 357.

73. Doran, "Women in the Philippine Revolution," 357.

74. Christa Weltring, "Die Frauenkoalition Gabriela: Zwischen Alle Fronten-Auf Allen Barrikaden?" Südostasien Informationen 7, no. 1 (1991): 52–55 at 52.

75. Weltring, "Die Frauenkoalition Gabriela," 52.

76. Weltring, "Die Frauenkoalition Gabriela," 52.

77. Weltring, "Die Frauenkoalition Gabriela," 52.

78. Mark R. Thompson, "Female Leadership of Democratic Transitions in Asia," *Pacific Affairs* 75, no. 4 (2002-2003): 535-55 at 547.

79. Thompson, "Female Leadership of Democratic Transitions in Asia," 551.

80. Thompson, "Female Leadership of Democratic Transitions in Asia," 551–555.

81. Sharmila Parmanand, *Saving our sisters: critical inquiry into sex trafficking discourses and interventions in the Philippines,* PhD Thesis (Cambridge: University of Cambridge, 2020).

82. Parmanand (2020), 2; Josen Masangkay Diaz, "Following La Pieta: Toward a Transpacific Feminist Historiography of Philippine Authoritarianism," *Signs: Journal of Women in Culture and Society* 44, no. 3 (2019): 693–716 at 702.

83. Diaz, "Following La Pieta," 693.

84. Diaz, "Following La Pieta," 693.

85. Mary John Mananzan, *Challenges to the Inner Room: Selected Essays and Speeches on Women* (Manila: Institute of Women's Studies, St. Scholastica's College, 1998), 166.

86. Peracullo, "Maria Clara in the Twenty-First Century."

87. Jamina Vesta Jugo, "[Opinion] The 'Noli' Trap." *Rappler* June 19, 2022, https://www.rappler.com/voices/thought-leaders/opinion-the-noli-trap-rizal/

88. Peter Bräunlein, "Negotiating Charisma: The Social Dimension of Philippine Crucifixion Rituals," *Asian Journal of Social Science* 37 (2009): 892–917 at 895.

89. Bräunlein, "Negotiating Charisma," 911.

90. Jonathan Nambu, "Developing Ministry Among Women in Prostitution," *Landas: Journal of Loyola School of Theology* 27, no.1 (2013): 73–101 at 78.

91. Ninotchka Rosca, "Commentary: Calling Filipinos Resilient is an Insult," *Yahoo!News*, November 18, 2013, https://news.yahoo.com/commentary%2D%2Dcalling-filipinos-resilient-is-an-insult-011053161.html
92. Rosca, "Commentary."
93. Rosca, "Commentary."
94. Eric Marcelo Genilo, "Crossing the Line: Church Use of Political Threats Against Pro-RH Bill Legislators," *Hapag: A Journal of Interdisciplinary Theological Research 7* (2010): 63–77; Jayeel Cornelio and Gideon Lasco, "Morality Politics: Drug Use and the Catholic Church in the Philippines," *Open Theology* 6, no. 1(2020): 327-41 at 328–30.
95. Sister M. Jean Frisk S.S.M., *Easter and Mary*, University of Dayton, https://udayton.edu/imri/mary/e/easter-and-mary.php

CHAPTER 14

Bangon Na, Pinays Rise Up: Reclaiming Pinay Power Dismantled by a Christian Colonial Past and Present

Cristina Lledo Gomez

In *The Pedagogy of the Oppressed,* Paulo Freire once said:

Parts of this article have been presented in different forums—namely at the INSeCT De/colonizing Theologies twin conference between Leuven, Belgium and Manila, Philippines, Mar 2023; the Munich School of Philosophy, Intercultural and Postcolonial lecture series, Germany, Apr 2023; and the Australian Catholic Theological Association Conference, North Sydney, Australia, Jun 2023. I thank my colleagues for their feedback on the ideas in this article and especially the online Women Shaping Theology group run by Prof. Jessica Coblentz who provided feedback on an earlier version of this entire chapter

---

C. Lledo Gomez (✉)
BBI-The Australian Institute of Theological Education,
Pennant Hills, NSW, Australia

Australian Centre for Christianity and Culture, Barton, ACT, Australia
e-mail: cristina.lledogomez@bbi.catholic.edu.au

© The Author(s), under exclusive license to Springer Nature Switzerland AG 2024
C. Lledo Gomez et al. (eds.), *500 Years of Christianity and the Global Filipino/a,* Pathways for Ecumenical and Interreligious Dialogue, https://doi.org/10.1007/978-3-031-47500-9_14

249

250   C. LLEDO GOMEZ

to surmount the situation of oppression, people must first critically recognize its causes, so that through transforming action they can create a new situation, one which makes possible the pursuit of fuller humanity.[1]

This chapter is about grappling with the effect of Christian colonization of the Philippines upon the *pinay* (the Filipina).[2] I argue that she can experience oppression intersectionally. That is, oppression on multiple and intersecting levels in terms of race, sex, and gender. For the racial oppression of *pinays* is deeply connected to their sex (as females) and gender (the socially constructed roles, behaviours, and expressions of what it means to be a woman in Philippine culture, a *pinay*). Further, these oppressions do not exist in isolation. They also exist because they are supported and reinforced on at least three levels—institutionally, interpersonally, and as internalized oppressions. This chapter is concerned with exploring the third level—internalized racism and internalized sexism. Thus, in terms of racial oppression, I will show that *pinays* can internalize being white European or American as superior (the races of the colonizers of the Philippines) and being *pinay* as inferior. Meanwhile, in terms of sex and gender, I show that their oppression is reinforced by a patriarchal and sexist Church. I argue that sexism occurs in more covert ways than overt, and by naming the ways they occur, this chapter hopes to encourage the Church to resist these covert forms of oppression. The chapter then briefly explores the turn to indigenous "Babaylans" as a form of feminist *pinay* re-empowerment and model for decolonizing. It lays out the possibilities and critiques of embracing "Babaylanism", and rather suggests Jesus Christ, as the incarnation of a God who is beyond gender, but also as "Christa", as an alternate feminist-*pinay* decolonizing model of liberation and empowerment. This can be an empowering turn for the Christian *pinay* who can feel ambivalent about her Christianity, as it is the colonizer's religion but also the religion which has helped many Filipin@s through difficult times. Christa has the potential to be an ongoing symbol of empowerment and healing for all, both "babaylans" and Filipinos in diaspora decolonizing.

The Colonial Oppression of Pinays

In *Internalized Oppression*, psychologist E.J.R. David defines oppression as "when one group has more access to power and privilege than another group, and when that power and privilege is used to maintain the status quo".[3] This group, the oppressors, oppress either through imposition or deprivation. Via imposition, a particular worldview is enforced and justified at the social, political, and institutional/systematic levels whilst resources are denied to the oppressed at those same levels. Enforced oppression occurs through law, policies, and "normative" practices which marginalize and inferiorize groups. Via deprivation, the oppressed are deprived of basic human needs: "of desired jobs, an education, healthcare, or living conditions necessary for physical and mental wellbeing such as food, clothing, shelter, love, respect, social support, or self-dignity".[4] In today's society, oppressions are more likely to occur covertly than overtly compared to the past. As the covert form, they are microaggressions: "subtle, everyday communications of discrimination and prejudice".[5] When experienced over a lifetime and intergenerationally, David argues that this "can lead individuals to internalize the messages of inferiority they receive about their group membership".[6] It can begin at a very young age such that internalized oppression becomes unconscious and involuntary.[7]

As a Catholic Filipina-Australian theologian, I think about how my people as brown and black-skinned, flat-broad nosed, with their beliefs in their connections to the land, waters and skies, the spirits (the *anitos*), and each other (*kapwa*), were dismissed and demonized by the Christian colonizer. For the colonizers, Filipin@s were viewed as uncivilized and in danger of destroying themselves. They were seen as needing to be rescued both spiritually and as a civilization.[8] In another essay, I spoke of coming to terms with my own internalized racial oppression, the internalized racial oppression of my Philippine kin, and the consequent detrimental effects to their health, ranging from anxiety, depression, and eating disorders to suicidality.[9] I spoke of socialization into whiteness as being the norm, due to the systems and practices in families, society, in academia, and even in churches. I felt shame for internalizing racial inferiority despite my theological education which told me all are equal under God—"There is neither Jew nor Greek, slave or free, male or female, for all are one in Christ" (Gal 3:28).

Psychologist, Lou Collette S. Felipe explains how persons like myself can internalize racial oppression:

> Though directionality or causality cannot be assumed, it is possible that repeated exposure to oppression, whether based on gender, race, or in combination, contributes to the development of negative internalizations about cultural identity. As recipients of dehumanizing treatment, *Pinays* may

embody the stereotypes imposed on them and move about the world accepting false notions of insignificance. With large numbers of Pinays in service positions, including nursing, the mail-order bride industry, domestic work, and prostitution, it is worthwhile to consider whether internalized inferiority plays a role in this worldwide phenomenon.[10]

The *pinay* might believe that she experiences no form of oppression, let alone multiple oppressions or intersectionality. Yet her actions can reveal otherwise. The typical act of the *pinay* mother massaging her daughter's flat nose at bedtime, in the hopes of making it "pointier like the European nose" is commonplace to this day. It is an unquestioned practice, passed from generation to generation, as a way that *pinay* mothers care for their *pinay* daughters. It unfortunately reveals the internalized oppression of the *pinay* for through the act, she shows her belief that to be beautiful, to be deemed worthy, the *pinay* must look like the white American or white European woman, with her white pointy nose, rather than the flat broad nose of the Philippine indigene.

Another example is the obsession with white skin. One of the first few greetings I would receive from Philippine uncles, aunts, grandparents, cousins, and friends would be how much my skin had become darker and that I would have to make sure I stayed out of the sun to become lighter. I grew up avoiding the beach because my skin would certainly become darker. On their recent visits to the Philippines, colleagues with white skin have lamented they could not find a single cream without a "whitening ingredient" in it. In Philippine cultural socialization, whiteness equals beauty. It equals superiority and something of value.

These exemplify what E.J.R David and Ozaki have named as the Filipin@s' experiences of colonial mentality resulting from colonization. [11] I have discussed this phenomenon in other publications.[12] I briefly list here the characteristics of Filipino colonial mentality as defined by David and Ozaki:

(a) denigration of the Filipin@ self (that is, feelings of inferiority, shame, embarrassment, resentment, or self-hate about being Filipin@).

(b) denigration of the Filipin@ culture or body (that is, the perception that anything Filipin@ is inferior to anything white, European, or American, including culture, language, physical characteristics, material products, and government).

(c) discriminating against less-Americanised Filipin@s (that is, distancing oneself from characteristics related to being Filipin@ and becoming as American as possible); and

(d) tolerating historical and contemporary oppression of Filipin@s and Filipin@ Americans (that is, the acceptance of oppression as an appropriate cost of civilization, believing maltreatment is well-intentioned).[13]

Oppression of another group by reasons of race, sex, gender, or by any other reason is dissonant with the Christian belief that all people are created by God, in God's image, and therefore with equal dignity (c.f. Gen 1:27). When God became incarnate in Jesus, God sought to proclaim the Good News of a different reality, a different reign. That reign involved no longer allowing people in power to dominate and further oppress the powerless (c.f. Gal 3:28).

Yet there are women themselves who believe their rightful place is to be secondary to man, even turning to Scripture (e.g. Genesis 2:22-23) to point to the woman as second to man because from his rib, the woman was formed. Other scriptural texts, such as the household codes of Colossians 3, Ephesians 5, Titus 2, and 1 Peter 2 which speak of the woman as submitting to the man's power, further justify this ideology. This is the consequence of the socialization of both men and women into a patriarchal world and a patriarchal Christian Church.

Internalized Sexism of the *Pinay*

"Sexism is defined as individuals' attitudes, beliefs, and behaviours, and organizational, institutional, and cultural practices that either reflect negative assessments of individuals based upon their gender or support unequal status of women and men and is mostly directed against women".[14] Like racism and colonialism, for Bearman and Amrhein (2014), sexism can be understood as occurring at three levels:[15]

(a) Institutionalized sexism occurs when sexism is woven into political, social, and economic institutions. Laws that limit women's rights, or media that portray women primarily as sex objects, are examples of institutionalized sexism.

(b) Interpersonal sexism occurs on a more individualized scale within interpersonal interactions. Someone expressing a stereotype that portrays women as inferior, and therefore deserving of fewer rights than men or sexual harassment wherein a man non-consensually treats a woman as a sex object, are examples of interpersonal sexism.

(c) Internalized sexism, often left out of the discussion, is acted out within or between women, even when no men are present. A woman believing herself to be inferior, and undeserving of equal rights, or women treating other women or girls as if their worth is based on their sexual attractiveness, are examples of internalized sexism.[16]

Since the days of colonization, in the history of the Philippines, many movements and many women themselves have risen up to fight their colonizers, to challenge dictators, and to give women access to basic rights such as voting and education. Such a history might present a false notion that sexism is not an issue among Filipin@s and that in fact the Filipina is a liberated and strong woman. But as the ASEAN Today reports:

> Philippine women remain vulnerable, and their basic rights are often violated. Millions of Filipinos are in extreme poverty...Prostitution is widespread, and according to UNICEF, the country is the number one source of child pornography and "epicentre of the live-stream abuse trade." Women peddle their children to make ends meet.[17]

In an opinion column of "CNN Life, Philippines", Julienne Joven blames sexism for keeping Filipina women poor, because of the valorization of motherhood and the unpaid labour of being a homemaker.[18] Meanwhile, Filipina theologian, Hope Antone, explains how sexism generally remains among Asians:

> There is ... the feeling that apart from being a western idea, feminism is not really needed in Asia. Many Asian men and women have invoked such sayings as "Behind the man is always a woman;" "The husband may be the head but the wife is the neck that moves the head around;" or "Father is the general and mother is the major: he makes *only* general decisions while she makes *the* major decisions." Many Asian men and women use these sayings to suggest that Asian women are already liberated, have power, and therefore, do not need any feminist movement. While there may be a few exceptions, such sayings would pale as deceiving when seen in view of the general reality of oppression and dehumanization of Asian women. Majority of

Asian women suffer from discrimination, inhuman treatment, harassment, abuse and violence before birth, after birth, and during their lifetime.[19]

Julia Christina Becker notes that overt sexism is no longer socially acceptable. Therefore, sexism today operates in "covert and subtle" ways, leading researchers to develop new concepts to accurately reflect new forms of sexism. Those concepts are "Modern Sexism/Neo Sexism" and "Ambivalent Sexism".[20] On the one hand, modern sexism appears as such:

(a) denial of discrimination against women,
(b) resentment of complaints about sexism, and
(c) resentment against special favours for women[21]

On the other hand, Neo sexism is described as "a manifestation of a conflict between egalitarian values and residual negative feelings toward women".[22] Both Modern sexism and Neo sexism mask the existence of sexism such that efforts made towards addressing the problem of sexism are deemed unnecessary and result in the maintenance of unequal gender relations and male privilege.

Meanwhile, ambivalent sexism results from the interplay between structural power ("control over economic, legal, and political institutions") and dyadic power ("power that stems from dependencies in relationships").[23] It is composed of both hostile sexism and benevolent sexism. Hostile sexism is the perception that women seek to control men through sexuality or ideology. It addresses dominative paternalism (the belief that men should have more power than women or that women seek to overpower men), competitive gender differentiation (the belief that women are less competent than men), and hostile heterosexuality (the belief that women are a danger to men because of their "sexual power").[24]

In contrast, benevolent sexism seemingly presents women positively. Yet women only "win" under this type if they behave according to sexist prescriptions, including "maintaining traditional gender roles" (being mothers, choosing the domestic rather than the public life, seeking to be in the shadows of successful men than becoming successful themselves) and not seeking to overpower men by using their sexuality. Benevolent sexism includes:

> protective paternalism (the belief that women should be protected and taken care of by men), complementary gender differentiation (the belief

that women are the "better sex", and have special qualities that few men possess, but only in ways suiting lower status and conventional gender roles) ... and heterosexual intimacy (the belief that heterosexual romantic relationships are essential for true happiness in life and that women fulfill men's romantic needs.)[25]

Because benevolent sexism appears to uphold women, even elevate them above men in certain ways, women can uphold the very system that oppresses them. They can become blind to sexism as a structural problem. They will tolerate gender discrimination and promote the seemingly innocuous system by rather aligning themselves with powerful men. Becker chillingly explains:

> Many women do not perceive benevolence as discriminatory for their own lives and do not realize the harm it causes for women as a category. As a consequence, Benevolent Sexism deflates collective resistance of women against it by offering them a way of coming to terms with a sexist system individually without having to challenge the structure of the system as a whole. Therefore, whereas Hostile Sexism is likely to elicit women's rebellion, Benevolent Sexism often obtains acquiescence and therefore works effectively and invisibly to promote gender inequality.[26]

Hostile sexism and benevolent sexism work together such that ambivalent sexism becomes a socially acceptable form of prejudice. Becker found that those who scored high in hostile sexism and benevolent sexism are ambivalent sexists, and "they reconcile their hostile and benevolent attitudes by classifying women into good (e.g. housewives) and bad subtypes (e.g. career women)".[27]

Turning to the Church, modern sexism, neo sexism, and ambivalent sexism appear when people highlight that more and more women are being appointed at leadership levels in the Vatican, the diocesan office, or the local parish and claim that the pope and the Church are doing all they can for women, and yet women are not only unequally represented at leadership and decision-making levels (including their prevention from ordination), but they also comprise of the majority who make priests' and bishops' lives easier by almost always being the ones called upon to arrange the flowers, to clean the altar cloths, to attend to the church or diocese's administrative paperwork, to cook, set up, and clean up at church events—for free or at minimal wages, in the name of building God's kingdom. In addition, "good women" are upheld through the ongoing promotion of

Mary, in her sexual purity and motherhood. They are rewarded for striving to be like her, whilst "bad women", including proponents of feminism and gender theory (couched as "gender ideology"), are ignored, condemned, silenced, or punished. The following words by Pope Francis, during a press conference on a plane in 2013, exemplify ambivalent sexism as it appears in the Church:

> as far as women's ordination is concerned, the Church has spoken and said: "No". John Paul II said it, but with a definitive formulation. That door is closed, but on this issue I want to tell you something. I have said it, but I repeat it. Our Lady, Mary, was more important than the Apostles, than bishops and deacons and priests. Women, in the Church, are more important than bishops and priests.[28]

On the one hand the pope affirms that priestly leadership is banned for women, simply because of their sex. On the other hand, he uses benevolent sexism (specifically complementary gender differentiation) to say women are more than men, just as Mary is more than the apostles. Benevolent sexism in the Church is promoted both in the valuing of women for their motherhood (exemplified in Mary) and in valuing them for their so-called feminine genius (as promoted in Pope John Paul II's *Mulieres Dignitatem* (cf nn.30-3). Pope Francis continues to promote this "feminine genius" but also recognizes that women are to be recognized as more than mothers.[29] Whilst he is against women's ordination, he also indicates in the Final document on the Synod on the Amazon that the Church might do well to turn to indigenous women as models of leadership of women within the Church.[30] In the Philippine context, decolonizers such as Leny Mendoza Strobel and Lily Mendoza, founders of the Center for Babaylan Studies, point to the indigenous women leaders of the Philippines, as the Babaylan. Could turning to these women help *pinays* and the Christian Church alike, to help imagine women as spiritual leaders of their communities and re-empower disempowered *pinays*?

THE *BABAYLAN* AS *PINAY* EMPOWERMENT FIGURE: POSSIBILITIES AND CRITIQUES

At a feminist forum, "She for She", in the Philippines, Benedictine nun, theologian, activist, and feminist, Sr Mary John Mananzan, began her presentation as follows:

Actually the title that was given to me [for this presentation] originally was "The contribution of the Catholic Church or the Church in feminism" and I said, "There is none. So will you please change the title of my talk to 'Women in the Catholic Church'", in the Philippines, of course.[31]

Mananzan then pointed out that Spanish colonizers often seem to claim to have uplifted the status of women in countries that they had "discovered". But in the Philippines, Mananzan suggests the unequal status of women and their oppression is due to the Christian colonizer's introduction of the concept of "virginity" to the Philippine egalitarian pre-colonial society. By not valuing virginity, Manazan argues, Philippine pre-colonial society treated women and men equally, and thus enabled women to move as freely as men amidst society. Mananzan then outlined in how many other ways women in pre-colonial society were equal: in the family (as opposed to the man as being the head), in being able to inherit, in education and training including sex education, in having the prenuptial and nuptial service costs paid by the groom (in contrast to India's dowry system paid by the bride), and in marriage. Such equality between men and women, she said, was exemplified by the woman's retaining of her name after marriage. Sometimes even, men were identified in terms of their spousal relationship to a woman. Further, divorce was a common practice. Mananzan, then, began to speak about such women as being leaders in their homes, societies, and most of all in the religious spaces, calling them the *Babaylan*, "priestesses", with no sign of male priests as we know them today in the Christian church. Mananzan further emphasized that one had to be a woman to be a "priest" (a medium between the divine and the people) in pre-colonial Philippine society.[32]

For the *pinay*, disempowered by internalized sexism and colonialism, discovering the babaylan as a formidable female figure of her nation's history and was also known to be part of or led resistance movements against colonizers of the Philippines can be very empowering. As Strobel and Mendoza explain:

Babaylan Tradition concerns the Filipino Wisdom and Power within us. Filipinos everywhere can be empowered by traditions preserved, upheld, passed on by Babaylan women and men. Filipino leaders can individually and collectively strengthen, evolve and uphold this intensifying, re-emerging respect for indigenous traditions and identity, and can in turn empower communities they serve.[33]

14 BANGON NA, PINAYS RISE UP: RECLAIMING PINAY POWER DISMANTLED... 259

But for Grace Nono, a Filipina singer, activist, scholar, and non-*babaylan* working among *babaylans*, this feminist *pinay* power reclamation must be critiqued, alongside the way *Babaylans* have been portrayed by Philippine feminists, historians, anthropologists, and decolonizers alike.[34] Nono's first critique is that they must be correctly referred to as "ritual specialists" rather than "*babaylans*". She argues there are many variations for what one might call a *Babaylan* depending on differing regions and peoples. Moreover, in several Philippine ethnolinguistic groups "ritual specialist titles have borne no resemblance to the term babaylan".[35] Second, she suggests these ritual specialists are not necessarily elderly, encountering herself living ritual specialists who are barely in their twenties and thirties. Third, Nono shows that there are differing accounts about their sex. Thus, they are not necessarily female and can be male or transgender. Fourth, the myth of their demotion in status due to colonization

> does not consider ... the discrepant social locations of different ritual specialists within the same ethnolinguistic groups ... ritual specialists have differed based on their respective communities' responses to the histories of colonization, resulting in greater hybridization in some areas than others with Christianity, or Islam, and/or secular modernity.[36]

Thus, in some spaces, their importance as spiritual healers and leaders of their communities have been replaced by the Christian male priest. But in other spaces, the ritual specialists continue to have status and have adapted their practice in a hybrid sense. Nono concludes: "the widely discrepant geographic, linguistic, and social locations of Native Philippine ritual specialists have rendered the notion of a unified babaylan identity untenable".[37] What Nono most importantly points out is the way the ritual specialists have been portrayed and co-opted into agendas, by non-ritual specialists, who have never engaged with ritual specialists themselves or have sought to give a platform to their living voices and actual oppressions. Nono says:

> The five centuries of babaylan discourses have seen many Native ritual specialists defined by languages not their own, deemed wanting of religious conversion, development expansion, and metaphoric and/or hyperreal representation by interests not necessarily their own.[38]

Nono suggests that three types of discourses have emerged from Spanish and American colonizers and Philippine scholars, as well as "diasporic gender and decolonial scholars and activists", creating three types of interlocking discourses which have served other agendas not necessarily in the best interests of real living ritual specialists today. The first is that they are "archaic witches and agents of superstition in a dying order". Nono shows this is not only far from reality, but also when viewed as a dying order, the ritual specialists "ceased to appear in Philippine history's pages", paving the way for the creation of other discourses during the late twentieth and twenty-first centuries.[39]

These discourses, formed by the second type, were created by feminists, gender and sexuality studies scholars, and LGBTQ activists. They sought to portray the ritual specialists as "archaic feminists and symbols of gender egalitarianism".[40] Portrayed as "protofeminists" and precolonial gender plural and transgender ritualists, the ritual specialists/*Babaylans* would under this second type become a source of re-empowerment for feminists and LBTQ activists alike—eventually leading them to ascribe the *Babaylan* roles and title for themselves, as Mananzan herself asserts:

> I have taken the power roles of the Babaylan—warrior, teacher, healer and visionary and priestess to characterize my various involvements for the last thirty years in the struggle for justice and social transformation.[41]

Mananzan ends her recollection of her journey towards feminist activism by stating: "May the spirit of the Babaylan continue to live in me and in all Filipino women!" Numerous conferences and publications have resulted from this second type of discourse, leading Nono to question where justice exists in this discourse for living ritual specialists. She suggests colonial complicity by the very people seeking to fight oppression in their own lives.[42]

The third type turns the ritual specialist into "contemporary, land-based figures of anti-colonial resistance". Under this type, *Babaylans* are imaged as survivors of colonialism and categorized as either primary or secondary *Babaylans*: The primary refer to living ritual specialists in the Philippines, whilst the secondary are those fighting multiple oppressions, often in urban and First World settings, and have gained "social privilege through colonial and neo-colonial tutelage".[43] Under this third discourse, the concept, "*Babaylan*" is a native resource for "empowerment and healing" for secondary *Babaylans*, but unfortunately they often have not encountered a single primary *Babaylan* themselves. Nono rightly asks, if the ritual specialist is to be turned into a tool of empowerment—"Whose empowerment are we talking about when those who get to participate in its acquisition are, indeed, struggling against the powers of domination, yet at the same time, have enough privilege to write out the voices of others?"[44] Though Nono acknowledges that there are proponents of the third type of discourse on babaylans who have engaged with indigenous communities on different lands and have sought to learn from them and give voice to their oppressions and realities. Strobel and Mendoza themselves are deeply engaged in the work of apology, reconciliation, and reparation with their local indigenous in the US.

While we can completely condemn the first type of discourse for degrading and demonizing the indigenous peoples of the Philippines, including the ritual specialists, and while we must acknowledge that oppressed peoples should not engage in silencing and colonialism themselves, the second and third types of discourses point to oppressions that still beg to be addressed. Further, we cannot dismiss the decades-long work of figures such as Mananzan, Strobel, and Mendoza. Thanks to these *pinay* elders, many people who have encountered them either through the Center for Babaylan Studies, their publications, classrooms, or public lectures have found a way to undertake the difficult journey of healing from colonial trauma, or from being the oppressed Filipin@. In calling all women to tap into the powerful *Babaylan* in themselves, Mananzan and other proponents of the second discourse have engaged in this type of discourse to empower the oppressed *pinay*. This *pinay* might be a trafficked person, domestic worker in poor conditions, slave labourer, domestic violence survivor or victim, the poor who have little or no access to basic rights and options, or simply the woman who always chooses abusive situations or limited options for herself because of her disempowerment. Mananzan and her colleagues are not wrong in seeking to find liberation for such *pinays* and if turning to one's own history can be that empowering tool, we are left with the question of how one can empower *pinays*, be inspired by "*Babaylans*" and other women of a nation's history, but without silencing the voices of Babaylans called into their roles by their community and the real oppressions they face as indigenous peoples.

Conclusion: Exploring Jesus as *Babaylan* and *Pinay*-Feminist-Anti-Colonial Figure

As a Christian theologian, an alternate figure of empowerment whom I wish to engage with, as someone who could uplift the disempowered Christian Filipina at the same time give voice to the babaylan/ritual specialist and their oppressions—is Jesus. I want to explore the possibility that the search for a symbol of pro-feminism, proto-feminism, gender-fluid-affirming, and de-colonial/anti-colonialism for *Pinays* and *Pinoys* alike, who still identify as Christian, might find in the second person of the Trinity, the Word, who has existed for all time but also as God incarnate, a liberating figure, symbol of both their oppression as brown persons but also a symbol of their full dignity leading to their empowerment.

I understand that this suggestion appears as a reinscription of coloniality. That is, a suggestion that Christianity again could replace Philippine indigenous spirituality in helping Philippine people to heal. As well, my putting forward Jesus as a figure of empowerment can appear as the classic feminist theological conundrum of the white man saving the brown female body. But I wish to engage in a deeper understanding of Jesus, beyond his colonial portrayal as the white man come to save the brown body. I want to take seriously that being Christian too does not necessarily negate my reembracing of my Philippine indigenous spiritual roots; both Christianity and Philippine indigenous spirituality evidence themselves an integration into their own of other symbols, thoughts, and practices.

On the conundrum of "Can a male saviour save a female?", feminists have often engaged in a Sophia Christology in which Jesus is seen beyond his male incarnation, the Eternal Word who whilst incarnated as a man, is also imaged as female, as a mother, in Christian tradition and the New Testament, showing Jesus as logos, as beyond gender.[45] Cecilia Deanne Drummond in fact sees the Logos as an extension of Sophia "so that sophia becomes logos and logos becomes *sarx* (flesh)".[46] Citing Athanasius in Denis Edwards, Niels Henrik Gergerson even states that "logos and Sophia must be one".[47]

The trinitarian God, incarnated in Jesus, is imaged in the Bible, too, as mother, father, lover, beloved, woman, crossing gender boundary lines. This is the same God who created first a genderless human, *ha'adamah* (Gen 1:26-27), from the earth, highlighting to believers that we are human first, in the *imago dei,* before we are other categories—male, female, transgender, Filipina, Filipino, white, brown, black, and so forth.

Peter Van Niekerk and Nelus Niemandt write that "Like God, who is beyond gender, Jesus' masculinity is not a necessity in order to reveal God and not a precondition to being the Saviour".[48] They say that Elizabeth Johnson's 1992 idea "that the Word might have become female flesh is not even seriously imaginable" given the thorough work of an androcentric Christology in erasing the full dignity of women as christomorphic in the community of disciples".[49]

But the incarnation of God in the human flesh is equally important to the identity of Jesus, as much as his divine nature as Logos. A critique of feminist Christologies centred on a Sophia-Jesus is its circumvention of Jesus' embodied reality in a certain time, place, and as a particular gender. The idea of "deep incarnation", coined by Niels Gregerson, over a decade ago, might be helpful here. It certainly broadened the anthropocentric approach towards Christology towards one that is more biocentric and cosmocentric. Deep incarnation connects all creation in such a way that our embodiedness comes from that fundamental level where the processes of biological life occur—intimately connecting us to each other. It is this same flesh in which God will be able to identify with the suffering of human beings and the wider creation so that it becomes redemptive for all. Lisa Isherwood in fact says that the incarnation "calls us to… a deep connection related to the physical ('bodies') – and not the metaphysical".[50] She says bodies are a "place of revelation and moral imperatives"[51] and that is why bodies must be heard and the flesh must become the Word rather than the reverse. Such a Christology would certainly provide a liberative word to the Filipina whose brown body is often the brunt of violence whether it is through domestic violence, prostitution, trafficking, slavery, in service jobs such as nursing and domestic work. It tells her at the fundamental level, she is the same in dignity and worth as others. That particularly her brown body that is rejected by white patriarchal heteronormative cultures is of value, a place where even God can and wishes to communicate Godself. Her brown indigenous body can be the site of God's revelation, enabling one to imagine that not only can she birth Christ, as the early Church fathers Ambrose and Augustine, called all Christians to do,[52] but reveal the Christa herself, in her femaleness, in her brownness, because the pinay is fundamentally connected to the cosmic Christ who shared her embodiedness and what that entails. Deep incarnation can also communicate to the pinay of a God who desires to walk with her in her suffering and who has experienced the suffering of being human. But the deep incarnational approach still does not address the question of why God chose to incarnate as a male over two centuries ago if the liberative action at this moment in time is for God to incarnate as a female. My own grappling with this question is that if God were to incarnate today, God would incarnate either as a female or transgender, because it is the Good News we desperately need today and she or they, would be heard. I considered the argument that God incarnated as a male 2000 years ago to break societal norms of what it means to be a man but given we still live in a patriarchal world today, the argument does not hold, given as I have suggested that the more liberative word for today would be God incarnating as a female or transgender.

As for the idea of colonial reinscription I wish to put forward Jesus/Christa as a replacement symbol for the Babaylan co-opted into decolonial agendas. We know that the Christian colonizers of the Philippines operated under a colonial mentality that is antithetical not only to who Jesus was, but the very Good News of the reign of God. The colonial mentality of the Spanish Christian invaders was also antithetical to the very God of Christianity. One could say that Jesus was tortured and put to death because he challenged colonialism—a mindset of empire expansion paired with oppression of peoples. Jesus was the person who put in the center those who had been marginalized by such colonial powers. The incarnation of God in Jesus thus is not a tool to destroy or diminish the marginalized but rather one who highlights their plight. In his cross and death, Jesus represents or symbolizes those who commit themselves to challenging abuse of power and colonial mindsets.

By entertaining Jesus/Christa as *Babaylan* then (as an Australian Indigenous or an African person might see Jesus as elder, spiritual ancestor, and healer), I am not suggesting the real living Babaylan be replaced as an important figure for healing the Filipino. Rather I am suggesting that the babaylan does not have to carry the burden of being the symbol of decolonization. Rather Christa can become that symbol of being oppressed as the colonized indigenous at the same time as being a symbol of full dignity and value as the Christological reality of deep incarnation tells us. Jesus/Christa as Filipina/pinay highlights her oppression as a woman, an indigene, a brown body. Jesus/Christa as pinay also highlights she is the image of the divine, a person of worth and value as brown and Filipina.

One of the ways Jesus sought to lift the marginalized, forgotten, and poor was not only to invite them to meals, "table fellowship", as his friends, but also to physically heal them, even bringing them back from the dead to show as a sign to the world not only that Jesus is God and could move between the human and divine worlds, but also that God Godself wanted to and continues to desire healing for the whole person— not just psychologically, mentally, or spiritually, but the entire self, including the body. One of such healings was of a little girl who was considered dead until Jesus gave the command: *"Talitha cum"* (Mark 5:41). Thereupon the girl rose from the dead and walked about as if she had never died. *"Talitha cum"* is often interpreted as "Little girl, get up!". Whilst Jesus' cross and death might represent the oppressions of the *pinay* and Philippine indigenous alike, as Jesus commanded the little girl to get up, might I suggest Jesus/Christa, too, can command the oppressed *pinay, babaylan,* and other Philippine indigenous to get up. *Bangon na. Pinays* rise up![53]

Notes

1. Paulo Freire, *Pedagogy of the Oppressed,* Trans. Myrna Bergman Ramos (London: Penguin, 2017), 21.
2. I wish to acknowledge Marilou Ibita for pointing out excellent resources on the Word as beyond gender and the Women Shaping Theology group for engaging with the chapter and providing helpful feedback.
3. E.J.R David (ed.), *Internalized Oppression: the psychology of marginalized groups* (Springer: New York, 2013).
4. D. W. Sue (ed.) *Microaggressions and marginality: Manifestations, dynamics, and impact.* (Hoboken, NJ: John Wiley and Sons, 2010) in E.J.R David, *Internalized Oppression,* 4.
5. E.J.R David, *Internalized Oppression,* 5.
6. E.J.R David, *Internalized Oppression,* 8.
7. E.J.R David, *Internalized Oppression,* 8.
8. See for example, President William McKinley's speech justifying the invasion of the Philippines, in Daniel B. Schirmer and Stephen Ross Kamm Shalom (eds.), *The Philippines Reader: A history of Colonialism, Neocolonialism, Dictatorship, and Resistance* (Boston: South End Press, 1987), 22-23. Thanks to Professor Lily Mendoza who pointed me to this reference in her chapter "Tears in the Archive: Creating memory to Survive and to Contest Empire", in *Among Us: Essays on Identity, Belonging and Intercultural Competence* 2nd edition, edited by Myron W. Lustig and Jolene Koester (Boston: Pearson, 2006), pp. 233-245 at 234.
9. Cristina Lledo Gomez, "Deleted and Reclaimed Borders: Embracing My Native Self", in Jione Havea, *Bordered Bodies, Bothered Voices* (Eugene, Oregon: Wipf and Stock, 2021), 119-138.

10. Lou Collete S. Felipe, "The Relationship of Colonial Mentality with Filipina American Experiences with racism and Sexism", *Asian American Journal of Psychology* 7.1 (2015): 25-30 at 29.
11. Victor E. Tuazon. Edith Gonzalez, Daniel Gutirrez, and Lotes Nelson, "Colonial Mentality and Mental Health Help-Seeking of Filipino Americans", *Journal of Counselling and Development* 97 (October 2019): 352-363, here 355. See also E.J.R. David and Dinghy Kristine B. Sharma, "Losing Kapwa: Colonial Legacies and the Filipino American Family", *Asian American Journal of Psychology* 8 (2017): 43-55; and Elizabeth Protacio Marcelino, "Towards Understanding the psychology of the Filipino", *Women & Therapy* 9 (Oct 2008): 105-128.
12. Cristina Lledo Gomez, "Noli Me Tangere: A Church for the Oppressed— Putting the Abused and Vulnerable at the Forefront of Ecclesial Activity and Change" pp. 67-76, in *Changing the Church: Transformations of Christian Belief, Practice and Life,* Pathways for Ecumenical and Interreligious Dialogue, edited by Vladmir Latinovic and Mark Chapman (London: Palgrave Macmillan, 2021); Cristina Lledo Gomez, "Overcoming tribalist colonialism", in *Tribalism's Troubles: Responding to Rowan Williams,* edited by Damien Freeman (Redland Bay, QLD: Connor Court Publishing, 2020), pp. 61-73 at 61-63; Cristina Lledo Gomez, "Deleted and Reclaimed Borders: Embracing my Native Self" pp. 119-138, in *Bordered Bodies, Bothered Voices: Native and Migrant Theologies,* edited by Jione Havea (Eugene, Oregon: Wipf and Stock, 2022).
13. Adapted from Tuazon et. al., "Colonial Mentality and Mental Health Help-Seeking of Filipino Americans", 355. See also David and Sharma, "Losing Kapwa" and Marcelino, "Towards Understanding the psychology of the Filipino".
14. Julia Christina Becker, *Women's Internalization of Sexism: Predictors and Antidotes,* Dissertation zur Erlagung des Doktorgrades der Naturwissenschaften dem Fachbereichh Psychologie der Philipps-Universität Marburg vorgeglegt (Marburg/Lahn, Germany, 2007), 1-189, at 5.
15. Steve Bearman and Marielle Amrhein, "Girls, Women, and Internalized Sexism" 191-225, *Internalized Oppression,* edited by E. J. R. David (New York: Springer, 2014), 192.
16. Bearman and Amrhein, "Girls, Women, and Internalized Sexism", 192.
17. ASEAN Today, *The continued oppression of Filipino women* (Feb 8, 2017), https://www.aseantoday.com/2017/02/the-continued-oppression-of-filipino-women/
18. Julienne Joven, CNN Life, *How sexism keeps Filipinas poor* (Mar 7, 2018), https://www.cnnphilippines.com/life/culture/2018/03/07/how-sexism-keeps-filipinas-poor.html

14 BANGON NA, PINAYS RISE UP: RECLAIMING PINAY POWER DISMANTLED... 267

19. Hope S. Antone, "Feminism, Womanism, and Asian Women" pp. 7-30, in *Babaylan: Feminist Articulations and Expressions* Vol 1, edited by Lizette Tapia-Raquel and Revelation Velunta (Manila: The Union Seminary Bulletin, 2007), kindle edition, location 229.
20. Becker, *Women's Internalization of Sexism*, 6-7.
21. Becker, *Women's Internalization of Sexism*, 7.
22. Becker, *Women's Internalization of Sexism*, 7-8.
23. Becker, *Women's Internalization of Sexism*, 9.
24. Becker, *Women's Internalization of Sexism*, 10.
25. Becker, *Women's Internalization of Sexism*, 10.
26. Becker, *Women's Internalization of Sexism*, 12.
27. Becker, *Women's Internalization of Sexism*, 10.
28. Pope Francis, *Press Conference During the Return Flight, Apostolic Journey to Rio De Janeiro on the Occasion of the XXVIII World Youth Day*, Sunday 28 July 2013, https://www.vatican.va/content/francesco/en/speeches/2013/july/documents/papa-francesco_20130728_gmg-conferenza-stampa.html
29. Pope Francis, *Press Conference During the Return Flight, Apostolic Journey to Rio De Janeiro on the Occasion of the XXVIII World Youth Day*.
30. Pope Francis, *Final Document of the Amazon Synod: New Paths for the Church and for an Integral Ecology*, 26 October 2019, http://secretariat.synod.va/content/sinodoamazonico/en/documents/final-document-of-the-amazon-synod.html. I explore Pope Francis' exploration of women's leadership in the Final document on the Amazon Synod in my essay "Mother Language, Mother Church, Mother Earth," in Rebekah Pryor and Stephen Burns (eds.), *Feminist Theologies: Interstices and Fractures*. Decolonizing Theology Series. Series Editor: Jione Havea (London: Lexington, 2023), 47-64.
31. Mary John Mananzan, "On Women and the Church", *She for She Forum* (16 May 2017), https://www.youtube.com/watch?v=QZvIJSsWFHk
32. Mananzan further explores these concepts in her books *Shadows of Light: Philippine Church History under Spain: A People's Perspective* (Diliman, Quezon City: Claretian, 2016) and *The Filipino Women: Before and After the Spanish Conquest of the Philippines* (St Scholastica's College, Manila: Institute of Women's Studies, 2003).
33. Centre for Babaylan Studies, *What is a Babaylan?*, https://www.center-forbabaylanstudies.org/history
34. Nono's activist work has seen her give platform for the voices of living babaylans in her books *Babaylan Sing Back* (2021) and *Song of the Babaylan* (2013). Cf. Grace Nono, *Babaylan sing back: Philippine shamans and voice, gender, and place* (Ithaca, New York: Cornell University Press, 2021); Grace Nono, *Song of the babaylan: living voices, medicines, spiritualities of*

Philippine ritualist-oralist-healers (Quezon City: Institute of Spirituality in Asia, 2013).

35. Nono, *Babaylan Sing Back,* 3.
36. Nono, *Babaylan Sing Back,* 3.
37. Nono, *Babaylan Sing Back,* 3.
38. Nono, *Babaylan Sing Back,* 4.
39. Nono, *Babaylan Sing Back,* 5.
40. Nono, *Babaylan Sing Back,* 5.
41. Mary John Mananzan, "The Babaylan in Me" pp. 59-67, in Strobel, *Babaylan,* 59.
42. Nono, *Babaylan Sing Back,* 6.
43. Nono, *Babaylan Sing Back,* 7.
44. Nono, *Babaylan Sing Back,* 9.
45. For the idea of the Word as beyond sex and gender, see for example, Van Niekerk, P. & Niemandt, N., 2019, 'The radical embodiment of God for a Christology of a new era', *HTS Teologiese Studies/ Theological Studies* 75(1), a5633. https://doi.org/ 10.4102/hts.v75i1.5633; McGory Speckman (2001) Feminist Notions in Christian Portraits of Jesus: Implications for A Gender Inclusive Christology, Acta Patristica et Byzantina, 12:1, 158-178, DOI: 10.1080/10226486.2001.11745695. See especially feminist grapplings with Mary Daly's classic question "Can a male saviour save us?" in Volker Küster, " ", *The Many Faces of Jesus Christ: Intercultural Christology.* Revised edition (New York: Orbis, 2023).
46. Cecilia Deanne Drummond, "The wisdom of fools? A theo-dramatic interpretation of deep incarnation", in N. H. Gregersen (ed.) *Incarnation. On the scope and depth of Christology* (Minneapolis, MN: Fortress Press, 2015), 177-202 at 179, in Niekerk and Niemandt, "The radical embodiment of God for a Christology of a new era", 2.
47. N. H. Gregersen, "Deep incarnation: Opportunities and challenges," in Gregersen (ed.) *Incarnation,* 362 in Niekerk and Niemandt, "The radical embodiment of God for a Christology of a new era", 2.
48. Niekerk and Niemandt, "The radical embodiment of God for a Christology of a new era", 3.
49. Niekerk and Niemandt, "The radical embodiment of God for a Christology of a new era", 3.
50. Lisa Isherwood, "The embodiment of feminist liberation theology: The spiralling of incarnation," *The Journal of Britain and Ireland School of Feminist Theology* 12 (2), 140-156 at 148, in Niekerk and Niemandt, "The radical embodiment of God for a Christology of a new era", 4.
51. Isherwood, "The embodiment of feminist liberation theology", 148, in Niekerk and Niemandt, "The radical embodiment of God for a Christology of a new era", 4.

52. Lledo Gomez, Cristina, *Church as Woman and Mother: Historical and Theological Foundations* (New Jersey, Paulist Press, 2018).
53. An area that I would have loved to explore in this chapter is the idea of Jesus as resistance fighter and the son of Mary who is herself a resistance fighter, the Virgen of Balintawak. This is another way the pinay can engage with the idea of resisting colonialism and oppression in her life, in her country, for her kapwa. There are other chapters in this anthology which briefly explore the Virgen of Balintawak as a model of colonial resistance. I think that this figure Mary is also a worthy figure of empowerment and emulation for the Christian pinay looking to decolonize and reindegnize.

CHAPTER 15

Re-Baptizing Spirit in Land and Ancestry: An Approach for Un-Doing Christian Colonialism

James W. Perkinson

This writing takes its burden from the sharp polemic of Asian liberation theologian Aloysius Pieris, offered in the 1980s, that Jesus began his vocation not by baptizing, but by *being* baptized.[1] *What* he was baptized *into* was the local watershed and a movement of people recovering the two millennium-old wisdom traditions of Israel's ancestors who had lived close to the land with their herd animals. In an age of apocalyptic "climate blowback," in which the Earth Herself is throwing up the kind of indictment Moses had promised earliest Israel (calling "heaven and earth to witness against" the people if they chose a death-dealing way of living; Dt. 30: 19), the conviction is prophetic and damning. Christianity in general must own a lion's share of the responsibility for generating a lifestyle of "docetic" pretense and profligate consumption, ravaging land, water, and

---

J. W. Perkinson (✉)
Ecumenical Theological Seminary, Detroit, MI, USA

University of Oakland, Oakland, MI, USA
e-mail: jperkinson@etseminary.edu

© The Author(s), under exclusive license to Springer Nature Switzerland AG 2024
C. Lledo Gomez et al. (eds.), *500 Years of Christianity and the Global Filipino/a*, Pathways for Ecumenical and Interreligious Dialogue, https://doi.org/10.1007/978-3-031-47500-9_15

271

272   J. W. PERKINSON

air as if they are of no consequence for things spiritual and eternal. And certainly, the last 500 years of white Christian-inspired, settler colonial take-over of the planet exhibits the pretense in hyper-delusional form. The future of the planet hangs in the balance of a return to indigenous sagacity in knowing how to "live in place." How indeed, do we "re-baptize" Christianity—if not an entire globe of capitalist destructiveness—in cross-generational land-accountability and watershed-community?

The offering here comes from a white settler charismatic, long-immersed in the harsh waters of a plundered inner-city Detroit, seeking to learn continuously from black cultural potency and more recently Three Fires and Wendet/Huron wisdom in surviving against the odds on the Strait between Lakes Huron and Erie, pushing to recover yet viable fragments of indigenous practice and memory back in an ancestry Celtic and Nordic before being crushed or coopted into Euro-supremacist colonial ventures. In that effort, re-immersion in land wisdom has become paramount. And such a turn to what lies beneath our feet has also entailed the need to cooperate politically in working toward the kind of de-colonizing "radicality" continually trumpeted by the likes of Winona LaDuke, Eve Tuck, and C.Y. Yang.[2]

INDIGENOUS INTERVENTION

She rose from the table and said, "Excuse me, but I have to stand to express myself. I've been listening to you talk about my people for two hours now, and your characterization is not reflective of the people I know. So, I need to have my say now." The meeting was a gathering in June of 2017, in the posh basement conference room at a hotel in Angeles, Pampanga, involving some 20 representatives of Clark Development Corp., Ayala Land, Inc., the Department of Education, faculty of the University of the Philippines, Clark (UPC), and three of us from the outside, invited into the two days round table to give input on the potential to develop a UPC-Sponsored Indigenous Studies Center. My partner, S. Lily Mendoza—given her writings, directorship of The Center for Babaylan Studies, and reputation as an international scholar[3]—had been asked for ideas by the Director of UPC, months earlier by email, and had immediately pushed back on the governing understanding that the imagined center should focus on "helping" the indigenous Ayta by supplying them with modern education and Western-inspired development skills. Mendoza's counter-charge was that the Ayta hardly needed "help" as historic hunting and gathering folk, living sustainably and self-sufficiently for eons in the area and only dispossessed into more desperate straits with colonial land grabs and Regalian Doctrine-inspired "property rights" claims.[4] What the Ayta needed instead was respect, justice, return of their ancestral domains, and legal protection. It was the rest of us modern-educated, urbanized, industrially dependent, "out-of-niche" casualties of neo-liberal globalization deluded into trying to live individualized life-styles at the expense of the entire planet, in service of colonial and corporate ventures of ruthless extraction, who actually needed help. She had proposed in the online exchanges that the Study Center focus rather on this kind of agenda and had been invited to weigh in (and potentially head up the initiative) in person when next back home from the United States, where she had been living and teaching "in diasporic exile" for nearly two decades.

Mendoza responded by agreeing to the round-table discussion, to be followed by a day-long workshop laying out her vision, and had invited an Ayta-heritage Methodist pastor, Carmen Scheuermann, and myself, her husband (and partner in re-learning indigenous wisdom), to assist. Scheuermann had been long working among the Ayta before attending Garret Theological Seminary in Chicago, where she solicited Mendoza to serve on her dissertation committee and discovered in her not only a faculty mentor but a *sympatico* soul in her own concerns for Ayta well-being and struggle. The first morning of the round table had largely involved Clark CDC, Ayala Land, Inc., and UPC faculty all offering testimony to the supposedly "backward" condition and impoverished desperation of the Ayta, seemingly begging redress in a concerted development intervention, when Scheuermann had had enough. She had ducked unobtrusively outside, picked up three small stones from the hotel grounds, brought them back and furtively handed one to each of the three of us to hold—and thus be "anchored by" at least a few tiny representatives of the natural world outside that artificial space—and then finally, pushed back from the table and stood up, to intervene in the flow of conversation. Disavowing the characterization of the Ayta thus far offered, and "apologizing" in pseudo-deference to "civilized" ideals of decorum, she then unleashed a long, crescendo-ing belly-wail that cut the entire room off at the knees like some suddenly appearing spirit-bolo. Aaaagggghheeeeee!

The effect was seismic. She then proceeded to lay out her own experience of the beauty and dignity and savvy of the Ayta, followed in short order by Mendoza, myself, and the Department of Education

274   J. W. PERKINSON

representative schooled by more than a decade of experience in Ayta community living, who altogether reinforced the set of counter-concerns so articulated. Within an hour, the tide of discussion had entirely flipped and continued apace in enumerating the kind of educational work necessary to halt continuing takeover, re-learning to "see" from an indigenous point of view, and then working collaboratively toward decolonization of (mainstream) people and land alike. The following day continued the confrontation in a seven-hour long exposition, rooted in earth-honoring ritual, and elaborated in a thorough-going excoriation of the Regalian template of Filipino land relations, foregrounding instead the beauty and efficacy of indigenous vision and skill in dwelling on, and belonging, to the land.

THE CRY OF GENESIS

The potency of Scheuermann's ad hoc belly-wail (detailed above) opens the intensity of the concern this writing seeks to address. Whether consciously intended or not, her intervention enacted a deep biblical tradition of rupturing the silences of oppression by venting a groan or cry. Indeed, the entire biblical corpus could be said to emerge from just such an outburst, memorialized in Exodus texts (Ex 2:23–24; 3:1–7) as the singular action that galvanizes the beginning of the slave walk-out and re-schooling as nomads in the sands of Sinai that ultimately issues in "Israel" coming into being in Canaan as a nascent experiment in recovering indigenous lifeways in the face of state control and urban predation. Though itself subverted (1 Sam 8:4–22; 12:16–18) into becoming an oppressive state organization ("like the peoples around") under Saul and the monarchical regimes that followed, before that seduction "early" Israel had, for at least a few centuries, re-instituted more earth-based living as a hybrid tribal-confederation of peasants escaped from Canaanite city-states and pastoral nomad *apiru* folk coming in off the southern deserts.[5] And in ritually nurturing and mythically consolidating her "genesis" out of the belly of Egyptian slavery, the experiment called "Israel" would underscore, in repeated tellings, her ancestral history, rooted in the archetypal "disappearance story" attending "civilizational" expansion—the murder by settled farmer Cain of pastoral nomad Abel, whose blood, swallowed by the "mouth" of the ground, emits a cry of unrequited grief, haunting the biblical text from Genesis (4:1–16) through the gospels (Mt 23:29–38; Lk 11:45–52) to Hebrews (11:4; 12:22–25) and Revelation (18:24).

All of which is to say—the biblical tradition *is*, in its deepest upwelling, the memory and recovery and ritual invocation and socio-political organization and prophetic elaboration of an ancient cry of violated land and disappeared indigenous.[6] Such at one overarching level is the subject of this writing.

Abel's cry underscores a profoundly indigenous understanding and marks a watershed in unfolding history. The move of a small fraction of our species out of exclusively hunter-gatherer relations with local ecologies and into the experiment of domestication roughly 10,000 years ago in the Fertile Crescent initiates a fundamental change in orientation.[7] Small wetlands settlements begin engaging in a flexible repertoire of food procurement, supplementing hunting and gathering with horticultural cultivation and small-scale pastoralism (goats, sheep, cattle, pigs, chickens, later horses and camels, etc.). After 4000 years of this earliest turn to taming certain sectors of the wild for human benefit, the project of re-engineering the environment in service of predictability issues in crossing what appears in hindsight as a definitive threshold. Domestication edges more and more toward outright enslavement, bending wild nature to human intention in the earliest city-state systems, coercing plants, animals, and human labor into surplus production to support elite lifestyles, presiding in palatial architectures and by means of sacred temples "over" their retinue of coopted "producers."

While the change was likely incremental and complexly negotiated, the alteration of social relations away from gift-economy reciprocity and toward surplus accumulation proves monumental (and perhaps, given the logic of such that we are witnessing today, ultimately catastrophic).[8] Such nascent city-state systems re-configured skill in the direction of a bilateral economy, anchored in peasant grain cultivation, supplemented by locally controlled pastoralism, each "side" exchanging with the other (grain, textiles, and pottery traded for meat, dairy, and hides). But the animal husbandry "wing" also provided a possibility of revolt and leveraged the earliest form of political resistance seen on the planet. Among those coercively pried out of their relatively relaxed lifestyles of egalitarian exchange with their riparian surroundings, to serve royal courts and landed aristocrats as cultivators and herders, the possibility for herders of flight to marginal lands to re-convene as self-sufficient bands of "outlaw" nomads (by 1400 BCE known as *apiru*) often appeared compelling.

Pastoral nomadism increasingly emerged in the ancient world, as the major viable alternative to effective "incarceration" in a coerced lifestyle of laboring drudgery, imposed debt (in the form of taxes), and likely demise in epidemics of urban-incubated disease. And while the history is far too complex and convoluted to detail in a short essay, in general, it is pastoral nomadism that embodies the first efforts of oppressed laborers to revolt, exit their oppression, and recover a more independent and self-sufficiently communal/tribal lifestyle, integrated back into the land (semi-arid grasslands in the case of the Mid East) by their herd animals. And of course, the early city-states branded them "outlaw" and feared them as "uncivilized" and "barbarian" (see an early description of Amorite nomads in Scott).[9]

The Abel-Cain incident likely gives emblematic representation of this on-going struggle between early mono-crop states and their "discontents." And it is telling, then, that the biblical tradition "proper," as a tradition about a particular people, begins with eponymous ancestor Abram told to exit Haran—that is, to leave urban life behind (Gen 11:27–12:6).[10] How did he then live? As a pastoral nomad, with his animals and his tents (Gen 12:16; 13:1–9). His progeny will also dwell in the land largely as herders (Gen 23–50), with Jacob, in particular, experiencing a primal "rock revelation" (he will even anoint his dreaming stone as a sacred memorial, naming it Bethel, "House of El" and negotiate with its resident deity for bread and clothing) while out in the wilderness on his way to secure a wife and his own herds from his Aramean ancestors (Gen 28:10–22).[11] Jacob will engage in all manner of pastoral nomad negotiation over water rights at the local well on arrival and (later) conflict resolution with his kin Laban on the way back to Canaan (Gen 28–29; 30–31). And Moses upon going feral and "outlaw" from Egypt, with a price on his head, will likewise hook up with a clan of Midianite nomads headed by a Kenite smith (Jethro), marry into the band and internalize their lifestyle— slowly having Egyptian imperial ways decanted out of him by learning how to live on the land—until finally at 80 years old he is capable of hearing a bush "speak" in the hallowed tones of the sacred (Exod 2–3).

Baptism in Place

All of this is background to the particular "testing" Jesus of Nazareth will face when he resolves to begin his own public campaign as a breakaway follower of John the Baptist. The latter receives press in the gospels as the initiator of Jesus—a veritable "wild man of the *wadis*," emulating ancestor Elijah in frequenting the rough-cut canyon-land east of the Jordan, searching out the cry of Rachel, apparently himself learning the land, compliments of the Bedouin herders there, whose dress and food he adopts, wearing leather and camel and eating locusts and wild honey (Mk 1:4–8; Jn 1:19–28).[12] This latter, according to exegete Jim Tabor, may well be a cipher for earlier Israelite experience upon leaving Egypt with Moses at head, given the command to "gather" (that is re-learn some hunting and *gathering* skill) a substance they do not recognize, puddling on the ground.[13] In their uncertainty they (sardonically?) name it "manna"—"what is it?"—and are explicitly cautioned by Moses to gather only enough for one day at a time, except every six days, when they are to take up two days' worth. This latter "seventh-day" admonition is Israel's origins story for the Sabbath memorial, honoring the ancient tradition of releasing humans, lands, and animals from any kind of labor designed to re-engineer the landscape's provision rather than simply enjoying its wild bounty "as is." Manna was likely aphid defecation—scale insects herded by ants, chewing up tamarisk leaves and pooping 130% of their body weight every hour—a "wild provision," puddling under tamarisk limbs in the Sinai and Jordanian/Syrian deserts that Arab Bedouin today call "man" (probably the Arabic cognate of the Hebrew "manna"), gather up regularly, and bake into honey loaves or other forms of sustaining carbohydrate.[14]

What we may then have in the cryptic accounts of wilderness prophet John is a subtle invocation of the escaped-Israelite-slaves' earliest memory of re-learning food security, no longer building storage cities for grain in Pharaoh's "food as weapon" program (Exod 1: 8–14; Gen 41:25–57; 47:13–26), but attending the land in its wild offering. The Great Baptizer is apparently schooled by the desert-dwelling indigenous herder clans who have the knowledge and "chops" to survive quite well without depending on imperial regimes of coerced labor and surplus production. Indeed, John's entire project seems to be focused on having the poor of Palestine "reverse" their settler colonial advent into Canaan, by going back "east" through the Jordan waters, to recover awareness of the time of wilderness-wandering as nomad herders, before "Israel" left the manna behind and turned to grain production and land tenure and ultimately predatory forms of state control (Josh 5:12; Mt. 3:1–6;).[15] When queried "what shall we do" by the people walking into the waters, John clearly commands a return to gift-economy relations—"those with food and clothing sharing with those who have not" (Lk 3:10–14)—anciently re-learned from herder life in the desert, when Israel first walked out of Egypt, and now epitomized by Sabbath practices invoking the manna-memory (about which, more below).

And it is this east bank terrain and this mythic memory of nomad ancestry that will become the prime teacher of Jesus. Under John's hands, the up-and-coming prophet of Nazareth plunges into "Judge River"—the riparian source of life in that part of the world, coming into being from the rain storms descending on Mt. Hermon in the north, coursing its way due south, finally to collect in the earth's nethermost basin (the Dead Sea), before evaporating back up into the sky and coalescing as cloud to begin the cycle again. Rivers, in ancient thinking, were considered portals to the spirit-world, as also to the ancestral domain of the dead.[16] Tradition has it that Jesus indeed traveled deep into the Other-World[17] for that brief moment in the Jordan, visiting spirits chained; announcing release (1 Pet 3:18–22; Eph 4: 8–9). On surfacing, the Heavens "open" and a Voice sounds—almost everywhere else in Hebrew writing, descriptions of a rainstorm pouring out blessing, accompanied by Thunder. YHWH, we must remember, across the entire range of Hebrew scripture, is above all else a Storm God, whose primary gift is rain, falling in a timely manner (the early rains in October, ending summer drought, as discussed below), ensuring field fertility.[18]

The land belongs to YHWH alone as king (see Lev 25:23). It is given as the initiating instance of gift-economy relations, articulated in what scholarship calls the "debt code,"[19] entailing obligations to a continuous recovery of mutuality, lest the gift become a curse. The obligations find most immediate expression in the weekly "release" of laboring humans and animals, and vegetation and land itself in Sabbath rest which is really a communal recognition of the claims of the wild to work its magic apart from human intervention. The weekly practice finds its more weighty convention in the Sabbath year requirements—admonition to dismantle debt and let fields lie fallow after every six years of plowing and planting, returning everyone to a "hunting and gathering" interaction with the land—an every seventh year "release" likely dictated in the deep past by the cycle of rains themselves, which habitually show up with "righteous" regularity[20] every October in the Levant, except for somewhat regular fluctuations occurring every seventh or eighth year.[21] Which is to say, "Sabbath" in its origins was probably a counsel of the land/rains themselves, demanding their due,[22] underscoring human indebtedness to such unmerited bounty, coming continuously from the mystery of sacred generativity as gift, but interrupting its own continuity with reminder: even the seasonal rains and fecund lands need regular liberation ("rest") from serving human food needs back into "doing their thing" as Wild Creatures on their own terms. Every seventh or eighth year, expect that they will step aside from their own "righteous" patterning of time (showing up every October like clockwork) into a deeper pattern of their own.

And of course, after every seventh time of honoring these "land sabbaths" (every "seven times seven" years, that is), a ram's horn was to be blown, initiating another year of release from planting, and indeed, mandating return of land occupancy "rights," under YHWH sponsorship, to every least clan and family that had been disenfranchised in the interim.[23] Festival sharing of the harvested bounty in feasts like the spring-time Passover (barley) celebration, and seven weeks later, the Pentecost (wheat) commemoration, and in the seventh month, the Sukkot (grapes) "New Year's" invocation, enacted the gift-economy priority as did the commands to leave corners of fields unharvested, or fallen grain un-retrieved, for those who would glean. Sukkot itself emerged in the deep past as an autumnal rain-fest—retaining that association even in Zechariah's prophetic imagination of an eschatological pilgrimage of the nations to Jerusalem to pay respects to the rains and their seasonal giver, YHWH (Zech 14:16–19).

Schooled by the Land

All of which is to say, Jesus' own initiation is a land apprenticeship. He accepts mentorship from John, goes into the watercourse marking "society" off from "wilderness," and is driven by a Spirit-familiar embodied as a Dove into the wilds east of the Jordan, where he re-capitulates some of ancestor Jacob's early experience.[24] The first "test question" of that outback terrain asks how stone can yield bread (Mt 4:3; Lk 4:3)—the very thing Jacob had thrown down as a test question *to* the numinosity of the wild place outside the Canaanite city of Luz where he dreamed of an open portal to heaven and saw a conduit for angelic ascent and descent when he first began his own journey "upstream" toward Haran and "back" in time to recover ancestral connections (Gen 28). Terrified in realizing this west bank "place" itself was sacred, Jacob had erected and anointed the dream stone as a pillar-shrine—an *axis mundi* or World-Pole between this world and the Spirit-World—and made a vow to the rocky terrain that he now called Beit-El, "House of God." The vow was predicated on this Place-Presence providing him bread and clothes on the way, which condition, if fulfilled, he would then honor, in returning and naming the Standing Stone "itself," as his Beit-El.

Much of Jacob's subsequent encounters with Landscape Powers (the "Camp of Elohim," and the unnamed "Night Wrestler of the Jabbuk"; Gen 32:1–2, 22–32)[25] will take place east of the Jordan on his return from Haran with herds and wives, after negotiating boundaries in that area with kinsmen Laban certified by standing stones and stone "heaps of witness" (Gen 28–29; 30–31)—in the very region where Jesus goes on "vision quest" after his baptism. In the case of Jesus, the question thrown up is *from* the landscape Haunt itself—the "Tester,"[26] as the gospels call that Vague Opposition Force of the outback—*to* Jesus, about the name the Thunder Voice had given him when he emerged from the Jordan waters ("If you are the Son of God, command these stones to become bread"; Mt. 4:2; Lk 4:2). Does he know how to bring out "food from rock?"— exactly the question the manna story had answered for the ex-slave Israelites after exiting Egypt. How does one live off the land (and especially rocky arid "desert land" like Sinai), when one steps outside empire (Exod 16:3)? Learn from those who already know—who are indigenous to the place—who already understand the sacrality of the terrain and its gift-economy provisions! And for Jesus—learn from John (who learned from indigenous Bedouin)!

There is no space here to elaborate this kind of reading[27]—which is reading *against* the overwhelmingly docetic ideas of mainstream imperial (and especially settler colonial) Christianity, which do not really take seriously the belief in an incarnate God—restricting "divinity in the flesh" to Jesus alone and even then, in actual practice, relegating the fully human God to a pedestal of uniqueness that effectively exempts followers from actually living the way enjoined by that figure (returning to gift-economy relations with each other and the land). The Bible itself explicitly denotes incarnation as at least involving not just Jesus, but a dove (Luke calls the passenger pigeon descending on Jesus at the Jordan the "Holy Spirit in bodily form"). The biblical corpus is full of personalized references to waters and trees and hills and mountains and animals and plants acting as agents of divine presence (Josh 3:16; Is 14: 8; 55: 12; 1 Kg 17:6; Num 22: 21–35; Jonah 4:6–8, etc.). In a very real sense, his testing in the wilds east of the Jordan is a grappling with angel-haunted stone[28]—whether in canyon cleft where he is asked about bread, or enslaved slab erected as "Temple artifice" in Jerusalem, or craggy outcrop as the ultimate source and image of bounty (rain storms falling on mountain heights running down in streaming rivers to ensure field fertility) that political leadership (such as "kingship") supposedly ensures and distributes (Mt 4:1–11; 5:45; Ps 72:6).

Indeed, the Jesus movement itself—as a Galilean peasant initiative frequenting the wild places of northern Palestine (Mk 1:35; 2:13; 3:7, 13; 4:1; 6:31, 46; 8:4; 9:2; 10:1)—would have been labeled as "pagan" by urbanized Roman Christianity after the first century, had they taken seriously the report of the gospels. *Pagani* was a term in the Latin of the time that referenced "rural-dwelling non-combatants"—peasants and forest-dwelling folk not (yet) conscripted into Rome's military machine—that was then adapted by city-dwelling Roman Christians to designate not yet evangelized populations living outside urban centers in the Empire.[29] Suffice it to note that much of Jesus' activity is "halo-ed" by wild natural agency—whether in the Seeds he invokes in teaching as emblems of his movement (Mk 4:1–32; Jn 12:24), the Winds and Storms that he has familiar relationship with on the lake (Mk 4:39; 6:51; Jn 6:18–20), the mountain-draping Cloud that addresses his disciples during a Sabbath-huddle on the heights to access ancestors (Moses and Elijah; Mk 9:2–8), or the Big Thunder Voice that ratifies his wild wheat sermonizing when he is confronting the Temple authorities for the last time (Jn 12:28–30). Against those authorities—and their commandeering of the rains in a half-shekel tax charged to the peasants to (supposedly) ensure the cloudbursts that grant field fertility—he will invoke "Living Water" as the embodiment of Spirit—a long-standing Jewish tradition that posited Wild Water (Is 55:1, 10) as the quintessence of Divine Blessing and Gift as long as it remained untouched by human technique and control (such as an aqueduct or a cistern; Jn 7:37–39).

And it is precisely the Heaven and Earth that Moses invoked—in the form of Cloud-Cover and Sun-Eclipse (Mt 27:45; Lk 23:44–45), or Ground-Quake and Rock-Split (Mt 27:51), or Lake yielding a mythically significant (153) abundance of Fish (Jn 21:1–14)—that will attest to the natural response to Jesus' crucifixion and resurrection, not to mention their anticipated confirmation of the hour of Apocalypse in Sun-Black and Moon-Dark, Star-Fall and Air Oscillation, Cloud-Sign and Wind-Transport and Leaf-Witness (Mk 13:24–28), much less Hail and Fire, Mountain-Collapse and Sea-Boil, Water-Poisoning, and Night-Dimming and Massive Extinction of Plants and Animals, Methane-Eruption and Locust-Infestation (Rev 8 and 9). Jesus is hardly the Lone Ranger Messiah of modernist individualism that our colonially "reduced" churches

282   J. W. PERKINSON

regularly preach. He is rather a Nature-Endowed, Wild Being, working through every level of In-Spirited Creation. He was taught by the Land. And he speaks from the Land.

IMMERSED IN DANCE

As contemporary counterpoint to this re-reading of an ancient Palestinian practice of "immersion," a brief indigenous iteration of "land baptism" in the Southern Philippines takes on added gravitas. One of Mendoza's comrades in contestation of colonial relations details a slowly galvanized project of re-awakening to ancestral land claims and earth-love in his 2000 CE book *Regenerating Energies in Mount Apo: Cultural Politics in a Contested Environment*. Long part of an on-going struggle all over the archipelago for indigenous peoples' (IPs) rights, Jesuit priest and cultural anthropologist Albert Alejo writes of the moment when his work with the Obo-Manobo folk displaced from their ancestral domain on the sides of Mount Apo west of Davao City, Mindanao (to make way for a governmentally approved geothermal plant), suddenly re-kindled their resolve, after years of depression and forced abandonment of their traditions. It began not in political organizing or filing legal challenges or writing newspaper exposés of the "theft," but with their choice to hold a family reunion animated by dance. Alejo managed to unearth some of the Manobo traditional instruments (*gongs* and *kulintang*, in particular) and once mused over and then played and danced by a local *datu* (tribal leader), the inchoate grief of loss so provoked, issued in a simple prescient lament: "how could we dance, if we are not secure on our land?"[30] Not enough to recover metallic reverb and body undulation. Sound and motion were immediately recast in their primordial genesis as born of the land. Indigenous genealogy traces such expression through human embodiment back to a ground-gift. Feet, hips, and lips are not simply human endowment but vital organs of particular landscapes. Absent the exact earth from whence they had long-ago irrupted in mirth and eloquence and celebratory gesture, any playing and dancing and chanting could only "evaporate" un-fallowed and out of place.

Alejo tracks the cultural re-birth that animated subsequent political contestation and mobilization, resulting in ancestrally based land reclamation. The flame slowly re-ignited over the course of the three-day reunion in 1996.[31] The event got rolling on a drizzly day with the ancestral mountain (Mount Apo) entirely hidden by mist. The rains were embraced as indicative of spirit participation. Instrument playing and epic poem chants punctuated that first day. A Protestant bible study service, with kitchen cooks attending a Catholic mass over radio, marked the beginning of the second day. Then after the ever-requisite Filipino photo shoot, the rest of the day was dominated by a new naming ritual. Those with Christian names were tagged with Manobo designations, gleaned from an unfinished clan genealogy in the process of being re-composed by one of the participant leaders. Though there had never been any traditional ritual for either baptism or naming, the folk improvised. Incantations, blessing of water in a bamboo jar, grouping leaf and nut offerings by sevens, and an offering of a red chicken for spirit-feeding accompanied the impromptu "christening" with native nomenclature. Then on to the business of choosing clan leaders, forming committees to aid in weddings and sick care, to put up communal farms, to sponsor children through high school, and to begin organizing to work for the return of ancestral land! The fest ended with a solemn agong-inspired dance in a nearby clearing by one of the elders that capped the re-surgent energies: a movement had been born!

Remarkably, this three-day "quickening" that issued finally in working toward securing legal recognition of a long-standing, pre-colonial land relationship never previously beholden to a colonial artifice like "title," in one sense inverted more typical understandings of Christian baptism. Many of the participants had already undergone Protestant or Catholic versions of immersion—but precisely *at the expense of* their long-standing relationship with land and ancestry and mountain spirits. What had emerged out of just the beginnings of recovery of a body-channeling of mountain gifts of sound, shaped from underground copper veins into *agong* and *kulintang* articulations of rhythm—giving the mountain a tongue of percussion—itself moved toward a re-baptism of the already baptized—this time in features of the entire ecosystem involving bamboo *bakkat* baskets, used to feed the resident spirits of place with sliced betel nut, betel leaves, tobacco, *apog*-lime, and a raw chicken egg (and this only after a ritually demanding, trance-induced "feeding" of the farming tools—knives and sickles—plunged into a rice mound both to satisfy the tools' need for vitality and to prognosticate the coming rice harvest by how many grains actually stuck onto the tool-blades when pulled out).[32]

The naming part of the ceremony, likewise required "immersion" in the realities of place and people—in this case, a *panuon*-leaf wrapped bamboo cup full of water, signifying both Manobo livelihood and character; a red chicken whose blood was offered first to the *bakkat*-basket, then laid on a rock on the western edge of the ritual space; and invocation of spirit-witnesses of the rite (*Tahavika, Panyagan,* and *Pantivug* as keepers of treasure/power, honeybee-good-life-sweetness, and fetal-caretaking and womb-protection, respectively). The heart of the naming liturgy centered on an elder priestess using a consecrated comb to stroke the newly embraced names (typically of plants, crops, stars, or family ancestors) into the hair of each those Manobo participants being (thereby) re-baptized.[33] This profound re-scripting of bodily being within the sensate touch of other ecosystemic symbionts and co-dwellers concluded with a visit to a local site of "re-baptism," understood as something land and water do *to* human occupants who seek to *belong to, rather than claim ownership of,* the place they live. Two trees were planted to mark the burial site of two community members recently drowned in the nearby river under suspicious circumstances—a "planting" understood politically by Manobo as simultaneously signifying, even in the very silence of the act, "a reclamation of the land."[34]

FLIPPING THE SCRIPT

The recitation here of the "mundane" materials of these ritual re-visitations goes to the heart of the necessary re-framing of baptism as a water-shed immersion rite. Ecosystems are never generic conjunctions of creaturehood. They are specific to the life-forms and element-beings (water, soil, rock, mineral, etc.) of a given place. And here, just maybe, having begun to re-read Jesus' own baptism with some degree of question about the non-human agencies of river, dove, cloud, and stone conducting the "messianic" initiation—*out of* Jesus' own settler colonial formation *and into* their own circle of pre-human eldership and wisdom—we can learn to open toward a more indigenous recovery of land-relations and ancestor-traditions such as that hinted at in the above-rehearsed Manobo "re-union." "Recovery," however, may be far too optimistic a word for the hour we suffer.

The science is daily direr. The changes already set in motion will not answer to human-scale conversion and begging for second chances. That we are, in fact, symbiotically embedded in relations with non-human "ancestors" and "elementary" co-dwellers of our respective watersheds will become daily, monthly, and annually more apparent. Having hubristically and violently "re-tooled" the entire regime of co-participant creatures into ever more elaborate technologies of enslavement for elite human benefit—no matter the consequences for said beings as indeed for a majority of our own species—such "techno-creativity" now shimmers for many even highly eco-sympathetic thinkers as the only way forward. We may well soon opt (if we haven't already in clandestine state interventions) to geo-engineer the air itself. Imagine a mid-twenty-first century re-writing of this paper with a cyborg Jesus, coming up out of the waters of a barbed-wire-protected swimming pool with a drone-dove descending upon his titanium shoulder! (China has indeed already begun making use of robot-pigeons doing drone-surveillance on public squares in Uyghur-land!) But whatever we who have the leisured privilege to write and speculate may conclude about our desperation to somehow perpetuate this 5000-year-old rampage of plunder and devastation we deludedly call "civilization," the rest of the biosphere would seem to be speaking in unavoidably apocalyptic tones of "promise." And here is the hard "rub" of the message. We are, I think, pretty clearly today, being *promised* an end of life as we know it.

But there is also this. No matter the brewing storm, the beauty of the beastly wilds of nature we now so fear continues. As does the beauty of indigenous commitments and practices honoring such—even up against the wall of continuing decimation and genocidal predation by one or another empire or corporation. We will die. We will go extinct. Soon... or much later. In the meanwhile, maybe we would do well to emulate the magnificence of all the little ones around us—even as they go extinct! And while they are still here—once again become *their* disciples and even "children"! Indigenous Filipinos, after all, tell stories of having descended from... bamboo.[35] And Jesus touts his Wisdom-Consort, his PhD-pedigree as coming from a Spirit-Familiar called... a dove.

Notes

1. Aloysius Pieris, *An Asian Theology of Liberation* (Maryknoll, NY: Orbis Books, 1987), 62–63, 90.
2. Winona LaDuke, *Recovering the Sacred: The Power of Naming and Claiming* (Cambridge, MA: South End Press, 2005); Eve Tuck, Eve and K. Wayne Yang, "Decolonization is Not a Metaphor," in *Decolonization: Indigeneity, Education & Society* 1, no. 1 (2012): 1–40.
3. See S. Lily Mendoza, *Between the Homeland and the Diaspora: The Politics of Theorizing Filipino and Filipino American Identities* (Routledge Series on Asian Americans: Reconceptualizing Culture, History and Politics) (NY & London: Routledge, 2002); rev. ed., (University of Santo Tomas

Publishing House, 2006); S. L. & Strobel, L. M. *Back from the Crocodile's Belly: Philippine Babaylan Studies and the Struggle for Indigenous Memory* (Santa Rosa, CA: Center for Babaylan Studies, 2013).

4. The Philippines' version of the Doctrine of Christian Discovery. See S. Lily Mendoza, "The Regalian Doctrine: The Philippine Case," *Doctrine of Discovery Project* (24 April 2023), https://doctrineofdiscovery.org/blog/philippine-doctrine-discovery/

5. Mark S. Smith, *The Early History of God: Yahweh and the Other Deities in Ancient Israel;* (Dearborn, MI: Eerdmans Publishing Co., 2002/1990), 6, 28; Jacob Rabinowitz, *The Faces of God: Canaanite Mythology as Hebrew Theology* (Woodstock CN: Spring Publications, 1998), 17–19, 81; Norman Gottwald, *The Tribes of Yahweh: A Sociology of the Religion of Liberated Israel*, 1250–1050 B.C.E (Maryknoll, New York: Orbis Books, 1979), xxiii; Jim Corbett, *A Sanctuary for All Life: the Cowbalah of Jim Corbett* (Englewood, CO: Howling Dog Press, 2005), 220–230; James W. Perkinson, *Political Spirituality for a Century of Water Wars: The Angel of the Jordan Meets the Trickster of Detroit* (New York: Palgrave Macmillan Press, 2019), 182–185.

6. James W. Perkinson, *Messianism Against Christology: Resistance Movements, Folk Arts, and Empire* (New York: Palgrave Macmillan Press, 2013), 27–37.

7. James C. Scott, *Against the Grain: A Deep History of the Earliest States* (New Haven, CN, Yale University Press, 2017), 6–9, 38, 44–50, 117, 121, 129.

8. The difference can hardly be overemphasized. Our ancient, globally shared indigenous *gift-economy* approach to human economic activity, in which the priority is a constant circulation of "wealth" and a respectful honoring of all of creation's gifts in a continually redressed "symbiotic balance" and giving of offerings (of shell beads or tobacco or even copper artifacts or weapons cast into lakes or buried) "back" to Wild Nature in return for the foods and materials taken in simply living, is the inverse of how economic activity is structured today. The organization of ancient city-states beginning around 3200 BCE shifts the emphasis from communal circulation to oligarchic *accumulation*, increasingly capitulating the ancestral domains of self-sufficient cultivators to the demands of creditors using imposed debt and compound interest to wrest away land and enslave labor (Scott, 2017) See note 7 above. While a book like *The Dawn of Everything* makes clear that some early cities apparently avoided top-down hierarchies and coercive inequities, by the third millennium BCE, the trajectory toward such became more and more evident (David Graeber and David Wengrow, *The Dawn of Everything: A New History of Humanity* (New York, NY: Farrar, Straus and Giroux; First Edition [November 9, 2021]). 5000 years later, the logic of that oppressive dynamic is realized in hyper-predatory form in

finance capital's marketing of indebtedness (from credit cards to credit default swaps) and privatizing of potentially the entire biosphere (land long ago rendered private as "property," but now water, and in cap-and-trade, even air commodified and "shackled" in the market in service of unlimited extraction). The logic of such now appears ever more starkly as utterly apocalyptic and biocidal.

9. Scott, *Against the Grain*, 215.

10. Corbett, *Sanctuary*, 221–222.

11. Perkinson, *Water Wars*, 242–243.

12. Ched Myers, "Elijah as the Archetypal Wilderness Prophet (talk at Wild Goose Festival, 2014; see also, recorded Webinar, "Elijah and the Wilderness Prophetic Tradition"), http://www.chedmyers.org/catalog/ecology-faith; James Tabor, "A 'Jesus Hideout' in Jordan," *TaborBlog*, http://jamestabor.com/2012/06/24/a-jesus-hideout-in-jordan/; Perkinson, *Water Wars*, 265–272.

13. James Tabor, "Did John the Baptist Eat Bugs, Beans, or Pancakes?" *TaborBlog*, http://jamestabor.com/2012/09/02/did-john-the-baptist-eat-bugs/.

14. Evan Eisenberg, *The Ecology of Eden: An Inquiry into the Dream of Paradise and a New Vision of Our Role in Nature* (New York: Vintage Books, 1999), 15–16.

15. Perkinson, *Water Wars*, 230.

16. Rachel Havrelock, *River Jordan: Mythology of a Dividing Line* (Chicago: University of Chicago Press, 2011), 185–186, 92; James G. Fraser, "On Certain Burial Customs as Illustrative of the Primitive Theory of the Soul," *Anthropological Institute of Great Britain and Ireland* 15 (1886), 65; Mike Williams, *Prehistoric Belief: Shamans, Trance and the Afterlife* (Stroud, Gloucestershire, UK: The History Press, 2010), 67–68, 72, 82, 109).

17. And from this point forward, I will often capitalize various phenomena of wild nature to give them an aura of Spirit (and indeed Agency and even Personhood)—to try to disrupt our modern way of speaking about the more-than-human world that typically disenchants and disparages Nature-Beings as merely "commodifiable objects" and thus, ultimately, "disposable trash."

18. Perkinson, *Water Wars*, 232, 189; James W. Perkinson, "Race War, Climate Crisis, Indigenous Witness and the Bible: The Word of Water," *Spiritus: A Journal of Christian Spirituality* 20, no. 2 (Fall, 2020), 222–224.

19. One of the scholars most responsible for delineating the way the debt and purity codes operate in Hebrew scriptures, Portuguese Christian Marxist Fernando Belo, for instance, says of the former (the debt code): "The earth which humans till and on which they live with their livestock can only *receive* the rain which is given to it to make it fruitful; thus a *gift* is the

288 J. W. PERKINSON

source of fruitful blessing. This basic fact explains the *principle of extension* that rest on the notion of giving; it says that what Yahweh has given to human beings, they must in turn give to their fellow humans who lack it... The victims [sacrifices] and tithes given to Yahweh, the Sabbath and feasts on which people stop working so that they may give the time to Yahweh— these simply make evident the gift that lies behind people's work and their abundance at table..." (Fernando Belo, *A Materialist Reading of the Gospel of Mark* (Maryknoll, NY: Orbis Books, 1981), 50; emphasis original).

20. Scholar of Israelite religion Jacob Rabinowitz notes that the Hebrew term for righteousness, *tsedeq*, has primary reference to "just order" whether used in reference to political or social or cosmic concerns. In connection with the latter, the term "is used of rain-fall sent at the right time,'" *lits-daqa* (Ps 85:12 ff; Rabinowitz, 46–48, 113). And this indeed, may well be its most primordial sense, as in the coronation psalm (Ps 72), the *tsedeq* king is compared to "rain that comes down on the mown field: the showers that water the earth" (Ps 72:6). The "just" king is (like) the mountain bringing rain and bounty to the people and the hills (and all creatures) (Ps 72:3).

21. Anders Jägerskop, quoted by Rachel Delia Benaim, "Depleted: Water and Patience are Running Out in Jordan," *The Weather Channel: Exodus: The Climate Migration Crisis*, posted 8/1/2018, accessed 9/2/19, https://features.weather.com/exodus/chapter/jordan/

22. There is indeed a hint within Hebrew scriptures, that the land, one way or the other, will act to enjoy its sabbath rests—if not observed cyclically as mandated in the covenant, then all at once, after Israel is taken into exile (II Chron 36:20; Lev 26:34f; Dan 9:2, 24). And likewise, there is suggestion that Israel's enemies will be held to a kind of "sabbath calculus" of account, as well (Jer 25:11–12; 29:10). Ultimately, the land does not respect national boundaries or adhere to nation-state identities.

23. What Michael Hudson calls "clean slate" debt cancellation was a long-standing Mesopotamian practice dating from at least the mid-3rd millennium BCE, wherein royal rulers upon coronation, or at times of military conflict or economic disruption when they needed to consolidate their support, proclaimed royal "debt forgiveness," returning lands lost to creditors by formerly self-subsistent laborers (Michael Hudson.... *and forgive them their debts: Lending, Foreclosure and Redemption from Bronze Age Finance to the Jubilee Year* [Dresden: ISLET-Verlag, 2018], 68). Such royal amnesties were not proclaimed out of some moral probity, but enacted out of the recognition that allowing creditors to permanently alienate land from smallholder cultivators would undercut the corvée labor and military service such cultivators supplied to the ruler as well as reduce the taxes conducing to temple and palace wealth and ultimately end in

overthrow as competing states took advantage of the weakened defense due to personal insolvency, debt bondage, and military defection (Hudson, x, 3, 17, 18, 23, 46, 64, 67). What is distinctive about the biblical tradition's "Sabbath Year" and "Jubilee Year" versions of such (after more than 1000 years of experience of Mesopotamian debt cancelations) is that the impetus is taken away from royal political calculation and re-rooted in a covenant relationship with the land itself. YHWH as "king" in effect roots such kingship in the land—or said another way around as discussed in the preceding footnote, it is land fertility as "embodied" in rain cycles that gives the most profound meaning to what "sacred rule" might look like (Rabinowitz, 46–48, 113). Cf. note 5 above.

24. Perkinson, *Water Wars*, 241–245; Tabor, "Hideout."

25. Perkinson, *Water Wars*, 214–218, 241–246.

26. Before becoming known as "evil incarnate" in the later thinking of the tradition, "Satan" was clearly embraced as part of the heavenly court, the "adversarial messenger/prosecuting attorney" *of* YHWH, who carried out a "testing" function that embodied YHWH's own intention (Job: 1 and 2; Num 22–24). See C. Breytenbach and P. L. Day, "Satan," in *Dictionary of Deities and Demons in the Bible*, eds. Karel van der Toorn, Bob Becking, and Pieter W. van der Horst, (Leiden, The Netherlands: Koninklijke Brill NV/ Grand Rapids, MI: William B. Eerdmans Publishing Co., 1999), 728, accessed June 25, 2022, http://www.friendsofsabbath.org/Further_Research/e-books/Dictionary-of-Deities-and-Demons-in-the-Bible.pdf

27. For deeper elaboration, see Perkinson, *Messianism*, 82; Perkinson, *Water Wars*, 226–227, 241–255. 9

28. Perkinson, Water Wars, 241–248. One way of reading this is that Jesus was likely a stonemason rather than a carpenter (the Greek *tekton* in Mark 6:3 actually means "craftworker" in general and is the root of the English word, "tectonic" as in the stone plates of the planetary crust). The prime building material in Galilee was stone, not trees. In much indigenous thinking, all wild nature is spirit-haunted, angel-aura-ed, deity-manifesting. Part of the testing of Jesus then would have been to break him out of only relating to stone as "building resource" or "material object," and initiating him into a recognition of the spirit-mediating power of everything in the wild, including rock—as his ancestry (Jacob and Moses, etc.) well knew.

29. Chadwick, Henry, 1990. "The Early Christian Community," *The Oxford Illustrated History of Christianity*, ed. J. McManners, New York: Oxford University Press, 61; Corbett, *A Sanctuary for All Life*, 195–212.

30. Albert E. Alejo, *Regenerating Energies in Mount Apo: Cultural Politics in a Contested Environment* (Manila: Ateneo de Manila Press, 2000), 94.

31. Alejo, *Regenerating Energies*, 89.

32. Alejo, *Regenerating Energies*, 101.

33. Alejo, *Regenerating Energies*, 101–102.
34. Alejo, *Regenerating Energies*, 102.
35. Mabel Cook Cole, *Philippine Folk Tales* (Chicago: A.C. McClurg & Co.: 1916), 187; Agnes M. Brazal, "Power-Beauty Feminism and Postcolonial Leadership," *Feminist Catholic Theological Ethics: Conversations in the World Church (Catholic Theological Ethics in the World Church)*, eds. Linda F. Hogan and A.E. Orobator, S.J. (Maryknoll, NY: Orbis Books, 2014), 72; see also Lane Wilckens, *The Forgotten Children of Maui: Filipino Myths, Tattoos, and Rituals of a Demigod* (CreateSpace Independent Publishing Platform, 2013).

CHAPTER 16

Toward Reclaiming the Wisdom of our Forebears: Nature and Environment from a Filipino Perspective

Ma. Florina Orillos-Juan

Our present knowledge about nature, environment, and disasters as Filipin@s are largely framed within European and Western epistemologies and ontologies since the Philippines was colonized by Spain and the United States. The traditions, customs, beliefs, and worldviews of the various ethnolinguistic groups in our islands were denigrated and dismissed as rudimentary, backward, and superstitious, and thus, we needed to be succored. The colonizers imposed upon us knowledge systems that were deemed as universal, practical, and scientific, in short, far more superior to our indigenous ways. The various ethnic groups who were neither pacified nor colonized were not acculturated and therefore were able to preserve their traditions and pass them on to the next generations, usually through oral tradition. However, such types of wisdom were vilified and ranked as inferior in the hierarchy of (Western/'civilized') knowledge, as imagined

---

M. F. Orillos-Juan (✉)
Department of History, De La Salle University, Manila, Philippines
e-mail: ma.florina.orillos-juan@dlsu.edu.ph

© The Author(s), under exclusive license to Springer Nature Switzerland AG 2024
C. Lledo Gomez et al. (eds.), *500 Years of Christianity and the Global Filipino/a*, Pathways for Ecumenical and Interreligious Dialogue, https://doi.org/10.1007/978-3-031-47500-9_16

291

and interpreted by the colonizers. In time, this way of thinking was sustained and perpetuated within the Philippines, which led us Filipin@s to believe that we were indeed an unsophisticated people.

It is at this point that the methods and approaches of postcolonial studies have relevance. One of the fundamental objectives of postcolonial studies is to critique and challenge such assumptions and presuppositions posited by our former colonizers. This chapter seeks to contribute to the body of literature on postcolonial studies, with reference to how early Filipinos, prior to Spanish contact in the sixteenth century already had a flourishing civilization and possessed a rich corpus of knowledge concerning their attitudes to, and perceptions of nature and the environment. It foregrounds the Filipino indigenous ontologies of nature, environment, and disasters which were unacknowledged and reviled by the colonizers as they insisted on their supposedly empirical and rational paradigms and epistemologies. This study is a modest attempt to provide agency to the early Filipinos who developed profound ecological wisdom and concept of environmental stewardship.

Filipino Indigenous Cosmologies

In his pioneering work, anthropologist Bronislaw Malinowski put forth an alternative way of interpreting myths rather than dismissing them as fiction or a product of the creative imagination of its composers. He argued that "myth...is a living reality believed to have once happened in primeval times and continuing ever since to influence the world and human destinies." [1] Malinowski elucidated his point further:

> ... myth fulfills in primitive culture an indispensable function: it expresses, enhances, and codifies beliefs; it safeguards and enforces morality; it vouches for the efficiency of ritual and contains practical rules for the guidance of man. Myth thus is a vital ingredient of human civilization; it is not an idle tale but a hard-worked active force; it is not an artistic imagery, but pragmatic charter of primitive faith and moral wisdom. [2]

Eminent Filipino anthropologist Felipe Landa Jocano posited that if we are to reconstruct our pre-colonial past, we must turn to myths of origin. [3] While it is true that myths are not factual, these serve a purpose for us. That is, they give us a glimpse of how our ancestors viewed the world and the natural environment that they lived in. Myths of origin do not just inform us about who the first humans were, but they also give us clues about how they understood the nature of things and how they perceived the environment and its elements. Our forebears learned to perform rites to invoke the help of the gods and deities in times of community planting or hunting. Rituals were likewise held to propitiate the deities, during the occurrence of plagues and calamities. The study of Philippine myths is a worthwhile undertaking as it reveals our integral link with nature and the environment.

Beliefs in a Supreme Being and Lesser Deities

Early Filipin@s believed in a variety of gods and deities, who inhabited different realms and abodes. They were responsible for creating the world, the four elements of air, water, fire, and earth, the skies with all the celestial bodies, the people, plants, and animals. Jocano posits that:

> These divinities ... were conceived as beings with human characteristics. Some of them are good and others are evil...Some of these deities are always near; others are inhabitants of far-off realms of the sky world who take interest in human affairs only when they are invoked during proper ceremonies...These supernatural beings are led by the highest-ranking deity and not by any one supreme divinity, for each has specific and some independent function.[4]

Among the Tagalogs, one of the largest ethnic groups in the Philippines, *Bathala* was the creator of everything—the sky, the land, the plants, and animals. *Bathala* is the keeper of the universe as it was his responsibility to guard nature and the creatures of the earth.[5] He was the Supreme Being revered by the people so that "no one ever dared question his demand for obedience and reverence from man."[6] However, if humans commit any kind of transgression, they would surely earn the ire of the *Bathala* who would punish them by sending lightning, a swarm of insects, or a deluge. There were other lesser deities in the Tagalog pantheon of gods who assisted *Bathala*—they kept guard over the mountains, seas, rivers and ruled over the rain and wind. Some of these lesser divinities could also cause misfortunes to people. In time, as the lifeways of the people became more elaborate and complex, *Bathala* sent down ancestral spirits to attend to the needs of the people.

In the southeastern side of the Cordilleras in Northern Philippines, the Ifugao people called the highest deity, *Kabunian* who lived in the fifth region of the universe—an abode located outside the realm of the skies.[7] *Kabunian* also had a long list of minor deities who acted in a benevolent manner and there were those who were not so kind especially to people who behaved unscrupulously. Just like in other ethnic groups, they did not act as keepers, or protectors of elements but as punishers and harbingers of harm.

The Sulod ethnic group who inhabits the Western Visayas region believed that the world is divided into three realms: the upper world was called *Ibabawnun,* the middle world was known as *Pagtung-an,* and the netherworld was referred to as *Idadalmunun.*[8] The most revered male and female divinities, *Tungkung Langit* and *Alunsina,* inhabit the *Ibabawnun.* Both were assisted by lesser deities who control time, seasons, lightning, and thunder, who protect the rivers, seas, mountains, and who keep an eye on humans.

One of the ethnic groups who live on the island of Mindanao is the Bagobo. They believe that the Supreme Deity whom they called *Pamulak Manobo* inhabits the upper world from where he keeps watch on what the people are doing. He is bequeathed immense power to control life and death; the rains and winds and bestow good harvest to the people.[9] *Pamulak Manobo* also has a retinue of deities who look after important life events, sanction rituals to propitiate the gods, and care for the different elements of nature.

Inang Kalikasan: Nature as Woman

Myths as discussed in the preceding sections give us clues as to how our forebears explained the nature of things—they sought answers to fundamental questions like how things began in this world, how can the existence of humans be explained, and what was their role vis-à-vis nature, among others. A scrutiny of these myths allow us to gain insights into the core elements of indigenous culture.[10]

One version of a myth of origin from the *Yligueynes* (*sic.*) tells the story of the first man and woman who came out at the same time from a reed that was planted by the god, *Captan.* The male was *Sicalac,* hence the local term for males is *lalac* (*lalaki,* boy); and the first woman was *Sicavay,* and thereafter, the term *babaye* (*babae,* girl) was used for females.[11] The fact that the two emerged simultaneously from the reed leads us to conclude that the local creation story reveals that both sexes were created equally. Women were the co-equals of men and they both performed their duties and chores together.

Women in pre-colonial Philippines were held in high esteem as *babaylan/catalonan* (priestesses). Salazar argues that the babaylan, who was usually a woman, and most of the time, an old woman, was one of the three key figures in a *barangay*. There was the *datu*, the local leader who managed politico-economic affairs; there was the artisan or *panday* (goldsmith), and the *babaylan* who was deemed as the expert in religion, culture, medicine, and different phenomena about nature.[12]

The story of Sicalac and Sicavay and the eminent position of the *babaylan* in pre-colonial society are relevant in the conceptualization of nature as feminine, hence the term, *Inang Kalikasan* (Mother Nature). While it is a fact that associating women with nature is almost a universal practice among world civilizations, it should also be underscored that there are variations in how Mother Nature's image is typified in local cultures. In the Philippines, its literal translation in the Filipino language is *Inang Kalikasan*. Nature is epitomized as a woman because of her intrinsic characteristics: nurturing, caring, and loving. Such conceptualization is imbued with a profound sense of spirituality. Moreover, *Inang Kalikasan* is personified—as a *diwata/lambana*—a goddess, guardian spirit, or forest nymph in local knowledge. There are three examples in Philippine lore: *Mariang Makiling, Mariang Sinukuan*, and *Lalahon*. All of them are associated with a mountain, which is considered sacred because it is the abode of the gods and deities. *Mariang Makiling* is believed to inhabit the mountaintop of Makiling, located on the southern shores of Laguna de Bay, deemed as the largest lake in the Philippines. She protects the mountain, and all its bounty, guarding it against abusive humans.[13] *Mariang Sinukuan* is the *diwata* associated with Mt. Arayat, a mountain that straddles two municipalities, Arayat and Magalang in the province of Pampanga. *Mariang Sinukuan* lives in a house made of gold located on one side of the mountain's peak. She and her retinue of twenty Acta (*sic.*) house helpers take care of the plants, trees, and animals inside Mt. Arayat.[14] *Lalahon* lives inside Mt. Kanlaon, an active stratovolcano located on Negros Island, Visayas. She is regarded by locals as the goddess of harvest.[15] When she is displeased with the arrogant behavior of the people, she sends locusts to destroy the crops. It is clear from the preceding lore that *Inang Kalikasan*, as epitomized by the three *diwatas* were benevolent and caring; however,

296   M. F. ORILLOS-JUAN

when people err and go astray, they could also demonstrate their relent-lessness to remind the people to change their demeanor.

Filipino Indigenous Ecologies and Worldviews

Worldviews are "mental lenses with which we view the world."[16] These constructs are the result of people's collective experiences throughout time. These worldviews are not static because they are periodically altered, as a response to critical events transpiring in the peoples' surroundings. Hart further elaborates that: "These are cognitive, perceptual, and affective maps that people continuously use to make sense of the social landscape and to find their ways to whatever goals they seek."[17]

Prior to Spanish contact in the sixteenth century, various groups of indigenous peoples that inhabited the Philippine archipelago evolved a distinct worldview about nature and their environment. Elements of nature like humans, animals, plants, land, water, air, celestial bodies, etc. were conceptualized and understood by our forebears based on their interactions and experiences with each component. Since the Philippines is an archipelago, these ontologies developed out of particular geographical and ecological settings—for example, riverine, coastal/littoral, and mountain communities.

Mga Bituin sa Kalangitang Pilipino (Stars in the Philippine Skies)

The early Filipinos had a thorough knowledge of celestial bodies because it affected their everyday lives. Planting and fishing seasons, depending on the areas inhabited by the indigenous folks, were determined by studying the constellations and stars in the skies. The most opportune time to hunt in the forest or sail on the vast ocean was likewise decided based on the meanings that the ethnic groups attached to the appearance and position of stars.

In his trailblazing research, Dante Ambrosio documented Filipino astronomical lore. He was able to establish that the *Sama Dilaut* (also referred to as *Bajau/Badjao*) ethnic group in Tawi-Tawi, Mindanao developed and evolved a complex knowledge of the skies. They had vernacular terms for these asterisms, some of which are: *Batik* (Orion's belt), *Mupu* (Pleiades), *Bubu* (Big Dipper), *Paliyama* (parts of Aquila), *Mamahi Uttara* (North Star), *Saloka* (Scorpius), *Anakdatu* and *Sahapang* (Alpha and Beta Centauri), *Bunta* (Southern Cross), *Lakag* or *Maga* (morning star), *Mamahi Kagang* and *Mamahi Pagi*.[18] The position and appearance of some of these stars at night or at dawn are observed and studied closely—for example, the *Paliyama* (parts of Aquila) and *Saloka* (Scorpius) are indicative of the different stages of *kaingin* (slash-and-burn agriculture) that they must perform. Usually, land clearing takes place anytime from December to February; drying the trees and grasses is best during the dry and hot months of March to May; planting is done at the onset of the wet season from April to May. Two of the most prominent group of stars across different Philippine cultures are *Moropóro* (Pleiades) and *Balatik* (Orion). Among the Mangyans of Mindoro, they called Pleiades "*Ulod Baboy*" [pig's maggots] and Orion "*Balatik Baboy*" [pig's spear trap].[19] The appearance of these groups of stars and constellations marked the agricultural activities of the different ethnic groups in the Philippines. Not only were these ethnolinguistic groups conscious of their surroundings, including the celestial bodies in the skies because it was natural for them to do so as they observed them every day or went about their daily lives. They were able to develop a rich body of astronomical knowledge because they used and applied it in practical terms—in planting and harvesting of crops, and in determining the right time for hunting, sailing, and fishing.

Laho and Bakunawa: Eclipse in Local Lore

Most indigenous groups would interpret astronomical phenomena like meteor showers, the appearance of comets, and solar and lunar eclipses as ominous signs coming from the heavens. This is also true for some ethnic groups in the Philippines. Ambrosio posits that there are at least three snakes in the skies, according to local astronomical lore: the *naga*, *bakunawa*, and *laho*, and these are associated with the Milky Way, as well as the occurrence of a solar and lunar eclipse.[20] Among the three, it is only the *bakunawa* that is often linked with both Milky Way and the eclipse. At a time when an eclipse could not yet be predicted, people would just be surprised that the sun would lose its brightness and the moon would gradually turn red. The people feared that they would lose their source of light, which increased their anxiety and uncertainty. They were anxious about living in perpetual darkness. From the perspective of the indigenous groups, the sun or the moon vanished because it was eaten or swallowed by the snake or dragon living in the sky. The Tagalog ethnic group called it *laho*, hence the expression, "*quinain nang Laho ang bouan*" (the snake swallowed the moon). The Bisaya and Bicolano ethnolinguistic groups attributed an eclipse to the *bakunawa*—Fray Alonso de Mentrida wrote this in his 1637 *vocabulario* (dictionary): "*binacunauahan ang bulan*" (the snake swallowed the moon).[21]

Aside from feeling sadness, fear, and anxiety, the people also responded to the eclipse: they thought that by making thunderous noises, they could scare away the snake. All sorts of things that would produce deafening sounds—pots, pans, gongs, drums, and trumpet horn—were used. The natives threatened to slay the snake with bamboo spears, bows, and arrows if it did not let go of the moon or the sun.

Stewardship and Interdependence

Various indigenous groups practice *kaingin/gasac*, the vernacular name for the following terms, which may have different connotations: swidden farming, slash-and-burn agriculture, and shifting cultivation.[22] The process follows different stages: a patch of land is usually chosen, months before the start of the planting season; during the dry season, trees and plants are burned to clear the area for cultivation; the ashes serve as fertilizer for the soil; at the onset of rains, planting would follow. This type of land use in the upland areas of the Philippines has been dubbed as the primary cause of environmental problems like deforestation, loss of habitat of animals, and even biodiversity loss. The colonial and the subsequent Philippine governments always blamed the indigenous folks for these multitude of problems. However, the type of *kaingin* practiced by the ethnic groups is largely based on indigenous knowledge about their locale and a spiritual connection with the land: humans are an integral part of nature, and that land is sacred. Harold Conklin, an anthropologist who lived with the Hanunuo Mangyan of Mindoro, argued that they practiced "integral *kaingin*" which refers to a more traditional, annual, community-wide, largely self-contained, and ritually sanctioned way of life.[23] The Hanunuo Mangyan has an extensive vocabulary of different types of fire, proof that their local knowledge base reflects a sustainable use of resources. Certain beliefs were associated with *kaingin* farming: for example, among the Manobo, Higaonon, and Tala-andig ethnic groups, when scouting for an area to be cleared, they would listen intently to sounds coming from the *limokon* (wild dove), an omen bird, which is believed to guide them to the right place.[24] Before the area is cleared of vegetation, a ritual is performed to ask for permission from the spirits—usually, chickens are offered as a sacrifice.

Then, as it is now, the indigenous groups of the Philippines nurtured a sacred, spiritual connection with the land. It is after all, land, that nurtures them and sustains their lives. Their cultural identity, rituals, beliefs, and traditions are rooted in land. The Supreme Being, the Divine Creator allowed them to live on the land, cultivate it, and harness its resources—therefore, the land is sacred. No mortal person could own the land because humans are humble stewards of land and nature. This is the reason why, before the land is utilized by the people, they must consult the gods and spirits who own it—"in the form of rituals which may include chanting, singing, dancing, praying, killing of animals such as chicken and pigs, wine-drinking and food-sharing during the communal meal usually at the end of the ritual."[25]

This attitude vis-à-vis the sanctity of land is still apparent in contemporary times: two indigenous leaders from the Matigsalug ethnic group of Bukidnon, Datu Dia-non and Datu Man-ukil declared: "God created land for the people. People die and are buried in the earth. Land the earth, owns the people. These are sacred places. Land is the place to live in, to use and to work for its fruits and then to be buried in and thus, finally be owned by it."[26] Land is a divine gift—ancestors and nature spirits own the land, with all its resources and bounty. This indigenous mindset and philosophy have always been invoked by various ethnic groups, even in contemporary times. For example, at the height of the controversy over the Chico River Hydroelectric Dam Project in the towns of Bontoc and Kalinga, a *pangat* (tribal leader) named Macli-ing Dulag from the Butbut tribe of Kalinga led and consolidated the efforts of all the indigenous groups whose ancestral lands would be severely affected by the dam project. As the Philippine government ridiculed the indigenous groups as sentimental for rejecting the dam project, Macli-ing uttered these words of wisdom: "You ask us if we own the land. And mock us, 'Where is your title?' Such arrogance of owning the land when you shall be owned by it. How can you own that which will outlive you?"[27]

Filipino Indigenous Concept of Disaster

A cursory survey of representative Philippine myths reveals stories about natural calamities, which in modern times are referred to as hazards or disasters. A predominant theme found in myths is the occurrence of a great deluge. One example is the Bisayan story of how the god Captan was so generous to the people and gave them everything, so they need not toil. But the people overlooked their duties to the gods at some point, even trespassing the abode of the *anitos* (ancestor or nature spirit, deities). Captan sent a great flood to discipline the people who had become insensitive and impertinent, unmindful of their obligations to the deities. The deities of the other indigenous groups like *Lumawig* of the Bontok, *Manama* of the Bagobo, and *Magbabaya* of the Bukidnon group did the same thing to punish the people who became too indolent to perform the rituals and offerings.[28] It is clear then, from the three stories that the gods wanted to remind the people about a moral order that they had to live by—the people had become complacent and irreverent and forgot to perform the needed rituals to propitiate the divine beings.

Another type of disaster that was periodically experienced by the natives was the eruption of volcanoes. There are two versions of the story of Taal volcano located in the middle of a lake called Bombon in the province of Batangas. The island where the volcano is located used to have lush vegetation and fruit-bearing trees. People were free to get as much as they needed, for as long they would consume it within the island. However, in time, the people got greedy and began to take more and more products out of the island. This ill behavior of the people did not go unnoticed and soon the spirits who guarded the volcano, personified as an old man, Nuno, and an unnamed beautiful maiden decided to teach the people a lesson.[29] They made the volcano emit smoke and fire, throw stones, and spew out ashes that reached the neighboring towns. Whenever volcanic unrest occurred, it served as a bleak reminder to the people of the consequences of what they had done. A similar story unfolds in the Mayon volcano in the province of Albay, Bicol region. It was believed that the Supreme Deity *Gugurang* lived inside Mayon.[30] The deity regularly received sacrifices from the people, but when he was displeased with their demeanor, he would make Mayon rumble, causing fear and anxiety to the people. This is a sign that they must perform *atang* (sacrifice) to pacify *Gugurang*. However, if the god was unsatisfied, he would cause the volcano to erupt and cause more harm. The preceding stories all allude to the fact that the people were impelled to abide by the moral order decreed by the local divinities.

COLONIAL CONSTRUCTIONS OF NATURE, ENVIRONMENT, AND DISASTERS

Colonialism and imperialism do not just involve the actual occupation of a territory, they also involve the imposition of colonial political-economic power, pacification, and acculturation of the people. The nature and environment are subjected to colonialism as well—both became an integral part of the imperialist pursuit. Nature became the target of colonial economic exploitation. The regard for nature gradually changed as foreign concepts were introduced to the locals. A different idea of what constitutes nature and what the humans' position within it was slowly introduced to us through religion, i.e. Christianity, in particular, Roman Catholicism, which was brought to the islands by the Spanish colonizers.

The Spanish conquerors were accompanied by the religious. It is important to take note of how they construed their role in the colonizing efforts of the Spanish Crown:

> Spanish missionaries viewed themselves as soldiers of Christ waging with spiritual weapons a war to overthrow the devil's tyranny over pagan peoples. They envisaged their work as a 'spiritual conquest' of the minds and hearts of the natives, a supplement to, and the ultimate justification for, the military conquest[31].

With the introduction of Christianity, the gods and spirits in Filipin@ indigenous society were replaced with the saints introduced by the friars and the Catholic Church. At times, some of them were declared as patron saints who would protect the people from disasters and calamities. Furthermore, the value and position of women were also articulated differently in the context of religion.

Nature and Woman Stereotypes

The author of an online article that tackles the United Nations Climate Conference held in Paris, France, in 2015 used a powerful and captivating title for her opinion piece: "The term 'Mother Nature' reinforces the idea that both women and nature should be subjugated."[32] Milner-Barry argues that inasmuch as old civilizations of the world associated the concept of nature with a woman, there was something spiritual in its context. She argues that "this language has been separated from accompanying traditions and belief systems; deeply meaningful terms have been co-opted by an ideology that actually values neither women nor nature."[33] Her arguments reinforce what other scholars and experts in the field of eco-feminism have articulated in the past. The tendency to dominate and control nature for humanity's own gains and interests was anchored in Western patriarchal society and so was the idea that since nature and woman shared inherent characteristics, women could also be overpowered. This idea was elaborated early on by Ortner, who published a seminal work wherein she put forth the idea that women's "pan-cultural subordination" was primarily due to her reproductive capability, and nurturing ability.[34] She added that due to this kind of association, "women are seen as closer to nature" while "men ...are identified with culture" and thus, if culture assumes a dominant, imposing role over nature, then it follows that woman, like nature, could also be controlled and subjugated.[35]

In the Philippine setting, the preceding ideas could be applied in the context of what Bankoff refers to (and criticizes) as "feminization of natural phenomena."[36] In an attempt to be familiar with the different types of hazards, natural phenomena, most notably typhoons, are epitomized as feminine. It has been a tradition, for example, to name a typhoon after the nickname of a woman that usually ends with "-ng"—as in "Reming" (international name Typhoon Durian) which devastated the Bicol region in November 2006; another example is "Diding" (international name Typhoon Yunya) which entered the Philippine Area of Responsibility while Mt. Pinatubo was erupting in June 1991. Since 2001 though, the local names given to typhoons are no longer exclusively female. But what does this practice of typifying hazards as feminine imply? It perpetuates baseless and unfounded stereotypes, i.e. women, just like nature have common attributes and tendencies like being unpredictable and temperamental.

Colonial Construction of Nature

The gradual subjugation of the native people and the environment occurred with the advent of colonialism in the Philippines in the sixteenth century. Corollary to the colonial project of engaging in trade and commerce, another significant objective of the Spanish colonizers was to inculcate their own concept of civilization—the worldviews, knowledge systems, language, alphabet, religion, etc. into the native population.

The pervasive European paradigm of the human's dominance and control over nature, as well as the human's ability to alter the environment, were translated to the enactment of colonial policies in Filipinos that were supposedly aimed at protecting its environment and natural resources. This could be seen, for example, in the creation of a colonial office in the second half of the nineteenth century called the *Inspección General de Montes* (Inspectorate General of the Mountains, roughly equivalent to a Forestry Bureau or Department).[37] The creation of this branch of colonial government was spurred by internal and external developments—the opening of the islands to international trade starting in the first half of the nineteenth century brought about sweeping social and economic changes to the colony. The high demand for timber and other forest products prompted the Spanish colonial regime to pass regulations that would allocate a sustainable quantity of these products for both domestic and international markets. Colonial officials were likewise alarmed at the rate of denudation of Philippine forests, and they blamed this on the natives' indiscriminate felling of trees and the practice of slash-and-burn agriculture locally known as *kaingin* or *gasac*. Essentially, the officers of IGM in the Philippines were guided with the state-of-the-art forestry practices in Europe at that time. In the nineteenth century, scientific forestry meant that the most economical, yet sustainable use of forests could be attained if these could be meticulously studied, surveyed, counted, listed, drawn, catalogued, and mapped. The IGM enforced forest legislations like the regulated and selective logging in certain areas, reforestation programs, classification of wooded lands, and the imposition of the forest tax code.

The indigenous knowledge systems that manifest sustainable practice were dismissed as inferior compared to the scientific models proposed by the colonizers: "Christianization has also undermined belief systems contributory to environmental protection and biodiversity conservation."[38]

Hegemony of Western Discourses in Disaster Studies

When the Spaniards colonized the Philippine islands in the sixteenth century, they did not only deal with problems and obstacles of pacification and proselytization of the indigenous population. They also had to face the challenge of dealing with a multitude of hazards in the island environment where the incidence of disaster is highly probable. Disasters that occurred frequently were volcanic eruptions, earthquake, inundations,

304 M. F. ORILLOS-JUAN

typhoon while agricultural disasters like locust or worm infestation and rinderpest struck periodically.

The idea of what caused a disaster was presented to the native population within the context of the evangelization efforts of the Spanish friars. A very early account written in 1572 revealed the misery of the natives of the island of Panay who had been experiencing famine and pestilence for about three years. The writer directly associated the occurrence of these disasters with the sins of the natives:

> When the governor was in that island there fell upon it—because of our sins and those of the natives, or God knows what—an extremely great plague of locusts, which has lasted three years and still continues. No field is sown which they do not destroy. A great famine and pestilence have sprung up among the natives of that island, so that more than half of them have died; and they will continue to die until God our Lord is pleased to remove his anger from over it.[39]

The occurrence of disasters was mainly due to the stubbornness of the people who refused to be proselytized and continued to follow animist ways. An unknown author who took note of the activities of the Jesuits in the years 1608–1609 vividly describes an event which showed how the natives of the town of Silan (*sic.*) practiced their religion: "It happened that some Indians turned aside from their journey to visit one of the inhabitants; and as they were taking out of a little chest some clothes that they were carrying with them, packed up, it happened that they took out along with them a tiny idol formed of a twisted mass of hair."[40] Upon witnessing this event, the townspeople were terrified and told the Jesuit friar about it. The priest then did everything and convinced the heathens to abandon this practice. The Jesuit prevailed and "...with the help of God she abjured the impious worship of hair, which she had before pursued, and also abandoned and corrected another sin of no small heinousness."[41] However, a terrible accident transpired—one night, as the people were preparing for a religious festival, there were strong winds, followed by torrential rains which soon toppled the natives' dwellings. They all sought refuge inside the church, as they prayed for safety and confessed their sins to the friar. These misfortunes were construed by the friars as the natives' retribution for being persistent in adhering to pagan practices.

Another instance of how disaster and disaster response were conceptualized by the religious is exemplified in the problem of locust infestation that destroyed the crops of the natives which eventually led to food shortage and starvation. From the point of view of the ecclesiastical officials, the swarms of these voracious insects were punishments sent by God so the natives should repent for their sins. The friars also suggested possible solutions to prevent the locusts from causing further harm to the people— most of these were anchored on religion: processions of images of saints in the rice fields, saying mass in the middle of the farmlands being devoured by the insects, blessing the fields using holy water to drive the locusts away, and appointing St. Augustine to be the patron saint against locusts.[42]

It could be inferred from the examples presented above that from the perspective of the Spaniards, those disasters were punishments that came from the Christian God because they were heathens. If they wanted to be spared from suffering and harm, they should have embraced the teachings of the Catholic Church and practiced the religion through piousness. The impact of certain disasters could also have been mitigated through piousness—e.g. the intercession of saints to prevent an agricultural disaster like locust infestation.

Due to its location, the Philippines is highly vulnerable to earthquakes. Two of the strongest earthquakes that devastated colonial Manila in the nineteenth century occurred in June 1863 and July 1880.[43] Both disasters resulted in damage to properties and loss of lives. As usual, the extent of damage to public buildings and infrastructure, including private properties was documented by colonial authorities to determine the magnitude of reconstruction work to be done. In the aftermath of these earthquakes, colonial policies vis-à-vis building regulations were thoroughly reviewed and consequently revised.

The example of the 1863 and 1880 earthquakes cited above clearly reflects a secular (in contrast to what was mentioned in the preceding sections) Euro-centric interpretation of disaster rooted in the nature-culture dichotomy.[44] Nature was seen as an entity that could be controlled by humans—this was part of the legacy of the period of Enlightenment/*La Ilustración/Siècle des Lumières*. Humans could be saved from catastrophes by relocating them to geologically safe environments. The scientific study and documentation of hazards would enable people to craft policies that would guide, for example, urban planning and zoning.

There is much evidence that at present, the conceptualization of disaster is framed within the knowledge systems of Europe and the West. The fundamentals of Western discourses on disaster studies pervaded our consciousness through education and governance and was deeply ingrained in

306   M. F. ORILLOS-JUAN

our minds ever since. We are at this propitious juncture to "...confront the Eurocentric/Western ontological and epistemological heritage of the Enlightenment and how it has sustained the imperialist and ethnocentric ideology promoted by the West."[45]

CONCLUSION

Postcolonial studies offer an opportunity for the former colonial subjects to articulate that local knowledge systems are as valid, logical, rational, and coherent as European and Western epistemologies, ontologies, and discourses. It is an opportune time to integrate the topic of historical legacies of imperialism in the conceptualization of nature and environment to establish how our forebears, the early Filipinos, developed a rich corpus of knowledge about nature, environment, and disasters. Our ancestors saw themselves as an integral part of nature; they maintained a deep spiritual connection with all its elements and knew that their relationship with nature was one of interdependence and mutuality. This is the right moment to reclaim and foreground the wisdom of our forebears for us to fully appreciate our identity as Filipinos.

NOTES

1. Bronislaw Malinowski, *Magic, Science and Religion and Other Essays*, ed., Robert Redfield (Boston, Massachusetts: Beacon Press and Glencoe, Illinois: The Free Press, 1948), 78.
2. Malinowski, *Magic, Science and Religion and Other Essays*, 78-79.
3. Felipe Landa Jocano, *Filipino Prehistory* (Quezon City: Punlad Research House, Inc, 1998), 99.
4. Felipe Landa Jocano, "Notes on Philippine Divinities," *Asian Studies* 6, no. 2 (1968): 169.
5. Felipe Landa Jocano, *Outline of Philippine Mythology* (Manila: Centro Escolar University Research and Development Center, 1969).
6. Jocano, *Notes on Philippine Divinities,* 170.
7. Roy Barton, *Mythology of the Ifugaos* (Philadelphia: American Folklore Society, 1955), 5-11.
8. Felipe Landa Jocano, "The Sulod: A Mountain People in Central Panay Philippines," *Philippine Studies* 6, no. 4 (1958): 422-423.
   Jocano mentions in footnote number 32 that these three are also mentioned in their epic, *Hinilawod*.

9. Fay Cooper Cole, *The Wild Tribes of the Davao District, Mindanao* (Chicago: Field Museum of Natural History, 1913), 106-107.
10. Jocano, *Filipino Prehistory*, 100.
11. Jocano, *Filipino Prehistory*, 100. The author mentions that he used the version recorded by a Spanish chronicler, Miguel de Loarca in 1582-1583.
12. See Zeus Salazar, *Ang Babaylan sa Kasaysayan ng Pilipinas* (Quezon City: Bagong Kasaysayan, 1999).
13. Damiana Eugenio, *Philippine Folk Literature Volume III The Legends*, (Quezon City: University of the Philippines Press, 2002), 214-215.
14. Eugenio, *Philippine Folk Literature*, 216-217.
15. For the original text in Spanish and the English translation, see Miguel de Loarca, Relación de las Yslas Filipinas [Arevalo, June 1582] in *The Philippine Islands 1492-1898 Explorations by early navigators, descriptions of the islands and their peoples, their history and records of the Catholic missions, as related in contemporaneous books and manuscripts, showing the political, economic, commercial and religious conditions of those islands from their earliest relations with European nations to the beginning of the nineteenth century Volume V 1582-1583*, eds. Emma Blair and James Alexander Robertson (Cleveland Ohio: The A.H. Clark Company: 1911), 127-128. The e-book format is also available at Project Gutenberg https://www.gutenberg.org/files/16501/16501-h/16501-h.htm.
16. Marvin Olsen, Dora Lodwick and Riley Dunlap, *Viewing the World Ecologically* (Boulder, San Francisco, Oxford: Westview Press, 1992), 2.
17. Michael Anthony Hart, "Indigenous Worldviews, Knowledge and Research: The Development of an Indigenous Research Paradigm," *Journal of Indigenous Voices in Social Work* 1, no. 1 (2010): 2.
18. Dante Ambrosio, "Mamahi: Stars of Tawi-Tawi," *Philippine Daily Inquirer*, January 26, 2008. See also Dante Ambrosio, *Balatik: Etnoastronomiya Kalangitan sa Kabihasnang Pilipino* (Quezon City: University of the Philippines Press, 2010).
19. Antoon Postma, "The Concept of Time Among the Mangyans," *Asian Folklore Studies* 44, no.2 (1985): 234-236
20. Ambrosio, *Balatik*, 136-148; Dante Ambrosio, "Eclipse and the Snake in the Sky: Bakunawa and Laho," *Philippine Daily Inquirer*, February 8, 2009.
21. Ambrosio, "Eclipse and the Snake in the Sky".
22. For the different connotations of the terms, see Ole Merz, Christine Padoch, Jeferson Fox et.al., *Human Ecology Special Issue: Swidden Agriculture in Southeast Asia* (New York: Springer Science and Business Media, 2009).

308   M. F. ORILLOS-JUAN

23. See Harold Conklin, *Hanunoo Agriculture: A Report on an Integral System of Shifting Cultivation in the Philippines* (Rome: Food and Agriculture Organization, 1957).

Owen Lynch elaborates what is meant by the term integral kaingin: "Integral swiddeners practice rotational agriculture by cutting and burning (usually secondary) forest cover and using the ash to fertilize the cleared field. An integral swiddener often intercrops a variety of plants and after one, two or, perhaps, three harvests stops planting annuals and, thereby, leaves the field in fallow. The fallow period allows the forest and topsoil to regenerate before the annual planting cycle begins anew." See Owen Lynch, *Whither the People? Tenurial and Agricultural Aspects of the Tropical Forestry Plan* (Washington DC, International Development and Environment, 1990), 12.

24. Ponciano Bennagen and Ma. Luisa Lucas-Fernan, *Consulting the Spirits, Working with Nature, Sharing with Others Indigenous Resource Management in the Philippines* (Quezon City: Sentro para sa Ganap na Pamayanan, 1995), 125.

25. Bennagen and Lucas-Fernan, *Consulting the Spirits, Working with Nature, Sharing with Others*, 8.

26. Bennagen and Lucas-Fernan, *Consulting the Spirits, Working with Nature, Sharing with Others*, 1.

27. "The Wisdom of Our Ancestors (from the Words of Macli-ing Dulag," *Alternative Futures*, (n.p.,1986)).

28. Stories of a great flood can be found in Damiana Eugenio, *Philippine Folk Literature Series Volume II The Myths* (Quezon City: University of the Philippines Press, 2001), 222-223; 236-237; 239-241 and 243.

29. Eugenio, *Philippine Folk Literature*, 175-176.

30. Eugenio, *Philippine Folk Literature*, 3-6.

31. John Leddy Phelan, *The Hispanization of the Philippines: Spanish Aims and Filipino Responses, 1565-1700* (Madison: University of Wisconsin Press, 1959), 54.

32. Sarah Milner-Barry, "The term 'Mother Nature' reinforces the idea that both women and nature should be subjugated," QUARTZ, June 35, 2022,   https://qz.com/562833/ the-term-mother-nature-reinforces-the-idea-that-both-women-and-nature-should-be-subjugated/

33. Milner-Barry, "The term 'Mother Nature' reinforces the idea that both women and nature should be subjugated."

34. See Sherry B. Ortner, "Is Female to Male as Nature is to Culture?" in *Woman, Culture and Society*, eds. M.Z. Rosaldo and L. Lhampere (California: Stanford University Press, 1974), 73.

35. Ortner, "Is Female to Male as Nature is to Culture?", 73.

36. Greg Bankoff, "In the Eye of the Storm: The Social Construction of the Forces of Nature and the Climatic and Seismic Construction of God in the Philippines," *Journal of Southeast Asian Studies* 35, no. 1 (2004), 92; Greg Bankoff, *Cultures of Disaster Society and Natural Hazard in the Philippines* (London and New York: Routledge, 2003).

37. Ma. Florina Orillos-Juan, "The Inspección General de Montes and Modern Forestry 1863-1898," in *Reassessing Imperial Modernization Achievements and Failures in the Transformation of the 19ᵗʰ Century Philippines*, eds. Maria Dolores Elizalde Pérez-Gruiso and Maria Serena I. Diokno (Madrid: Ediciones Polifemo, forthcoming).

38. Bennagen and Lucas-Fernan, *Consulting the Spirits, Working with Nature, Sharing with Others*, 2

39. Anonymous, "Relation of the Conquest of the Island of Luzon, Manila, April 20, 1572" in *The Philippine Islands 1492-1898 Explorations by early navigators, descriptions of the islands and their peoples, their history and records of the Catholic missions, as related in contemporaneous books and manuscripts, showing the political, economic, commercial and religious conditions of those islands from their earliest relations with European nations to the beginning of the nineteenth century Volume III 1569-1576*, eds. Emma Blair and James Alexander Robertson (Cleveland Ohio: The A.H. Clark Company: 1911), 149. The e-book format is also available at Project Gutenberg https://www.gutenberg.org/files/13616/13616-h/13616-h.htm

40. Anonymous, "Jesuit Missions 1608-09," in *The Philippine Islands 1492-1898 Explorations by early navigators, descriptions of the islands and their peoples, their history and records of the Catholic missions, as related in contemporaneous books and manuscripts, showing the political, economic, commercial and religious conditions of those islands from their earliest relations with European nations to the beginning of the nineteenth century Volume XVII 1609-1616*, eds. Emma Blair and James Alexander Robertson (Cleveland Ohio: The A.H. Clark Company: 1911), 60. The e-book format is also available at Project Gutenberg https://www.gutenberg.org/files/15530/15530-h/15530-h.htm#d0e754

41. Anonymous, "Jesuit Missions 1608-09", 60.

42. Ma. Florina Orillos-Juan, "Box 32.4: Facing Locust Swarms in the Philippines," in *The Routledge Handbook of Hazards and Disaster Risk Reduction*, eds. Ben Wisner, JC Gaillard and Ilan Kelman (London and New York: Routledge, 2012), 394. See also Ma. Florina Orillos-Juan, *Kasaysayan at Vulenrabilidad: Ang Lipunang Pilipino sa Harap ng Pananalanta ng Pesteng Balang 1569-1949*, (Manila: De La Salle University Publishing House, 2017).

310   M. F. ORILLOS-JUAN

43. See Francis Gealogo, "Historical Seismology and the Documentation of Post-Disaster Conditions: The 1863 and 1880 Luzon Earthquakes," *Philippine Studies* 64, nos. 3-4 (2016): 359-384; Kerby Alvarez, "The June 1863 and July 1880 Earthquakes in Luzon, Philippines: Interpretations and Responses," *Illes i imperis* 22 (2020): 147-169; Susana Ramirez Martin, *El Teremoto de Manila de 1863: Medida Politicas y Economica* (Madrid: CSIC, 2000).

44. See Chap. 2 "Genealogy of Disaster Studies" in JC Gaillard, *The Invention of Disaster: Power and Knowledge in Discourses in Hazard and Vulnerability* (London and New York: Routledge, 2022); Ben Wisner, JC Gaillard and Ilan Kelman, eds. *The Routledge Handbook of Hazards and Disaster Risk Reduction*, (London and New York: Routledge).

45. Gaillard, "Genealogy of Disaster Studies", 2.

Index[1]

A

Aetas (Aeta Community of Sapang Uwak, Ayta), 29, 30, 35, 36, 39, 164

Aglipay, Gregorio (Gregorio Aglipay y Labayan), 16, 102–104, 108–110, 112, 113, 115, 116n4, 119n23, 121n50, 126, 128–132, 135, 136, 231

Aglipayan Church, 104, 112, 231

Alejo, Albert, 165, 167, 170, 175n21, 190, 193, 282

Anito, 39, 149, 150, 159n12, 187, 195n1, 197n17, 251, 300

Anti-colonialism/resistance, 262

Anti-Jewish, 92–95

Apo Namallari, 39

Appropriation, 15, 29–41, 60, 153, 188

April 14, 1521, 3, 15, 33

Asian hate, 16, 95

Assumption, 216, 239, 241, 292

Astronomical knowledge, 297

B

Babaylan
  babaylan discourse, 259
  babaylan/catalonan, 5, 14, 18, 41, 151, 152, 162, 165–171, 181, 192, 195n4, 229, 250, 257–265, 267n34, 295
  Babaylanism, 250
  baylans, 193, 195n4
  Centre for Babaylan Studies, 12
  primary babaylans, 261
  secondary Babaylans, 260

Bacon, Francis, 187

Balintawak, 109, 232

Baptism, 3, 5, 30, 33, 39, 57, 149, 276–280, 282–284

Bathala, 145–152, 155, 293

[1] Note: Page numbers followed by 'n' refer to notes.

© The Author(s), under exclusive license to Springer Nature Switzerland AG 2024
C. Lledo Gomez et al. (eds.), *500 Years of Christianity and the Global Filipino/a*, Pathways for Ecumenical and Interreligious Dialogue, https://doi.org/10.1007/978-3-031-47500-9

311

312   INDEX

Bautista, Julius, 83, 85–89
Benedict XV, Pope, 7, 98n45
Bernad, Miguel, 60, 102
Biblical hermeneutical methods,
    88–95, 209–221, 271–285
Blood pact, 33, 38, 39
Bourdieu, Pierre, 16, 48, 49, 52, 60
Brillantes, Pedro, 105, 106
Burgos, Jose, 6, 108, 112

C

Canaanite
    reading, 213
    woman, 218–220
Capitalocene, 205, 208n17
Carlos, 35
Catequesis, 130, 131
Catholic Bishops Conference of the
    Philippines (CBCP), 8, 89, 93
Catholicity, 101, 111, 113–115, 127,
    128, 133–136
Cebu, viii, 3, 4, 15, 29–41,
    120n40, 149
Centurion, 209, 210, 218–220
Christa, 18, 250, 263–265
Christian diaspora, 9–15
Christianity, 1–19, 36, 41, 65, 66,
    68–74, 76–78, 80n30, 82n46,
    123, 144, 150, 152, 167,
    174n13, 187, 200, 202, 205,
    206, 210, 211, 214, 215, 228,
    250, 259, 262, 264, 271, 272,
    280, 301
Christianization, 4, 16, 17, 68, 69,
    151, 154, 170, 201, 205, 206,
    228, 230, 231, 303
Christology
    Sophia Christology, 262
Chronicles of Antonio Pigafetta, 15
Churches of the Anglican
    Communion, 133, 135–136
Civilizing mission, 66, 68–74, 181,
    210, 218

Colonial
    construction of nature, 302–303
    evangelization, 48–50, 54, 95
    mentality (CM), 11, 12, 15, 163,
        198n37, 252, 264
    missions, 15, 16, 47–60, 152, 154
    resistance, 269n53
Colonialism, 2, 13, 14, 18, 76,
    136, 162, 163, 174n15, 185,
    205, 208n17, 213, 253, 258,
    260, 261, 264, 269n53,
    301, 302
    settler colonialism, 161, 167, 168
Communion, 124–126, 128, 129,
    132–136, 200, 201
Confessionarios, 58
Conquistadores, 4, 5, 51
Constantino, Renato, 49, 52,
    53, 60, 186
Conversion, 4, 5, 30, 34, 56–59, 70,
    72, 75, 78, 80n30, 151, 179,
    205, 259, 284
Crocodile god, 192

D

Dangal, 164
de Benavides, Miguel, 53
de la Costa, Horacio, 51, 60
de las Casas, Bartolome, 4, 52
de los Reyes, Sr., Isabelo, 102, 104,
    105, 112, 115, 116n2, 126, 130,
    132, 134, 136
de Montesinos, Antonio, 52
de Salazar, Domingo, 4, 52, 53, 295
de Urdaneta, Andrés, 53
de Vitoria, Francisco, 52
Declaration of Utrecht, 125, 129
Decolonization, 15, 17, 18,
    164–166, 168–170, 173, 206,
    264, 274
Decolonizing, 12, 17–19, 161–173,
    234, 250
Deep incarnation, 263, 264

INDEX

Disaster
Filipino indigenous concept of disaster, 299–300
studies, 303–306
Discrimination, 12, 74, 78, 103, 113, 154, 251, 255, 256
Dispu, 37
Diwata, 148–151, 295
Doctrina Cristiana en Lengua Española y Tagala (Doctrina Christiana), 153
Doctrinas y Reglas Constitutionales (DRC), 104, 118n17
Doctrine of Discovery, 14, 15, 19, 186
Double verité (Double-truth of practice), vii, 16, 48, 60

E

Earth, 67, 170, 189, 195, 200–206, 208n18, 210, 211, 239, 262, 271, 278, 281, 282, 287n19, 293, 299
Easter Sunday Mass, 38
Eclipse, 297–298
Ecocentric, 205, 206
Ecology, 275, 296–299
Ecumenism, ecumenical, 124, 125, 132, 136
EDSA (1986 People Power), vii, 9
Emotional, 56, 86–88, 160n23, 234, 239
Empire, 15, 50, 51, 94, 168, 170, 184, 193, 209, 211, 216–220, 224n33, 231, 264, 280, 281, 285
Encomienda, 4
Ensounded body, 86, 87
Environment, 19, 75, 86, 168, 203, 208n17, 234, 275, 291–306
Episcopal Church, 106, 132–134, 136
Epistolas Fundamentales, 104
Ethnic, 12, 37, 84, 89, 95, 163, 169, 193, 291, 293, 294, 296–299
ethnicity, 16, 84, 88–95, 103, 172

Euro-Christian, 201
Evangelization, vii, 4, 5, 37, 40, 48–52, 54, 57, 69, 95, 202, 304

F

False gods, 35
February 22-25, 1986, 9
Feminine genius, 257
Feminist, vii, viii, 15, 18, 157n3, 213, 230, 236, 238, 242, 250, 254, 257, 259, 260, 262, 263
Fiesta, 155, 181, 191
1521, 2, 3, 15, 29–41, 66, 67, 144, 149
Filipin@s, 83–95, 250–254, 291–293, 301
Filipino primal religion, 148, 150, 151, 155, 159n12
Filipinos, 10–13, 15–17, 19
primal religion, 17
spirituality, 13
First Baptism (in the Philippines), 3, 30–36
First Mass (in the Philippines), 15, 30–36
First Synod of Manila, 53
Folk Catholicism, 147–149, 151, 152
Francis, Pope, 144, 257
Fundamental Epistle, 104–106

G

Genesis, 59, 84, 92, 112, 187, 253, 274–276, 282
Ginhawa, 170
Global, vii, viii, 15–17, 41, 69, 76, 77, 83, 123, 124, 136, 163, 170, 199, 211, 220, 228, 234
Globalization, 9–15, 41, 163, 220, 273
Glocal, 16, 83–95
Gomez, Mariano, 6, 108
Gran Cordillera Central, 18, 201

314 INDEX

H

Hermeneutics of Serendipity,
17, 143–157
Herzog, Eduard, 16, 126–128,
130–132, 135
Hispanophiles, 49, 54
Holocaust, 91, 94, 190
Holy Week, 54, 59, 83, 85, 87, 88,
90, 95, 181
Hudyo, 89–95
Humabon, Rajah, 3, 33, 35,
36, 38, 149
Humamay, Hara, 3
wife of Rajah Humabon, 3, 34, 39
Hybridity, 2, 6, 48

I

Ibalois, 200
Iglesia Filipina Independiente (IFI),
vii, 6–7, 16, 17,
101–115, 123–136
Igorot, 18, 200–204, 227
Ileto, Reynaldo, 6, 59, 85, 86, 88, 93,
217, 230
Imperialism, 18, 210, 211, 213–215,
217, 218, 230–233, 301, 306
*Inang Bayan—Mother Country or
Mother of the Nation*, 232
Inang Kalikasan, 294–296
Independence, vii, 2, 7, 20n1,
101–110, 112, 115, 121n50,
126, 128, 131, 136, 184
Independent church, 101, 107, 108
Indigenization, 15, 29–41, 164, 230
Indigenous
cosmologies, 292–296
ecologies and worldviews, 296–299
hospitality, 33, 36, 37, 39
inculturation, 17, 143–157
Mary, 109
religions, 5, 57, 68, 211

Interdependence, 217, 298–299, 306
Interfaith, 77
Internalized racism, 15, 250
Interpretation, 47, 49, 52, 76, 79,
115, 131, 133, 194, 207n13,
210–213, 216–218, 232, 305
Intersectional oppression, 18
Investments, 87, 89

J

Jeepney, 210–221
Jeepney hermeneutics, 18, 209–221
Jesus, 13, 18, 25n55, 30, 59, 76, 85,
88–93, 95, 120n49, 149, 156,
158n7, 209, 210, 212, 217–220,
225n39, 228–230, 242, 253,
262–265, 269n53, 271, 276,
278–281, 284, 285, 289n28
Jesus movement, 281
Jew/Jewish, 16, 40, 84, 89–95,
98n45, 220, 251, 281
John Paul II, Pope, 257
July 4, 1902, 103

K

Kabunian, 202, 203, 207n15, 294
kagandahang-loob, 148, 155, 164, 187
Kaingin, 297, 298, 303, 308n23
Kapwa, 164–170, 183, 187, 196n16,
251, 269n53
Kolambu, Rajah, 31, 33, 36, 38

L

La Guadalupana of Mexico, 231
Lalahon, 295
Land, viii, 4, 5, 9–11, 14, 19, 32, 52,
68, 72, 74, 89, 104, 113,
121n50, 161, 162, 164,
166–170, 173, 184, 187, 190,

195n1, 201–204, 206, 215, 217, 220, 221, 251, 261, 271–285, 293, 296–299, 303
Landa Jocano, Felipe, 292
Leitourgia, 206
Liberation, 6–8, 18, 54, 59, 74, 85, 88–90, 101, 114, 184, 213, 239, 240, 242, 250, 261, 271, 279
Local, 4, 5, 15, 16, 50, 55–57, 66, 73, 76, 78, 83, 85, 87, 88, 107, 144, 149, 154, 161, 162, 168, 170, 181, 182, 203, 212, 228–230, 242, 256, 261, 271, 275, 276, 282, 284, 294, 295, 297–298, 300–302
Local knowledge, 295, 298, 306
Loob, 6, 183
Lopez de Legaspi, Miguel, 4

M

Machismo, 229
Macho Messianism, 241
Magdarasal, 151
Magellan, Ferdinand, 2, 3, 15, 17, 30–40
Maggay, Melba, 162, 182, 194
Mananzan, Mary John, 165, 215, 238, 257, 258, 260, 261
Martial law, 8–9, 74–76, 78
Mary, Virgin, viii, 18, 85, 92, 105, 109, 181, 227–242, 257, 269n53
  Chinese-Filipino Marian, 230
  Filipino Marianism, 230
  Latine Marianismo, 230
  Mama Mary, 237
  Mariang Makiling, 230, 295
  Mariang Sinukuan, 295
  Marianism, 18, 229, 242
  Marianismo, 229, 230

Our Lady of Fatima, 30, 228
Our Lady of Guidance, 231
Our Lady of Piat, 228
political Marianism, viii, 235, 239
"Virgin Mary With the Mobile Phone," 234
Virgin of Balintawak, 109, 231–233
Massaua (Limasawa), 31
Maternal politicians, 235–238
Matthew's Gospel, 18, 217
May 1, 1521, 35
McKinley, William, 72, 163, 184
Migrant, migrants, viii, 4, 9–13, 17, 18, 233, 234
Misogyny, 229
Missionary conquest, 201
Moors, 31, 40, 66, 153
Mungan, 171–173
Myths of origin, 292, 294

N

National Council of Churches in the Philippines (NCCP), 8
Nationalism, 101, 111–113, 115, 126, 230–233
Nationalists, 49
Nature
  as woman, 294–296
  and woman stereotypes, 301–302
Nostra aetate, 76, 77, 93
Novenari
  Novenario de la Patria, 109
Novenario, 109, 231, 232

O

Obispo Maximo, 102, 112, 126, 127
Old Catholic Churches, 17, 124–126, 128, 133–136
Overseas Filipino workers (OFW's), viii, 10, 11, 89, 162, 233–234

316 INDEX

P

Pabasa, 84, 86–90, 92, 95
Pachamama, 41
Pagdama, 147, 148
Pais, 217–221
Pastoral nomadism, 275, 276
Pasyon
  Pasyong/Pasiung Henesis, 86
  Pasyon/Pasiung Pilapil, 86
  text, 84–92, 94, 95
Patriarchal church, 250, 253
Patronato Real, viii, 48, 50–54
Payson
  chanting, 83, 86
  performance, 83–89, 95
People's movement
  people power revolution, 8–9
  people's power movement, 13
Philippine Christianity, viii, 2, 15,
  17, 54, 205
Philippine Independent Church, 16,
  101–115, 126
Philippine ritual specialists, 259
Philippine-US Relations, 7, 184–186
Pieris, Aloysius, 271
Pigafetta, Antonio, viii, 15,
  30–40, 149
Postcolonial, viii, 2, 5, 6, 15, 19, 47,
  48, 126, 132, 136, 144, 145,
  151, 154, 186, 213, 292, 306
Post-human, 199
Prechtel, Martin, 168, 188, 192
Pro deo et patria, 106, 111, 113, 126
Pudong, 18, 199–206

Q

Quiapo Black Nazarene, 17,
  146–149, 158n7

R

Racism, 11–13, 15, 170, 215,
  244n50, 250, 253
Rafael, Vicente, 56, 59, 162
Reducción, 54–57
Religious intolerance, 13, 75
Religious Philippinism, 126, 132
Rinkel, Andreas, 17, 133–135
Rizal, Jose, 53, 108, 145, 217, 235
Robredo, Leni, 235, 237, 238, 240
Roman soldiers, 90, 91, 218
Roosevelt, Theodore, 103

S

Sabbath, 200, 204, 277–279,
  288n19, 288n22
Sacrifice, 30, 37, 38, 44n34, 49, 87,
  109, 233, 235, 239, 241,
  288n19, 299, 300
Sama Dilaut, 296
Santo Niño, 30, 34, 38, 39, 149
Scalice, Joseph, 85, 88, 89
Scheuermann, Carmen, 273, 274
Schism, 104, 106, 114, 124
Scripture, 105, 205, 212, 213,
  215, 241, 253, 278,
  287n19, 288n22
Second Vatican Council, 7, 76
Sentimental, 87, 299
September 21, 1965, 135
September 24, 1903, 108, 135
Serendipity, 17, 143–157
Sexism
  ambivalent, 255–257
  benevolent, 229, 255–257
  neo, 255, 256
  overt, 255
Siani, Rajah, 31, 33, 36

INDEX   317

Silang, Gabriela, 235, 236
Sinakulo, 14, 41, 85, 89, 90
Spanish empire, 50, 51, 94
Spanish missionaries, 49, 68, 149, 152, 153, 301
Stewardship, 19, 145, 167, 190, 292, 298–299
Storytelling, 92, 167, 170
Suffering, 59, 83, 86–89, 93, 95, 190, 228, 238, 239, 241, 263, 305
Surplus of meaning, 50, 60
Synod of Manila (1582), 4, 5, 53

T
Tao po, 37
Tengao, 204, 207n13
Transgender, 5, 259, 260, 262, 264
Translation, 55–57, 133, 295
Tydings-McDuffie law, 7

U
Ubaya, 204, 207n13

Unión Obrera Democrática (UOD), 102, 106

V
Vatican, 144, 256

W
Watershed ecology, 271–285
Way of the Cross, 83
Whiteness, 13, 251, 252
Worldview, 38–40, 126, 132, 147, 170, 179, 186, 187, 251, 291, 296–299, 302

Y
Ygollotes, 199–206
Yligueynes, 294

Z
Zamora, Jacinto, 6, 108, 112

Printed in the United States
by Baker & Taylor Publisher Services